Cityscapes of Modernity

Critical Explorations

David Frisby

D1556367

Polity

First published in 2001 by Polity Press in association with Blackwell Publishers Ltd

Editorial office:
Polity Press
65 Bridge Street
Cambridge CB2 1UR, UK

Marketing and production:
Blackwell Publishers Ltd
108 Cowley Road
Oxford OX4 1JF, UK

Published in the USA by
Blackwell Publishers Inc.
350 Main Street
Malden, MA 02148, USA

ISBN 0-7456-0967-8
ISBN 0-7456-2625-4 (pbk)

A catalogue record for this book is available from the British Library and has been applied for from the Library of Congress.

Typeset in 10 on 12pt Times
by Graphicraft Limited, Hong Kong
Printed in Great Britain by MPG Books Ltd, Bodmin, Cornwall

This book is printed on acid-free paper.

Contents

Illustrations

Illustrations are reproduced by kind permission of the Historisches Museum der Stadt Wien and the Direktion der Museen der Stadt Wien (5.1 to 5.6) and the Stiftung Archiv der Akademie der Künste, Sammlung Baukunst, Berlin (7.1 to 7.5).

Acknowledgements

The essays contained in this volume are largely the result of research and reflections over the past seven years. The first chapter on the figure of the flâneur in social theory originally appeared in a volume edited by Keith Tester, *The Flâneur* (London: Routledge, 1994), pp. 81–110. I am therefore grateful to Routledge for permission to reprint this essay in a slightly extended form.

The second chapter on the figure of the detective relates to an ongoing work on the prehistory of the detective novel. The essay has not been previously published. As a paper it originally carried the title: 'Yeggmen and Legmen – We Never Sleep'. The references in this title are to the slang term for safebreakers (Yeggmen) and detectives (Legmen). Those who know something of the history of the Pinkerton National Detective Agency will recognize 'We never sleep' as the company's motto, beneath the logo of an open eye. I would like to take this opportunity of thanking the staff of Pinkertons at their world headquarters in Encino, California, who afforded me every assistance in working in the archive on the Agency. Since then it has been wisely decided on grounds of preservation to move the material to the Library of Congress. Versions of the essay were presented as talks, most recently at the Whitney Humanities Center, and Morse College, both at Yale University, and in the sociology seminar programme at Columbia University, and thanks are due to participants for their critical comments.

The third chapter on Simmel's analysis of the metropolis arises out of an attempt to explore his contribution to our understanding of the modern city from a somewhat different perspective. The essay has not been published previously but has been presented in various versions in talks at the architecture departments in Edinburgh University and Columbia University in 1999. Here, I wish to acknowledge Iain Boyd Whyte at Edinburgh and Mary McLeod at Columbia for their invitations to speak and to the respective audiences for their comments.

The fourth chapter is a version of a paper given at a conference on 'Werner Sombart and "American Exceptionalism"' at Erlangen–Nürnberg University in July 1999 and organized by Mark Thompson, in their Political Science Department. I am extremely grateful to Mark for the invitation to speak at this conference and to participants for their critical comments.

The fifth chapter on Otto Wagner's Vienna has not been published previously. Some of its content relates to a much more comprehensive examination of Otto Wagner and modernity that originally constituted my Master of Architecture dissertation awarded at the Mackintosh School of Architecture in the Glasgow School of Art in 1998. A revised and expanded version of the thesis is appearing shortly as *Metropolitan Architecture and Modernity: Otto Wagner's Vienna* (Minneapolis: University of Minnesota Press). A version of the essay that appears here was given as a talk to the Sociology Department of Yale University in February 1999 when I was visiting professor there. I wish to acknowledge the critical commentary of colleagues at Yale. The later discussion of valorizations of Old and New Vienna was given as a paper in July 2000 to a conference in honour of Carl C. Schorske's eighty-fifth birthday on 'The Generational Dynamics of Cultural Analysis' organized by the Internationales Forschungszentrum Kulturwissenschaften (IFK) in Vienna and held in the Akademie der Wissenschaften. I am grateful for commentary there on my paper. An extended version was also given in the Departments of Art and Archaeology and History at Princeton University in October 2000, and I wish to thank Esther da Costa Meyer for the invitation to speak, and the audience for critical commentary.

The sixth chapter on the relationship between social theory and German Expressionism originally appeared in the catalogue of an exhibition on *Expressionist Utopias* at the Los Angeles County Museum of Art in 1993, organized by Dr Tim O. Benson, now Curator of the Rifkind Center at LACMA. The essay 'Social Theory: The Metropolis and Expressionism' was first published, in slightly different form, in *Expressionist Utopias: Paradise, Metropolis, Architectural Fantasy*, © Museum Associates/Los Angeles County Museum of Art, 1993; 2nd enlarged edn, University of California Press, 2001.

The final chapter appears here for the first time. It is an expanded version of a paper given at the Whitney Humanities Center, Yale University, in March 1999. The occasion was a colloquium on 'The Spirit of the City in Modernity', and forms part of the research funded by the Getty on 'The City and Spirituality in Modernity', together with Iain Boyd Whyte and Volker Welter. I wish to thank especially the discussant to this paper, Joan Ockman, along with other participants.

Many of the essays assembled here were developed or expanded during a period of study leave from Glasgow University. Part of that leave in the winter of 1997/8 was spent as Visiting Fellow at the IFK in Vienna. I wish to express my thanks to the staff of that institute – and especially its Director Gotthart Wunberg and its Scientific Secretary, Lutz Musner – for providing an ideal working environment. Since October 1998 a further period of leave has been funded by a Getty Research Grant, jointly with Iain Boyd Whyte and Volker Welter (both Edinburgh University), and thanks are therefore due to the generous support of the Getty for research on 'The Spirit of the City in Modernity'.

Research for this volume was undertaken in a number of libraries and archives, and I wish to take this opportunity of expressing my thanks to the library and research staff of the following institutions: the Stirling Memorial Library and the Mudd Library, both at Yale University; Mary Daniels in the Special Collections section of the Loeb Library in the Harvard Graduate School of Design; the periodicals section of the library at the Technische Universität, Vienna; the Österreichische National-bibliothek in Vienna; the archive of the Akademie der Künste, Berlin; the Research Institute Library at the Getty; the University of California, San Diego Library; the Southern Regional Library Facility (on the UCLA campus); and the Sächsische Landesbibliothek in Dresden.

At various times, many of this volume's chapters have been given as papers to seminars at Glasgow University and I am grateful to colleagues and graduate students for their commentaries.

I have greatly benefited from conversations and discussions in recent years with Iain Boyd Whyte (Edinburgh), Christian Hermansen (Glasgow), Klaus Christian Köhnke (Leipzig), Lutz Musner (IFK, Vienna), Gotthart Wunberg (IFK, Vienna), Moritz Czàky (Graz), Rudi Laermans (Leuven), Birgitta Nedelmann (Mainz), John Czaplicka (Harvard). Responsibility for the views expressed in this volume is, of course, mine.

I wish to thank Maureen McQuillan and Ann Settle for typing the final version of this text. If the final version of the manuscript has greater coherence, then this is due to the comments made by the ubiquitously anonymous reader, and to Louise Knight at Polity who encouraged me to follow them up. Finally, a word of gratitude for their forbearance is due to Gill Motley and Louise Knight at Polity Press who waited patiently for the final completion of the manuscript.

David Frisby, Glasgow

Introduction

One can distinguish two kinds of images of the city: those that are consciously formed, and others that reveal themselves unintentionally. The former emerge out of an artistic intention that is realised in squares, perspectives, groups of buildings, which Baedeker usually illuminates with a small star. The latter, in contrast, emerge without having being previously planned. They are not compositions that, like the Pariser Platz or Place de la Concorde, owed their existence to a unified building conception, but rather they are fortuitous creations that do not permit themselves to be called to account.

Siegfried Kracauer, 'Aus dem Fenster gesehen'

A person matters, his or her experiences matter, but in the city, where experiences come by the thousands, we can no longer relate them to ourselves; and this is of course the beginning of life's notorious turning into abstraction.

Robert Musil, *The Man Without Qualities*

I am not satisfied with the expression 'street image'; I would prefer to say 'street landscape' or 'cityscape', for what it refers to is the actual landscape total image, which is produced by the arrangement and forming of masses in the same manner as the natural landscape emerges out of the grouping of mountain masses and vegetation.

Anon [Walter Rathenau], 'Die schönste Stadt der Welt'

I

There exist a series of tensions in modernity that manifest themselves as ambiguities and contradictions. The processes of modernization that generate the 'modern' dimensions of modern societies appear to be driven by unilinear and ostensibly inexorable forces, be they – *inter alia* – capital accumulation or rationalization. These processes appear to create modes of ordering society and its structures. However, this ordering of social formations is accompanied by processes of disintegration of human experience, creating fundamental discontinuities in the life worlds of modernity. In other words, the orders and structures of modernization and their putative totalizations simultaneously generate basic modes of fragmentation of everyday experience. What appear as processes of the 'rational' ordering of economic, political and social systems are accompanied not merely by commitment to irrational or non-independently groundable ends but also, and more fundamentally, by the disintegration of modes of experiencing basic features of the life world, a discontinuous experience of time as transitory, space as fleeting and causality negated as the fortuitous and arbitary.

At the same time, the dynamic movement that we experience as the presentness of modernity creates illusions of infinite movement of that which appears similar. If it is the case that a large part of our experience of modernity on the surface of everyday life takes place within the spheres of circulation, exchange and consumption, then these spheres are capable of generating an indifference to other modes of differentiation, be they those of gender, class or ethnicity. The immediate moments of exchange, for instance, are moments of dedifferentiation, of equivalent relations between apparently similar entities.

The responses to such experiences of modernity – of modes of experiencing the newness, the presentness of modern society – are varied. Modernity has been both celebrated and critiqued in a plurality of aesthetic representations as modernisms. Modernity has been resisted in movements of anti-modernity, sometimes in ambiguous anti-modern modern movements. The dedifferentiating dimensions of modernity have also generated, as responses and spaces of resistance, differentiated counter-cultures around class, gender and ethnic formations.

Such tensions and contradictions also manifested themselves in those bodies of reflection upon modernity that sometimes even identified themselves with modernity itself. This was particularly true of the social sciences since the eighteenth century, and especially at the points of their emergence as diverse disciplines a century later. Some of these disciplines – and this is particularly true of sociology – not merely took modernity to be the object of investigations that might provide an analysis of contemporary modern society, but also, less frequently, reflected upon their own position within this modernity.

Indeed, the social sciences abound in theories of modernization – social, economic, political, psychological and cultural explorations of how and through what processes that which has been termed modern society emerged. Such accounts have often rested upon a juxtaposition between traditional and modern societies, between static and dynamic socio-economic formations. Yet an account of modernity, understood as modes of experiencing that which is 'new' in 'modern' society, would presuppose an account of transitions to modern society, but without itself being reduced to a theory of modernization. Similarly, the aesthetic representations of transitions to modern society and modernity since the second half of the nineteenth century have given rise to a series of aesthetic modernisms, often accompanied by avant-garde manifestos announcing the arrival of absolutely new, modernist movements and exploring, aesthetically, 'the shock of the new'. The closer the concept of modernity is to that of modernization, the more it is likely to become a conceptualization of historical periodization. Where the concept is closer to aesthetic modernisms it is more likely to become a conceptualization of modes or qualities of modern social experience. A third, more recent, conceptualization of modernity is as a historical project. None of these concepts of modernity is without analytical and methodological problems.

Indeed, there has been considerable uncertainty surrounding the concepts of the modern, modernity, modernization and modernism in some historical periods, such as the turn of the nineteenth century and perhaps in recent decades, when the concept of modernity has come to encompass or be fused with all these related concepts. Indeed, the common associations of modernity with changes in historical and time consciousness, with an emphasis upon accelerating change and an identification of the present as modernity does raise the issue of historical periodization.

The historical periodization of modernity often relies on abstract chronologies and temporalities and contextualized stages of presentness. Modernity as emergent in the (late) Renaissance around 1500 and in its successive phases – 1500–1789, 1789–1900 and 1900 to the present – relies upon an abstract conception of historical epochs. Modernity as co-terminus with the development of the capitalist mode of production makes sense only if the processes by which capitalism as a socio-economic formation transforms social relations and experience into modernity can be delineated. Modernity as a project co-terminus with the Enlightenment and auto-nomous reason can be said to rest upon a demonstration of the continuity of this intellectual project since Kant. The most ambitious attempt to abandon the connection between modernity and periodization and turn to modernity as process in the past and present – Walter Benjamin's 'prehistory of modernity' – itself retains elements of periodization of capitalism (Baudelaire, for instance, is viewed as a poet of 'high' capitalism by Benjamin).

Nonetheless, accounts of the transition to modernity and the contemporary analysis of the present modernity were always associated with a critique of modernity, rather than merely a celebration of the present modernity. Even then, and more commonly in the early decades of the twentieth century, this did not preclude the development of theories of an 'anti-modern' modernity and the mythological and 'post-historical' political projects associated with Fascism.

Since the introduction of the concept of modernity around the mid-nineteenth century, and especially in the proliferation of reflections upon its features in the late nineteenth century (partly stimulated by the emergence of new academic disciplines and their claim for resources in universities), *one* of the possible sites for the study of modernity was the modern metropolis. The modern city was not the *only* site for such investigations. For some, such as Marx, the capitalist mode of production was clearly of greater importance. For others, such as Emile Durkheim, the nature of social solidarity in modern society was of primary concern. For some, like Max Weber, the historical investigations of the origin of modern western rationalism and its most consequential product, modern western rational capitalism, were paramount. But in these and other instances in which the city did not appear to play a prominent role in the delineation of modernity, this did not mean that the modern metropolis was not without its significance.

Indeed, a brief overview of some of the contributions to understanding modernity suggests that the metropolis was of importance to a greater or lesser extent. For Charles Baudelaire, the metropolis was the site on which the spectacles of modernity were played out. The city as aesthetic object was to be rendered poetic by both the poet and the flâneur. Less than two decades earlier, Engels had depicted the modern metropolis as the site of modern capitalist estrangement in his naturalistic descriptions. This analyst, however, possessed a transformative interest in the object of study, in the transformation of the alienating relations of capitalism. And although many of Marx's explorations of the modern capitalist mode of production implicitly had an urban dimension, the latter was not a central concern in his drive to discover the 'laws of motion' of this system.

By the late nineteenth century the metropolis had assumed a greater significance in some social theories at least. Although not usually viewed as an urban theorist, Durkheim's studies of the abnormal forms of the division of labour (and the moral/social density of urban life) and the weakened levels of moral regulation and integration in the metropolis indicated a concern with some of the pathologies of modern urban life and a remedial and prescriptive interest in their amelioration. For Durkheim's exact contemporary, Georg Simmel (both were born in 1858), with his postulation of an interpenetration of the mature money economy and the modern metropolis, the city was the crucial site of the intensification of the features of modernity and the attendant transformation of human experience. Simmel's interest, as he pointedly remarked at the close of his essay on the metropolis, lay in the direction of an interpretation or description of modernity that could aid our understanding of the new forms of social interaction in modernity.

The modern metropolis also received explicit treatment from a more negative standpoint in the otherwise quite diverse social analyses of modernity provided by Ferdinand Tönnies and Werner Sombart. For Tönnies, the modern metropolis was the very epitome of the negative, empty contractual and abstract social relations that pertained in modern society, generated, in part, by an arbitrary will devoid of any communalistic tendencies. Sombart, on the other hand, explored the metropolis much more extensively both in its historical development in early capitalism and in its modern form. The modern metropolis, for Sombart, was dominated by mass phenomena (commodities and individuals), quasi-independent technology and rapid transformation, producing a new urban culture, an 'asphalt culture' whose features and tendencies were viewed negatively.

A more analytical focus upon the historical development of the metropolis – which owed not a little of its original impetus from a confrontation with Sombart's historical interpretation of the emergence of modern capitalism and the city – was provided by Max Weber's historical analytical investigations of the city as economic market and political military development. On occasion, Weber reflected more freely in discourse and correspondence on the nature of modern urban existence. And although specific features of the city in which his analytical investigations were taking place seldom surfaced, the inner life of the modern metropolis in the often distorted self-understanding of the experience of its inhabitants was explored by Freud as part of a broader study of the pathologies of everyday life. In turn, this focus upon a nervous individual culture in the metropolis had some affinities with Simmel's more general explorations, with the latter's desire to drop soundings beneath the surface of everyday life.[1]

II

If modernity is characterized by contradictions and ambiguities, then is the same true of the concept of a cityscape? So many of the representations of our experience of modernity are tied up with our experience of the metropolis that the presentation and representation of the city are likely to share in modernity's contradictions. The issue as to how to represent modern experience of the metropolis is central to discussions within the aesthetic modernisms that modernity generated. The representation and reading of the modern metropolis manifested itself in crucial differences between modernist movements, each of which was ostensibly diametrically opposed to its predecessors, at least as far as the proclamations of their avant-garde manifestos were concerned.

At the same time, giving a name to that which was being represented or, better, to that *mode* of representation itself also became an issue. Beyond the call to depict the modern city and our experience of it that is shared by Baudelaire, the Impressionists, the Expressionists, the Surrealists and so on, there lay the problem of identifying the mode of representation itself. The 'panorama' of the city differs from the 'snapshot', just as the 'narrative' differs from the 'image'. In part, these differences were contingent upon the development of new techniques of representation. But, at the same time, the observer of the city and the practices associated with that observation were also changing. Different observers, as potential sources of representing the city, were located at different distances (and different tempos) from their object. For instance, the portrayal of the city embedded *in* the landscape is to be distinguished from the portrayal of the city *as* landscape and, in turn, from the portrayal of the city's *streetscape* as if it were from a perspective *within* the streets themselves.

Whilst some questioned whether the modern metropolis could constitute a landscape, others searched for new terms to describe what they took to be a new object of study. The former issue is indirectly addressed in Simmel's 'Philosophy of Landscape' ('Philosophie der Landschaft', 1910), in which he implies that the modern streetscape cannot be a landscape,[2] and contrasts with his earlier representation of the modern city in 'The Metropolis and Mental Life' (1903).[3] Yet the search for new terms was already evident in Walter Rathenau's anonymous essay 'The Most Beautiful City in the World' ('Die schönste Stadt der Welt', 1899)[4] where he sought to redefine the notion of the 'image' of the city. The context is the question as to what are the conditions under which a city requires beautiful buildings. Where there is no beautiful landscape setting, no prospect of the sea or a broad river and such like, then it is necessary to create 'a significant and well set out image of streets (*Strassenbild*)'. However, Rathenau expresses his dissatisfaction with this concept and prefers that of 'street landscape'[5] (*Strassenlandschaft*) or 'cityscape' (*Stadtbild*) on the grounds that what is at issue is

the genuine landscape total image that is produced by means of the arrangement and formation of masses in the same manner as is the natural landscape from out of the grouping of mountain masses and vegetation.

Those who have ever walked in Trafalgar Square or Place de la Concorde, Piccadilly or the Piazza della Signoria can appreciate what deep impression has been called forth to produce urban scenery purely as total image and not as the effect of individual works.[6]

Rathenau was clearly struggling here with the transition from landscape to streetscape and cityscape, to the humanly formed constellation of a total effect of streets and cities. Less than three decades later the notion of a cityscape or streetscape became central to the investigations of the modern metropolis by Franz Hessel,[7] Walter Benjamin,[8] Siegfried Kracauer[9] and others.[10] And in some cases the focus had shifted away from merely visual response to spatial effects of streetscapes and cityscapes. Benjamin, for example, argued that 'every architecture worthy of the name ensures that it is the spatial sense as a whole, and not just the casual gaze, that reaps the benefits of its greatest achievements'.[11] Or elsewhere he maintained that 'what is crucial in the observation of architecture is not seeing but rather the coming through of traces of structures. The objective effect of built structures upon the conceptual existence of the observer is more important than their "being seen" '.[12] Thus, when such reflections are applied to the cityscape, it becomes apparent that its exploration is by no means exhausted in our attention to the image of the city, to its 'image space'. Rather, a more complete exploration should open up a broader constellation of experience of its spatial and temporal (historical) existence.

One of the ways of accessing other dimensions of the cityscape is to examine the figures who populate it. More specifically, social theories of modernity have often had recourse to real and metaphorical figures in order to illuminate their methodology and substantive theories. Walter Benjamin, for instance, in his ambitious prehistory of modernity, had recourse to the figures of the archaeologist and critical allegorist, the collector (including the rag collector, the *chiffonier*) and the flâneur in order to amplify the nature of his methodological approach to the construction of the site of the prehistory of modernity, namely Paris as capital of the nineteenth century. Other social theorists have populated their analysis of modernity and the cityscape with other figures. One somewhat neglected juxtaposition of figures must suffice as indicator of the fruitfulness of such explorations.

III

In the course of one of several replies to the critics of his 'Protestant ethic' articles[13] – and the two essays did not constitute a monograph – Max

Weber addresses a question posed by one of his critics, Felix Rachfahl, one that he 'haunts me with in the most helpless manner'. If the question is asked,

> within the total image of modern capitalism *which* figures could and should quite unconditionally *not* be understood from the standpoint of 'inner worldly asceticism', then I reply: the *'adventurer'* of capitalist development – taking the concept of the 'adventurer' here in the same sense as it has recently been delineated by G. Simmel in a beautiful, short essay. As is well known, its economic historical significance especially (but not only) within the history of early capitalism is extremely important – and yet nonetheless in the increasing domination of capitalism over the whole of economic life, in a certain sense and *cum grano salis*, one can roughly treat alike the *development of economic opportunity profit into an economic system*; and the genesis of the capitalistic 'spirit' in my sense of the word, the development *from the romanticism of economic adventurism to the traditional economic system of life* (*Lebensmethodik*).[14]

Clearly, Weber is here primarily concerned with justifying his thesis concerning the development of the spirit of capitalism and the distinctive nature of modern western rational capitalism, as compared to earlier (and sometimes surviving and recurring) forms of capitalism. In passing, one might ask what the connection might be between this notion of adventurer capitalism and Marx's earlier discussion of 'original' (and not, as appears in the English translation, 'primitive') accumulation. Both historical and recent examples from post-communist societies suggest that original and adventure capitalist accumulation has not disappeared. Rather, such accumulation quite rapidly seeks to 'legitimate' itself by transforming itself into 'rational' and 'legitimate' economic activity. This would suggest that the demarcation that Weber tends to draw as a sharp distinction between 'romantic' and 'rational' capitalism may not be one that holds historically with the same rigour that he assumed.

However, our present concerns go in a different direction. An implication of Weber's distinction between the adventurer capitalist and the 'rational', systematic capitalist is that the former is *premodern* whereas the latter is *modern*. It is true that Weber does acknowledge that adventure capitalism can also be significant in modern capitalism. But the main thrust of his argument lies in establishing a sharp demarcation between adventure capitalism (which could not itself generate modern western rational capitalism) and modern systematic capitalism, whose origins are related to inner-worldly asceticism. The distinction between the premodern and the modern which Weber draws in this context does not confront the implications of his acknowledged source for a model of the adventurer, namely Simmel's essay on 'The Adventure'.[15] His exploration of the adventure and the attitude of the adventurer makes no reference to capitalism (though it does contain an important reference to gambling). Simmel's essay does, crucially, define the adventure in terms of experience divorced from or torn out of everyday existence and as demanding a heightened consciousness of absolute presentness. At first sight, such features are still compatible with Weber's usage of adventure capitalism, insofar as adventure capitalism is not a systematic, routinized activity but something dependent upon fortuitous opportunities, and insofar as rational economic life – since its *capitalist* variant is devoted to ever-renewed profit or capital accumulation – must have a future orientation as well as a location in the present. (Though generations of commentators have notoriously viewed *working-class* orientation to 'rational' economic life – in its capacity as formally free wage labour – as one that is not fixed upon future horizons but upon *present* satisfaction.)

But if we examine the adventure from Simmel's perspective do we reach similar conclusions to those which Weber clearly drew from this essay? Is not the adventurer, in Simmel's context, the equivalent, for example, of the flâneur? Does the focus upon absolute presentness and total disregard for history not make the adventurer the epitome of modernity? Or could we see the experience of the adventure and the systematic 'rational' life system as *two dimensions of modernity* rather than as instances of the premodern and modernity?

Certainly *calculability* and *fortuitousness* appear, at first sight, to be contradictory orientations. They are, however, interrelated insofar as the search for, and introduction of, calculability is a process whose aim is the eradication of fortuitousness or at least the mastery of the arbitrary and the random. Calculability and fortuitousness can also be linked together in our image of the city. When Simmel describes our impression of the metropolis – and he largely has streetscapes in mind – as one of bombardment of the senses with diverse impressions and criss-crossing interactions, he also reveals that this view of urban existence is contingent upon precisely calculated interactions, meetings, timetables, etc. If our personal/functional/transport and other timetables broke down momentarily (for instance, to give Simmel's own example, if all the clocks stopped at the same time) then the existing chaos (of individual impressions) would become total.[16]

Yet are there, nonetheless, grounds for regarding calculability and fortuitousness as separate and even contradictory processes? If we remain with images of the city for the moment, then the fortuitous images derived from strolling or walking the city (examined in their different ways by both Kracauer[17] and de Certeau[18]) clearly differ from those that are, as it were, already preconstructed or framed for us by guidebooks. The ready-mapped (and already 'read') city of the tourist guide can be instrumental in routinizing responses to that upon which it bestows attention. It is the routinized response that is also anticipated or expected in the calculability of rational economic processes, be they in the sphere of production, circulation or consumption. Since we are dealing with modes of experience and their representation, these reflections may be advanced by exploring the figures in the landscapes of calculability and fortuitousness. The figures clearly associated with the fortuitous are, for Weber, the adventure capitalist, for Simmel the adventurer and the gambler and for Benjamin, the flâneur and the gambler. In the case of figures associated with calculability, it is only Weber who could unambiguously offer an instance – the practitioner of formal rationality and, above all, the rational capitalist dedicated to a vocation of capital accumulation. This should not imply that figures such as the adventurer, the gambler or the flâneur are not accumulating experiences or images but merely that, in Weber's terms, they do not do so *systematically*. It is only Weber's rational capitalist (and 'rational' worker) who appear directly associated with production and the whole production process in modern western rational capitalism.

For both Simmel and Benjamin there are other figures in the urban landscape or cityscape, whose relationship to the processes of calculability and fortuitousness may be more ambiguous. In Simmel's case, the stranger and (as collectivity) the poor would be confronted, amongst others, in his cityscape. Neither is necessarily associated with modernity, although each may acquire modern forms. Yet there is one figure whom Simmel identifies unambiguously both with the mature money economy and modern metropolitan experience – the blasé person. This figure is identifiable through their response to the metropolis and the modern money economy as being blasé, that is, as adopting an attitude of (apparent) indifference to what both have to offer. When Simmel introduces the blasé person in the context of the modern money economy, this figure is preceded by one who is also to be found in the metropolis, namely the cynic. Not to be confused with the positive figure of the cynic in Greek antiquity, the modern cynic proliferates in the money economy – whose centre is the modern metropolis – and responds to 'the baseness of the highest values and the illusion of any differences in values'.[19] Not surprisingly, 'the nurseries of cynicism are . . . those places with huge turnovers of commodities and money.' These same 'nurseries' – extended to things themselves – are the sites of the proliferation of the blasé person,

> who has completely lost the feeling for value differences. He experiences all things as being of an equally dull and grey hue, as not worth getting excited about . . . [an] indifference to . . . [the] specific qualities . . . [of things] from which the whole liveliness of feeling and volition originates.[20]

Unlike the cynic, however, the blasé person still seeks 'the attractions of life' in the metropolis and the money economy. Hence, the blasé attitude has a further aspect, namely:

> the craving today for excitement, for extreme impressions, for the greatest speed in their change . . . the modern preference for 'stimulation' as such in impressions, relations and information. . . . The search for mere stimuli in themselves is the consequence of the increasing blasé attitude through which natural excitement increasingly disappears.[21]

If the blasé figure is the one 'unreservedly associated with the metropolis' and the mature money economy, then this figure is surely not one devoted to calculation – which requires being attuned to value differences – but rather to the fortuitous stimulations that the sites of modernity offer. As a modern response to the calculability of everything, the blasé attitude accords with a situation in which 'something definite' at the centre of our existence is missing. The conscious distance and indifference which metropolitan dwellers develop as defence mechanisms, and which give the impression of coolness and reserve, are only part of their response to the capitalist metropolis. There exists, too, a 'secret restlessness', a 'helpless urgency that lies *below* the threshold of consciousness', which propels us towards ever-new stimulations. Hence, Simmel argues:

> we become entangled in the instability and helplessness that manifests itself as the tumult of the metropolis, as the mania for travelling, as the wild pursuit of competition, and as the typically modern disloyalty with regard to taste, style, opinions and personal relationships.[22]

But these features, too, are related to the 'rational economic system of life' insofar as circulation in the metropolis, travel, taste and style are all commodified. The 'adventurer' in the modern metropolis, seeking new sensations and stimulations and seeking to break out of everyday mundane existence, is likely to pursue those stimulations that are themselves constitutive of the 'rational economic system of life'.

The calculating individual, who features in Simmel's cityscape and in Weber's vision of modern western rational capitalism, employs what Simmel terms 'calculative functions' when 'coping with the world and in regulating both individual and social relations' through conceiving of the world 'as a huge arithmetical problem . . . [with] events and the qualitative distinction of things as a system of numbers'.[23] Qualitative values are thereby reduced to quantitative ones. Is this not another version of the blasé individual, exemplifying the 'measuring, weighing and calculating exactness of modern times'? And is this commitment to calculability and quantification – that Weber saw as a crucial feature of modern rational capitalism – also indicative of both formal rationality and the fortuitous appearance of quantitative connections in economic and many other trans-actions in the modern metropolis?

This is merely one instance of the way in which the exploration of figures in the cityscapes of social theories reveal the ambiguities and contradictions of modernity. It would go beyond the scope of the present introduction to develop other instances, but Benjamin's flâneur, prostitute, gambler and other figures in his prehistory of modernity,[24] along with Simmel's fashion addict in the modern metropolis, might prove equally revealing.[25]

IV

The chapters in the present volume explore various dimensions of the struc-turing, representations and modes of experiencing the modern metropolis. They make no claim to be exhaustive investigations but, if they succeed, then they will have raised some significant aspects of metropolitan experi-ence that might encourage further study. They extend from the analysis of what appears to be a most trivial activity, that of strolling the metropolis with an eye to images of it and its population – the pursuit of flânerie – to the examination of attempts to construct the rational city in the city planning activities of Martin Wagner in Weimar Berlin. But, as with all dimensions of modernity, things are seldom what they appear. As Benjamin suggested, the flâneur or flâneuse may appear to be strolling aimlessly but is, in reality, in search of a market for his or her images of the city. The apparently most systematic and rational organization of the modern metropolis – in this case, Martin Wagner's vision of a new Berlin – in fact culminates in its opposite: the dissolution of the metropolis into 'satellite' towns with a population of 50,000 inhabitants. Such ambiguities and contradictions are present to a greater or lesser extent in the other explora-tions in the present volume.

The first chapter on the role of the flâneur in social theory should be read in the context of a much wider and expanding literature on the sign-ificance of the figure of the flâneur for our understanding of modernity. The essay appeared originally as a contribution to a broader exploration of this deeply ambiguous figure. In particular, Priscilla Ferguson invest-igated the historical emergence of this figure. Challenging Benjamin's loca-tion of the flâneur in Paris from the 1830s and 1840s, she demonstrated that the figure emerged several decades earlier.[26] My essay seeks to challenge four other aspects of the discourse on the flâneur. The first is Benjamin's own claim that with the development of the grand boulevards and the department store, the arcades that had 'housed' the flâneur themselves declined, and with their economic demise the figure of the flâneur also disappeared – to be replaced by the consumer. Yet Benjamin's reviews of the work of his friend Franz Hessel in Weimar Germany, and the title of one of those reviews, 'The Return of the Flâneur',[27] suggest that this decline of flânerie lacked finality. More compelling is Benjamin's own activity as flâneur, not merely in Paris and Berlin but, equally significantly, as an intellectual or research flâneur in the Bibliothèque Nationale.

The second, related aspect of flânerie, is the positive evaluation of flânerie that is implicit in Benjamin's own writings. If his judgement of the historical role of the flâneur is often a negative one in the context of early nineteenth-century Paris, then this contradicts his frequent recourse to the figure of the flâneur in order to clarify his own historical method. In this context (and in the historical analysis of the flâneur) a neglected dimension of flânerie is revealed, namely the flâneur as *producer* (of texts, images, etc.).

The third aspect of flânerie highlighted here is the contribution of this activity both to sociological knowledge and to our understanding of its generation. The scientist claims of some sociological histories and the accompaning canonization of sociologists and their 'knowledges' erase the conditions under which a great deal of that knowledge is *produced*. These include not merely the observational and experimental settings of much interactional sociology but also the manner in which historical archival knowledge is generated. To return to Benjamin for a moment, it is instructive to note that when he declares to Kracauer that he is in the arcades, he is in fact in the Bibliothèque Nationale in Paris. The manner in which Benjamin's *own* archive is produced is illuminated by flânerie.

Finally, an implication of our broader exploration of flânerie is that it is not confined to mere observation or images. If the flâneur is a producer, then the reconstruction of experience – and primarily modes of metropolitan experience of modernity – must extend beyond the merely *visual* grasp of metropolitan interaction.

As Benjamin suggested, the figure of the private detective is prefigured in that of the flâneur, at the moment in which the flâneur's gaze becomes directed towards specific persons and objects. Far too little attention has been given to the training of individuals for the activity of detection, in comparison with studies of detection in its literary and, from the twentieth century onwards, cinematic representations. Perhaps no other figure has become so identified with their representational embodiment in a metropolitan context (outside of which, the 'cowboy' in the US could not compete with as compelling a representational trajectory). Not surprisingly, the emergence of the figure of the detective (as opposed to the government agent) appeared in literature at the same time as detective forces were being formed in both the public and private sectors in several countries.[28] The 1850s saw the appearance of Inspector Bucket in Dickens's *Bleak*

House (1853) as well as the founding in Chicago of the Pinkerton Detective Agency (1850).[29] In turn, in a European context this crucial decade witnessed the creation of several forms of protection against criminality, but more especially against civil unrest and revolution after the failure of the 1848 revolutions. In Paris, Haussmannization coincided with the creation of national police forces elsewhere. In the United States, the consolidation of federal power took several decades to complete after the Civil War. In the intervening period prior to a more comprehensive federal system of law enforcement, many capitalist institutions had to rely upon private forces such as Pinkertons for their protection.

When Allan Pinkerton drew up the rules for his detective agency he sought to identify its activities as *modern* (as against earlier informer-based systems of policing). The rule-governed nature of the activity of detection that is evident in Pinkerton's set of principles and, as the agency expanded, the increasingly bureaucratic nature of its organization by the turn of the century around 1900, already contrasted with the emergent representation of the private detective as an independent agent. It also contrasted with the absence of rules for those with a managerial overview, except with respect to the bureaucratic organization of the agency. There was, in turn, one exception here, namely that operatives should have no access to the knowledge generated by other operatives and, still less, an overview of a whole operation. As such, Pinkerton's agency is an interesting early example of the knowledge industry, but one whose subsequent representational form was the individual 'private eye' and not the waged operative within a bureaucratic enterprise.

But the activity of detection in its modern form was also predicated upon new forms of, and possibilities for, *secrecy* opened up by the growth of the metropolis and a developed money economy and corresponding attempts at *revelation* of secrets. The ability to remain hidden within these two networks of the metropolis and an increasingly sophisticated money economy, both of which in their own ways provided increasing anonymity for both the hunted and the hunter, required the creation of new modes of detection. In addition, the perceived development of urban masses also created new modes of secrecy and prompted the search for new modes of *individual* differentiation (most often based upon the typification of *individuals*) instanced in photography and fingerprinting. Thus, once more, the search for the (scientific) means for *calculating* criminal activity and behaviour (enhanced in another industry, that of insurance, by the calculation of *probability*) coincided with the representation of detection – and the crucial role of the discoveries of *clues* – as performed by individuals confronted in an urban context by the *fortuitous* nature of the discovery of hidden relations between individuals and groups. The ostensibly rule-governed nature of detection by operatives in Pinkerton's agency was presumably intended, in part, as a means of giving a semblance of a modern system to detection and as a counter to the seemingly arbitrary or fortuitous nature of the discovery of clues.

The exploration of the 'secrets' of the modern metropolis was also undertaken by several emergent academic disciplines in the late nineteenth and early twentieth centuries, most notably by social theorists. Prominent amongst their number is Georg Simmel, whose essay 'The Metropolis and Mental Life' is perhaps one of the most cited in literature on the modern metropolis. For that reason, amongst others, it runs the danger of being both fetishized and decontextualized. If we wish to examine more fully Simmel's contribution to the interpretation of metropolitan modernity, then we need to locate his famous lecture in its context and to integrate his other contributions and explorations of the metropolis into a broader constellation. In this way, the essay which is so often veiwed in isolation can be treated as an intersection of thematic circles of interpretation of the modern metropolis.

The more we explore Simmel's other writings aside from his metropolis essay, the more extensive the urban location of much of his analysis of modern society and modernity becomes apparent. This is, in part, because the two major sites of modernity for Simmel, the metropolis and the mature (capitalist) money economy are inextricably linked. However, in the present context, an attempt has been made to examine other dimensions of Simmel's richly diverse analyses that are relevant to a fuller understanding of his interpretation of the metropolis.

Indeed, if we confined our attention merely to Simmel's 1903 metropolis essay, then a number of *absent* dimensions of the modern metropolis would become apparent. These would include the sphere of production, political power, gender relations and gendered experience of the metropolis, spatial dimensions of the metropolis (including both representations of the city and its architecture) and the aesthetics of the metropolis. To varying degrees, these and other aspects of modern metropolitan life are explored in other Simmel texts. The latter include reflections upon urban space (including its boundaries and the inside/outside dialectic), architecture, representations of the city, female culture, domination and subordination and network analysis, interactions with the other, figures in the metropolitan landscape, pathologies of metropolitan modernity, distractions in the metropolis and beyond, and the dialectic of objective and subjective culture. This should not imply that all these reflections are located in other places devoted specifically to the metropolis, but merely that, at the very least, aspects of these other texts are evidently relevant to a fuller exploration of Simmel's interest in the modern metropolis.

If there is a *textual* context within which Simmel's essay 'The Metropolis and Mental Life' can be located and even reconfigured, then this is also true for its *historical* context. Originally a lecture as part of a series in Dresden prior to the opening of the first major celebration of the modern German metropolis at the German Metropolitan Exhibition in 1903, Simmel's contribution proved not to be what its organizers had anticipated: a positive statement on the institutional, intellectual and cultural life in the city. Instead, and unlike all the other contributions to the lecture series which contained a substantial historical, comparative element, Simmel's lecture focused upon the inner life of the individual in the metropolis, and drew upon little historical and certainly no statistical evidence. His emphatic concentration upon the mental or inner life of the contemporary metropolis (with an occasional historical reference to Athens or Weimar) and the potential for individual freedom within its expanding objective culture gave it a more philosophical and social psychological import than several of the lecture series' participants and organizers desired. In a broader historical context, Simmel's lecture/essay appeared seven years after his essay on the Berlin Trade Exhibition of 1896,[30] which signalled that city's elevation into a world city as far as many contemporaries were concerned, and three years after his most sustained examination of crucial aspects of modernity – his *Philosophy of Money* – was published in 1900. After the metropolis essay of 1903, there were no further substantial treatments of the modern city by Simmel.

In terms of *theoretical* threads in his exploration of social, cultural and psychological processes in the modern metropolis, they can perhaps be viewed as a series of contradictory tensions that may be concentrated in the metropolis but which are present in other contexts explored by Simmel. Such tensions and antinomies would include the widening gap between objective and subjective culture, the simultaneous presence of processes of differentiation and dedifferentiation, the juxtaposition of calculability and fortuitousness in social interactions, the simultaneity of proximity and distance in the metropolis, the boundaries of inside and outside (not merely in terms of private and public spheres, but also the boundaries between publics) and the relationship between the totality and the fragment.

Although Simmel refers only once to Berlin in his essay on 'The Metropolis and Mental Life', it is evident that *his* metropolis – despite the fact that he visited many others – is Berlin.[31] And although there is no instance of comparison of metropolitan centres in Simmel's various explorations of the modern metropolis, such comparisons were not uncommon amongst his German contemporaries. In the present context our major focus is largely upon Berlin and Vienna. Paris is represented through Benjamin's exploration of the flâneur and elsewhere, American cities are implicit in the account of detection in the Pinkerton Agency, and German cities are implicitly present in the discussion of German Expressionism.

In the German context of the late nineteenth and early twentieth centuries, a number of issues emerge in discourses on the metropolis. The first is what constitutes a city and a world metropolis. By the last decades of the nineteenth century, and prompted by the dramatic expansion in urbanization after German unification in 1870, it was agreed – by social statisticians, urban researchers and others – that a city (*Grossstadt*) should have a population in excess of 100,000. This had the consequence that urban conurbations in the Rhine–Ruhr area possessed a large number of cities which, because they were not consolidated into a single unit, never constituted a single metropolitan centre, even though they comprised the largest urban area in Germany. At the same time, before their incorporation into Greater Berlin, cities such as Charlottenburg or Rixdorf constituted separate metropolitan entities even though they were effectively an extension of the Berlin urban nexus. Where the issue as to what constituted a world metropolis was resolved quantitatively at a population in excess of one million, then at the turn of the century only Berlin qualified for such status (with Hamburg with its over 900,000 inhabitants in second place).

Yet the nature of the metropolis was evidently not merely a quantitative issue (or even, as Durkheim was aware, one of social or moral density). The symbolic representation of the city was also decisive, as in the correlation between Berlin's 1896 trade exhibition and its self-recognition as world city. At the same time, other regional metropolitan centres such as Munich could lay claim to be cultural capitals whose influence extended well beyond their regional boundaries. But more importantly, the comparisons that were being made *between* cities said much more about the representations of metropolitan existence. Our focus is upon two instances.

The first is the comparison drawn between Berlin and American cities (notably Chicago, but also New York).[32] If Berlin's expansion after 1870 was dramatic in a German and wider European context, then it could be compared with the even more rapid explosion of populations in such cities as Chicago – and Berlin was sometimes referred to as 'Chicago on the Spree'. Again, however, such contemporary comparisons did not merely focus upon quantitative expansion. The identification of Berlin as an American city did not rest merely upon its expansion within a relatively short timespan. Rather, this putative comparison and even identification was directed inwards towards a discourse upon the negative effects of urbanization, often in the context of an anti-urban ideology. Berlin as American city could be read as America in Berlin in Germany. American civilization could be read as Berlin metropolitan culture.

Indeed, the second significant comparison made in the same period was between Berlin and Vienna. And here almost invariably the representational context was that of Berlin as symbol of civilization and Vienna as symbol of culture. One could also reconfigure this constellation as modern

American civilization compared with historical, European (German) culture. In part, the mode of *evaluation* of such symbolic constellations rested upon whether this comparison was being made from a Berlin or Viennese perspective. But more crucial in deciding the evaluation of these representations was the stance vis-à-vis modernity itself. In turn, this could be rendered more complex by an anti-modern analysis of modernity such as Werner Sombart provided. Berlin as the symbolic representation of a (negative) modernity could be contrasted with the historically rooted cultural capital, Vienna.

Within Vienna itself, around the turn of the century, there existed an often vitriolic conflict between the forces of modernization and tradition, between 'New Vienna' and 'Old Vienna'. In part, this was not a new conflict but rather one that was embedded in the first major restructuring of the city from 1857 to the late 1880s associated with the Ringstrasse development. That project had already called forth a nostalgic literature on Old Vienna (i.e. pre-Ringstrasse), but the extension of the city boundaries in 1890 and the competition for a new city plan for the creation of a 'modern' metropolis – as 'Gross-Wien' – gave the 'Old Vienna' ideology a new impetus. Unlike Berlin, Vienna had retained a largely intact medieval, Renaissance and baroque core around which the new Ringstrasse zone formed a historicist modernity, and beyond which were the originally older urban developments increasingly subjected to modernization.

This was only part of the context within which the notion of designing a modern metropolis was likely to prove problematical. The capitalist industrialization of Vienna proceeded more slowly than was the case in Berlin. In turn, that capitalist development was located in the context of a substantial agrarian land empire of which Vienna was the capital (increasingly challenged in pace of development at least by Budapest, the capital of the Hungarian portion of that empire since its separation in 1867). The multinational and multicultural nature of the Hapsburg Empire and the waves of migration into Vienna gave the city an additional horizontal dimension of stratification (based on ethnicity, culture, language, etc.) to the dual vertical stratification systems of an estate society (based on rank) and a class society. This multidimensionality, combined with a large bureaucratic sector to administer the largest land empire in Europe outside Russia, rendered modernization a contested project that would be strongly resisted.

Hence, an architect such as Otto Wagner, with his 1896 manifesto for a modern architecture that should reflect modern life – whose epitome was the modern metropolis – and who had already been successful in winning the competition for the general plan of New Vienna in 1894 as well as for the new city railway, was likely to encounter considerable resistance in Vienna. Yet the notion of modernity with which Wagner operated, despite his persistent call for a modern architecture and a modern metropolis, was neither internally coherent nor consistent.

Nonetheless, beyond Wagner's somewhat naive plea for a structural homology between modern life and modern architecture, many significant issues were raised in his *Moderne Architektur* of 1896.[33] His attack on the orgies of historicism in the recent past (the Ringstrasse zone development and, by implication, some of Wagner's own earlier work) focused not merely on its inappropriate stylizations in the modern world but upon a more interesting issue – which he himself neither fully articulated nor solved – as to the *intelligibility* of (modern) architecture. Although Wagner's argument was that contemporary historicisms were unintelligible to the modern urban dweller, the issue of architecture's and, implicitly, the modern city's intelligibility had much wider implications.

At one level, this issue was about the textuality of the metropolis and its architecture. For contemporary architects and observers/users/dwellers, this architecture could be conceived as *text in the process of being created or produced*. At the same time, the creation of a new modern architecture in the context of a historically existing urban and architectural constellation also implied *the destruction of text*. This was particularly relevant to the Viennese context (as it had been earlier on a larger scale in Haussmann's 'creative destruction' of mid-century Paris) in which part of 'New' Vienna would be built upon 'Old' Vienna. Indeed, this problematic of intelligibility had already been raised in Camillo Sitte's 1889 volume on city planning and the ensuing debate on the seemingly somewhat obscure issue of straight or crooked streets.[34] Sitte (drawing almost all of his non-Viennese examples of irregular squares and crooked streets from Italian Renaissance and baroque cities) maintained that the long straight avenue and the large modern square constituted urban spaces that created pathological responses in modern city dwellers. More importantly, the obsession with problems of traffic circulation and public hygiene (sewage systems, etc.), generated a mode of town planning that was preoccupied with technical rather than aesthetic dimensions of the metropolis. As Sitte stated in one of his many newspaper attacks upon the plans for New Vienna (often directed at Wagner), the issue before the modern city planners was whether they wished to create the metropolis as 'a work of art' or as 'a human storehouse'.[35] Wagner himself did not directly respond to Sitte in the press, nor did he directly participate in this debate on straight or crooked streets (whose principal protagonists were Joseph Stübben – for straight streets and a modern metropolis – and Carl Henrici – supporting Sitte's position).

Wagner's *Modern Architecture*, however, does contain many implicit attacks upon Sitte's position. But his main concern is to argue for a modern architecture appropriate to modern metropolitan life. The modern metropolis as the epitome of modernity will be subject to unbounded expansion and extension. The correlation between modern architecture (and the modern metropolis) and modern life made it encumbent upon Wagner to specify the features of modern life that its modern architecture would 'reflect'. Although not coherently presented, these features of modern life centre around the process of *abstraction, circulation and movement* and *monumentality*: unbounded expansion of the city, permanent progress, technological advance, democratization, levelling of life-forms, purposive orientation to time and money, increasing mobility, and acceleration in circulation (and fashionability) and monumentalism (including the street as monument). As both symptom and response to several of these features, Wagner lay emphasis upon the domination of the rented apartment block (as a 'conglomerate of cells').

Aside from the somewhat uneasy location of fashion within these putative features of modern life, the desire for a new, modern monumentalism is worth noting. Only those conceptions of modernity that conceive of it as a calculated ordering and structuring of the built environment would argue for an increase in public monuments and a new monumentalism. If modernity is conceived as experience of the transitory, fleeting and fortuitous, then *its* monumental representation could be conceived only as the temporary, fleeting and fortuitous structure, or the imploding structure. The logic of Wagner's somewhat positivistic delineation of the features of modern life pointed only in the direction of a systematic and even symmetrical ordering of built forms. Modern public monumentalism required *political* support and this was not forthcoming after the shift in political power in Vienna to Dr Karl Lueger's Christian Social Party (with its anti-Semitic ideology), however much Wagner sought its support.[36]

If we return to the notion of the imploding structure of the city, to the representation of its street life as fleeting and fortuitous impressions, then the movement that perhaps came closest to realizing this conception in some of its declarations and representations of the modern metropolis was the short-lived German Expressionist movement. Whereas Otto Wagner conceived of the constantly expanding modern metropolis in circles radiating outwards from its centre and was best articulated in his short monograph *Die Grossstadt* (1911),[37] some Expressionist Utopians conceived of the radical dissolution of the modern metropolis and the creation of new cities of glass – as 'city crowns' – in the mountains.[38] However, our concern is less with what Benjamin later referred to as 'the well-ventilated Utopia' of such conceptions that were conceived but never realized by Taut and others, as with possible affinities between Expressionist artistic and literary representations of the modern metropolis and contemporary social theory in Germany. The chapter on Expressionism thus explores not merely some of the affinities between social theorists' representations of the city and metropolitan modernity and those of Expressionist artists, but also Expressionism *in* social theory, most notably in the work of Ernst Bloch.[39] A fuller treatment of this interface might wish to explore, say, the impact of Simmel's social theory and philosophy upon Erich Mendelsohn, Kurt Hiller and, beyond the Expressionist movement, Adolf Behne, Martin Wagner and others.[40]

One dominant mode of representing the Expressionist city was to focus upon the inner life of the human subject in the city streetscape bombarded with all dynamic effects upon the individual. Here, the street at a distance, the street viewed from above familiar to many Impressionist representations of the metropolis, was replaced by an increasingly fragile human subject buffeted by the throng of the chaotic urban crowd, its traffic and its threatening built structures, an urban nexus imploding upon the individual. Any affinities between this mode of representation of the modern metropolis and contemporary social theory would be located in those social theories that explored expressions of emotional or other psychological responses to the tumult of the modern city. Another possibility would be the development of a mode of expressing such experiences in social theory that was consonant with Expressionism itself. Amongst social theorists the primary instance of the latter is the work of Ernst Bloch, who remained committed to this mode in subsequent decades.

In the 1920s, after what many saw as the demise of Expressionism in Germany, several of the architects who had been prominent in creating Expressionism's Utopian visions of the modern city, and who had participated in the revolutionary councils for art and architecture in the period around the failed German Revolution of 1918, were active in what some saw as the construction of new, rational Utopias of the modern metropolis. By the end of the 1920s journals announced the creation of another 'New' Vienna, the 'New' Frankfurt and, above all, the 'New' Berlin. The joint editor of the short-lived *Das neue Berlin* (the other editor being Adolf Behne), and city planner of Berlin since 1926, was Martin Wagner.[41] The journal displayed the achievements and projected works in Berlin that emphasized two spheres of preoccupation – public housing and the reconstruction of the centre of the city (most notably, Alexanderplatz) – that contributed to giving Berlin the appearance (once more) of being the most modern capital city in Europe. In turn, the problems of traffic circulation in an expanding metropolis and the questioning of the site of that expansion (within the metropolitan core or at its periphery and beyond) also raised the issue of the accelerated 'turnover time', as it were, of the built environment itself.

The preoccupation with the modern metropolis in the 1920s in Weimar Germany called forth a number of Utopian and not realized models. One of the most radical and not realized was the dystopian vision of Ludwig

Hilberseimer with high-rise blocks and a radical separation of traffic forms, whose overall alienating effect (although realized in many cities from the 1960s onwards in advanced capitalist societies) caused even Hilbersheimer to lament that they were 'more a necropolis than a metropolis'.[42] In contrast, the housing schemes conceived by Martin Wagner, and sometimes realized in association with Bruno Taut and others, displayed the hallmark of careful, realistic calculation. The same was true of his extensive writings on housing and, in a negative manner, of his commitment to rationalization of the building industry. Some of these writings pleading for rationalization serve as confirmation of Max Weber's argument that rationalization was likely to be carried forward more systematically by socialists than capitalists.

Nonetheless, few had such an overall conception of Gross-Berlin as Wagner in the late Weimar Republic's years. Although his concern for the development of public housing schemes and for the heart of the Berlin metropolis was not unique, even his opponents recognized his achievements in what were the most difficult years of the increasingly crisis-ridden Republic. City planning as encouragement of the acceleration of motorized circulation of individuals and commodities took on a logic of its own when Wagner declared that the dynamic nature of the traffic points or squares (such as Alexanderplatz) implied that the buildings surrounding them could have a life of no more than 15 or, at most, 25 years. Modernity, as the eternally transitory, had been recognized with respect to aspects of the built structures of the modern metropolis. The plans of Wagner and others were not realized for the Alexanderplatz (nor incidentally for the Platz der Republik or the Potsdamerplatz – the future form of all of which have been once more the subject of the most heated debate in Berlin in the last decade) but for quite other reasons – notably Allied bombing raids on Berlin in the Second World War. The amortization of the buildings around the Alexanderplatz hardly survived Wagner's 15 year minimum.

The increasing political deadlocks in the last years of the Weimar Republic in Berlin and increasingly bitter internicene political struggles prompted Wagner to resign from the Social Democratic Party. Within a very short space of time he was dismissed from his position in 1933 to face uncertain years in Berlin and then exile first in Turkey (Istanbul) and subsequently in the United States. But one year before his dismissal, Wagner – almost in desperation – outlined another Utopia of the modern Berlin metropolis, namely its demise and dispersal into cities of 50,000 population in the countryside, not unlike other contemporary conceptions of satellite towns. In this respect, therefore, the presumed dissolution of the city, of which many Expressionists had dreamed and then committed to paper but never realized, might perhaps have come to fruition in the writings of one of the most formally rational city planners.

V

It should be apparent that the present volume consists of a series of explorations of a number of dimensions of the city in modernity. To varying degrees, attention is given to examining aspects of *space* and the metropolis. With the exception of the study of detection, all the other explorations largely focus upon dimensions of cityscapes of modernity in Berlin and Vienna. In other words, there is an implied shift in focus upon modernity eastwards. Even the discussion of the flâneur takes as its central orientation the writings of Walter Benjamin on the figure of the flâneur, who is usually located in Paris. Benjamin originally set out from Berlin with Franz Hessel to write two articles on the Parisian flâneur, a move which, for Benjamin, generated his unfinished Arcades Project. In this respect, we are reading a Berlin perspective on what was often claimed to be a Parisian figure.

The spatial explorations of modernity commence with the *spatial practices* of the flâneur, initially as outlined by Benjamin but also demonstrating their relevance for sociological investigations. At one level, the flâneur is located within Benjamin's meticulous exploration and excavation of the origins of modernity in nineteenth-century Paris. His multilayered reading of the city is one that gives attention to the seemingly most trivial traces, to the refuse, to the scraps left behind by a history written by victors. The texts and images upon which he draws are referencing material entities – spaces, representations and practices. They are textual and visual remains that document the spaces of nineteenth-century Paris and the origins of modernity. This should clarify the significance of Benjamin's statement to Kracauer that he is in the arcades, when in fact he is in another space – the Bibliothèque Nationale in Paris. As Bettine Menke has argued, our reading of Benjamin's Arcades Project is a reading of that project's textual spaces as well as the spaces of the modern metropolis. This is especially true of the memory spaces that Benjamin is redeeming:

> The 'memory spaces' that are to be found in modernity in the cities are, however, spaces of texts, of allusions and intersections, of inscriptions, of the extension and transcription of texts. The memory space of Paris is . . . [staged] in Benjamin's reading of the 'capital of the nineteenth century' . . . [as] the quotation space of his *Arcades Project*.[43]

For our purposes, what this implies is that any examination of the spatial practices of flânerie must also explore the textual and image spaces of the products of flânerie.

The exploration of the not unrelated activity of the detective also involves an examination of the spatial practices of detection. 'Walking the city' takes on a definite intention and goal. The testing of potential detectives in Pinkerton's Agency for their skills in 'shadowing' and 'roping' (drawing into conversation) is a test and training in specific social and spatial practices. The training in detection took place in metropolitan centres such as Chicago, New York, Philadelphia and San Francisco. By the First World War, Pinkerton's Agency was established in most major cities in the United States. Thus, although the activity of detection also clearly took place in rural areas, training for this spatial practice was undertaken in the city. Similarly, although the *representations* of detection were not confined to urban spaces, specific genre were associated more with the modern metropolis and its mysteries.

Walking the city as detective requires training the 'eye' for acute observation *and*, in the case of shadowing, recognition of appropriate spatial distance.[44] Gathering information through conversation, often as if the detective is someone else, requires a trained recognition of the dialectics of spatial proximity and secrecy. The transgressions of the boundaries of proximity and distance that are implied in detection practices are also present in the relationship between the public and private spheres of urban existence. The private eye is distinguished from the public police 'eye'. But the privacy implicit in the former's activities suggests a much greater transgression of the private sphere and, by virtue of a cultivated anonymity, a greater command of public space than is permitted the visible, public police force. This putative superior access to the (potentially open) spaces of the city is accentuated in literary representations of detection. Although the representation of the metropolis in detective fiction in its *noir* variants, and indeed in its earlier forms, has often been a powerful one, it has not been alone in providing compelling images of the city.

As Simmel observed, the metropolis can be represented in displays of itself in exhibitions. Prior to his most famous essay/lecture on the modern metropolis (1903), which itself had its origin in an exhibition of modern German cities in 1903, he had already explored, however briefly, the spaces of representation of the metropolis – in this case, Berlin – in his 1896 essay on the city's trade exhibition and in 1890 on art exhibitions in relation to the city. Taken together with his explicit, detailed examinations of significant dimensions of social space in 1903, we can see a developing focus upon spatial configurations of social life in general and the metropolis in particular. At the same time, we should recognize that the essay on the metropolis and mental life is itself not merely an exploration of our representations of the city in our mental life, as it were, but also a compelling representation of the metropolis. Despite its omissions and often limited treatment of specific dimensions of metropolitan existence, the essay and other relevant pieces by Simmel on urban existence in turn had a significant impact upon literary and artistic representations of the metropolis. This is not intended to detract from the substantial analytical and interpretive force of Simmel's exploration of urban existence. Rather, it is to acknowledge that its reception in some cultural and artistic circles may well have been as a powerful representation of the modern metropolis.

Despite earlier affinities with Impressionism,[45] viewed as an extension of the realist tradition, Simmel's representation of the modern city is one that, in conjunction with later writings, could be drawn upon by strands of the German Expressionist movement. Within some strands of Expressionism that focused upon the city it was not the calculating exactness of metropolitan transactions that was compelling in Simmel's portrayal of the city, but rather the chaos of the bombardment of sense impressions and the emotional impact of the city's myriad encounters that were manifested in some Expressionist images. The regulated spaces of metropolitan circulation were transposed into imploding chaotic spaces that impinged forcefully upon the 'mental life' of its inhabitants. In turn, this spatial deregulation in Expressionism's representations was to be interpreted as potentially Utopian by one of Simmel's students, Ernst Bloch.

In contrast, what was perceived as the most modern European city, Berlin, came, for some, to be the embodiment of a spatial dystopia that, by virtue of its sheer quantification of everything within it, already symbolized the crass materialism endemic to American cities and 'Americanism'. In order for such an imaginary to come into its own, it often required a counter-instance, another urban space positively filled out. That urban space was Vienna, conceived as city of culture, a definite place in contrast to the anonymity of Berlin's spaces, an embodiment of culture in contrast to civilization and even, for some, a bulwark against Americanism. Of course, this third imaginary, America, was most often an imaginary representation of an unvisited and unresearched space.[46]

Not surprisingly, therefore, projects to design and *produce* a modern metropolis often met with powerful opposition. The projects of architects and city planners to produce new urban spaces in and of modernity never commenced with a tabula rasa. Indeed, response to Otto Wagner's intention to produce a modern architecture for a modern metropolis – which implied the transformation of *fin-de-siècle* Vienna into a modern metropolis – reveals not merely the systematic resistance of Old Vienna to New Vienna but an attempt at a spatial demarcation of these two modes of valorization of the city into an inside (for the old) and an outside (for the new). The defence of the inner core from substantial modernist incursions, despite some transgressions, was largely successful. At the same time, the cultural imaginaries of old and new could also mask other valorizations of these spaces, namely the significance of these spaces as urban capital. Culture *and* capital form and inform these spaces.

Almost four decades after the debate on New Vienna had commenced in 1890 the project for a New Berlin was advanced by the city's chief planner Martin Wagner. During the last years of the Weimar Republic, and despite the catastrophic collapse of the world economy and of the still most modern European city, the dynamic spaces of circulation – of commodities, traffic and individuals – were to be transformed at the heart of Berlin, most notably on the Alexanderplatz. At the same time, the dynamic mobility of modern life was to be given spatial form in the transformation of one of the seemingly least dynamic spaces, the house. The expanding, 'growing' house was displayed at the historical juncture when the economy was deeply in crisis. The problems faced by the inner city in this crisis led Wagner to conceive of the Utopian city as dissolved into smaller units (his 50,000 units) dispersed in the countryside. The spaces of the metropolis were to give way to the smaller urban units of satellite towns. The crisis of metropolitan space was dissolved into the rationalized spaces of *urbs in rures*.

1

The City Observed

The Flâneur in Social Theory

Flânerie is a kind of reading of the street, in which human faces, shop fronts, shop windows, café terraces, street cars, automobiles and trees become a wealth of equally valid letters of the alphabet that together result in words, sentences and pages of an ever-new book. In order to engage in flânerie, one must not have anything too definite in mind.

Franz Hessel, *Spazieren in Berlin*

The city as a mnemotechnical aid for the solitary stroller calls up more than his childhood and youth, more than its own history. What it opens up is the immense drama of flânerie that we believed to have finally disappeared.

Walter Benjamin, 'The Return of the Flâneur'

In the article I wrote about the city I leaned rather heavily on the information I had acquired as a reporter regarding the city. . . . Sociology, after all, is concerned with problems in regard to which newspaper men inevitably get a good deal of first hand knowledge. Besides that, sociology deals with just those aspects of social life which ordinarily find their most obvious expression in the news and in historical and human documents generally. One might fairly say that a sociologist is merely a more accurate, responsible, and scientific reporter.

Robert E. Park 'Notes on the Origins of the Society for Social Research'

I

Any investigation of the flâneur in social theory must commence with the
contribution of Walter Benjamin towards a history and analytic of this
ambiguous urban figure, whose existence and significance was already
announced a century earlier by Baudelaire and others. In so doing, we are
compelled to recognize that, in his variously termed 'prehistory of modernity', his excavation of 'Paris, the Capital of the Nineteenth Century', his
Arcades Project and in his many other writings, Benjamin revealed himself
to be not merely an outstanding literary critic and writer in his own right,
nor merely a subtle philosopher of history, nor indeed merely a stimulating
and often unorthodox Marxist – and all of these groupings have claimed
their Benjamin as *their* own – but also a *sociologist* and, in the context
of his still unrivalled investigation of the origins of modernity, an astute
practitioner of historical sociology.[1] Such a claim must be made against
the background of Benjamin's own resistance to sociological orthodoxy,
to 'the detectivistic expectation of sociologists',[2] to 'the euphemistic whisperings of sociology',[3] and also in the light of his praise for Siegfried
Kracauer's *Die Angestellten* (*The Salaried Masses*), whose author has fortun-
ately left 'his sociologist's doctoral hood behind'.[4] (In fact, Kracauer's doc-
torate was in architecture, although he had also published on sociology.)

The fundamental *ambiguity* of the figure of the flâneur, sometimes
verging on that of the mere stroller, at other times elevated to that of the
detective, to the decipherer of urban and visual texts, indeed to the figure
of Benjamin himself, was amplified by Benjamin's own analysis. It is
necessary to trace some of the dimensions of Benjamin's own history of
the flâneur in the context of his prehistory of modernity and to distinguish
this figure from the idler, the gaper (*badaud*) and others in Benjamin's
historical explorations.

Yet the flâneur functions, for Benjamin, not merely as a historical figure
in the urban context, but also as a contemporary illumination of his own
methodology. In this sense, the flâneur/detective is a central, albeit often
metaphorical, figure that Benjamin employs to illuminate his own activity
and method in the Arcades Project, together with the archaeologist/critical
allegorist and the collector/refuse collector. An investigation of flânerie
as *activity* must therefore explore the activities of *observation* (including
listening), *reading* (of metropolitan life and of texts) and *producing* texts.
Flânerie, in other words, can be associated with a form of *looking*,
observing (of people, social types, social contexts and constellations); a
form of *reading the city* and its population (its spatial images, its architecture, its human configurations); and a form of *reading written texts* (in

Benjamin's case both of the city and the nineteenth century – *as* texts and of texts *on* the city, even texts as urban labyrinths). The flâneur, and the activity of flânerie, is also associated in Benjamin's work not merely with observation and reading but also with *production* – the production of distinctive kinds of texts. The flâneur may therefore not merely be an observer or even a decipherer; the flâneur can also be a producer, a producer of literary texts (including lyrical and prose poetry as in the case of Baudelaire), a producer of illustrative texts (including drawings and painting), a producer of narratives and reports, a producer of journalistic texts, a producer of sociological texts. Thus, the flâneur as producer of texts should be explored both with regard to Benjamin's historical investigation from the conjuncture of the emergence of the flâneur and the production of the physiognomies of urban life in the 1830s and 1840s down to the presumed decline in the possibility of flânerie, as well as with regard to Benjamin's own research activity and textual production, especially within his Arcades Project.

Insofar as the flâneur is a significant figure for elucidating Benjamin's own unorthodox historical investigations – and to the extent that the serious and directed observations of the flâneur announces, for Benjamin, the emergence of the (private) detective or investigator – the exploration of this paradoxical figure of the flâneur and the ambiguous activity of flânerie can also illuminate some modes of sociological practice. It is possible that such investigations can deepen our understanding of the practice of social research as detection, both with respect to historiography (for instance, when Benjamin declares, 'I am in the Arcades', he is in fact in the Bibliothèque Nationale in Paris)[5] and to urban ethnography (as in Benjamin's excavation of the 'mythological topography of Paris',[6] or his explicit aim with respect to mid-nineteenth century Paris 'to build up the city topographically, ten times and a hundred times over').[7] Benjamin also detected a connection between the flâneur and the journalist, thereby pointing, in turn, to an affinity between the flâneur–journalist and social investigation from Henry Mayhew, through many other urban explorations in the nineteenth century to some of the work of Georg Simmel, Robert Park, Siegfried Kracauer and others, including Benjamin himself.

Such connections have often been obscured by sociology's own desire to lay claim to its academic credentials as a scientific discipline, as *the* science of society, by purging its historical development of any figures other than the most scientistically and often formalistically acceptable. In reality, however, sociology's contacts with more modest and sometimes dubious occupations may reveal procedures for acquiring knowledge of social experience that do not immediately set up an abstract distance from everyday experiences of modernity and replace them with what Benjamin referred to as 'the euphemistic whisperings of sociology'. The question as

to how knowledge of the social world is made possible may be explored
in ways other than recourse to such self-referential abstractions as are
generated today in rational choice theory or micro–macro debates, and
other such paradigms borrowed parasitically from another 'dismal' social
science's century-old paradigms, in the hope of gaining some of the latter's
presumed but illusory scientistic status and grandeur.

An exploration of the flâneur in social theory should therefore turn to
an examination of the contributions of those who were not recognized as
sociologists at all, such as Benjamin, or those whose work has often been
incorporated into the negative caricature of formal sociology, such as
Simmel, or those who were installed in sociology's 'shirt-sleeved' hall of
fame, such as Robert Park, or those whose sociological contribution was
seldom even acknowledged in Anglo-American discourse, such as Siegfried
Kracauer.

II

In one of his earliest references to the flâneur, in the notes on the Arcades
Project from the late 1920s, Benjamin already intimates the connection
between flânerie and modern representations of the city: 'Surrealism –
vague de rêves – the new art of flânerie. New past of the nineteenth
century – Paris its classical location'.[8] It is the past that is revealed to us
in the present through a reading of surrealist texts, above all of Aragon's
Paris Peasant and Breton's *Nadja*, as revelations of the dream-worlds of
the city, of the 'primal landscape of consumption' in the decaying arcades.
And, in keeping with the surrealist exposure of the dream, there is 'the
figure of the flâneur. He is similar to the hashish eater'.[9] But already
Benjamin wishes to break out of the dream-world of the metropolis, to
destroy its mythology in the historical space that is now first revealed to
us as the world of modernity of the nineteenth century. The flâneur is
immersed in this world in contrast to the person who waits: 'the person
waiting as opposite type to the flâneur. The apperception of historical
time to be insisted upon in the case of the flâneur against the time of the
person waiting.'[10]

What is to be emphasized here in these early notes is, first, the recognition of the figure of the flâneur in the nineteenth century as the result of
reading the then avant-garde literature of surrealism (not itself part of
the current avant-garde in Weimar Germany). Second, the flâneur, through
this reading, is associated with the dream-world of the surrealist perspective on the city – an intoxicated world, a particular form of remembrance
or recall of the past as an immediacy in our present. Third, even in these

earliest notes on the Arcades Project, there is indication of a not yet fully explored attempt to go beyond the revelation of the mythical dream-world of modernity. And in these earliest notes, it is not yet clear what role the flâneur might play in such a critique. Finally, Benjamin is already convinced that the origins of the flâneur as figure lay in Paris: 'Paris created the flâneur type. . . . It opened itself to him as a landscape, it enclosed him as a parlour.'[11]

Yet even by 1929, in his critical assessment of surrealism as 'The last snapshot of the bourgeois intelligentsia', Benjamin had already turned away from the mere intoxicating representations of modernity on the grounds that:

> the most passionate investigation of the hashish trance will not teach us half as much about thinking . . . as the profane illumination of thinking about the hashish trance. The reader, the thinker, the loiterer, the flâneur, are types of illumination just as much as the opium eater, the dreamer, the ecstatic. And more profane.[12]

What were the origins, then, of this profane illuminator, of the flâneur as Parisian urban figure?

Although Benjamin was the first to recognize the flâneur as a significant cultural figure of modernity and to excavate the historical location of this ambiguous figure in mid-nineteenth-century Paris, some of Benjamin's own analyses, read in isolation from his other texts, are apt to produce their own ambiguities. In Benjamin's writings on Baudelaire translated into English, which contain a section on the flâneur (*Charles Baudelaire*),[13] the flâneur as historical figure is seen largely as a social type who flourished in the period after the Revolution of 1830 down to the period of the development of the grand boulevards and department stores. In particular, the flâneur as figure flourished in the same period as the Parisian arcades, during the Second Empire of Louis-Philippe. In fact, in the period from 1799 to 1830 a total of 19 arcades were constructed in Paris and down to 1855 a further seven were erected. In Benjamin's account, the flâneur is located in relation to the arcades, to journalism and especially the feuilleton and physiologies of the 1830s and 1840s and to the urban crowd.[14] The flâneur is an urban stroller, observer, even idler (Benjamin cites taking a turtle for a walk as a demonstration against the division of labour). At times, the figure of the flâneur is close to that of the dandy (as a down-wardly mobile aristocratic and gentry figure) and the bohemian. As indicated earlier, Benjamin also views the flâneur as producer of texts in this period – the feuilleton's emergence in the 1830s and 1840s – and this also included feuilleton pieces on the figure of the flâneur as part of the much wider production of physiognomies. Benjamin's analysis of this form of literary production is, of course, critical, since it is the production of a literature that renders the dangers of the metropolis harmless, through the creation of caricatures of figures in the urban crowd, whose figures from the 'dangerous classes' are transformed and incorporated into part of the bourgeois bonhomie.

Similarly, Benjamin emphasizes that such literary texts are produced by a social figure who is intimately associated with the commodity form, indeed who circulates like a commodity himself and who, in seeking a marketplace for his literary productions, goes in search of the magical field of commodity circulation. There are two important implications of this identification. The first is the affinity with the crowd and the commodity:

> The *flâneur* is someone abandoned in the crowd. In this he shares the situation of the commodity. He is not aware of this special situation . . . [which] permeates him blissfully like a narcotic that can compensate him for many humiliations. The intoxication to which the *flâneur* surrenders is the intoxication of the commodity around which surges the stream of customers.[15]

The flâneur and his productions as commodities are here seen as caught up in the narcotic intoxication of the mass (of individuals and of commodities) that stand like a veil between the flâneur and his goal. However, in the previous paragraph, Benjamin also intimates the social context for the demise of the flâneur – the development of the department store, the shift from the street as *intérieur* to the department store as its commodified embodiment:

> If the arcade is the classical form of the *intérieur*, which is how the *flâneur* sees the street, the department store is the form of the *intérieur's* decay. The bazaar is the last hangout of the *flâneur*. If in the beginning the street had become an *intérieur* for him, now this *intérieur* turned into a street, and he roamed through the labyrinth of merchandise as he had once roamed through the labyrinth of the city.[16]

The implication here is that the transformation of the flâneur's social place and social space in the arcade and the street, with the development of the department store and – what Benjamin mention elsewhere – Haussmann's grand boulevards, signifies the decline of flânerie and the figure of the flâneur in this guise.

Yet we should not lose sight of the fact that Benjamin's Arcades Project came increasingly to focus upon Charles Baudelaire as flâneur. In its earlier projections, the figure of the flâneur remains ambiguous and contradictory. This is most evident in the 1935 'exposé' – 'Paris, the Capital of the Nineteenth Century' – and the section there on Baudelaire, where Benjamin declares that Baudelaire's lyrical poetry with Paris as its object, betrays 'the allegorist's gaze',

> the gaze of alienated man. It is the gaze of the *flâneur*, whose way of living still bestowed a conciliatory gleam over the growing destitution of man in the great city. The *flâneur* still stood at the margin, of the great city as of the bourgeois class. Neither of them had yet overwhelmed him. In neither of them was he at home. He sought his asylum in the crowd. . . . The crowd was the veil from behind which the familiar city as phantasmagoria beckoned to the *flâneur*. In it, the city was now landscape, now a room.[17]

Again Benjamin concludes these reflections with reference to the department store as 'the flâneur's final coup', thereby signifying once more the decline of the flâneur. But attention should be drawn here not merely to the flâneur (in this case Baudelaire) as producer of lyrical poetry and prose poems thematizing metropolitan life, but also the *marginality* of the flâneur's location within the city (seeking asylum in the crowd) and within his class (marginal to the bourgeoisie and, presumably downwardly mobile). In addition, the flâneur's gaze upon the city is 'veiled', 'conciliatory' and presented as a 'phantasmagoria'. It is the metropolis at a distance.

But in this same section, Benjamin draws a connection between the figure of the flâneur and that of other figures and groups revealing a problematical *political* dimension to his analysis. He maintains that:

> As *flâneurs*, the intelligentsia came into the market-place. As they thought to observe it – but in reality it was already to find a buyer. In this intermediate stage . . . they took the form of the *bohème*. To the uncertainty of their economic position corresponded the uncertainty of their political function. The most spectacular expression of this was provided by the professional conspirators, who without exception belonged to the *bohème*.[18]

The flâneur is here linked socially and politically to the *bohème*, the analysis of whom constitutes the opening section of his 1938 draft on 'The Paris of the Second Empire in Baudelaire'. This political connection virtually disappears in the 1939 article 'Some Motifs in Baudelaire', written after Adorno's critique of the 1938 draft, perhaps as a result of the narrower focus upon Baudelaire. Be that as it may, the flâneur appears in 'Some Motifs in Baudelaire' largely in the context of the crowd and the shocks of metropolitan existence.

We can read of the flâneur in all these drafts as if this is a transitory figure, whose literary productions were conditional upon the market for the feuilleton sections of the new press,[19] whose identification of the street with an *intérieur* 'in which the phantasmagoria of the *flâneur* is concentrated is hard to separate from the gaslight',[20] and whose habitat is challenged by the decline of the arcades, the advent of Haussmann's grand boulevards and, associated with them, the department stores. However, such a reading can be challenged in a number of ways, not least by reference to Benjamin's other writings (including his review of Franz Hessel's *Spazieren in Berlin*[21] entitled 'The Return of the Flâneur' ('Die Wiederkehr des Flâneurs', 1929)[22] and his extensive notes on the flâneur in *Das Passagen-Werk*[23]). Susan Buck-Morss, for instance, in *The Dialectics of Seeing* has pointed to the contemporary political relevance of many of Benjamin's remarks on the flâneur as a critical warning to intellectual flâneurs in the inter-war period – exemplified with obvious reference to protofascist journalists – in such notes as: 'Flâneur-sandwichman-journalist-in-uniform. The latter advertises the state, no longer the commodity.'[24] The *contemporary* relevance of the flâneur is drawn out more dramatically in another passage cited by Buck-Morss on the *flâneur* and the crowd, as a 'collective' that

> is nothing but illusory appearance (*Schein*). This 'crowd' on which the flâneur feasts his eyes is the mold into which, 70 years later, the '*Volksgemeinschaft*' was poured. The flâneur, who prided himself on his cleverness . . . was ahead of his contemporaries in this, that he was the first to fall victim to that which has since blinded many millions.[25]

Buck-Morss here draws attention to an unexplored political dimension of flânerie in totalitarian societies, in which mere strolling becomes suspicious behaviour and the activities of the stranger do contain, as Simmel suggested, 'dangerous possibilities'. The full consequences of the ambiguity of the flâneur's stance in relation to the market place and to socio-political movements are not drawn out by Benjamin.

There is another sense in which the discussion of the flâneur and flânerie cannot be confined to a single historical conjuncture. In his detailed study of the literary history of the flâneur, Eckhardt Köhn in his *Strassenrausch* has traced the relationship between *flânerie* and the short prose form from 1830 down to 1933, commencing with Louis-Sébastien Mercier's *Tableau de Paris*[26] (in book form in 1781), through the Second Empire; and then, shifting his perspective to Berlin, he traced this urban literary form from the 1850s to the turn of the century (and such figures as Robert Walser), before devoting half of his analysis to three twentieth-century figures: Franz Hessel, Walter Benjamin and Siegfried Kracauer. Such a configuration suggests that we should look more broadly at Benjamin's discussion of the flâneur, in the context of which he can also be seen as a flâneur, in which some of his writings are the literary products of flânerie and in which his reflections upon his own method of textual production may open up a wider relevance of the flâneur as illuminating some aspects at least of social investigation.

III

Benjamin creates not merely one of the first attempts at a history of the flâneur; he also provides us with an analytic of flânerie that reveals potential affinities between this activity and the sociologist's investigation of the social world. In part, this analytic emerges out of Benjamin's own reflections upon his methodology for the Arcades Project. It shifts the focus on the flâneur from the negative conception of the stroller and producer of harmless physiognomies to the notion of the more directed observer and investigator of the signifiers of the city.

This may become clearer if we start out for the moment with Benjamin's 1938 draft of 'The Paris of the Second Empire in Baudelaire' and, in particular, with his examination of the relationship between the flâneur and the detective. This connection brings out the possibilities of flânerie as a *positive* activity of individuals not totally submerged in the crowd (and its phantasmagorias). It distinguishes this activity from that of the passive spectator: 'In the *flâneur*, the joy of watching is triumphant. It can concentrate on observation; the result is the amateur detective. Or it can stagnate in the gaper; then the *flâneur* has turned into a *badaud*.'[27]

Benjamin, with Baudelaire and Dickens as counter-instances, goes on to observe that 'the revealing presentations of the big city have come from neither' – i.e. the flâneur, or the *badaud*; rather from 'those who have traversed the city absently'. Such a judgement must be challenged in the light of Benjamin's own literary production, his own analysis of flânerie and the social investigative activities of figures such as Henry Mayhew, Simmel, Park and others.

The connection that Benjamin draws between the flâneur and the detective, however, is one that breaks the confining identification of flânerie with the Second Empire and its 'soothing' physiologies, since the latter 'were soon passé'. In contrast:

> a literature which concerned itself with the disquieting and threatening aspects of urban life was to have a great future. This literature, too, dealt with the masses, but its method was different from that of the physiologies. It cared little about the definition of types; rather, it investigated the functions which are peculiar to the masses in a big city.[28]

If, for Benjamin, the masses are 'the asylum that shields an asocial person from his prosecutors' and if this 'menacing aspect' is 'at the origin of the detective story', then we would wish to claim some affinity with the origins of urban social theory and investigation. To anticipate later discussion, a plausible case can be made for the kind of connection between the masses and sociology that Simmel makes and for social investigation of more general social typifications (again Simmel's studies of processes, such as conflict, and typifications such as the stranger, the poor, the blasé person), away from individualistic explanations of the social world and a preoccupation with individual types common to the physiologies.

If we accept this interpretation, then we can read Benjamin's suggestive comments on detection not merely with reference to the origins of detective literature, but also as an explication of dimensions of flânerie that illuminate the nature of social investigation. In addition, his own notes on detection and his own methodological procedures are relevant for an understanding of his own activity of investigation and his own textual productions. The flâneur author as producer also applies to Benjamin himself. Such an interpretation thereby challenges the largely negative interpretation of the flâneur which confines this figure to that of seeing, observing and, in general, being confined to a mere spectator. In the historical explorations destined for his Arcades Project, Benjamin's activities surely qualify for inclusion within, while at the same time critically transcending, the procedures that Robin Winks outlined some time ago in his *The Historian as Detective*[29] as exemplary of a form of detection and inferential practices in historical research, in which

> the routine must be pursued, or the clue may be missed; the apparently false trail must be followed in order to be certain that it is false; the mute witnesses must be asked the reasons for their silence, for the piece of evidence that is missing from where one might reasonably expect to find it is, after all, a form of evidence in itself.[30]

In this context, the flâneur can engage in his or her intellectual flânerie in an archive, in a library, indeed in an *intérieur*, perhaps even as Adorno portrayed Kierkegaard: 'Thus the flâneur promenades in his room; the world only appears to him reflected by pure inwardness'.[31] In fact, Benjamin's own sojourns in the Bibliothèque Nationale proved a rich, dynamic and innovate source for his investigations of the historical arcades and much else.

But let us return for the moment to Benjamin's exploration of detection and flânerie. For Benjamin, 'the figure of the detective is prefigured in that of the flâneur'.[32] But, on occasion, the flâneur is 'turned into an unwilling detective'.[33] Such occasions are those of political crisis, of social crisis, of periods of terror. Hence, 'in times of terror, when everyone is something of a conspirator, everybody will be in a situation where he has to play detective'.[34] This role is best achieved through strolling, which in such situations is a politically charged activity that is hinted at by others, such as Simmel's notion that the detached stranger's view 'contains dangerous possibilities' or Hessel's opening account of flânerie in Berlin entitled 'The Suspicious Person' that refers to 'the suspicious role of the spectator'.[35] Benjamin, for his part, cites Baudelaire's view in this context that 'an observer is a *prince* who is everywhere in possession of his incognito',[36] before commenting that the flâneur's seemingly passive spectator role

> only seems to be indolent, for behind this indolence there is the watchfulness of an observer who does not take his eyes off a miscreant. Thus the detective sees rather wide areas opening up to his self-esteem. He develops forms of reaction that are in keeping with the pace of a big city. He catches things in flight; this enables him to dream that he is like an artist.[37]

This 'watchfulness of an observer, this figure who 'catches things in flight' can signify the detective, the artist of modernity, the journalist and certain types of urban sociologist. And, unlike the detective, the flâneur is interested in murders *and* rebellions.

The flâneur as urban observer who 'goes botanizing on the asphalt', collecting and recording urban images, social interactions and social typifications, is someone clearly at home in the metropolis and capable of combining observation, watchfulness and the preserving of his incognito. Hessel's insistence upon the suspicious activity of the flâneur and Baudelaire's emphasis upon the flâneur's incognito together provide the elements of that which Benjamin refers to as 'the dialectic of flânerie: on the one hand, the man who feels himself observed by everyone and everything, the totally suspicious person, on the other, the completely undiscoverable, hidden person.'[38]

This hidden figure, who is totally at home in the urban milieu, however strange it may appear in the course of his explorations, possesses the capacity for reading the signs of the crowded impressions of the metropolis, including the faces of the crowd. This is what Benjamin refers to as 'the phantasmagoria of the flâneur: reading off the occupation, the social origin, the character from the faces'[39] in the street and the crowd. Flânerie is an activity that requires training – in order not to overlook the obvious in one's own city and in order to engage in meaningful collection of images – and a particular social habitus. For Benjamin, 'the flâneur is an uprooted person. He is at home neither in his class nor in his birthplace but rather only in the crowd'.[40] Such marginality creates a distance between this figure and that which is observed. Similarly, the 'watchfulness' and capacity to catch 'things in flight' in the metropolis is accompanied by a necessary reserve with regard to his intentions. The capacity for rapidly reading off social characteristics from fleeting appearances and the slightest clues led Benjamin to insist upon 'how urgent must the interest in the hiding of his motives be in order to create a place for such thread-like theses'.[41]

The flâneur as observer cannot therefore be reduced to the passive spectator, to the mere idler or to the gaper (*badaud*). Rather, the activity of watchful observation in the modern metropolis is a multifaceted method for apprehending and reading the complex and myriad signifiers in the labyrinth of modernity. 'For the flâneur "there is always something to see".'[42] When the flâneur 'seems to be indolent', this apparent idling can be suddenly transformed into acute observation. In this context, Benjamin draws an analogy with other figures and their apparent idling: 'the spontaneity that is common to the student, the gambler and the flâneur is perhaps akin to that of the hunter, in other words to the oldest kind of work that above all may be closely interlinked with idling'.[43] The flâneur as prefiguring the detective also draws this figure closer to the hunter, to that transformation of the flâneur from a 'philosophical stroller' into a 'werewolf' in the social wilderness of the metropolis, which Benjamin took to be the theme of Poe's 'The Man of the Crowd'.[44]

It has often been pointed out that Benjamin's conception of observation and recording of metropolitan modernity is by no means confined merely to the activity of seeing or viewing the signifiers of modernity. Rather, in many places, Benjamin insists upon the significance of a *tactile* ability in the flâneur that brings this figure in proximity to that of the collector as ragpicker (*chiffonier*), as well as the less well-drawn figure of the archaeologist, all three of whom are important for understanding dimensions of Benjamin's methodology. Here it must suffice, for the moment, to take seriously his comment that the flâneur is nourished 'not merely from that which appears seriously there before his eyes, but often will seize upon mere knowledge, even dead data, like experienced and lived-through data'.[45] The flâneur must listen carefully to sounds, stories, scraps of quotations as well as search for clues amongst the 'dead data' of the metropolis – just like the detective; or in the archive – just like a historical social investigator such as Benjamin himself.

If, as David Grossvogel has argued for the detective story, 'the detective is traditionally an "eye" in a story about acuities of seeing . . . a "private" eye inasmuch as his sight is his alone',[46] and if we accept the affinities between flânerie and detection, then flânerie as observation involves modes of seeing and of reading. The location of this activity is the metropolis as a complex labyrinth of spaces, structures and populations. Indeed, 'the city is the realization of the ancient dream of the labyrinth. Without knowing it, the flâneur goes in search of this reality'.[47] But although 'the city is the genuine holy ground of flânerie', its actual reality is not necessarily that which the flâneur confronts; rather, 'a new romantic view of landscape emerges that appears instead to be a cityscape'.[48] What remains an open question here is the extent to which the flâneur contributes to the reproduction of a romantic cityscape in his own textual productions. Benjamin's acquiescence to Baudelaire's praise of Constantine Guys and Charles Meryon suggests other possibilities. At all events, Benjamin at times views the relationship between the flâneur and the city as one of estrangement: 'To the flâneur his city – even if he was born in it, like Baudelaire – is no longer home. For him it represents a showplace'.[49] Again, elsewhere, Benjamin suggests that one needs to be schooled in a particular form of estrangement in order, as in 'A Berlin Chronicle' and 'Berliner Kindheit um Neunzehnhundert' ('Berlin Childhood around 1900'), to read one's own earlier images of the city.

The flâneur, however, is also interested in the social space of the metropolis. Not only does the flâneur gaze starry-eyed at space but 'the "sensational phenomenon of space" is the fundamental experience of the flâneur'.[50] There is a concern with the sensational *intérieurs* of the nineteenth century but, above all, a preoccupation with streets and their architecture, both of which together constitute for Benjamin a further 'dialectic of flânerie: the *intérieur* as street (luxury), the street as *intérieur* (poverty)'.[51]

The streets and their architecture, the ostentatious architecture of mass transit (railway station), mass of spectators (exhibition halls) and mass consumers (department stores), to which the flâneur is drawn, remain also to be read and deciphered by Benjamin as flâneur. But it is not merely the spaces and structures of the metropolis to which the flâneur is drawn. The flâneur also explores the labyrinth of the populace, the metropolitan masses. This mass

> lies like a veil before the *flâneur*: it is the newest intoxication of the isolated person – it erases, secondly, all traces of the individual: it is the newest asylum of the hunted – it is, finally, in the labyrinth of the city, the newest and least researched labyrinth.[52]

This human labyrinth is researched in different modes by the flâneur as physiologist, as journalist, as 'sensational' and realist novelist (such as Zola) and as social investigator. In his own investigations, Benjamin focuses only upon the physiologist (of the 1830s and 1840s), the journalist and the early detective story writer (such as Poe's detective stories or Dumas's *Mohicans of Paris* where 'criminological sagacity [is] coupled with the pleasant nonchalance of the flâneur').[53]

What all of these figures might have in common is their connections at some time with journalism. Indeed, Benjamin insists that 'the social foundation of flânerie is journalism' – a thesis also developed by Kracauer.[54] The flâneur wishes to sell his or her images of the metropolis, to sell his or her socially necessary labour time spent on the boulevards, traversing the signifiers of modernity. The extensive literature of flânerie extends into our own century with some of the work of Hessel, Kracauer and Benjamin, as well as Simmel, Park and others. The positive evaluation of such textual production is perhaps hampered by Benjamin's own concentration upon explorations of the flâneur's milieu in the mid-nineteenth century and a correspondingly largely unreflected relevance of *his own activity* as flâneur for his own textual production. At all events, the two sets of explorations are seldom brought together. Exceptions, including a positive assessment of flânerie, are scattered in his notes for the Arcades Project and other writings, as well as in his reviews of Hessel's *Spazieren in Berlin*. In the 1939 notes for reworking the flâneur chapter of his Baudelaire study, he decisively distinguishes flânerie from mere distraction: 'Distraction and amusement as contrast to flânerie. The *badaud* of the distracted. Isolation and nonconformity of the flâneur. Contemplative residual elements transformed into the armed watchfulness of the hunter'.[55]

A positive evaluation of the flâneur in our century was provided by Benjamin himself a decade earlier in his review of Hessel's *Spazieren in Berlin*, entitled 'The Return of the Flâneur'. The origins of Benjamin's own Arcades Project lay in a visit to Paris with Hessel a few years earlier, with the intention of writing an article on the Parisian arcades. In his review, Benjamin contrasts a stranger's reading of a city that focuses on the exotic, the picturesque, with that of one of its inhabitants: 'to acquire an image of a city as a native requires other, deeper motives. Motives for which extend into the past instead of the distance'.[56] The city as an aid to historical memory opens up 'the immense drama of flânerie that we believed to have finally disappeared'.[57] Hessel's exploration of Berlin, his own sense of flânerie as 'a kind of reading of the street', is portrayed by Benjamin as an instance of 'the perfected art of the flâneur', namely:

> the knowledge of living. The primal image of living, however, is the *matrix* or the casing (*Gehäuse*). . . . Indeed, if one merely recalls that not only human beings and animals but also spirits and above all images inhabit, then it is abundantly clear with what the *flâneur* is concerned and what he seeks. Namely, images wherever they are housed. The *flâneur* is the priest of the *genius loci*. This inconspicuous passer-by with the dignity of the priest and the detective's sense for clues'.[58]

And, in contrast to much of his critical commentary upon the *flâneur* of the mid-nineteenth century, Benjamin suggests that this figure is capable of grasping concrete historical experience (*Erfahrung*) and not merely subjective lived-out experience (*Erlebnis*): 'Individual experience (*Erlebnis*) seeks the unique and the sensational, concrete experience (*Erfahrung*) the ever-same.' The flâneur, personified by Hessel, creating a topographical 'register' of the city, 'remembers like a child', and 'insists firmly like the sage upon his wisdom'.[59] Hessel himself insists at the end of his Berlin flânerie that he should not be accused of having overlooked important things. Rather, he suggests to the reader: 'go yourself just like me without destination on the small journeys of discovery of the fortuitous'.[60]

IV

Hessel was not alone in making important contributions to the literature of flânerie, nor was he alone in seeking a living from journalistic activities. Benjamin himself, without a salaried occupation throughout his life, was also engaged in endless flâneries. The activity of the flâneur is not exhausted in strolling, observing or reading the signifiers of the modern metropolis. Benjamin's *own* actvity in producing the hitherto most illuminating account of the flâneur involved the *reading* of texts *on* metropolitan modernity and the *production* of texts on that modernity. In addition, as Köhn and others have insisted, many of Benjamin's other texts belong to the literature of flânerie. It is precisely the author of an article entitled 'The Author as Producer', who should prompt us to look at how Benjamin himself produces texts and to ask what is distinctive about the flâneur as producer.

When Benjamin announced to Kracauer in March 1929, 'I am in the arcades – "it's as if I were in a dream", "as if it were a piece of myself" ' ,[61] he was referring to one of the many intense periods of working on his Arcades Project, an intense sense of being embedded in the context of the Parisian arcades of the nineteenth century. In fact, this intensive work on the textual reconstruction of 'Paris, the Capital of the Nineteenth Century' was undertaken in the Bibliothèque Nationale. This was the site of his excavations. His friend Stephan Morgenroth (Lackner) could declare that Benjamins 'pride was introducing me to the secrets of the Bibliothèque Nationale'.[62] Here and elsewhere Benjamin, like the flâneur, would go in search of the traces, literally read the traces of the nineteenth century from hard-earned clues and insist upon the 'necessity of listening for every accidental quotation, every fleeting mention of a book over many years'.[63] Like the flâneur as detective, Benjamin sought to assemble the facts into concrete constructs: 'Formula; construction from facts. Construction through the complete elimination of theory. That which only Goethe attempted in his morphological writings.'[64] Yet this early insistence upon citation – 'I have nothing to say, only to show' – and the montage principle, gave way to the notion of dialectical images of modernity. And here, again, there is a connection with the flâneur, namely in the notion of illustrative seeing: 'The category of illustrative seeing is basic for the flâneur. He writes just as Kubin did when he wrote "The Other Side", his dreamings as text to the illustrations.'[65] The graphic nature of Benjamin's texts and his creation of a 'metaphorical materialism', renders an orthodox analysis of them difficult.

Benjamin's Arcades Project constitutes an astonishing ensemble of quotations and commentaries that are systematically ordered under central themes with cross-referencing possibilities. The most diverse texts, quotations, scraps of information are placed together in a constellation of meaning that is rendered possible by their similarity. In this respect, Benjamin's procedure may be seen as a combination of a flânerie through the extensive archives of the Bibliothèque Nationale and a desire to bring some order to the scraps of information and citations gathered that is suggestive of one of the other figures who is illustrative of his method, namely the collector, both as learned collector and as *chiffonier*. This dimension of collection, of placing the similar in conjunction with one another, is a feature, too, of detection, of that activity which assumes importance with the increasingly serious nature of flânerie. This reading, recording, extracting, ordering, reconstituting, deciphering and the like that is an essential feature of historiography and archival research may also be viewed as a form of *ethnography*. This seems particularly apposite in Benjamin's case where his object is the construction of constellations of objects, figures and experiences in Paris in the mid-nineteenth century. His research and 'viewing' of its streets, its social types, its buildings, its whole topography, layer by layer, has affinities with other forms of urban ethnography.

There is a third illustrative figure for comprehending Benjamin's methodology, namely the reader of texts that remain to be deciphered. This figure, at times the critical *allegorist*, at others the *archaeologist*, is one whose activity emphasizes both the significance of language and the research for traces of the past in the layers of its representations from the present downwards. This activity and the specific configuration of concern for language and traces is brought together in Benjamin's brief reflection 'Ausgraben und Erinnern' ('Excavate and Memory'):

> Language has unmistakably signified that memory is not an instrument for the reconnaissance of what is past but rather its medium. It is the medium of that which has been lived, just as the soil is the medium in which ancient cities lie buried. Whoever seeks to gaze more closely at one's own buried past must proceed like a man who excavates. Above all, he must not shy away from coming back time and time again to one and the same fact – scatter it just as one scatters earth, root it up just as one roots up the soil. . . . Indeed the images that are extracts from all earlier contexts stand as valuables in the frugal chambers of our later insight – like torsos in the collector's gallery.[66]

In addition, Benjamin insists upon the necessity for a hermeneutic intention in such excavations insofar as 'a good archaeological report must not only indicate the strata from which its discovered object emanates, but those others above all which had to be penetrated'.[67] This intention is evident in Benjamin's own ordering of objects for his Arcades Project that extend through an A to Z of objects, and an incomplete low case collection from a to v, and includes such objects as 'A Arcades, department stores, calicot'; 'H The Collector', 'I Intérieur, the trace', 'L House of dreams, museums, spa', 'Y Photography', all with cross-references to other objects.

The flâneur, as embodiment of all these dimensions of exploration, traverses metropolitan modernity in search of that which is hidden: the ever-same in the new; antiquity in modernity; representatives of the real in the mythical, the past in the present and so on. But it is not merely the flâneur exploring the city, it is also Benjamin exploring the texts of the city, the texts on the experience of modernity, the representations of modernity, all of which are themselves as labyrinthine as the metropolis itself. This constellation of the city and text and the text as city is explored by Michael Opitz in his essay 'Lesen und Flanieren' ('Reading and Flânerie: On the Reading of Cities, on Flâneries in Books').[68] To explore Benjamin's theories of language and the doctrine of similarity and mimesis and the art of reading would take us away from our theme. But this is the context within which Optiz locates the detective dimension of the flâneur and Benjamin himself. The flâneur as marginal figure, collecting clues to the metropolis, like the ragpicker assembling the refuse, like the detective seeking to bring insignificant details and seemingly fortuitous events into a meaningful constellation – all are seeking to read the traces from the details. Benjamin's Arcades Project with over a thousand pages of notes, commentaries and the like is a complex *inventarium* that is also to be rendered meaningful. In this context Opitz draws out the dialectical relationship between flâneur and reader:

> 'The text', Benjamin writes in the Arcades Project, 'is a forest in which the reader is a hunter. Not every reader is struck by inspiration'. The reader as hunter and the flâneur as reader of traces; they are both in search of something. Benjamin took a notion of Adorno's as being 'outstanding' (V, p. 1112) that viewed the city as a 'hunting ground'. To the reader and to the flâneur the book and the city become a hunting ground.[69]

Similarly, the 'illustrative seeing' so fundamental to the flâneur is placed in conjunction with reading: 'Like the astrologer, the flâneur interprets from the signs of other constellations. The flâneur reads the city. In so doing, he is guided by the streets and buildings just as is the reader of the text by the script.'[70] Benjamin's construction of the prehistory of modernity and its projection into our present requires a distinctive mode of remembering. The painstaking construction of the origins of modernity in the Arcades Project is built up out of details and traces into dialectical images and the 'tiger's leap' into our present. This construction commenced from a myriad of fragments whose meaning could often not be recalled except through their construction and re-presentation in a new constellation. In this process, the flâneur and Benjamin played a crucial role As Opitz concludes:

> In order to be able to see things in their hardly still remembered significance, the flâneur had to wrest the details from out of their original context. To read them means to produce new constructions, means to derive more meaning from them than they possessed in their own present. 'That which is written is like a city, to which the words are a thousand gateways' (VII, p. 877).[71]

Benjamin excavates Paris, capital of the nineteenth century as a text, just as the Berlin of his childhood is a text. He does so not merely through texts *on* the city, but also through recognizing the text *as* a city.

The preceding study has sought to shift the discussion of the flâneur and flânerie from the restricted negative application to the Second Empire on the grounds that it neither does justice to the more extensive elucidation by Benjamin nor does it bring out the wider relevance for some forms of social investigation and textual production. Indeed, research still needs to be undertaken on the relevance of the flâneur and flânerie for elucidating social investigation and textual production. This is quite apart from the use made by researchers in other fields such as art history in their contextualization of some movements such as impressionism and metropolitan modernity. Drawing upon Benjamin and Simmel's discussion of the stranger, Robert L. Herbert in his *Impressionism: Art, Leisure, and Parisian Society*[72] has developed the connections between the flâneur artist as investigator of urban life and observer of *intérieurs* in the impressionist tradition of self-avowed flâneurs such as Manet and Degas. The exploration of metropolitan modernity, with its myriad cross-cutting interactions, its momentary shocks, its fleeting impressions and all that which Baudelaire signified as 'the transitory, the fleeting and the fortuitous', posed problems – in different ways – for artists, writers and social investigators alike.

If a case has been made for regarding the flâneur as producer of texts, it is important to examine the nature, however briefly, of the texts themselves. In addition, although the preceding discussion has concentrated upon the work of Benjamin, it seems fruitful to outline how far the flâneur and flânerie may be of wider significance in social theories of the metropolis and explorations of modernity. Thus far, a number of configurations have been intimated between flâneur and journalist, flâneur and detective and, more generally, the flâneur as producer of texts resulting from flânerie, which might suggest possible connections between forms of investigating metropolitan modernity and reporting and narrating this modernity in textual forms.

To remain with Benjamin for the moment, there are evident connections between flânerie and a number of his textual productions, above all *One-Way Street, Berlin Childhood* and the Arcades Project itself. To take but one example, *One-Way Street* is itself a constellation or 'construction' of aphorisms as a street 'just like, for instance, the famous stage set of Palladio in Vicenza: the street'.[73] Köhn suggests that the contents of *One-Way Street* do not indicate a random sequence of titles that is common in many aphorism collections, but rather that they

> are taken from the linguistic material of the street, or more precisely mirror the written material of the street as it is offered to the observer in a stroll down a metropolitan street on nameplates, posters, advertising hoardings, house façades, shop windows and exhibition showcases. What at first sight looks like a register of inscriptions of everyday street signs, nonetheless for Benjamin stands in the context of the street as a constructive idea of presentation.[74]

The reader is invited to stroll along the textual one-way street, that is itself the product of a kind of flânerie. In this context, Köhn asks 'who traverses the textual street built out of urban linguistic material? No longer as earlier in urban literature, the figure of the flâneur, but rather a mode of thought engaged in flânerie (ein flanieren des *Denken*)'.[75] In the case of some of Benjamin's other texts, such as the Arcades Project itself, only essays relating to the whole project were published in his lifetime. The Project itself remains 'a torso', an *inventarium* of research in Paris and elsewhere.

If we turn to other writers who have strong affinities with the figure of the flâneur and flânerie in social theory, then one of them must be Georg Simmel, who is strangely accorded brief attention in Köhn's study of textual forms of flânerie. Simmel's early foundation for a sociology that can investigate any and all forms of social interaction or sociation starts out from a recognition of social rather than individual explanations of social life as a result of the emergence of complex mass societies and mass social movements. The customary identification of his sociology with the problem of the relationship between individual and society obscures the extent to which that sociology is frequently concerned with a mass of individuals as part of a wider problematic of social differentiation.

However, what is distinctive about Simmel's investigations of metropolitan modernity is his concern to capture this dynamic reality through its 'delicate invisible threads', through 'the fortuitous fragments of reality', through exploring the intersection of social circles' as well as the broader processes of sociation and social differentiation. In my *Sociological Impressionism*[76] an attempt was made to locate Simmel's distinctive approach with that of a 'sociological flâneur'. Perhaps drawing too heavily on the negative associations of the flâneur from some of Benjamin's discussion of this figure in the Second Empire, and by seeking to encompass all his social investigations within this mode, the study failed to do justice to the full and systematic range of Simmel's achievement.[77] Nonetheless, the exploration of the figure of the flâneur and that of the stranger with reference to Simmel's approach to metropolitan modernity remains an illuminating one. In what follows, further lines of investigation are merely indicated rather than fully substantiated.

The affinities are most striking with respect to Simmel's essays and, in particular, his early often anonymous newspaper and journal articles. In all probability, the number of anonymous newspaper articles attributable to Simmel could be greatly increased with further investigation. The connection with journalism is strengthened by the knowledge that Simmel's brother Eugen was himself a journalist by profession.

The multiplicity of themes relevant to an exploration of metropolitan modernity by someone who, as Kracauer remarks, 'seeks . . . in his work – and this is very typical – to preserve his incognito, often even nervously,[78] calls for a fuller examination of Simmel's Berlin milieu. Similarly, the acknowledged mastery of the essay form requires not merely a recognition of the essay's significance as a texual production but also its place within modernity. This suggests not merely an investigation of discussions of the essay form by those with an interest in modernity itself, such as Lukács, Adorno and others, but also an examination of Simmel's own essay production within the modernist tradition. As Matthias Christen has argued, Simmel's statement of Rodin's aesthetic modernist problematic as one in which 'art no longer merely mirrors a world in flux, rather its mirror has itself become dynamic' can apply to Simmel's own practice in his *Philosophische Kultur*, namely 'to offer a mirror image of modernity with the *Philosophische Kultur*'.[79] In other words, we need to investigate further how far Simmel produces dynamic presentations of the modernity that he wishes to grasp in motion.

Earlier in the preface to his *Philosophy of Money*, Simmel also seeks to bring his *presentation* of the exploration of the site of modernity, the mature money economy, into some accord with the *object* of study itself:

> The significance and purpose of the whole undertaking is simply to derive from *the surface level of economic affairs* a guideline that leads to the ultimate values and things of importance in all that is human. . . . The

unity of these investigations does not lie . . . in an assertion about a particular content of knowledge . . . but rather in *the possibility . . . of finding in each of life's details the totality of its meaning.*[80]

This exploration of 'the symbol of the essential forms of movement within the world' is one that retains methodologically elements from that to which Simmel often referred, namely the 'snapshots *sub specie aeternitatis*'. In a sense, this most systematic of Simmel's works, with its symmetrical construction, is the culmination of over a decade's investigation of 'fortuitous fragments of reality', 'the superficial and transitory'.

In his excellent and original study of the Chicago School of Sociology's urban sociology, Rolf Lindner[81] points out that, as an inspirational figure in the naturalistic observation of the metropolis, Robert Park seldom wrote much on the methodological presupposition of his approach. As a newspaper journalist, both reporter and editor in the period 1887–98 in New York, Chicago and elsewhere, Park's investigations of the metropolis were to be fundamental for his subsequent sociological urban analysis. So, too, was his period of study with Simmel in Berlin and his acquaintance with a sociological programme that focuses upon the forms of social interaction and sociation, and in particular the forms of sociation in the metropolis. For Park it was the acute observation of metropolitan interaction in specific locales that not merely accords with the activity of the flâneur as investigator but also makes intelligible both his seemingly simple methodological advice, distinguishing between 'acquaintance with' and 'knowledge about' in favour of the former: 'It is, in the last analysis, from acquaintance knowledge and nowhere else that we derive the raw materials for our more recondite and sophisticated ideas about things',[82] and his view of the exemplary nature of the metropolis as the site for sociological investigation. In his 1915 essay 'The City', Park declared that:

> a great city tends to spread out and lay bare to the public view in a massive manner all the characters and traits which are ordinarily obscured and suppressed in smaller communities. The city, in short, shows the good and evil in human nature in excess. It is this fact, more than any other, which justifies the view that would make of the city a laboratory or clinic in which human nature and social processes may be most conveniently and profitably studied.[83]

The plurality of forms of differentiation and heterogeneity opened up the possibility for a plethora of studies of social types, spatial locations, social milieu, social groups and, in fact, the wealth of studies with which the members of the Chicago School and its students were concerned in the inter-war period.

As Park himself pointed out, his own version of urban ethnography had strong affinities with that of the newspaper reporter[84] and, though Park does not make this connection, with the flâneur-as-detective's directed gaze at urban life. Park's remarks on journalism, too, could apply to the urban ethnography of the Chicago School: 'The newspaper is, like art to the artist, less a career than a form of excitement and a way of life.'[85] The explorations of 'low' life, of forms of existence previously only sensationalized, recalls an earlier tradition of social investigation in the mid-nineteenth century as practised by figures, such as Henry Mayhew, who also had an interest in social reform.[86]

In the 1920s, when students of the Chicago School were investigating 'the city as a natural phenomenon', the 'journalist' Siegfried Kracauer was conducting his explorations of metropolitan modernity in Berlin and elsewhere.[87] Kracauer was certainly driven in Paris and probably elsewhere by 'an urge to engage in flânerie', and a desire that at various times was stated as the 'mastery of the immediately experienced social reality of life',[88] or later, in correspondence with Ernst Bloch, as an interest in 'the most superficial things', in 'the instances of superficial life'.[89]

Such urban explorations, even of the contemporary Berlin metropolis, often retained a strong historical sense, especially in his comparisons of Berlin as city of modernity and Paris as city of historical tradition. This led Kracauer in exile to work on a study – contemporary with Benjamin's Arcades Project in Paris in the mid-1930s – of the Paris of Jacques Offenbach which, like Benjamin, draws attention to the flourishing of flânerie and journalism on the boulevards.[90]

But, in addition, Kracauer also retained a wider interest in the figure of the flâneur. Two examples must suffice here. The first (from 1931) emerged out of a brief visit to Paris from Berlin. In a section headed 'Flânerie', he draws a contrast between the two cities as follows:

> Speed is a result of the mode of building cities. Can a person in Paris adopt the tempo of Berlin even though they are in a total hurry? They cannot do it. The streets in the inner sections of the city are narrow, and whoever wishes to pass through them must exercise patience. . . . And even though the grand boulevards are broadly set out, they nonetheless connect thickly populated districts with one another. The urge to engage in flânerie is indeed a sweet one, and seldom is such a wonderful virtue made out of the necessity of limited space. Unfortunately, it is very difficult to transpose such activity to Berlin. Our architecture is dreadfully dynamic: either it shoots undisturbed in a perpendicular line upwards or seeks out breadth in a horizontal manner. And the streets themselves – if I think, for instance, of the Kantstrasse, then I am immediately overcome by the irrestistible urge to dash without stopping at all towards its vanishing point, that must lie somewhere in infinity, close to the Berlin Radio House (*Rundfunkhaus*).[91]

Such reflections upon the spatial and temporal preconditions for flânerie were taken up again several decades later with reference to the representation of life on the street in film. In his *Theory of Film* (1960), subtitled 'The redemption of physical reality', Kracauer returned, on occasion, to the experiences of the flâneur. In particular, he singles out the street and the masses as preconditions for the flâneur's continued existence in the context of the new technology of the film and, earlier, photography. The street is

> a place where the flow of life is bound to assert itself. Again one will have to think mainly of the city street with its ever-moving anonymous crowds. The kaleidoscopic sights mingle with unidentified shapes and fragmentary visual complexes and cancel each other out, thereby preventing the on-looker from following up any of the innumerable suggestions they offer. What appear to him are not so much sharp-contoured individuals engaged in this or that definable pursuit as loose throngs of sketchy, completely indeterminate figures. Each has a story yet the story is not given. Instead, an incessant flow of possibilities and near-intangible meanings appears. This flow casts its spell over the *flâneur* or even creates him. The *flâneur* is intoxicated with life in the street – life eternally dissolving the patterns which it is about to form.[92]

These metropolitan streets gain their forceful impact from their populations – the historical emergence of the masses and their motion. Kracauer recalls Benjamin's observation that:

> in the period marked by the rise of photography the daily sight of moving crowds was still a spectacle to which eyes and nerves had to get adjusted. The testimony of sensitive contemporaries would seem to corroborate this saga-cious observation: The Paris crowds omnipresent in Baudelaire's *Les Fleurs du mal* function as stimuli which call forth irritating kaleidoscopic sensations; the jostling and shoving passers-by who, in Poe's *Man of the Crowd*, throng gas-lit London provoke a succession of electric shocks.[93]

The new technology of photography – unlike earlier art forms and techniques – was

> equipped to portray crowds as the accidental agglomerations they are. Yet only film, the fulfillment of photography in a sense, was equal to the task of capturing them in motion. . . . It is certainly more than sheer coincidence that the very first Lumière films featured a crowd of workers and the confusion of arrival and departure at a railway station.[94]

Kracauer's concern here is, of course, with film. But his own early interest in this medium coincided with his intoxication with metropolitan existence and the attempt to bring to life the analysis of crucial dimensions of mass urban experiences. In undertaking this latter project, in individual articles, in the *Frankfurter Zeitung*, in brief snapshots (as in the series 'Berliner Nebeneinander') and in monograph form (notably the highly successful *Die Angestellten* (*The Salaried Masses*)[95] it is often evident that Kracauer was influenced by the new technology insofar as it opened up new approaches to presenting documentary material.

It is not possible here to develop the depth of Kracauer's mostly brief, feuilleton-length explorations of the modern metropolis and especially Weimar Berlin.[96] But, in the context of Weimar Berlin, mention must be made of his exploration of white-collar employees in Berlin – *Die Angestellten* – published in article form in the *Frankfurter Zeitung* at the turn of 1929/1930 and in book form in 1930.[97] This investigation of the structure of the life experience and situation of white-collar workers in Berlin drew upon extensive interviews with workers, employers and others. It was an exploration of a social stratum 'whose life is more unknown than that of the primitive tribes whose customs white collar workers marvel at in films'. It drew upon documents, interviews and articles or, as Kracauer put it, 'quotations, conversations and observations' constitute 'the foundation of the study'.[98] However, such 'data' 'are not to count as examples of some particular theory, but rather as exemplary instances of reality'.[99] Convinced that 'there also is a flight into the concrete', is not descriptive reporting, 'the reproduction of what is observed' appropriate here? Kracauer rejects reportage in favour of what he terms a 'constructive standpoint':

> A hundred reports from a factory do not lend themselves to being added to the reality of the factory, but rather remain for all eternity a hundred views of the factory. *Reality is a construction.* Certainly life must be observed for it to come into being. But in no way is it embodied in the more or less arbitrary series of observations of reportage. Rather it is embodied solely in the *mosaic* that is assembled together from out of the individual observations on the basis of knowledge of its content. Reportage photographs life; such a mosaic would be its image.[100]

In a more pointed formulation, Kracauer states that 'reality does not emerge out of uncontrolled descriptions but out of the dialectical interplay of viewpoints and concepts'.[101] Or elsewhere, in the descriptions of a then popular reportage, 'one describes reality, instead of coming upon *the traces of its errors of construction*'.[102] Of course, Kracauer insists upon an investigation of 'normal existence in all its imperceptible dreadfulness', of 'minor events out of which our normal social life is composed' but, at the same time, his concern is with that which a title of one of his 1931 articles indicates lies, 'Beneath the Surface' ('Unter der Oberfläche').[103]

His 'constructive' standpoint also is 'directed towards a destructive procedure. It must unmask ideologies'.

Kracauer's reflections upon the nature of textual production and modes
of representation of social life remain in his later writings too. Although
they do not necessarily resolve all the methodological problems which they
raise, they do indicate the difficulties to be encountered in social investigation, including the flâneur's collection of documentation of metropolitan
modernity. The conclusion in Kracauer's article 'The Challenge of Qualitative Content Analysis' from 1952[104] contains the statement:

> Documents which are not simply agglomerations of facts participate in the
> process of living, and every word in them vibrates with the intentions in
> which they originate and simultaneously foreshadows the indefinite effects
> they may produce. Their content is no longer their content if it is detached
> from the texture of intimations and implications to which it belongs and,
> taken literally, it exists only with and within this texture – a still frag-
> mentary manifestation of life, which depends upon response to evolve its
> properties. Most communications are not so much fixed entities as ambi-
> valent challenges. They challenge the reader or the analyst to absorb and
> react to them.[105]

Of Kracauer's own 'documents' and 'communications', it was *Die
Angestellten* (*The Salaried Masses*) that had the greatest impact, 'indeed
created a sensation and had a major influence on discussion of the internal
political situation'.[106] That would probably not have been the case had it
appeared in another form. In one of his two reviews Benjamin suggests
that 'at one time, this text would have been called "Towards a Sociology
of White-Collar Employees". Indeed it would not have been written
at all'.[107] Rather, for Benjamin, its virtue lay precisely in avoiding 'the
euphemistic whispering of sociology'.

2

The City Detected

Representations and Realities of Detection

Words – printed ones especially – are murderous things.
E. A. Poe, 'Marginal Notes'

Ask yourself: How does a person acquire an 'eye' for something? And how is such an eye to be used?
Ludwig Wittgenstein, *Philosophical Investigations*

A man whom I was shadowing went out into the country for a walk one Sunday afternoon and lost his bearing completely. I had to direct him back to the city.
Dashiell Hammett, 'From the Memoirs of a Private Detective'

I

Benjamin's statement that 'the figure of the detective is prefigured in that of the flâneur' is grounded more in his reading of the literature of flânerie and the literary representations of the detective than in his first-hand know-ledge of the practices of detection. The flâneur *as* detective does figure in Benjamin's metaphorical materialism and in his investigation of the origins of modernity largely with respect to his reflections upon his own *method-ology* and research practices in his prehistory of modernity project. The flâneur/detective figure operates with the collector/ragpicker and the allegorist/archaeologist in a complex dialectical configuration, not merely of these pairs but also of the whole constellation of these figures in Benjamin's enterprise.[1]

The flâneur as *producer* transcends the role of mere spectator, stroller or observer in favour of the production of images of the metropolis, its artefacts, its populations. The modes of representation of the metropolis are extensive, but include the representation of the metropolis as itself a *mystery* and the representation of a figure – the *detective* – who investigates the city's mysteries. A prehistory of modern detective and mystery fictions would have to explore the symbiosis of the emergence of the city as mystery and the figure investigating the city's mysteries in continuous literary and, later, visual representations. In turn, the mutations in these representations and their origins would also be the subject of research. The study of the city investigated would have to draw upon the histories of *surveillance* and *detection* and the social organization of their respective techniques.[2]

Whilst it is not possible here to develop the prehistory of the detective novel in any detail, some brief indication of key dimensions of its origins and development is necessary in order to place in context the main body of this chapter – an extract from the history of the *social* construction of surveillance and detection in the metropolis which grounds the representation of the *individual, private* detective, the 'private eye'.

The city itself as mystery is explicitly announced in the title of Eugene Sue's *Mysteries of Paris* (1845), whose resounding success prompted not merely immediate foreign translations but also a rapid succession of imitations featuring other cities.[3] In turn, the mystery novel of urban life (both the city's labyrinthine *public* topography and stratified social groupings and its interiors as *domestic* sites for crimes) soon came to be complemented by a literature on the dark side of the city (the city by lamplight, light and shadow in the metropolis, etc.). As an urban genre, it may well have been associated with a fear of the 'dangerous classes' (Louis Chevalier) in the expanding metropolis and a periodically perceived, felt or imagined absence of public order ('crime waves').[4]

As part of his orientation to a critical study of Sue and Dickens in *The Mysteries of Paris and London*, Richard Maxwell points to the fact that:

> the novel of urban mysteries emphasizes the role of paper and paperwork. Allegory has always been associated with 'the book of the world'; the notion that city life constitutes a 'close and blotted' text is a less traditional idea but, by the mid-nineteenth century a familiar one: Carlyle, always a wonderful phrasemaker, dubbed modern times the Paper Age. . . . [More recently] Henri Lefebvre asserts that the city begins as writing on the ground; Lévi-Strauss suggests that 'the only phenomenon with which writing has always been concomitant is the creation of cities and empires, that is, the integration of large numbers of individuals into a political system, and their grading into castes or classes'.[5]

The mystery of the city presupposes that it can be deciphered or 'solved'. In turn, this presupposes a notion of reading the city as text. In the present context this has two dimensions. The first is the (fictional) detective/decipherer as the reader of the city which could be *either* the classical *puzzle* detection, where *detached* reason is applied to problem-solving, or the 'hard-boiled' tradition in which the private eye engages in detection *in the streets*. The second is *our own* reading of detective fiction in which detective fiction is *itself* reading the city, and in which our satisfaction as reader of this genre is derived from the fact that the city can be read as a text that is ordered and under control. As Dana Brand argues in this context, the detective 'comforts city dwellers by suggesting that the city can be read and mastered, despite all appearances to the contrary'.[6]

The theme of the city as mystery is not confined to Sue's popular work. It can also be found, as Benjamin intimated in his concern for excavating the topography of nineteenth-century Paris, in the work of Hugo, Balzac and other writers of 'mysteries'. To take but one example, Balzac's story 'Ferragus: Chief of the Dévorants'[7] locates its mystery in the city of Paris and the elaborate topographical differentiation and social stratification of its streets – 'low streets where you would not care to linger and streets in which you would like to live'. As instances of the former, Balzac reflects:

> Is not the Rue Traversiere Saint Honoré plainly a shameless street, with its villainous little houses for mistresses, a couple of windows in width, and vice, and crime, and misery on every floor? And there are thoroughfares with a northern exposure visited by the sun only three or four times in the year; deadly streets are they, where life is taken with impunity, and the law looks on and never interferes.[8]

Later, when the detective novel emerged as a continuous genre in the 1860s, one of the earliest proponents and creators of the genre in France, Emile Gaboriau, occasionally described the new expanding city of Paris (consequent upon Haussmann's plans for its restructuring). In his last major detective novel, *Monsieur Lecoq* (1869), Gaboriau presents the search for clues whose

> way led through an unfinished street that had not even been named, full of mud-puddles and deep holes, and obstructed with all sorts of rubbish. There were no longer any lights or drinking saloons; no footsteps, no voices; nothing but solitude, gloom and silence. One might have supposed oneself a hundred leagues from Paris, had it not been for the deep and continuous murmur that always arises from a large city, like the hollow roaming of a torrent in the depths of a cave.[9]

The analogy with natural settings – and we should not forget the major impact which James Fenimore Cooper's novels had upon the detective and mystery genre, with the figure of the hunter in the wilderness searching for traces – returns in another context for Gaboriau. In *File No. 113* (1867), the detective's search for clues is highlighted with the following analogy:

> When the savage discovers the footprints of an enemy, he follows it persistently, knowing that falling rain or a gust of wind may efface the footprints at any moment. It is the same with us; the most trifling incident may destroy the traces we are following up.[10]

But the destruction of traces may be both fortuitous and deliberate.

In the mystery genre of the mid-nineteenth century, including its variants in what was described and denounced as the 'sensational novel',[11] the obscuring of traces and of relations between things and people is one of the most compelling metaphors that guides the narrative structure from near total obfuscation to the unravelling of hidden connections and relationships. One of the most striking images in this period is in the opening passage of Dickens's *Bleak House* (1853), a novel that introduces the detective in the form of Inspector Bucket into English literature. There, after commencing with the mundane location 'London. Michaelmass Term lately over, and the Lord Chancellor sitting in Lincoln's Inn Hall' and the rain and mud-soaked streets of the metropolis, Dickens evokes the London fog as metaphor for the obfuscation of social relations in the metropolis and with respect to the characters in the narrative of *Bleak House*:

> Fog everywhere. Fog up the river, where it flows among green aits and meadows; fog down the river, where it rolls defiled among the tiers of shipping, and the waterside pollutions of a great (and dirty) city. Fog on the Essex marshes, fog on the Kentish heights. Fog creeping into the cabooses of collier-brigs; fog lying out on the yards, and hovering in the rigging of great ships; fog drooping on the gunwales of barges and small boats. Fog in the eyes and throats of ancient Greenwich pensioners, wheezing by the firesides of their wards; fog in the stem and bowl of the afternoon pipe of the wrathful skipper, down in his close cabin; fog cruelly pinching the toes and fingers of his shivering little prentice boy on deck. Chance people on the bridges peeping over the parapets into a nether sky of fog, with fog all round them, as if they were up in a balloon, and hanging in the misty clouds.
>
> Gas looming through the fog in divers places in the streets, much as the sun may, from the spongy fields, be seen to loom by husbandman and ploughboy. Most of the shops lighted two hours before their time – as the gas seems to know, for it has a haggard and unwilling look.[12]

It is fog on the river that also symbolically opens the novel in which Dickens develops a more fully elaborated conception of society in the urban mystery form: *Our Mutual Friend* (1869).[13] There, in its opening chapter, the discovery of a body in the Thames and the problem of identification announce typical elements in the mystery novel's *fabula*.

An uncontrollable *nature* (fog, the river, etc.) as the metaphorical location for urban mysteries located in *second nature* (the construction of the city and its social relations) proved to be a powerful symbol in the nineteenth century and beyond. At some time shortly after mid-century, the mystery novel as a continuous genre came into being in several modernizing societies. So, too, did a literature on the city which sought to capture – often in elaborate historical and topographical description and narrative and accompanied with profuse illustrations – the *transformation* of the city into a modern metropolis and the confrontation of the new metropolis with the old city. Walter Thornbury's *Old and New London* (no date, but roughly 1869),[14] running to six volumes, should be cited in this context, but comparable volumes appeared in other cities such as Paris, Vienna and New York within the next two decades. Introducing 'London as it was and as it is', Thornbury, too, had recourse to nature for a metaphorical image of the complexity of engaging upon such an enterprise:

> Writing the history of a vast city like London is like writing a history of the ocean – the area is so vast, its inhabitants are so multifarious, the treasures that lie in its depths so countless. What aspect of the great chameleon city should one select?[15]

Unable to answer that question except with a naive empiricist desire to cover all the facts, Thornbury is left to 'wander from street to alley, from alley to street, noting almost every event of interest that has taken place there since London was a city'.[16] Although the figure of the detective lacks the historical intensity of such an interest in the city, such topographical intentions were shared by the detective who emerged in real and in fictional form during the same decades. The detective, however, was concerned not merely with the topography of the metropolis but also with the physiognomy of its inhabitants.

II

It has been argued by Dana Brand that the representation of the figure of the detective (and earlier that of the flâneur) in mystery fiction served to reassure the reading public that the apparent chaos of sense impressions and the overwhelming diversity of relations and experiences in the nineteenth-century metropolis was both intelligible and legible. This was effected through the creation of a

> fantasy of a spectatorial subjectivity capable of establishing epistemological and aesthetic control over an environment commonly perceived to be

threatening and opaque. By reducing the city to a legible model or emblem of itself, and by demonstrating his control over its production, such a subjectivity assumes a paternalistic or heroic role in relation to an urban literary audience.[17]

The detective figure in the fiction of Poe – the major source of the model of the domination of *ratio* over urban chaos and its illegibility – thus serves to create a threatening and not merely confusing *urban crowd* and cityscape and at the same time to provide a figure – the *private detective*, Dupin – who possesses the capacity to create an overview of the metropolis that can render it intelligible.

However, as Tony Bennett points out, the initial unintelligibility of the metropolis as text was not confined to mystery and other fictional genre of the urban landscape. And, more importantly, he continues:

> nor were the responses to it merely imaginative. As Benjamin points out at some length, the development of a position of imaginative spectatorial dominance afforded by detective fiction was accompanied by, and corresponded to, the development of new mechanisms of surveillance which – precisely through their bureaucratic reduction of individuality to a set of knowable traces – rendered the city legible to the gaze of power.[18]

As Bennett goes on to argue, the gaze of power emerges as a multifarious means of organizing, disciplining and controlling a society in transformation. The seemingly unregulated dynamics of modernization became increasingly subject to attempts by the state to regulate and control their unwelcome manifestations. It is in this context that Foucault all too briefly outlines his arguments as to the emergence of detective fiction in *Discipline and Punish*.[19] For Foucault, the genre's emergence coincides with the end of public executions and the end of its accompanying literature, the broadsheet on the heroic aspects of the condemned *criminal's exploits*, and the emergence of a new narrative on the *investigation* of criminality.

Such investigations were carried out on behalf of the state by emergent police forces and the somewhat later establishment of detective forces. Such investigations also came to be fictionally organized as *police procedurals*. But the more powerful literary tradition established by writers such as Poe was the representation of investigation by a *private detective*. The characteristics of Monsieur C. Auguste Dupin that enable him to successfully carry out independent, successful investigations are revealed by his narrator to be that he is: an *independent* young *gentleman* of *independent income* which ensures *impartiality* and the *leisure* to pursue investigations; one who has experienced downward mobility and is therefore able to mix in different levels of society as well as with those marginal to it (with the implication that the *declassés* are capable of resolving class differences); one who possesses a *stock of knowledge* capable of being applied to *problem solving*; one who leads a secluded life given over to thought, to *ratiocination*; one who is an *expert* available for consultation, and whose expertise and reasoning is capable of giving meaning to material things, of recognizing their *true significance* (i.e. that they *signify* something that was not apparent or evident to other observers); and one who by virtue of his successful investigations has been transformed from an aristocrat to a capitalist capable of translating matter (the world of things) through signification into money.[20]

Many of these characteristics – essential for this mode of detection – are also shared by Sherlock Holmes. At the same time, however, as a figure whose fictional appearance spans four decades, Holmes as private detective is a more fully drawn investigator, with other features that reveal the significance of this representation of private detection. As Franco Moretti has argued,[21] Holmes is devoted to detection for its own sake (and not for personal gain). Holmes is also a dilettante enjoying the pleasures of work (detection) and other activities (music, recreational drugs). Above all, Moretti identifies Holmes's activity as detective as possessing a cultural goal. Holmes

> is not a policeman but a private detective: in him, detection is disengaged from the purposes of the law. His is a *purely cultural* aim. It is preferable for a criminal to escape (as, in fact, happens) and the detection to be complete – rather than for him to be captured and the logical reconstruction be pre-empted. But the corollary of this is that the cultural universe is the most effective means of policing. Detective fiction is a hymn to culture's coercive abilities: which prove more effective than pure and simple institutional repression. Holmes's culture – just like mass culture, which detective fiction helped found – will reach you anywhere. This culture knows, orders, and defines all the significant data of individual existence as part of social existence. Every story reiterates Bentham's Panopticon ideal: the model prison that signals the metamorphosis of liberalism into total scrutability.[22]

Moretti, like Brand and others, views detective fictions as representational forms of solutions to the problems of social control in a dynamic capitalist urban milieu. The activity of detection by the late nineteenth century is aided by the new media of communication that at the same time open up the possibility for new forms of *criminal* activity. The individual detective – in this case, Holmes – can still make the connections in an increasingly complex and opaque urban milieu. This enables detective fiction to resolve

> the deep anxiety of an expanding society: the fear that development might liberate centrifugal energies and thus make effective social control impossible.

This problem emerges fully in the *metropolis*, where anonymity – that is, impunity – potentially reigns and which is rapidly becoming a tangled and inaccessible hiding place. We have seen detective fiction's answer to the first problem: the guilty party can never hide in the crowd. His tracks betray him as an individual, and therefore a vulnerable, being. But detective fiction also offers reassurance on the second point. All Holmes's investigations are accompanied and supported by the new and perfect mechanisms of trans-portation and communication. Carriages, trains, letters, telegrams, in Conan Doyles's world, are all crucial and *always* live up to expectations. They are the tacit and indispensable support of the arrest. Society expands and be-comes more complicated: but it creates a framework of control, a network of relationships, that holds it more firmly together than ever before.[23]

This process of detection in which the individual detective engages posits a relationship between this privileged process of problem solving (as if it were entirely logical and scientific) and the society that is ostensibly being investigated. Moretti draws two inferences from this process as it is represented in detective fiction. First, that single problems have single solutions, such that it is individuals who are guilty, whilst society is innocent. This feature can be explained by the fact that:

> detective fiction . . . aims to keep the relationship between science and society *unproblematic*. What, indeed, does detective fiction do? It creates a problem, a 'concrete effect' – the crime – and declares a sole cause relevant: the criminal. It slights other causes (why is the criminal such?) and dispels the doubt that every choice is partial and subjective. But, then, discovering that unique cause means reunifying causality and objectivity and reinstating the idea of a general interest in society, which consists in solving *that* mystery and arresting *that* individual – and no one else. In finding one solution that is valid for all – detective fiction does not permit alternative readings – society posits its unity, and, again, declares itself innocent.[24]

Second, this activity of applying reason to solving problems signifies not the glorification of science but rather the ideology or mythology of science. It is true that there exists a range of pseudo-sciences of appearances that are promulgated by Lombroso and draw upon Bertillon's 'science' of phys-ical traits as well as on the new techniques of fingerprinting developed by Galton and others.[25] But in detective fiction it is the ideology of science that is represented in the investigation process. It seems, therefore, that initially one may view

> detective fiction as 'scientific', and certainly it mimes the univocality of scientific language. Yet, unlike the assertions of the empirical sciences, the solutions of detective fiction are literary, and so non-referential. Detective fiction, therefore, furnishes only the sensation of scientific knowledge. It

perfectly satisfies the aspiration to certainty, because it rigorously avoids the
test of external reality. It is science become myth; and hence self-sufficient.
Detective fiction empties the proto-bourgeois ideal of experimental culture
by subordinating it to a literary structure that is anything but experimental.
The cultural model it promulgates must not be coherent with external reality,
but only with itself.[26]

It possesses a 'perfect self-referentiality'. Hence, this process of ratiocination is not tested by any *external* reality. It is purely internal to the fiction
itself and therefore satisfying for the reader too.

This model of a superior *homo cogitans*, a 'pseudo *logos*' (Kracauer),[27]
remained the dominant motif in detective fiction for several decades. Its
corresponding conception of society was, as Kracauer put it, 'the idea
of the thoroughly rationalized, civilized society', the 'stylization of one-
dimensional unreality', revealing

a state of society in which the unbounded intellect has gained its ultimate
victory, a merely more alien juxtaposition and jumble of figures and things
that seem both lucid and perplexing because it distorts into a caricature the
artificially eliminated reality.[28]

The prevalence of the puzzle tradition in the detective fiction genre seems
more aptly characterized by Kracauer here than are other sub-genres. The
puzzle tradition of the inter-war period often displayed a preference for
non-urban milieu, exemplified in the country house murder and, satirized
by Colin Watson as the 'snobbery with violence' tradition.[29]

Although the critical reflections of Kracauer, Bloch and Benjamin have
illuminated many dimensions of the social and philosophical context of
detective fiction, their reflections are largely confined to the superior *homo
cogitans* tradition. This is especially true, for historical reasons, for
Kracauer's illuminating analysis of the detective novel which dates from
the period 1922–5.[30] Benjamin's extensive reading of detective fiction
extends through the 1930s, often revealing a preference for the detective
fiction of Simenon, with its settings in a petit bourgeois Paris and its
exploration of the psychology of the criminal.[31] Bloch's later reflections
hardly take up the implications of a different sub-genre that emerged in
the late 1920s in the United States – the so-called 'hard-boiled' genre.[32]

III

Like earlier detective fiction, the development of the hard-boiled tradition was also associated with changes in the production and distribution

of popular fiction. Production was connected with the development of seri-alization, the cheapening of production, the development of mass journal publications and an expanding market for a new reading public – in the mid-nineteenth century with the 'penny dreadfuls', later in the United States with the 'dime novel'.[33] In the case of one of its variants, the 'sensational novel' of the 1860s, contemporaries saw its distribution as made possible by the development of circulation libraries and the expansion of railway travel (which itself became a new and modern site for crimes), which created a time/space vacuum for the modern traveller that was filled in by reading. A contemporary reviewer in 1863[34] ascribed the huge popularity of the mystery or 'sensation' novel (such as Wilkie Collins's *The Woman in White* or Mary Braddon's *Lady Audley's Secret*) to the expansion of periodicals satisfying empirical and transitory interest, to the circulating library ('it is to literature what a *magasin de modes* is to dress') stimulat-ing the consumption of the new and the fashionable and to the creation of railway stalls (with lurid book covers to create temporary excitement and attraction). The content of these novels was seen to comprise 'incident', 'action', 'game' (puzzle) and to aim at 'electrifying the nerves'.

At first sight, such features in a different context can also be ascribed to the hard-boiled tradition, with its pulp fiction, lurid covers and sensation. But although there may be some affinities between the sensational novel and the pulp fiction emerging in the United States from the late 1920s onwards, there are crucial differences between this hard-boiled tradition and the earlier detective fiction whose solution rests upon ratiocination.[35]

An initial reflection upon the difference between these two traditions is provided by Raymond Chandler's appreciation of Dashiell Hammett, one of the originators of the hard-boiled tradition in the 1920s. Chandler maintains that:

> Hammett took murder out of the Venetian vase and dropped it into the alley; it doesn't have to stay there forever, but it looked like a good idea to get as far as possible from Emily Post's idea of how a well-bred debutante gnaws a chicken wing.
>
> Hammett wrote at first (and almost to the end) for people with a sharp, aggressive attitude to life. They were not afraid of the seamy side of things; they lived there. Violence did not dismay them; it was right down their street. Hammett gave murder back to the kind of people that commit it for reasons, not just to provide a corpse; and with the means at hand, not hand-wrought duelling pistols, curare, and tropical fish. He put these people down on paper as they were, and he made them talk and think in the language they customarily used for these purposes. . . .
>
> He was spare, frugal, hard-boiled, but he did over and over again what only the best writers can ever do at all. He wrote scenes that seemed never to have been written before.[36]

Amongst the implications of Chandler's appreciation of Hammett's crime fiction are a return to urban realism away from the increasingly formal puzzle tradition, the use of the everyday dialogue of the street and the utilization of a style of writing that was efficient, 'spare' and 'frugal'. The latter reference to a frugal style is sometimes used to place Hammett in the tradition of Hemingway and others. But there is an equally plausible source for the features of Hammett's writing as related by Chandler.

One of the most distinctive features of the hard-boiled school of representation of detection (in the *Black Mask* magazine, amongst others) is that the activity of detection is regarded as *work*. The figure of the detective is no longer that of *homo cogitans* but rather *animal laborans*.[37] This work is in fact routinized wage labour. If the figure of the reader of this detective fiction is still, in Moretti's terms, *homo palpitans*, then the detective is no longer referred to as a gentleman but as a 'sleuth', a 'shadowman', a 'gumshoe' or a 'legman', all of which refer to work activity. Hammett's critical reflection upon the distance between the early figure of the private detective and the figure portrayed in the hard-boiled tradition leads him to say of the modern figure:

> He's more or less of a type: the private detective who oftenest is successful: neither the derby-hatted and broad-toed blockhead of one school of fiction, nor the all-knowing infallible genius of another. I've worked with several of him.[38]

Somewhat more prosaically, Hammett describes the figure portrayed in his own early stories about the 'Continental Op' – the operative working for the Continental Detective Agency:

> I see in him a little man going forward day after day through mud and blood and death and deceit – as callous and brutal and cynical as necessary – towards a dim goal, with nothing to push or pull him towards it *except that he's been hired to reach it*.[39]

Similarly, Hammett's reviews of contemporary detective fiction often reveal his contempt for its ignorance of detective work. In one review he suggests that:

> In some years of working for private detective agencies in various cities, I came across only one fellow sleuth who would confess that he read detective stories. 'I'd eat em up', this one said without shame. 'When I'm through my day's gum shoeing I like to relax: I like to get my mind on something that's altogether different from the daily grind; so I read detective stories'.[40]

Unlike many of his contemporary detective fiction authors, Hammett had himself worked for the world's largest detective agency.

But to remain with Hammett's fictional account of the detective's activity for a moment, the world of the Continental Op, as Steven Marcus has argued, is that of an unlimited, acquisitive capitalist society still existing in Hobbes's state of nature in which 'society and social relations are dominated by the principle of basic mistrust. As one of his detectives remarks, speaking for himself and for virtually every other character in Hammett's writing, "I trust no one".'[41] In this context, the operative is confronted with the flawed world of criminality *and* of the world of clients who hire the Continental Dectective Agency (and their operatives) for their purposes. The operative is governed only by the rules of his detective agency

and they are 'rather strict'. The most important of them by far is that no operative in the employ of the Agency is ever allowed to take or collect part of a reward that may be attached to the solution of a case. Since he cannot directly enrich himself through his professional skills, he is saved from at least the characteristic corruption of modern society – the corruption that is connected with its fundamental acquisitive structure. At the same time, the Op is a special case of the Protestant ethic for his entire existence is bound up in and expressed by his work, his vocation.[42]

How was this work structured when Hammett himself worked as an operative in Baltimore in 1915 and again in San Francisco in 1920 for the Pinkerton National Detective Agency?[43]

IV

Hammett was first employed by the Pinkerton National Detective Agency in 1915 – as Sam Hammett for $21 per week. He said that 'an enigmatic want-ad took me into the employ of Pinkerton's National Detective Agency'.[44] Although the Pinkerton archives do not reveal this particular want-ad, they do contain an 1897 instance for New York which merely states:

Wanted. Healthy able-bodied men, not over 35 yrs of age, must have fair educ. and good references from actual employers and be willing to work for moderate salary. Address, stating age, previous occups. and references. None others needed. Cosmopolitan, 44.
Herald Downtown.[45]

At least since the 1880s, prospective employees were required to complete an application form stating their: 'name, age, height, build, complexion, where born, married or single, secret societies of which a member, foreign languages spoken and written, places resided in, trades or professions and previous employments, statement of previous career'.[46] If accepted, the applicant was tested by the agency several months after employment for further suitability. Thus, to take one instance, John Fraser, originally employed by the agency on 28 June 1880, was tested by the Superintendent of Detectives on 28 October 1880. Fraser's 'general deportment and appearance' was judged to be that of a 'young mechanic'. Of greater significance was the assessment of his abilities as an operative. As to the level of society in which he could readily mix, the questionnaire reads: 'Classes of society can become readily adapted to; whether higher or laboring class, sportingmen or thieves.' Fraser was judged to be at ease with 'young laborers and mechanics'.[47]

The operatives were tested with respect to two classes of surveillance activity: their ability to 'shadow' and their ability to be a 'roper'. The report form does not elaborate on shadowing, but 'the class of "roper"' is amplified: 'whether makes acquaintance easily, and ability to obtain friendship and confidence'. Before returning to these two facilities, the remainder of the report tests for: ability for making investigations, knowledge of criminals, whether moderate in expenditures or inclined to be extravagant, impulsive or cautious, determined or timid, secretive or talkative, self-reliance and ability to originate a plan of operations beyond instructions, and failings to be guarded against. In this 1880 test, Fraser was judged to be medium or moderate for most of these tests and the Superintendent commented that 'this is a young man but lately employed bids fair to make a good operative'.

The ability to become a good 'shadow' or 'roper' makes clear that the operative's task was to gather information (knowledge) through engagement in these two activities. The activities themselves differ in significant respects. Success as a shadow requires a good 'eye'. Shadows are natural and unavoidable. There is a *natural* casting of a shadow, but in the city a *social* ability can be developed to hide within shadows. The shadow should not be visible to the shadowed, but the task is to create vision. The 'shadow' is not visible but is preoccupied with the visible. The eye is capable of surveying unobserved, which is a constituent element of surveillance. The 'roper' collects knowledge and information through social interaction. The acquisition of information and knowledge is secured by direct (but hidden) means. The roper is *visible* but his or her intention is *hidden* or *invisible*. The roper enters into natural communication *as if* it were natural.

These two processes for the acquisition of knowledge are a prominent feature of detective fiction. In his 1924 story 'Zigzags of Treachery', Hammett relates the four rules of shadowing (almost certainly derived from his Pinkerton Agency training): 'stay behind your man as much as possible; do not ever try to hide from him; act naturally, regardless of what happens; never look him in the eye'.[48] In fact, Hammett received his own training in the Agency in the same year (1915) as William Pinkerton was revising the rules of the detective agency for publication on 1 January 1916. 'The General Principles and Rules of Pinkerton's National Detective Agency' had previously been expanded in 1878. The latter, in turn, were similar to those of 1873 and were outlined earlier by the agency's founder Allan Pinkerton.[49] Research by Wayne G. Broehl, Jr. on one of Pinkerton's most notorious cases, the Molly Maguires case – which revealed the organization's complicity in crushing an early labour organization in Pennsylvania – brought to light an earlier rule book published in Chicago in 1867 (and thus shortly after the end of the Civil War) under the title *General Principles and Rules of Pinkerton's National Police Agency*.[50] By 1873 the Agency's name had been changed to that of the National Detective Agency. 'Policing' in the immediate aftermath of the end of the Civil War may have sounded appropriate for the times, but 'detection' may have been more acceptable in the 1870s, though the content of the basic principles remained unchanged.

Allan Pinkerton (born in Glasgow in 1819) established his detective agency in Chicago in 1850. Its dramatic expansion and prominence before the American Civil War and Pinkerton's political connections led to him being secured by Abraham Lincoln as head of the newly established Secret Service in the Civil War for the Unionists. The infiltration of Confederate lines and other espionage work is related, ostensibly by Pinkerton himself, in *The Spy of the Rebellion*.[51] The early records of the detective agency's work in Chicago were unfortunately destroyed in the Chicago Fire of 1871. In what follows on the organization of routinized surveillance work by the agency, the major sources are the rule books of 1873, 1878 and 1916 and a number of operatives' reports. In particular, extensive use is made of the 1878 rule book, not least in order to indicate how early the parameters for detection were drawn up in a systematic manner. To anticipate, the detective agency is an exemplar of the bureaucratic organization of knowledge collection strategies as far as the activity of detection is concerned. In addition, the agency employed security guards to protect the transport of money, the banks, and commercial and industrial enterprises. Thus, although the agency covered crimes such as murders, robberies and frauds, it also engaged extensively in strike-breaking, industrial espionage and general anti-trade union activity. Therefore, when Moretti argues that detective *fiction* is not interested in production, the activities of this and other agencies demonstrate that the *reality* of detective work indicates otherwise (as does Hammett's story 'Poisonville').[52] In particular, the surveillance and social (physical) control of social groups intent upon social transformation – and the Molly Maguires, the Homestead Riots and the Pullman strike are only a few of the instances in which the Pinkerton Agency was active – created the strong impression that the Agency was opposed to trade union activity, forcing it periodically to publish denials of its anti-union stance.[53]

By the 1870s the Pinkerton Agency had adopted the logo of an open eye beneath which was inscribed 'We never sleep'. Not surprisingly, this motto is transformed into one of the rules of the agency (Rule 6: Devotion to Business):

> The entire time of the Detective is expected to be devoted faithfully to the service. He is subject to be called upon at any time of night, on Sundays and in all kinds of weather – *his labors may not cease when the honest sleep; crime does not stand still* and the Detective must ever be on the alert. He is engaged for the seven days in the week.[54]

The motto 'We never sleep' draws attention not merely to the detective's response to active nocturnal criminal activity but is also predicated upon a transformation of the metropolis *at night*. The implications of 'the honest sleep' at night is that the moral universe is transformed at night. As Joachim Schlör has argued, the discourse on the city at night is transformed in the 1840s with the development of metropolitan modernity.[55] The differential experience of the city at night by different groups is manifested in differential reports on night-time in the metropolis: by the police and detectives in 'forbidden' areas of the city; by opponents of the city night; by religious and reform groups who view morality as threatened at night; by newspaper reports and reviews revealing aspects of the city at night. These diverse reports reveal a conflict between those who wish to maintain order in the metropolis and those who wish to challenge it. The areas of conflict are security, morality and accessibility, areas that overlap in contemporary discourses. Access to the city's night by diverse social groups with greater mobility creates new problems of security. The very openness of the city, including its open forms of sexuality, becomes threatening to those wishing to maintain a strict moral universe and, in turn, affects excursions into the night – from one enclosed space (usually an interior) to another (interior) with the least time spent on the street (as the space subject to the least control).[56]

That 'we never sleep' therefore implies a new acute attention to the changing physiognomy of the metropolis by night. The shadows of the metropolis called forth a new literature that comprised both the urban fictional mystery and the ostensibly objective reporting of the dark side of the city at night. On the one hand, there is the narrator in Poe's 'The Man of the Crowd' in London, initially observing the urban crowd from the security of a coffee house in a principal thoroughfare, observing that, as the darkness came on, the throng momently increased; and, by the time the lamps were well lighted, two dense and continuous tides of population were rushing past the door. At this particular period of the evening I have never before been in a similar situation, and the tumultuous sea of human heads filled me, therefore, with a *delicious novelty* of emotion.[57]

There follows a detailed exploration of the various social strata and types in this crowd, which was transformed 'as the night deepened'. In this process:

not only did the general character of the crowd materially alter (its gentler ones retiring . . . and its harsher ones coming out into bolder relief, as the late hour brought forth every species of infamy from its den), but the rays of the gas-lamps, feeble at first in their struggle with the dying day, had now at length gained ascendancy, and threw over everything a fitful and garish lustre. All was dark yet splendid.[58]

Like the operative, subsequently the narrator follows 'the man of the crowd', the face of a stranger in 'full night-fall' when 'a thick humid fog hung over the city, soon ending in a settled and heavy rain'. The stranger is followed 'along a route which brought us to the verge of the city' to:

the most noisome quarter of London, where everything wore the worst impress of the most deplorable poverty, and of the most desperate crime. By the dim light of an accidental lamp, tall, antique, worm-eaten, wooden tenements were seen tottering to their fall, in directions so many and capricious that scarce the semblance of a passage was discernible between them. The paving-stones lay at random, displaced from their beds by the rankly growing grass. Horrible filth festered in the dammed-up gutters. The whole atmosphere teemed with desolation.[59]

Eventually, following this stranger, the narrator is led back to the main thoroughfare from where this tracking commenced and, when the narrator gazed at the stranger, 'he noticed me not'. This is the procedure of the operative, except that the operative is directed towards specific strangers for shadowing.

The narrator moves openly through this city's spaces, observing and reading the social milieu, the diverse strata of the crowd and the physical and social space of the built environment. It is remarkably close to the activity of the operative. Of course, not all operatives would have viewed this passage through the crowd in terms of 'delicious novelty', 'dark yet splendid' and culminating in 'horrible filth' and 'desolation'.

Elsewhere, the city's shadows were also explored by another literature which, like Pinkerton's volumes on his detective cases, purported to be objective. This urban literature, however, had a moral aim, one which drew guarded conclusions with respect to the accessibility of the whole metropolis. In the United States, it broadly coincided with the period in which Pinkerton's agency became established and the decade (the 1870s) in which the rules of the agency took on an elaborated form. In *The Secrets of the Great City* (1868),[60] for instance, a volume that takes the reader through high and low life in post-bellum New York, the mystery of the city is threatening: 'New York is a great secret, not only to those who have never seen it, but to the majority of its own citizens. Few living in the great city have any idea of the terrible romance and the hard reality of the lives of two thirds of the inhabitants'.[61] And although the descriptions contained in the volume are 'a simple narration of actual facts', its purpose is a *moral* one: 'to warn the thousands who visit the city against the dangers and pitfalls into which their curiosity or vice may lead them . . . The city is full of danger.' However, the crucial advantage of this volume and that of subsequent ones in the same vein – and the variants of the crime narratives too – is that the reader's 'curiosity can be satisfied in these pages, and he can know the Great City from them, *without incurring the danger attending an effort to see it*'.[62] The dangerous city can thus be observed, in whatever detail the reader may be offered, from the comfort of the reader's secure *interior* – the view from the armchair was assured and insured. Such reassuring physiognomies and ethnographies of the metropolis were popular in all metropolitan centres. Matthew Hale Smith's *Sunshine and Shadow in New York* (1872), as another instance of this genre, ran to many editions.[63] It was already somewhat less menacing in tone than some of its predecessors, proclaiming that 'the joy and good in New York abound over sorrow and evil'. And this is despite the fact that 'a worse population than can be found in New York does not inhabit the globe. The base men of every nation, and the crimes, customs and idolatries of every quarter of the world, are here.' Stereotypes of 'base men' follow: 'the lowest order of the Jews'; 'the Italians . . . dangerous, turbulent, stealthy and defiant . . . [their] very tread . . . suggestive of the stiletto'; 'no locality [is] viler, more repulsive, or more wicked than that occupied by the low French'; 'the Chinese herd together, without the decency of cattle. They smoke their opium, burn incense, and worship idols.'[64] But the light and shadow is seen as inherent to the very nature of the modern metropolis and New York is no exception. Within this city, 'a portion . . . is Paradise: a large part is Pandemonium'.[65]

That pandemonium required containment. This urban literature itself contributed to the containment by creating barriers for its reader, transforming the mental topography of the city into safe and unsafe areas. But policing, including the employment of private detective agencies, became an increasing process as more areas of the city, and in the United States the expanding frontier, were subject to regulation and police surveillance. The remilitarization of the city and the building of large troop garrisons and arsenals provided a more powerful support where necessary. In conjunction with new means of communications, this neglected factor of a substantial military presence in many European cities itself affected urban development. To give but one instance, the city railway in Vienna, designed by Otto Wagner and largely completed in the period 1894–8, ran *around* the city centre and not *into* the centre. One reason for this was to prevent potential political movements having direct and rapid physical access en masse to the centre of the city, with its imperial and governmental sites and aristocratic and *haute-bourgeois* residences.[66]

As far as the operatives working for the detective agency were concerned, they had to develop a sense of the portions and divisions in the city and, if they were successful 'ropers', had to enter into communication with a variety of social strata and negotiate the differentiated spaces of the modern metropolis. How far they were successful depended, in part, on their training. In the case of the Pinkerton Agency it should be asked whether its rules for employees provided this training.

V

When an operative had been accepted by the Pinkerton National Detective Agency, they entered into a contract with the Agency.[67] The operative – and other employees – agreed to be 'guided by and act upon the General Principles' as set out by the Agency and to conform to, observe and abide by all 'Rules, Regulations and General Orders' that had been made. This is already an indication that the operative had entered into a contract with a distinctive bureaucratic organization. Further, an employee, including the operative, was never to ask for a reward, bonus, gift or gratuity or compensation from the Agency's clients. The regulation of operatives as wage labourers was to preclude supplementation of their wages by such additional emoluments. In the language of an employment contract, it was stated that all information and knowledge acquired by the operatives 'shall be considered and treated by the said party of the second part [the operative] as *the exclusive* property of the said parties of the first part [the Agency]'. Here, the contract was quite unambiguous with respect to the Agency's aim to collect information and knowledge that would give it exclusive access to such information. Finally, given the dangers involved in the operatives' work, the contract ominously stated that the 'Agency accepts no responsibility for damage to the party of the second part', i.e. the operative.

The acceptance of and adherence to the 'General Principles and Rules of Pinkerton's National Detective Agency' (1878) was required of 'the General Superintendent, Superintendents, Officers, male and female Detectives, and of the Clerical force'. Although the number of 'female Detectives' remained extremely small, the very fact of their employment as operatives cast an interesting light upon the notion of the 'invisible flâneuse'.[68] Already in 1856, Allan Pinkerton had employed Mrs Kate Warne, a widow, as the first female detective. In 1881, shortly before his death, Pinkerton was requesting George Bangs, his General Superintendent in New York, 'to employ female detectives'. Writing to Bangs, he states:

> I suppose you have not yet hired a female detective, but I think with some effort you will. I now give you a description of the class of woman you will require. Say a lady about 35 years old, about five feet six or seven inches high, hair dark, black or auburn. I don't think blonde would do. She should be either married or single, but if married her husband must be dead [!], face oval, forehead large and massive. Her hair should be worn plain or very little braided or banged, eyes should be large, whether black, blue or gray, her feet moderately small. An easy talker but careful and one who can keep her own counsel, yet be able to carry on a conversation on any subject and be always self possessed and natural, although assuming a character.[69]

Clearly, Pinkerton was convinced that female operatives could be trained as good 'ropers', readily entering into conversation and adept at disguise. As later research revealed, Pinkerton's attempts to employ female detectives, including the proposed establishment of a female department in Phildelphia in 1876, met much opposition, also from his son Robert. Nevertheless, his aim was 'to use females whenever it can be done judiciously. I must do so or falsify my own theory, practice and truth.'[70] The oppositon to his intentions meant that the employment of females operatives remained limited.

What was the nature of the employment offered to operatives? It was a *modern profession*, whose aim was the *detection* of crime (to be distinguished from the *prevention* of crime, which was dealt with by 'the Preventive Watch' in the city of Chicago and elsewhere). Detection was associated with modernity and newness: 'The character of the detective is *comparatively new*.' Although there were earlier activities associated with detection,

> the manner and style of these operations were entirely different from those of the Modern Detective. The existence of the Detective, as an officer, should be entirely unknown. All his acts should be surrounded with secrecy, and, in fact, so far from his being known as a Detective, he should be the very last upon whom such a suspicion would be likely to fall'.[71]

The modern detective force is part of 'the enlightened intelligence of modern times' and must match the fact that 'crime, itself, has become more scientific'. The specialized training and the search for knowledge (which should be monopolized) render detection a *modern profession*. Indeed:

> The profession of the Detective is a high and honourable calling. Few professions excel it. He is an officer of justice, and must himself be pure and above reproach.[72]

The necessary qualities for entry into this profession are integrity, 'considerable intellectual power', 'such a knowledge of human nature as will give him [the detective] a quick insight into character', 'a keen analytical mind . . . so that he may be ready for any emergency', and '*the player's faculty* of assuming any character that his case may require, and of acting it out to the life, with an ease and naturalness which shall not be questioned'. The *speed of reaction* to new situations and contexts, the analytical skills for *preparing for emergency* and the *instant disguise* (of self and motives) are all features that are developed in metropolitan modernity but heightened in the profession (and training) of the detective. However, for those unable to develop these skills, Pinkerton, in a Durkheimian manner, suggests that they will be commissioned to do the class of work for which they are best fitted by nature and education.

But in both the general statement or principles of detection and in the subsequent specific rules pertaining to detectives, there is one feature of this activity that Pinkerton emphasizes above all others, namely *secrecy*. Less than a decade after the Civil War, in 1873, the statement of the general principles of the Agency – reproduced in the 1878 version of the rules – asserts that:

> secrecy is the prime condition of success in all . . . [Detectives'] operations. It is the chief strength which the Detective possesses beyond that of an ordinary man. His movements should be quietly conducted; his manner should be unobtrusive; and his address agreeable. He should be able to adapt himself to all persons, in all the various grades of society. . . . [W]hilst engaged in the detection of Crime . . . all his movements should be as silent as the 'snow-flake that falls upon the sod'.[73]

The qualities associated with secrecy – quiet movement, unobtrusive manner, agreeable interaction, adaptation to varied social settings – are extensions of the operatives' test, outlined earlier, for being a good 'shadow' and a good 'roper'. Secrecy, as a prime attribute of activity, is also associated with the Secret Service of which Pinkerton was appointed the Union's head in the Civil War. In this context, the principles of 'private' detection intertwine with those of 'state' espionage and vice versa.

The interaction with individuals in diverse (and often criminal) social settings on the basis of apparent equality may require *deception* on the part of operatives. Infiltration of other (potentially hostile) social groups was a feature of both the Civil War Secret Service *and* the destruction of the Molly Maguires. It called forth a further figure who does not play a prominent role in the general principles and rules of detection – namely, the *informer*. In part, this is because Pinkerton wished to distinguish his efficient, modern detective force from earlier inefficient systems of policing that had relied heavily (and often unreliably) upon elaborate informer networks. Nonetheless, this did not mean that the Agency did not make extensive use of informers; merely that the moral expediency of the operatives was asserted to be superior to that of informers.

However, there is clearly an ethical problem at the heart of detection that Pinkerton had to address. The General Principles recognize that, on occasion:

> the Detective . . . [must] pretend to be a Criminal. . . . It is, unfortunately, necessary to resort to these deceptions, to save society from its enemies. . . . The Detective has at times to depart from the strict line of truth, and to resort to deception, so as to carry his assumed character through thoroughly and successfully.[74]

This process of deception is justified from the point of view of the operative insofar as, once the deception is completed and justice has been done, the operative 'will return . . . unblemished by . . . [his] fiery ordeal . . . and take his place once more in society'. The process is justified by the *Agency* on the grounds that 'it is held by this Agency that the ends being for the accomplishment of justice, they justify the means used'.

The reference to the 'fiery ordeal' of the operative, presumably in the hell of criminality, gives more than a hint of Calvinist fervour, a Protestant ethic of detection. This is confirmed with reference to the consumption of alcohol and money. With respect to alcohol, it is demanded that:

> While associating with Criminals, the Employees of the Agency must abstain from using intoxicating liquors, except when it is absolutely necessary; and never . . . to influence the mind of the Criminal with whom the Detective may be brought in contact.[75]

There is, of course, a practical reason for such abstention, namely 'the inadmissibility of such evidence procured by these means in a court of law'.[76] The practice is also detrimental to the profession of the detective who has to resort to such means. Rather (again in a Calvinist mode):

> The Detective must not do anything to farther sink the Criminal into vice
> or debauchery; but, on the contrary, to win his confidence, by endeavour-
> ing to elevate him, and to impress him with the idea of his [the Detective's]
> mental and moral superiority.[77]

This evangelistic spirit is extended to the convicted criminal, and it is
the duty of those who come into contact with him during a prison sen-
tence 'to elevate and enable him' for rehabilitation in society. For his
part, the detective should apply 'kindness and justice' in his dealings with
the criminal since 'no human being [is] so degraded but there is some
little bright spark of conscience and of right still existing in him; and,
whenever it is possible, the Detective should endeavour to reach this and
cultivate it'.

The General Principles conclude with an affirmation of the detectives'
truthful and impartial reporting of knowledge of suspects (both for and
against their cases). Therefore, data collected by the detective 'should be
founded upon knowledge only, and if upon hearsay, the same must be
fairly expressed. All suspicions must be verified by facts.'

The moral rectitude of the detective and the ethical issues involved in
the practice of detection were not always treated in such a sanguine
manner. Indeed, an alternative view was that the detective – at least as
employed in public office – belonged to the class of oppressors in modern
society, engaging in constant deceptions. In George McWatters, *Knots
United* (1871),[78] with the ominous subtitle of *Ways and By-Ways in the
Hidden Life of American Detectives* and purportedly written by an ex-
officer of the New York police force, the author associates the modern
detective with 'the oppressors' and 'the tramplers':

> He is dishonest, crafty, unscrupulous, when necessary to be so. He tells
> black lies when he cannot avoid it; and white lying, at least, is his chief
> stock in trade. He is the outgrowth of a diseased and corrupted state of
> things, and is consequently, morally diseased himself. His very existence is
> a satire upon society. He is a thief, and steals into men's confidences to ruin
> them. He makes friends in order to reap the profits of betraying them. . . .
>
> His position is paradoxical in a measure. He has the satisfaction of
> knowing that if he lies and cheats, he is no worse for this, in a business
> way, than his neighbors, and that his frauds are exercised to protect them
> in keeping whatever ill-gotten gains they may have in the shape of prop-
> erty, from being stolen from them by some of the rest of his (and their)
> neighbors; or in the discovery of criminals, such as murderers and assassins,
> in order that they may be punished, to satisfy the majesty of the law, made
> by the society which made the criminals. In this sense he is a public bene-
> factor, and better entitled to the honors he wins in society than is, perhaps,
> any other useful citizen of the governing classes.[79]

Such critical reflections upon the role of the detective in society had no place in the almost entirely positive representation of this figure by Pinkerton.

VI

The more detailed requirements of the Agency's employees as set down in 1878 already indicate that the Agency was a hierarchical, bureaucratic organization for the collection of knowledge. A stratification of the work-force is indicated by the fact that all 'Officers' – from superintendents to cashiers – and 'the Clerical Force' have *duties*, whereas the 'Detectives' – in the 1916 version they are now 'Operatives', a more generalized and socially less prestigious category – are subject to *rules* (in the 1878 version, 41 in all).

The duties of the General Superintendent (by 1916, General Manager, a title also indicative of a shift to a large-scale bureaucratic organization) include the prevention of nepotism by employing 'but one of a family in the Detective or Clerical Forces of the Agencies'. The business of the Agency excludes work for reward, payment or fee, collection of money or property involving collusion with criminals, 'the business of cities and towns' and divorce cases.

The organization of the detective force by the superintendent involves the personal detailing and instructing of the detectives and ensuring that detectives are not brought into contact with 'the patrons of the Agencies'. For other reasons, detectives are not to be brought into contact with one another when engaged on operations. The superintendent

> must exercise extraordinary circumspection, to the end that the Detectives know as little of each other's Operations as the interest of such operations will permit, and will positively require that the Clerical and Detective Forces do not associate, either in, or out, of the Agency.[80]

The element of secrecy is therefore to be applied to the activities of the detectives in relation to one another. Being detailed for *specific tasks* excludes knowledge of the whole operation. This separation and secret activity of detectives is to extend to knowledge of the patrons of the Agency. Secrecy should also be maintained in the relationship of the detective to the Agency since:

> the value of a detective is dependent upon his being unknown as such, and in this view he is positively required to keep his connection with the Agency a secret.[81]

For the same reason, wherever possible, detectives should not be called as witnesses in prosecutions since 'the Detective becomes further and further known, and, finally, irretrievably "spotted"'.

The detailed regulation of the activities of detectives is accompanied by comprehensive written accounts of all operations, expenses, etc. In contrast to most detective fiction, the personal initiative of the detective is secondary to their ability to follow rules. Success of an operation 'is often not so much due to the natural ability of the Detective, as to his obedience to instructions'. Rule-following is, of course, a key feature of all bureaucratic organizations.

Indeed, 'Rule 1' governing the detective (in 1916, 'operating') force is to read the rules and general principles of the Agency 'carefully'. Although it is not possible to summarize the succeeding 40 rules, some of them should be highlighted. Again the moral rectitude of the detective is emphasized, and even when it is necessary 'to apparently put on the garb of crime' operatives must 'maintain their integrity and manhood'.[82] Operatives 'are not permitted to indulge in the habitual use of intoxicating beverages' and all consumption in the course of detection must be justified.

With respect to secrecy, the rules again emphasize not merely its significance for knowledge collection but also for the safety of the operatives. At the same time, there is a recognition that this knowledge could be divulged to third parties. Secrecy is a multidimensional entity. It is secrecy that ensures that the detective has *no knowledge* of what is going on in the whole operation. Thus:

> Every Detective attached to the Agencies is *positively forbidden* from prying into the business being transacted by the same by getting access to the Reports when they are being written.[83]

It is secrecy, also, that ensures the success and safety of the operative:

> The power of the Detective can be best exercised when he is entirely unknown. This efficiency is thereby increased, and the risk of personal danger diminished . . . The Detective will, therefore . . . [use] every precaution to keep strictly secret his connection with the Agencies.[84]

It is secrecy, further, that ensures that only the Agency possess the overview of the total situation in a particular operation:

> On the Street, and in public places, Detectives attached to the Agencies will not recognise each other, nor any of the employees of the same; and must not walk or be seen together, or be in company in coming to, or going from, the Agencies.[85]

The isolation of the individual operative is not merely to be maintained with respect to fellow operatives but also with regard to family members or relatives, who are expressly forbidden to accompany the operative. The lone 'eye' has its foundation in this rule. This isolation is maintained also in written communication, which must only take place through the Agency and must hide the location of the operative when engaged upon investigations. The Agency therefore controls all communication between operatives, one with another, *and* between operatives and the outside world.

Since the organization of a detective agency has as its prime concern the collection of knowledge (information), this knowledge must be assembled in such a manner that it can become *the exclusive property* of the Agency. The presentation of knowledge collected in a systematic and accurate form is therefore of crucial significance to the Agency. It is a form of *total knowledge* that encompasses not merely the *knowledge that has been collected* but also the *knowledge of the operative's movements* (i.e. how it was collected). Hence, Rule 16 states that:

> Written reports are required from each member of the Detective Force, setting forth in detail the manner of the employment for every hour during the whole day . . . They should be written in ink, and a pencil will only be used for this purpose when it is impossible or unsafe to have ink.[86]

The significance of the written report is confirmed by the *degree of detail* expected of them, 'giving the most minute particulars of all that may be observed, heard, or said by the Detective, which may in any way affect the matter under investigation, or in the remotest degree be of interest to the Agency'.

Not only must the precise details of time, place, source and circumstances be given in the report but also, 'in repeating what is said by themselves or others, *the language as near as possible must be given*; and, at all events, the substance of the conversation'. This language of criminals and informants and *representations of it* is, for its part, a crucial dimension of the hard-boiled school of detective fiction. It is one of the features of the narration that gives it the semblance of realist veracity.

The reports should also have precise regard to *topography* and *physiognomy*. Pinkerton requires of the reports that:

> In describing houses or locations in country places, make the description sufficiently plain, so that they may be found by a stranger without inquiring. In describing houses in cities, write the streets and numbers plainly, state the name of the occupants when known, and whether the houses are dwellings, and if not, the character of the business . . . In describing persons, state in the following order their age; height; build; complexion; color of

eyes, color of hair and beard, and how worn; marks; shape of features and limbs; and dress and jewellery worn.[87]

Again, this dense and precise description is a feature of Hammett's early Continental Op stories.

Reports should also indicate *changes in climatic conditions* that might affect the nature and veracity of the evidence provided. Here the rule is that:

> Detectives, when on special night service, must set forth in their Reports the character of the night, such as dark, cloudy, clear, starlight, rainy, snowing, frosty, cold, warm, etc., and should the weather change during the night, the Report should also set forth the time when the change took place.[88]

This was often crucial in court evidence, when the nature and degree of visibility of suspects was questioned. In the city, the nature of street lighting became important with the technical development of forms of gas lighting prior to the introduction of electric lighting.[89]

The *transmission* of reports requires special care and attention. Reports whilst on operations were to be mailed to the Agency and 'memoranda of all circumstances' should be prepared if this was not possible, in order subsequently to complete the report. As Simmel pointed out, the letter as a form of communication can be seen in the context of protecting the secrecy of its contents.[90] Here, the mundane rule is that:

> All letters must be numbered 1, 2, 3 etc, always commencing a new series of numbers upon a change of service. This is necessary in order that it may be known that all letters are received. Detectives are enjoined to be sure that their envelopes are *securely gummed* and bear a *sufficient number of stamps to cover the postage* and to see that the same properly *adhere* to the envelopes.[91]

The actual *content of the reports* should not display any prejudice on the part of the operative for or against any of the parties involved in the operation. Indeed:

> The truth is all that is required, and that only must be Reported. It is no proof that the Detective is unfit for his business because he may not obtain evidence of guilt. If the whole facts are reported, the guilt or innocence will soon be apparent.[92]

The reports themselves are to be completed in the Agency office as quickly as possible, 'so as to be in readiness to enter upon any business at a moments notice'.

The reports are usually accompanied by *Expense Bills*. All expenses are to be kept to a minimum. A revealing list of expenditures that will not be permitted include, aside from expensive hotels, the following:

> When it is necessary for Detectives to use a street conveyance, as from, or to, Railroad Stations, they are required to take the cheapest mode, and not to engage a hack or hotel omnibus when a cheaper conveyance, such as a street car, can be used.[93]

The loss of the operative's own possessions cannot be claimed for, nor can they claim for

> cigars, while travelling in a Baggage Car; or for cigars, drinks, tickets to places of amusement, or extra meals while 'shadowing' except when positively and Absolutely necessary . . . and no charges will be allowed for fees or gratuities to Stewards, Chambermaids, Waiters or Porters; . . . for Baths, Boot Blacking, Shaving or Hair Cutting, unless for disguise and by special orders of a Superintendent.[94]

Similar degrees of social control pertained to the Agency's offices. The rooms for detectives were to be vacated by 10 p.m. at the latest, whilst in sleeping rooms operatives were to retire by 11 p.m. In neither is 'loud and boisterous talking and laughing, or disorderly, or filthy conduct . . . card playing . . . use of profane or improper language . . . discussions on political or religious topics . . . and spirituous liquors' permitted, and tobacco only 'so long as the rooms are not soiled by those using it'.[95]

This compendium of rules for the operatives has more in common with the rational, bureaucratic organization of information and knowledge collection than it does with the hard-boiled tradition of the private eye. The clear attempt to secure a monopoly of knowledge and regulation of entry into the occupation does mark the activity out as a profession. Indeed, it is a *modern* profession.[96]

However, there are also affinities and connections with the fictional tradition of the private eye. The exclusion of the operatives from the overview of the whole investigative operation, and indeed the systematic exclusion of this bird's-eye vision of it, contributes to the private-eye tradition insofar as the eye does not know what is happening. This produces a kind of *structured disorientation* in detective work. What this means, however, is that the gaze of power (Foucault) is not that of the operative but of the detective agency itself.

There is a conception of urban space as an open city, available to the gaze and even experience of the operative. In one sense, there appears to be a *cognitive mapping* on the part of the operative which enables him to *know* the city in its highly differentiated dimensions. Indeed, Rule 33 states that the agency desires that operatives

> become thoroughly conversant with the various localities they may be detailed to operate in and that they acquire an acquaintance with the inhabitants of such localities, so that they may be able, when called upon, to operate with facility and amongst any class of people.[97]

However, although urban space *appears* open for the gaze of the (private) 'eye', the *actual* gaze of power (which requires the most complete knowledge possible) is not that of the operative but of the organization (the agency) itself. The operative *gathers* information through being a 'shadow' and 'roper'. But the overview, the total gaze, is only available to the heads of the organization itself. As the rules for the operative emphasize, detection is most successful when it is conceived as rule-following and this has primacy over any individual initiative on the part of the operative.

VII

But if we return to the *collection of knowledge and information*, it is clear that it possesses a *density*, which is implied in some of the rules and which extends beyond them to the realms of so-called 'true' crime accounts and to detective fiction (of writers such as Hammett). In other words, the issue of *intertextuality* emerges when we examine more closely the nature of *reportage* by operatives and others in the Agency. The most obvious textual layers are those derived from the informer's letters, the notes or 'memoranda' of operatives, the formal reports required by the Agency, reports and publications on aspects of criminality, the operations written up as true crime accounts (ostensibly by Allan Pinkerton but actually by a coterie of ghost writers) and the 'fictional' representations of detection (by such writers as Hammett) that draw upon the experience of being an operative in the Pinkerton National Detective Agency. Ideally, it would be instructive – although not possible here – to take these various levels in relation to a single operation or case. However, the differentiating features of the levels of reportage are still apparent from diverse and unconnected sources drawn from several cases.

The communications of informers by letter display a familiarity with the social setting upon which they are reporting and, in the instance provided here, a 'knowing' response to the agency's superintendent in New York. In 1900 a report from 'XYZ' – a not uncommon nomenclature for those who wish to remain unknown, as evidenced decades earlier in one

of the cases of Waters's *Recollections of a Detective Police-Officer* (1875)[98]
– to the agency in New York (probably to Seymour Butler) written from
The Henking Hotel, Springfield, Massachusetts, commences as follows:

> Friend Seymour,
> This town and Worcester are getting to be Yeagg headquarters.
> In Worcester they frequent 84 Southbridge St. a saloon owned by one
> O'Connell or Connell and where a nephew of the proprietor and a former
> Yeagg Pete man tends the bar. A mob passed through here the other day
> after beating the P.O. at Petersham Mass. for $600.[99]

On the same operation, 'XYZ' also reports from Montreal on May 28 with
the following:

> Friend S.
> The people who have been operating around Toronto and who have tackled
> 3 or 4 Jugs around that Section make their Montreal headquarters at Joe
> St. Ongs road house, near Queen's Park, Verdun, Montreal.
>   They are 'Yeaggs' and this place is the headquarters of all Yeaggs visiting
> Montreal. He says two Yeaggs named Dublin Murphy and Black Billy were
> the principals in that Brewery stickup at Pawtucket. . . . If you want him
> (Murphy, Kid Huddle) for any of your jugs, Ongs say he is around the
> Yeagg joint in the Bowery.
> Expect to see you in a few days. By, By, XYZ[100]

These two texts, revealing information on the activities of various Yeaggs
– specifically safe-burglars but the term was used more generally for
criminals – in Canada and Massachusetts and of their links in New York
are written in a familiar mode of direct reporting.

   Their counter-text is perhaps the paper read by William A. Pinkerton
in June 1904 to the Annual Convention of the International Association
of Chiefs of Police on 'The Yeggman: Bank Vault and Safe Burglar of
Today'.[101] Complete with statistics on crimes and convictions of 'burglars
of the "Yegg" class' and an array of photographs of prominent Yeggs
such as 'Topeka Joe', 'Denver Harry', 'Mass Dick', 'Frisco Slim',
'Shenandoah Red' and the like,[102] the report on Pinkerton's speech contains details of the 'origin, methods, habits and characteristics' of
'Yeggmen', of which:

> nine-tenths of this class are made up of so-called driftwood of humanity
> in this country, composed of about one-half natives, one-quarter foreign
> descent and one-quarter foreign birth; most of these are mechanics or
> have been railroad men, iron workers, or originally in some trade and have
> lost their places of employment through labor troubles, and stealing rides

on cars, or tramping from one city to another they formed the acquantance of criminals, gradually becoming criminals themselves.[103]

Pinkerton also reflected upon the etymology of the term Yegg (which appeared to have more than one spelling):

> The word 'Yegg' or 'Yeggman' originated with the gypsies. When a particularly clever thief is found among a gypsy tribe he is selected as the 'Yegg' or chief thief. This expression is now adopted by the better class of thieves among the tramps or 'hobos' of this country. As late as twenty years ago, one tramp meeting another and wishing to be sure of his identity as a professional tramp, would address him as 'Ho-Beau'. This expression subsequently developed the word 'hobo'. If a tribe or band of tramps found among their number a particularly persistent beggar or daring thief, they, using the expression of the gypsies, called him a 'Yegg'. Then came the name of 'John Yegg' and finally the word 'Yeggman'.[104]

This somewhat questionable etymology is accompanied by details of the activities of Yeggs throughout the United States.

More in keeping with the rules governing the operatives and their reporting of information collected is the memorandum of an operative employed on shadowing a number of figures associated with the largest bank robbery in the United States in the nineteenth century – the Northampton, Massachusetts, bank robbery by the Scott–Dunlap gang in 1876.[105] In one of the few operatives' memoranda found in the Pinkerton headquarters archive, an operative has set down, in a small notebook, the notes for a fuller report in accordance with the Agency's rules. The 'shadow's' detailed notes cover a number of suspects in New York in 1881. The initials inserted against some of the descriptions suggest that more than one operative was involved in the shadowing operation. The notes commence with the following:

> In connection with the watching of
>
> 'Butch' McCarthy
> No. 343 East 83rd St.
> About 40 years of age; 5ft 7in
> height; medium build, dark hair
> dark brown full beard and moustache;
> beard parted in center; wore broad
> bruin black soft felt hat; dark blue frock
> overcoat; carried a cane.
> Jan 12. Visited Bakery No. 118 Fulton St. NY
> Jan 15 About 2 p.m. visited No. 1332 Third
> Avenue (Mary Wheelen) and remained

one hour
At 4.50 p.m. entered passengers
waiting room. Brooklyn-City R. Road
24th St. and 3rd Avenue Brooklyn
had probably been to Leary's house
as Kate and her sleigh was seen in
the neighborhood shortly afterward
Jan 18 Visited at 3 p.m. Harry Jennings,
Dog Fancier corner of Broome St. and
Center Alley. And left 15 minutes later
with man 45 to 50 years of age; 5ft 8 inches
high stout build; dark complexion, short
black side whiskers and moustache mixed
with grey. Wore Derby hat and light
colored suit of clothes. Appearance of English
sporting man.[106]

Here are descriptions of 'the man of the crowd', totally mundane and, as the sparse notes indicate, the knowledge of the person shadowed after a whole day's shadowing is meagre. The routine activity of detection is tedious and often unrewarding. A later entry, still for McCarthy relates:

Jan 25 Visited Harry Jennings and remained
2 hours – came out accompanied by man
about 35 to 37 years of age; 5ft 9 or 10 inches
high; medium build; dark or sallow complexion;
black straight hair; black moustache. German
features. Wore Black Derby hat; dark overcoat
and dark pants. Went to 'Butch's' house
and $1^1/_4$ hours afterwards they both went to
picnic grounds on Ave B between 83rd &
86th Sts; East River and were lost there.[107]

This thin notebook contains brief descriptions of other suspects who had been shadowed. The memoranda would have been amplified and systematized in reports to the Agency.

An instance of a complete report in connection with a drug-dealing operation indicates a fuller text in which actions are elaborated upon. Again an informer is involved in the case, for which there is an operative's report for Saturday, 22 April 1899 by F. M. Hawes on C. C. Silas Operation. It reads as follows:

Today in New York
Continuing on the above operation under instructions from Asst. Supt.
H. W. Bearce. I left the agency at 9.45 a.m. and proceeded to Hanover Sq.
where I met the informant Davies. We went into the cafe at Hanover

Sq. and sat down at a table where I could take Davies statement. Plause told Davies last night that he could get any amount of Drugs on 48 hours notice. He said it made no difference how large the order was. He said he had enough on hand to fill a hundred order swell [?] as he said [?] Mr. Spangenberg & Boyd last night. He gave Davies to understand that there was a man back of the business who had lots of money. He did not give any names. He said Flood let him in on the deal about two months ago. He stated that Flood knew a lot of Drugists. There is a man in a Drugstore at 725 Fulton St. Brooklyn who is a friend of Floods.

[There follows an elaborate shadowing operation and the handing over of a numbered $5 bill to Davies etc. The operative is later to meet up with another operative at another drug store. The report proceeds as follows:]

Not seeing opr. Webster there I went up to 8th Ave. and met him shadowing Plause from his dinner. Plause went into the pool room at 251 – 8th Ave. I gave Opr. Webster the information I got from Davies.

I then returned to the agency leaving there again at 4.00 p.m. and proceeded to 410 W 22nd St. where I instructed Operative Webster to keep up the shadow on Plause and let Opr. Carter shadow Flood as Carter knew Flood and some of the people that Flood meets. Operative Carter was not there. Webster said he went to pier to watch the steamer Adirondach for the purpose of getting the name of the officer that Plause met on the steamer. I discontinued at 6.00 p.m.

Yours Respectfully

F. M. Hawes

Car fares	.35
Cigars	.50
Expense Money to Davies	4.00
	$4.85[108]

Such elaborate reports could form part of the basis for complete write-ups of cases. The everyday, mundane account in ordinary language (complete with misspellings and other errors) is not reproduced in the volumes of true accounts of cases assembled, purportedly, by Allan Pinkerton, but almost certainly written by the ghost writers he employed.[109]

These 'true' accounts of detection were enormously popular and ran to 18 substantial volumes from the 1870s onwards. The claim that is made for these texts is not their literary quality but rather their *veracity*. A typical preface by Allan Pinkerton is the March 1875 note to *Claude Melnotte as a Detective*, which states that:

The stories which compose this volume are taken from the author's original notes on three actual cases, which were placed in his hands several years ago. Whatever else may be said of these tales, they cannot be denied the merit of strict truthfulness; and it is to this quality, more than to any pretensions to literary excellence, that the author trusts in presenting them to the public.[110]

The success of these volumes rested in part upon the notoriety of some of the cases themselves – such as railroad robberies on the Central Illinois Railroad, major bank robberies in Chicago, New York and other cities, the notorious Molly Maguire case and the Agency's involvement in the apprehension of the Jesse James Gang, Butch Cassidy and others.[111] The Agency's success in generating business from many of the major railroads and banks greatly extended its operation into the West (and hence the involvement in the apprehension of the Jesse James Gang), a success that was maintained until the closing of the Frontier and the gradual establishment of a structure of national law enforcement through a system of Federal Marshalls. Some of the cases were not without interest with respect to the development of modern means of communication. *Professional Thieves and the Detective* (1881), for instance, contains a case entitled 'Lightning Stealers and the Detective' from 1867, involving two criminals hooking up to the telegraph wires in the Midwest and sending bogus claims to the New York Stock Exchange.[112] Each new technology was already creating its own appropriate crime.

So successful were these true cases that by the 1880s imitations purporting to be Pinkerton stories were being published.[113] In addition, it has been suggested that, already in the 1870s, Pinkerton as detective became a model for the enormously popular dime novel series featuring 'Old Sleuth'.[114] These texts, catering to a less literate public, were often quite ambiguous in their response to crime. As Michael Denning has shown, the dime novel reflected contradictory responses to criminality.[115]

To remain with the *representations* of detection for a while, Pinkerton's 'eye' is part of a rational organization of systematic detection, bureaucratically structured with a command system from above and with little space for initiative from below (obedience to rules is paramount for operatives). In the private-eye literary genre, the representation of detection by an 'eye' is, however, usually that of an individually, (privately) directed activity by an 'eye'. There is often a contrast with the incompetent detection by others (usually the police, that is, the 'official' investigators). The narrative structure dramatically reduces the time-frame of detection and its fictional time is accelerated by rapid activity (in contrast to many Pinkerton investigations that extended over years).[116]

In short, the representation of detection often favours the independent figure, whether it be Dupin, Holmes, Poirot, Sam Spade or Philip Marlowe. But, at the same time, the 'true crime' tradition is significant for the development of the detective novel genre, both in terms of the latter's frequent recourse to actual cases and, more importantly, its extensive use of devices to create the veracity of its narratives. Pinkerton appears in Conan Doyle's Holmes stories, and Doyle himself was active in investigating real cases.[117]

In the case of Dashiell Hammett, as a significant creator, along with others, of a hard-boiled tradition within the genre, we have an author who, in his early work at least, draws extensively upon his own experience as an operative. This is true of his anecdotes in 'From the Memoirs of a Private Detective' (1923)[118] (including 'I knew a detective who once attempted to disguise himself thoroughly. The first policeman he met took him into custody.'), his rules on shadowing in 'Zigzags of Treachery' (1924) and, above all, the stories of the Continental Op.[119] The latter even contain fragments from, probably, Hammett's own Pinkerton experience. In 'The Golden Horseshoe', for example, when the Op confronts an individual calling himself John Ryan, his response is: 'I chalked that up against him. I don't suppose there are three old-time yeggs in the country who haven't used the name at least once; it's the John Smith of yeggdom'.[120] Later in the same story, the Op is to meet up in a hotel lobby with another operative who has a finger bandaged with adhesive tape:

> I passed him and stopped at the cigar stand, where I bought a package of cigarettes and straightened out an imaginary dent in my hat. Then I went out to the street again. The bandaged finger and the business with the hat were our introductions. Somebody invented those tricks back before the Civil War, but they still worked smoothly, so their antiquity was no reason for discarding them.[121]

The 'antiquity' of such tricks suggests that they were handed down through generations of operatives' training in the practice of detection as opposed to being part of the rules governing the operatives' activities in Pinkerton's General Principles. The practice of detection is only hinted at in the tests for prospective operatives. But when Hammett was first accepted into the Agency, the parameters of his activity as an operative had already been drawn up several decades earlier. When we as readers take up Hammett's early stories for the first time, the manner in which the activity of detection is practised appears new (in comparison with the ratiocination tradition). It was, however, already at least 50 years old. The routine of detection as portrayed by Hammett has affinities with the routines actually followed several decades earlier. And Hammett did not have access to the Pinkerton archives. His archive of knowledge of detection was created from his own experience of surveillance practices.

VIII

Much of the detail on detection has been deliberately and specifically drawn from Pinkerton archive material. But are there more general issues that can be raised regarding the relationship between surveillance and the city? It has already been argued that the Pinkerton National Detective Agency was, organizationally, a large-scale bureaucratic structure. Indeed, the organizational structure of the Pinkerton Agency, as outlined in its rules as early as 1878 and amplified in the 1916 rules, accords remarkably closely with Weber's analysis of bureaucracy that is 'fully developed', he argued, 'in the private economy, only in the most advanced institutions of capitalism' or in 'the large modern capitalist enterprise'. In Weber's analysis, bureaucracy is characterized by 'the principle of fixed and official jurisdictional areas' (set within the Pinkerton Agency but having regard to other jurisdictions such as the public police forces), within which the activities of the organization are 'distributed in a fixed way as official duties' (in the Agency defined as a set of rules) carried out only by those 'who have the generally regulated qualifications to serve'[122] (the training of operatives as indicated in rule-following and training for detection).

The hierarchical structure of a bureaucracy implies 'a firmly ordered system of super- and subordination in which there is a supervision of the lower offices by the higher ones', and when fully developed 'the office hierarchy is monocratically organised'.[123] In the case of the Agency, it is not merely the office that is organized monocratically but also all those employed in carrying out its functions. Similarly, when Weber argues that 'the management of the office follows general rules', then this, too, must be taken to include all the Agency's employees. Just as Weber maintains that 'office holding is a "vocation"' in a bureaucracy, so, too, Pinkerton insists upon the vocational dimensions of detection as a modern 'calling'. Those employed must pass through 'a firmly prescribed course of training' and remain loyal to the organization. In this context, Weber indicates that 'modern loyalty is devoted to impersonal and functional purposes'. Pinkerton insisted that the 'career' of detection possessed 'social esteem' (Weber), rewarded with a 'fixed salary' (Weber).[124]

Amongst the significant factors responsible for the development of the modern bureaucracy, three stand out as pertinent to the development of the Agency. First, 'the development of the *money economy*' (Weber) was crucial to the Agency's early cases associated with the dramatic increase in the mobility of monetary means (bullion movements) and the storage of money (the often unregulated banking system). The Agency in its early decades secured contracts from both banks and railroads. Second, as Weber notes 'railroads . . . are intimately concerned with the development of an inter-local traffic of mass goods'.[125] Third, and equally importantly, Weber refers to the fact that 'the increasing demand of a society, accustomed to absolute pacification, for order and protection ("police") in all fields exerts an especially persevering influence in the direction of bureaucratization'.[126] That protection was offered not merely to banks and railroads but also to capitalist enterprises threatened with labour unrest.

More familiar in Weber's analysis are the grounds for the technical superiority of bureaucracy, which 'operates like a technically rational machine' that is characterized by 'precision, speed, unambiguity, knowledge of the files, continuity, discretion, unity, strict subordination, reduction of friction and of material and personal costs',[127] and, with respect to its rationality, 'rules, means, ends, and matter-of-factness dominate its bearing'.[128] Operating with a set of impersonal rules requiring procedural correctness and consistency, the Agency generates 'knowledge of persons and events'. That knowledge is itself, in turn, set down in reports and files whose production is subject to rules governing their creation. As Weber suggests, 'the management of the modern office is based upon written documents ("the files"), which are preserved in their original or draft form'.[129] The assemblage of such knowledge forms an archive in the Agency. Its collection 'according to *calculable rules* and "without regard for persons" '[130] is protected by secrecy. The knowledge obtained from detection is only made available to third parties at the behest of the heads of the Agency. Pinkerton's emphasis upon secrecy in the collection and transmission of knowledge is echoed in a somewhat different context by Weber, when he maintains that:

> Every bureaucracy seeks to increase the superiority of the professionally informed by keeping their knowledge and intentions secret. Bureaucratic administration always tends to be an administration of 'secret sessions'. . . . The tendency towards secrecy in certain administrative fields follows their material nature: everywhere that the power interests of the domination structure toward the outside are at stake . . . we find secrecy.[131]

In the Agency's case, secrecy and discretion have an economic price that its clients must pay. At the same time, the immediate collectors of the Agency's knowledge – the operatives – are themselves not merely subject to rules of secrecy; they themselves are also not to know the purpose of the knowledge they collect. Their relations with the outside world are not what they seem to others, as the activities of shadowing and roping indicate.

The Agency as a large-scale enterprise in the knowledge industry stored its knowledge in reports and files in its urban offices – by 1916, 35 offices in cities across the USA. But even several decades earlier the Agency was already a significant employer in this modern industry, whose expansion generated new techniques of surveillance and 'scientific' classificatory systems. A March 1887 report on the Pinkertons in *The Detective* states that at that time the Agency had offices in Chicago, New York, Philadelphia, Boston and, since 1886, Denver. The Agency 'as it stands today has a list of about 750 regular employees, and besides that, has from 300 to 400 specials. At the present writing the pay roll shows over 1100 names'.[132] The offices of the Agency, from which the business of detection is directed,

> are all fitted out with a most complete set of photographs of rogues from all parts of the world, and with all the improved weapons and appliances which would assist in the detection of criminals of all grades. To the student of human nature, no place could possess more interest for a day's study than the picture gallery and cabinet, at Pinkerton's famous agency.[133]

The detective 'student of human nature' could draw upon knowledge and experience of the similarities in ways of doing things, of the similarities in sites chosen for criminal activity and so on. In his *Thirty Years a Detective* (1884), Pinkerton notes that:

> everyone has a particular way of doing things, and . . . their every action is bound to bear some resemblance to each other, both in character and method; and this peculiarity applies with equal force to those who . . . commit unlawful deeds.[134]

This knowledge, based on the experience of detection, facilitates the assembly of a 'certain well-defined classification' of *modes* of working, the *social milieu* of operating, and the choice of *locality* favoured by criminals.

The 'student of human nature' and the large surveillance agencies also already had access to an elaborate photographic system for indexing criminals into various types. The development of 'scientific' surveillance also extends to physiological details, most notably in Alphonse Bertillon's systematization of physiological traits (ears, mouths, foreheads, etc.), on the assumption that a classification of criminal features could be developed. Support for such assumptions (not least their racist ones) could be drawn from texts such as Cesare Lombroso's *L'Homme criminel* (*Criminal Man*, 1876) and many later works.[135] 'Scientific' surveillance later came to synthesize with scientific racism and discourses on the degeneracy of classes of persons and races.

In metropolitan areas the recognition of mass criminality required the introduction of systems of control and classification. The mass and the crowd became the object of a rapidly expanding literature by the 1890s, of which Gustav le Bon's *The Crowd* and Gabriele Tarde's *Les Lois de l'imitation* (*Laws of Imitation*) were significant instances.[136] The dynamics of collective behaviour was only one aspect of this discourse and of attempts to understand and classify urban populations. The identification of individual persons from out of the mass, the possibility of a precise identification and 'readings', of 'the man of the crowd' were also being developed. In Francis Galton's *Finger Prints* (1892) a new means of individual identification – fingerprinting – is only one of many that Galton says are justified:

> In civilised lands, honest citizens rarely need additional means of identification to their signatures, their photographs, and to personal introductions. The cases in which other evidence is wanted are chiefly connected with violent death through accident, murder, or suicide, which yield the constant and gruesome supply to the Morgue of Paris, and to corresponding institutions in other large towns.[137]

In 'distant countries' – and by implication, less civilized ones – even honest citizens may be falsely identified. But the major problem that is highlighted in such countries is personal identification from the mass. Galton reports on the difficulties in the identification of 'Hindoos', 'Chinese residents in our Colonies and Settlements', 'coolies' and presumably all those native populations that 'look alike' en masse.[138] Yet the same problem holds true for the mass urban population and, especially, for the dangerous classes in modern urban societies.

Looked at in another context, therefore, what is often viewed as a crisis of personal identity in relation to *fin-de-siècle* modernity must be seen simultaneously as the problematic relationship between *individual* identity and the development and recognition of masses of human beings as *masses*. To remain with Galton's investigations, and *one* of the ways in which this problematic is being expressed, an issue for detection is not merely the identity of one individual compared with another (including the possibility of *false* identity, and the *Doppelgänger* syndrome that was often so central to 'sensational' and mystery fiction in the nineteenth century and beyond), but also the more difficult issue of the hitherto *unknown* individual. Galton assumes that whilst the former may be dealt with through the development of fingerprinting, the latter requires a more elaborate register and classification system. Hence, Galton argues:

> For most criminal investigations, and for some other purposes also, the question is not the simple one . . . 'Is A the same person, or a different person from B?' but the much more difficult problem 'Who is this unknown person Y? Is his name contained in such a register?'[139]

Galton is impressed by the scale and apparent success of the sets of measures devised by Bertillon ('by the end of 1887 no less than 60,000 sets of measures were in hand'), even given the lack of sufficient staff to measure all prisoners and difficulties in some measurements (such as limbs).

Without following the detailed elaboration of *Bertillonage*, and whilst recognizing Galton's racial and class stereotyping, there are some general features of modern detection that Galton himself reveals. There is a close correlation between the development of 'scientific' detection and statistics (we should remember that a contemporary reviewer of Poe's tales of *ratiocination* commences from a discussion of Laplace's probability theory).[140] In turn, the assembly of an elaborate classificatory system or archive requires full utilization of existing technologies (photography) and the development of new ones (fingerprinting).[141] The more general issue of identification of individuals that this whole process focuses upon requires *searching an index* of features of individuals (*identities*) and *comparison* of one with another (*likeness*). The latter rests upon the recognition of what is *typical* (which raises other statistical problems of frequency and tests for error).[142]

In other words, rather than regarding the late nineteenth century as a period of the emergence of systematic reflections upon the relationship between the individual and society in some abstract sense (which is where the emergence of the 'new' independent discipline of sociology is often located), we should turn our attention to the specific spheres and modes of confrontation of issues of individual identity (including the 'crisis' of personal identity, which may have been by no means universal) and their relation to problems of dealing with masses of (unknown, anonymous) persons.

But there is a further implication of this preoccupation with parts of the body as indices of identity for detection and for its fictional representation. There is not merely a (private) *eye* in the streets of the metropolis – which accords with a *visual* preoccupation with the city – but also an operative as a human *body* that is in pursuit of other bodies with their own lives. The operative's attention to body size and (distinctive) external appearance is emphasized in Pinkerton's rules for operatives. In the fictional accounts of detection in the hard-boiled tradition, the vulnerability of the human body is also a feature of the narrative. And so, too, is the damage (including lethal damage) incurred by the human body. The detailed description of such damage in the hard-boiled tradition contrasts with the absence of such detail, both in the earlier ratiocination tradition and in the contemporary 'Golden Age' of puzzle detection (Christie, Sayer, etc.).

This preoccupation with external features in the hard-boiled tradition led commentators such as Albert Camus (in *The Rebel*)[143] to regard the tradition as revealing a pathological view of modernity that is anything but realist. The technique employed in these narratives consists in describing men by their outside appearances, in their most casual actions, of reproducing, without comment, everything they say down to their repetitions, and finally by acting as if men were entirely defined by their daily automatisms. On this mechanical level men, in fact, seem exactly alike, which explains this peculiar universe in which all the characters appear interchangeable, even down to their physical peculiarities. This technique is called realistic only owing to a mis-apprehension . . . it is perfectly obvious that this fictitious world is not attempting a reproduction, pure and simple, of reality, but the most arbitrary form of stylization. It is born of a mutilation, and of a voluntary mutilation, performed on reality. The unity thus obtained is a degraded unity, a levelling off of human beings and of the world. It would seem that for these writers it is the inner life that deprives human actions of unity and that tears people away from one another. This is a partially legitimate suspicion . . . [but] the life of the body, reduced to its essentials, paradoxically produces an abstract and gratuitous universe, continuously denied, in its turn, by reality. This type of novel, purged of interior life, in which men seem to be observed behind a pane of glass, logically ends, with its emphasis on the pathological, by giving itself as its unique subject the supposedly average man.[144]

Camus' references to 'daily automatisms', 'mechanical' repetition and 'levelling off' suggest a systematic representation of the human body and its behaviour that is itself created out of reductionist systems of data collection on human types, physiological affirmities and behavioural peculiarities. In part, this can be traced back to the knowledge collection system of detection inaugurated in the nineteenth century. The historical specificity of the representation of this world – what Camus refers to as a 'degraded unity' – in the hard-boiled tradition may be the result of another conjuncture.

In an ostensibly very different context, Benjamin reflected upon the poverty of representations of experience after the First World War.[145] He argued that human beings returned from that war not richer but poorer in expressible experience to live in a new post-war world. They returned from that war

poorer in communicable experience . . . a generation that was still transported to school with the horse-drawn omnibus stood under the open sky in which nothing remained unchanged except the clouds, and in the middle, in the force-field of destructive currents and explosions, the small fragile human body.[146]

One response to this, as Benjamin relates, was to retreat into another world, an escape world of alternative belief systems and lifestyles. From Camus's perspective, the war was another universe of degradation of human beings, requiring a massive bureaucratic collection of information on physical and mental capacities, actual mutilation (classified by body parts) and death. What would require further analysis is the historically specific reasons for the variety of responses to that war experience with respect to the detective genre. The 'Golden Age' of the puzzle tradition and the hard-boiled tradition existed side by side for a large part of the inter-war period.

IX

Pinkerton's rules for his operatives required that they 'become thoroughly conversant with the various localities they may be detailed to operate in'. Thus, the operatives required not merely a knowledge of *inhabitants* but also of *habitus* in order to operate 'with facility and amongst any class of people'. In other words, the operative should be trained in the *recognition of the social and physical space of the metropolis* and its interiors. The rules are silent on how this training could be effected. It can only be assumed that it emerged gradually out of the routine practices of detection activity itself. And, in passing, it should be noted that 'routine practices', recognition of 'natural settings' and 'definitions of the situation' pertain not merely to social scientific investigations but are almost paradigmatic for the fields of detection itself. Again, the much more difficult process of investigation, the routine practices of detection, could not remain content with any general principles and rules of detection drawn up by Pinkerton or anyone else.

The *fictional representations* of detection and urban mystery often do rely greatly and in different ways upon the urban setting (both as exterior and interior). At different periods in the development of the mystery and detective genres, the metropolis and its spaces have been drawn upon, often in an emblematic manner, to signify mystery. The specific dimensions of the city and its interiors have varied in response to historical and social conjunctures. The hard-boiled tradition and later *film noir* have forefronted the street, specific interiors such as the hotel lobby (highlighted, presciently, by Kracauer in the early 1920s) and sexually charged interiors (compare the frequency of bedroom settings in Chandler with Conan Doyle's Holmes stories).[147] And although much feminist research has focused upon the gendered spaces of *film noir*, the mystery and detective genre as a whole, extending back to the mid-nineteenth century, is in need of fuller investigation.[148]

The initiation of investigations often commence in the habitus of the detective. Rather than the private residence of Dupin or Holmes, the public office (most often rented by the 'private' eye) of the detective is where the narrative commences. The representation of the office in the hard-boiled and *noir* traditions does not suggest that this is the space of the archive of detection. More frequently, it is the private eye who is the embodiment of the archive. The Pinkerton Agencies, however, like others (including the more elaborate *state* archives), housed their archives in the office rooms away from the clients. Thus, the office into which clients entered was like that of other offices in which established professions offered their personal services. A contemporary newspaper description from 1875 depicts the exterior and interior of the Pinkerton Agency New York office as follows:

> The New York Bureau is in a narrow street that runs out of Broadway, adjoining Wall Street. An unpretentious sign is fastened at the side of the entrance way to one of those stately, dark and gloomy buildings down town which seem to frown away everything but business of the most serious nature. Once upstairs the whole floor is found to be subdivided into Pinkerton's rooms. One enters the visitors apartment to find several people nervously waiting already. It is furnished with the ordinary office paraphernalia of green table, directories, cane bottom chairs, a desk, messenger telegraph and any quantity of cheap pictures. Glass doors lead out in several directions. Two or three hatless boys-in-waiting are ready to take your card, and you sit down and reconnoitre. The only thing at all significant is the conduct of the other visitors. All else wears the dull business air of a lawyer's ante-room.[149]

The 'unpretentious' and 'gloomy' dimensions of the exterior are in keeping with an organization whose purpose is the collection of information that may reveal hidden connections and secrets.

Presumably, the operatives were exiting this building by another entrance than that used by the Agency's clients. An operative's report (21 September 1897: H. J. Hallawell) confirms this:

> Left agency at 11.15 a.m. and went to side entrance on Exchange Alley of building at 55 Broadway where I took up position to get spot on man as he left agency. He came out at about 11.50 a.m.[150]

This shadowing of someone who had visited the Agency may not have been uncommon. Once in the streets of the city, the operative was to shadow the person wherever they went.

The hard-boiled tradition certainly focuses upon detection as *work* in the streets of the city and its interiors. It differed in many respects from the earlier ratiocination tradition, not least in rendering the city once more a mystery and in locating *action* often in the public space of the street. The nature of these streets in terms of their physical layout, the density of building along them, the density of population in the buildings themselves and the transport available along them – and by the end of the century under them but sometimes above them – was being transformed. The fields of vision, so crucial for surveillance, were being opened up in many cities. The extensive use of large plate-glass windows in shops, bars and other public buildings ostensibly opened them up to an exterior and closer gaze and, importantly, the transformation of lighting systems (even before the introduction of electric lighting) altered the ability to shadow at night.[151] Indeed, department stores themselves became Pinkerton clients. The creation of a mass of customers opened up the possibility of stealing from such stores on a significant scale. As Elaine Abelson has argued, the detection came to focus upon what was regarded as a female pathology – kleptomania.[152]

There was, in Germany and Austria at least, also a heated debate (commencing in 1890, although the theme was initially dealt with in 1877 by one of the debate's participants) on the virtues of straight or crooked streets.[153] Although this debate commenced in part from aesthetic concerns, the omniscience or not of the gaze of power by the surveyor (a key real and metaphorical figure examined by such writers on city planning as Patrick Geddes in the same period) is relevant to the problems of surveillance.[154]

The potential for the street as the site of crimes rests not merely upon its physiognomy, but also upon its population and its relationship to the street. When Benjamin declared that Eugène Atget's photography of empty Parisian streets and squares rendered them into the scenes of a crime, then this could equally have been said of Charles Marville's photography some decades earlier.[155] The emptiness of the streets (which Kracauer also detected in West Berlin in late Weimar Germany as creating the impression of an empty terror)[156] does not reveal their secrets. The labyrinth of the streets of the metropolis, as Benjamin remarked, does not compare with 'the newest and least researched labyrinth' – the urban mass.[157] It is the relationship of the mass to its habitus – rather than merely the physiognomy of the city's streets and squares – that creates the difficulties for surveillance and for shadowing.

The labyrinth of the city's streets is therefore compounded by the labyrinth of its population. This connection was already made in the opening scene of Eugene Sue's *Mysteries of Paris* when Rodolph enters into the Cité at the end of October 1838:

> into that labyrinth of obscure, narrow, and winding streets which extends from the Palais de Justice to Notre Dame.
>
> Although limited in space, and carefully watched, this quarter serves as the lurking place, or rendezvous, of a vast number of the very dregs of society in Paris, who flock to the *tapis-franc*. . . .

On the night in question, the wind howled fiercely in the dark and dirty galleys of the Cité: the blinking and uncertain light of the lamps which swing to and fro in the sudden gusts were dimly reflected in pools of black slush, which flowed abundantly in the midst of the filthy pavement.

The murky coloured houses, which were lighted within by a few panes of glass in the worm-eaten casements, overhung each other so closely that the eaves of each almost touched its opposite neighbour, so narrow were the streets. Dark and noisome alleys led to staircases still more black and foul, and so perpendicular that they could hardly be ascended by the help of a cord fixed to the dank and human walls by holdfasts of iron.[158]

Less than a century later, such images of the city came to be favoured by some of the German Expressionists.[159] The emblematic image of the labyrinths of stone closing in on its furtive population is a powerful one. As far as its population is concerned, their ability to escape detection is contingent upon their knowledge and experience of this labyrinth. Again, as Benjamin points out, the physiognomy of the streets signifies something quite different to those who inhabit it than it does to those who are mere passers-by.[160] It is this kind of knowledge that the operative must master in the metropolis, confirmation of Benjamin's pointed connection between the flâneur and the detective. It is in the labyrinth of the mass and its interaction with the built labyrinth of the city, rather than in the empty streets of the metropolis, that secrets are revealed.

X

In the General Principles and the specific Rules of the Agency, Pinkerton placed the greatest emphasis upon the importance of *secrecy* for the success of any detection enterprise. Secrecy was seen to be vital to the movements and intentions of operatives, to the relations between operatives' schedules on an operation, and perhaps most importantly of all, the total operation was to remain a secret to operatives, thereby preserving the Agency's gaze of power within its own organization. Operatives were not to be called as public witnesses in trials since they would be 'revealed' for what they are. And even though applicants to the agency were asked on their application form whether they had been members of any secret societies, an affirmative answer did not disbar them from employment. Perhaps, on the contrary, their experience of a secret society would be viewed as a positive advantage.

The detective agency is not itself a secret society. As a private company offering its services to the public this would not be the case. However, the service offered is attractive by virtue of the fact that both it and its results can remain secret at the wishes of a client. One of the justifications for the practices of the detective agency is that many of those subject to surveillance are themselves engaged in secret (criminal) activity and are, sometimes, organized as secret societies. The agency must, correspondingly, also act in secret. It has further been suggested that there is a connection between the rules governing detection within this private agency and the organization of a secret service by Pinkerton during the Civil War. The Agency's subsequent extensive involvement in strike-breaking and anti-trade union activities also required infiltration of worker organizations. For all these reasons, the issue of secrecy is central to the activity of detection.

Yet the secret and secrecy, so fundamental to social interaction in all societies, has not received the attention it deserves. As is so often the case in the study of neglected properties of social interaction, it was Simmel who made a first significant contribution to understanding these phenomena. In a series of articles – 'The Secret: A social psychological outline' (1907), 'The Letter: From a Sociology of Secrecy' (1907) and more fully in 'The Secret and the Secret Society' (1908)[161] – Simmel made a phenomenology and a sociology of knowledge contribution to the study of secrecy. Although some sociological interest in secrecy has drawn upon Simmel's work, it has tended to focus upon features of secret societies (as in Hawthorn's and Hazelrigg's contributions).[162] An exception, dealing with secrecy's macrosociological dimensions, has been provided by Birgitta Nedelmann,[163] which raises issues that are relevant to the study of detection in metropolitan modernity.

Analytically, as Nedelmann has shown, secrecy is significant for Simmel as a form of *interaction*. Its key dimensions are: *sharing* a secret (by two or more) as common knowledge and as their exclusive property; *hiding* this knowledge from others as an excluding strategy or 'aggressive defensive' technique; the excluded person's attempts to *discover* the secret (as a result of recognizing this exclusion from knowledge) and adopting an 'aggressive offensive' technique; and secrecy as *organized* behaviour; the *dualisms* present in secrecy (which both unites those with knowledge of it and creates a barrier against those excluded from it); and the *psychological life* of secrecy, which generates emotions attached to secrecy (including trust).

At a more general level, Simmel views the secret, defined as 'the hiding of realities through positive or negative means – [as] one of the greatest intellectual achievements of humanity'.[164] The transformation of our relationship to reality is effected by secrecy in a remarkable manner insofar as 'the secret offers, as it were, the possibility of a second world alongside the manifest one, and the latter is most strongly influenced by the former'.[165]

This 'second world' to which Simmel alludes is undoubtedly one of the attractions of the mystery and detective genre. It is an attraction attached to the secret that is 'unified in a remarkable manner with its logical apposite: its revelation. The secret contains a tension that finds its release in the moment of its revelation'.[166] Potentially, this tension is one that is shared by the activity of actual detection as well as in its literary and other cultural manifestations.

But how does secrecy relate specifically to modern social formations? At the societal level, as Nedelmann indicates, Simmel identifies two features of modern society that facilitate secrecy as social interaction: *individualization* and the *money economy*. Individualization in modern society has two dimensions. The first is 'the process by which the individual's total role-set is divided into an increasing number of *segments*'.[167] The second is 'the process in which individuals develop a consciousness of the *uniqueness* of their personalities'.[168] The practice of secrecy in the first setting refers to an individual's ability to keep different role segments apart from each other . . . the *technique* of *segmentation*. At only one point do they all come together: at a person's funeral. As Nedelmann remarks: 'the only participant at funerals who has a professional interest in experiencing the effects of cross-cutting circles is the detective'. The practice of secrecy in the second setting refers to an individual's ability to demarcate themselves from others through discretion and trust. The maintenance of privacy requires the establishment and maintenance of a boundary of secrecy, a boundary that may vary according to individuals and social contexts.

As we have seen, the issue of the uniqueness of individuals, their *traits* and *traces*, is of prime concern to the detective. The *recognition* of the other as distinctive and (as assumed in fingerprinting) unique, without the operative being recognized (in the case of 'roping') *as* an operative, is at the heart of detection. The detective's task, to use Simmel's notion, is to penetrate the 'second world' created by the techniques of secrecy. But, as Simmel emphasized, the development of modern capitalist societies, grounded as they are in a massive expansion of the spheres of circulation and exchange, is accompanied by a corresponding expansion of the mature *money economy*. Money, as the universal equivalent of all value, is simultaneously the *reification* of exchange relations. The relations between human beings are transformed into the relations between things. Detection must concern itself, therefore, not merely *with individuals and their traces* but also *the traces of things*.[169]

However, Simmel is more specific in his exploration of the relationship between secrecy and the money economy. He argues that in 'small and tightly enclosed circles', the maintenance of secrecy is rendered more difficult by the frequency of close personal contact with others and the

likelihood of revelation in such settings. In larger and more extensive
social milieux, however, the maintenance of secrecy is made easier by the
abstraction, infrequency and lack of intensity of social relations. In this
context, the money economy reveals 'most clearly the specific traits of
the large circle' of relationships. Indeed:

> Ever since economic transactions have been carried out by monetary means,
> an otherwise unattainable secrecy has been made possible within them. Three
> qualities of the money form of value are important here: its *compressibility*
> (*komprimierbarkeit*) which permits someone to be made a rich man by a
> cheque sliding unnoticed into his hand; its *abstraction and lack of qualities*
> by virtue of which its acquisition and change in ownership can be made
> in a secret and unknown manner, such as is impossible in the case of
> extensive and undoubtedly tangible objects; finally its *effect over distances*
> (*Fernwirkung*) by means of which one can invest it in the most distant and
> continuously changing objects and thereby totally remove it from the eye
> of the immediate environment.[170]

The development of the money economy has thus created massive 'possibilities for concealment' (*Verbergungsmöglichkeiten*) for stock companies
and the state and – we can add – for criminal activity. Although in the
Philosophy of Money Simmel draws particular attention to the possibilities
for bribery and corruption facilitated by monetary transactions in the
economic, social and political spheres of life, it is only part of the much
larger potentialities for secrecy opened up by the money form.[171]

But, as Simmel recognizes, the maintenance of secrecy itself arouses its
opposite: attempts to discover secrets. 'Every secret concerning public
affairs reveals, however, its inner contradiction in the fact that it immediately creates the counter movement of revelation of secrets and espionage'.[172] The same may hold not merely for public affairs but also more
generally. Indeed, Simmel assumes, somewhat optimistically, that public
affairs have lost their secrecy. What is interesting in the present context is
not so much the veracity of this statement but the connection he makes
with another modern development, namely that:

> politics, administration and law have lost their secrecy (*Heimlichkeit*) and
> inaccessibility in the same measure as the individual has gained the pos-
> sibility of even more complete reservedness, and to the same extent that
> modern life created a technique of discretion, of the secreting of private
> affairs in the midst of metropolitan crowdedness as it was earlier produced
> solely by means of spatial isolation.[173]

Not only is a dialectical relationship between the public and the private predicted here; there is also a connection between secrecy and the

metropolis. This enables us to bring together the strands of Simmel's discussion of secrecy in a central modern focal point. As Nedelmann argues:

> The metropolis is the focal point for the development of secrecy as a form of interaction. Urbanization and the institutionalization of secrecy are two developments which run parallel in the process of cultural evolution. But in addition, the metropolis has an autonomous influence upon the development of secret behaviour. . . . Individuals exposed to the crowds of the city have to learn certain attitudes by which they can protect their personal sphere from the environment. Simmel calls this attitude . . . [that] of being 'blasé' or aloofness. It allows metropolitan dwellers to develop an amount of personal freedom which was not possible to achieve in traditional settings. . . . Furthermore, because of the exactness of the rhythm of urban life, the applicability of the techniques of secrecy (segmentation and demarcation) is facilitated.[174]

Thus, it is the modern metropolis with its labyrinth of streets and buildings and its 'newest' labyrinth, the masses, which is a source for a literary genre concerned with the process of revealing its secrets. At the same time, the opportunities for secret activity call forth attempts to reveal the secret nature of such activity itself by secret means. The city always remains to be detected.

3

The City Interpreted

Georg Simmel's Metropolis

From the outset, the world of things in no way confronts the mind,
as it might appear, as a sum total of problems whose solution it has
to gradually master. Rather, we must first extract them as problems
from out of the indifference, the absence of inner connection and the
uniform nature with which things first of all present themselves to us.

Georg Simmel, 'Über Massenverbrechen'

'The fact is, my dear Watson, that you are an excellent subject', he
said. 'You are never blasé. You respond instantly to any external
stimulus. Your mental processes may be slow but they are never
obscure, and I found during breakfast that you were easier reading
than the leader in *The Times* in front of me'.

Arthur Conan Doyle, 'The Field Bazaar'

The most important single article on the city from the sociological
standpoint.

Louis Wirth on Simmel's metropolis essay

I

George Simmel wrote a number of essays on the metropolis as well as
several that take up, however briefly, aspects of the city and its architecture. But only one essay was published under his name on Berlin, and
that piece dealt with an exhibition, with the *representation* of the city in
its products. Even then, given its topic, it is somewhat surprising that

'The Berlin Trade Exhibition' (1896) was not published in Berlin but in Vienna.[1] This 1896 essay is clearly eclipsed in its impact by Simmel's much more wide-ranging essay 'The Metropolis and Mental Life' – an essay that clearly draws upon Simmel's Berlin experience (even though the city is mentioned only once in the text) – which was published in 1903 in Dresden.[2] This piece, one of Simmel's most famous essays, is actually concerned with cities in the plural (*Die Grossstädte*). It is an essay which, like some of his other pieces such as 'The Stranger', has come to live a life of its own divorced from its original context.[3] A similar fate has befallen other seminal essays by others.[4] It is therefore one of the aims of this essay to bring together Simmel's writings on the modern metropolis as an intersection of texts, just as he argued in his sociology that individual identities do not develop in isolation but rather as the intersection of social circles.

'The Berlin Trade Exhibition' and 'The Metropolis and Mental Life' essays – however different their ostensible themes – have a number of features in common. First, as already intimated, neither was published in Berlin, suggesting that the context of publication is worth investigation.

Second, both may be read in relation to Simmel's exploration of metropolitan modernity and to his wider investigation of modernity. The exhibition essay coincided with Simmel's important lecture on 'Money in Modern Culture' ('Das Geld in der Modernen Kultur'), given in March 1896, and was also published in the liberal Viennese newspaper *Neue Freie Presse*.[5] This lecture constituted his first overview of themes developed more fully in his *Philosophy of Money* (1900).[6] At the end of the metropolis essay, Simmel notes that its major themes are expanded upon in more detail in his *Philosophy of Money*. The metropolis and the money economy are interrelated sites and thematic constellations.

Third, the occasion for both essays was an exhibition on the metropolis: in the case of the 1896 essay, the Berlin Trade Exhibition and, in that of the metropolis, the First German Municipal Exhibition in Dresden (1903). In other words, the occasion for both pieces is the representation of the city: in 1896, Berlin, and in 1903, modern German cities in general.

Fourth, there are some revealing intersections between these two essays. The Berlin exhibition essay commences with a quotation from Karl Lamprecht's *Deutsche Geschichte*. Lamprecht was one of the leading figures in historical and cultural studies at Leipzig University.[7] Simmel's lecture was one of a series of lectures in Dresden given in the winter of 1902–3, all of whose participants were either members of the Leipzig circle or had strong links with it.[8] It should be added here that, although today we might look to Simmel's *Philosophy of Money* for a significant turn-of-the-century account of modernity (especially in the last chapter), many of Simmel's contemporaries might have turned to the supplementary volumes of Lamprecht's *Deutsche Geschichte* for a more specifically German-orientated account, but one that also drew attention to the nervous culture of modernity.[9]

Fifth, there is a connection between the two exhibitions of 1896 and 1903. Due, in part, to opposition from other German states, jealous and fearful of Prussian hegemony, the 1896 exhibition was named merely the Berlin Trade Exhibition and not the German Exhibition.[10] Given the popularity and above all prestige of exhibitions in Europe and elsewhere since the London Great Exhibition of 1851, it is surprising that there was no such international exhibition in Germany in the late nineteenth century. Be that as it may, it was perhaps as a result of the tension between the German states that the 1903 Dresden exhibition of German municipal authorities was conceived – six years earlier – as a counter to the earlier Berlin exhibition. The timing of the decision to mount such an exhibition is revealing. As the sociologist Howard Woodhead – a pupil of Albion Small's in Chicago and of Simmel, amongst others, in Berlin – wrote in his opening remarks to his report on the Dresden exhibition (published by Small in the *American Journal of Sociology*):

> In 1897 the Oberbürgermeister of Dresden proposed to a meeting of German municipal officials at Karlsruhe an exposition of the great development of German municipalities in the last decades. The plan was heartily seconded, and at a meeting called soon thereafter it was concluded to hold a German municipal exposition in Dresden this year (1903).[11]

Woodhead's account of this important exhibition as a major, positive representation of metropolitan life in Germany remains the best detailed account in English of its content. It was to be followed by other exhibitions on the metropolis in Germany before the First World War, including the major competition for plans and designs for the enlargement of Berlin itself in the *Gross-Berlin* competition of 1910.[12]

The fact that the two sites of Simmel's essays on the modern metropolis are devoted to the *representation* of the city suggests that there may be a wider interest on Simmel's part in exhibitions and representation. This leads us to include in the ensuing discussion further pieces by Simmel on Berlin and on exhibitions as well as other essays relevant to the metropolis. In particular, there are good grounds for including his neglected early essay 'Über Kunstausstellungen' ('On Art Exhibitions', 1890), especially since he regarded such exhibitions as *symbolic* (representation) of the modern metropolis. This early essay appeared anonymously – under the authorship of 'S' – in the journal *Unsere Zeit* in 1890, and is possibly Simmel's first attempt at analysing the representation of the metropolis.[13] It also predates his seminal essay on 'Sociological Aesthetics'

('Soziologische Ästhetik') by six years,[14] but it is one of the first sustained attempts to analyse a significant aspect of the aesthetics of modern metropolitan life. The key argument linking art exhibitions and the metropolis is made by Simmel in 1890 in terms of a reciprocal relationship of cause and effect. For Simmel:

> precisely the specialization of our times produces the rush from one impression to the other, the impatience for enjoyment, the problematical strivings to compress together in the shortest possible time the largest possible sum of acquisitions, interests and enjoyments. The colourfulness of metropolitan life, both on the street and in the drawing room, is both the cause and the consequence of this continuous striving, and art exhibitions encapsulate this symbolically in a restricted space.[15]

Already in this early statement we can see Simmel working with different dimensions of his key concept of reciprocal effect (*Wechselwirkung*) or interaction. The relationship between the metropolis and one of its 'restricted spaces' – in this case, art exhibitions – is not merely one of homology but rather of both cause and consequence. The metropolitan existence that is the key to this reciprocity possesses both an outside (the street) and an inside (the drawing room). For their part, art exhibitions are a symbolic fragment whose exploration reveals the effect of the totality of metropolitan life. In 1896, in 'Sociological Aesthetics', this relationship between the fragment and the totality is given fuller expression with the claim that:

> the essence of aesthetic observation and interpretation lies in the fact that the typical is to be found in what is unique, the law-like in what is fortuitous, the essence of things in the superficial and transitory . . . Every point conceals the possibility of being released into absolute aesthetic significance. To the adequately trained eye, the *total* beauty, the *total* meaning of the world as a whole radiates from every single point.[16]

The earlier essay on art exhibitions has a somewhat more modest importance. Art exhibitions there 'form a miniature image of our intellectual currents'; they 'belong to the symbols of our transitional times'.[17]

Alongside Simmel's resonant contemporary remarks on city planning in his 'Sociological Aesthetics' essay, there are a number of other pieces on Berlin as well as essays raising more general issues on the metropolis in relation to space, landscape and architectural models. At an even more general level, as Simmel himself indicated, much of the analysis in his *Philosophy of Money* is relevant to a delineation of facets of the modern metropolis. What, then, are the features of the modern metropolis in which Simmel was interested and chose to analyse?

II

It is evident from his early essays in the 1890s that one of Simmel's interests in the metropolis emerges out of its *modes of representation* and its
manifestation in *other* entities rather than in a direct confrontation with
features of the metropolis. In particular, Simmel explores some of the
forms in which metropolitan existence is *displayed.* Prominent in this
respect are *exhibitions* of economic and cultural productions. In other
words, Simmel is interested in forms of presentation (*Darstellung*) and
exhibition (*Ausstellung*) of 'the culture of things'. Further, as he later
observes, such an interest is significant not least because this culture of
things (*Sachkultur*) *is* our human culture. Thus, his initial treatment of the
Berlin Trade Exhibition of 1896 is as an exemplar of world exhibitions
(and earlier annual fairs) viewed as a 'fundamental type of human sociation
(*Vergesellschaftung*)'.[18] What Simmel chooses to explore in this context is
aspects of amusement and consumption (of impressions of things), the
external (architecture) and internal (forms of display) modes of exhibiting the world of things (commodities), and the representation of the
metropolis in and through its economic and cultural products. But before
examining Simmel's analysis of the Berlin Trade Exhibition in detail, its
broader significance and context should be explored since – aside from
Simmel's recognition that it symbolizes the fact that 'Berlin, despite everything has became a "world city" ' – this is not revealed in his text.

The 1896 Berlin exhibition is usually viewed (and was viewed by contemporaries) as a symbolic indicator of the city's transition from a metropolis (*Grossstadt*) to a world city (*Weltstadt*).[19] At the same time, its very
installation arose out of the rejection of a German exhibition to succeed
London, Paris, Vienna, Philadelphia, Chicago, etc. On more than one
occasion, the official guide to the exhibition refers to the uncertainty as
to whether it is a Berlin, German or world exhibition, without revealing
the hostility and resentment of other German states to a perceived Prussian
hegemony.[20] But after being 'reduced' to a Berlin exhibition, the intention
was still to exceed the displays of the recent Paris (1889) and Chicago
(1893) exhibitions. However, the very title of the exhibition sounded somewhat archaic – a trade (*Gewerbe*) exhibition rather than an industrial
exhibition. This archaic aura was reinforced by the design for the cover
of the official catalogue – a hand grasping a hammer emerging out of the
earth with the silhouette of the city of Berlin in the far distance, hiding
images of the massive industrialization of production in such major
enterprises as Borsig, AEG and Siemens. Instead, the exhibition's catalogue cover design announced other attractions than the products of

3.1 Cover of commemorative album for the Berlin Trade Exhibition, 1896

Berlin's trades, namely 'Old Berlin' and Cairo. Thus, the new world of commodities was displayed alongside the construction of an 'Old Berlin' using 'genuine materials' by the architect Karl Hoffacker. The reconstruction of the old was complemented by constructions of the exotic (in turn complementing similar displays in panoramas) in the form of an 'Alpine Panorama', a colonial display (of one of Germany's few colonies, New Guinea) and a construction of the streets of Cairo (which the catalogue declared to be better than the Cairo construction at the Paris Exhibition of 1889). Again, the exhibition did not actually bear the title of 'Colonial' or 'Imperial' Exhibition (unlike many British and French exhibitions subsequently). However, the Imperial dimension was satisfied, in part, by the official opening of the exhibition on 1 May 1896 by the German Emperor and Empress, who arrived in the steamer 'Alexandria', and by the display of the Emperor's steamboat 'Bremen' as an exhibition

3.2 Reconstruction of section of Old Berlin for the 1896 exhibition by Karl Hoffacker

item. The official catalogue does not seek to justify the choice of opening date. The attraction of the exhibition and its amusement potential (which is one of Simmel's major concerns) can be seen as a counter to the significance of the first of May for the labour and trade union movements.

The representation of the metropolis, its streets and its architecture in this exhibition is thus quite distinctive. The city of Berlin had its own exhibition area (but was by no means one of the most significant), but if the visitor were to seek out the streets of the metropolis, then they were located only in their nostalgic form in 'Old Berlin', or in an exotic form in 'Cairo'. The 'modern' architecture of the metropolis was to be found in the neo-Gothic central administration building designed by Hoffacker, the many other exhibition areas, the main restaurant and, above all, the main industrial exhibition building designed by Bruno Schmitz, with its 'snow white front', red-tiled roof and aluminium-covered towers. Like several other structures, this major exhibition building was constructed in a 'Spanish style', no doubt influenced by exemplars in the 1893 Columbia Exhibition in Chicago.[21] In this respect, therefore, *modern* Berlin was represented less in its architecture than in its commodities displayed *within* the structures erected in the Treptow Park, whose overall effect was that of a late-nineteenth-century Disneyland. In this context, Simmel's emphasis upon amusement in such exhibitions is not out of place.

As Klaus Strohmeyer has argued, most of these broader dimensions of the exhibition's significance are absent from Simmel's text. Instead, Strohmeyer maintains that 'the Trade Exhibition is, for him, a paradigm of modernity that was breaking through the capital city with destructive force'.[22] But even this goes too far. Simmel's primary interest in this exhibition lay in the direction of the exhibition as a form of sociation into the culture of things, a sociation involving amusement and consumption of display forms of commodities.

For Simmel, the exhibition contains an overwhelming plethora of objects assembled together, the only unifying factor being 'that of amusement'.[23] The sheer heterogeneity of things 'crowded together in close proximity paralyses the senses' and creates 'a veritable hypnosis' of the spectator, whose finer feelings are 'violated and deranged by the mass effect of the merchandise offered'. The force of 'contradictions', the 'stimuli' and 'diversity of consumption' that we confront in modern life (and in the metropolis) is felt dramatically in the world exhibition. The latter offers a 'richness and variety of fleeting impressions [that] is well suited to the need for excitement for overstimulated and tired nerves'.[24] It is a metropolitan phenomenon whose features are reproduced in the confined space of the exhibition.

But Simmel also draws attention to two contradictions in this sociation into the world of things in the exhibition. The first is that, although the configuration of the world of things in the exhibition appears to create

3.3 Industrial exhibition hall designed by Bruno Schmitz, 1896

'an outward unity', in fact it hides beneath this apparent unity 'a vigorous interaction [that] produces mutual contrasts, intensification and lack of relatedness'.[25] The aesthetic veil of the totality hides a contradictory diversity. Second, and more importantly, the process of the *production* of commodities does not have the same effect upon the individual as does the process of their *consumption*. The 'differentiation on the side of production', with its 'ever greater specialization' and 'one sidedness of function', does not extend to the sphere of consumption. On the contrary, Simmel declares that our

> one-sided and monotonous role in the division of labour will be com-
> pensated for by consumption and enjoyment through the growing pres-
> sure of heterogeneous impressions, and the ever faster and more colourful
> change of excitements. The differentiation of the *active side of life* is
> apparently complemented through the extensive diversity of its *passive and
> receptive side*.[26]

The activity ascribed to the process of production and the passivity ascribed to the process of consumption is here combined with a compensatory theory of consumption, insofar as the latter is an escape from the excessive specialization, uniformity and monotony of the production sphere.

The notion of consumption as escape from production might presuppose that, for consumption to have this effect, it requires to be located and housed elsewhere. In the present context, Simmel draws out the distinctiveness of a 'specific exhibition style' for the housing and encasing of commodities on display. If, elsewhere, Simmel declares that 'each style has its own syntax', then the key to the exhibition style is its *transitory* nature. This fundamental feature of modernity is embodied in the architectural style of the exhibition in a distinctive manner. In many other building designs, the architect is committed to creating something permanent, 'to incorporate the permanence of form in transient materials'. But in the case of exhibition structures, they

> look as if they were intended for temporary purposes; because this lack of
> permanence is unmistakable they are absolutely ineffective as unsolid build-
> ings. . . . It is this conscious denial of a monumental style that has produced
> a new and positive shape . . . here the attraction of the transient forms its
> own style. . . . In fact the architects of our exhibition have succeeded in
> making the opposition to the historical ideal of architecture not a matter of
> absurdity or lack of style; rather they have taken the point last reached in
> architecture as their starting point.[27]

Despite Simmel's claim that this particular architecture signifies 'the point last reached in architecture' – which would have been true of some earlier

3.4 Bird's-eye view of Berlin Trade Exhibition: a 'temporary' architecture for 'amusement'

and subsequent exhibition architectures – his emphasis upon the lack of permanence accords fully with the aim of transient structures of modernity.

What he terms 'the aesthetic output of the exhibition principle' is manifested not merely in the housing of the world of things, but also within their outer casing in the visual stimuli and modes of representation of the commodity. The aesthetic veil of the commodity, this 'shop window quality of things' in the exhibition, has its origins in the need for commodities to circulate. As Simmel states it, 'the production of goods under the regime of free competition and the normal predominance of supply over demand leads to goods having to show a tempting exterior as well as utility'.[28] In order 'to render the graceless graceful for consumers', attention must be drawn to 'the external stimulus of the object, even the manner of its presentation'. The display of commodities in exhibitions confers upon them a new aesthetic significance akin to that being developed 'in the relationship between advertising and poster art'.[29]

Yet not merely commodities are being displayed and represented in world exhibitions. Their metropolitan sites are being represented too. In other words, visitors to these exhibitions participated in the consumption of representations of the modern metropolis itself. Such exhibitions 'form a momentary centre of world civilization' through the concentration of the world of things in a restricted space. The world city is not merely represented through the display of 'all the important styles of the present cultural world' but also 'through its own production a city can represent itself as a copy and a sample of the manufacturing forces of world culture'.[30]

On a more modest scale, a 'totality of cultural production' is also provided in the spatial configuration of the art exhibition and museum. The thematic content and the categorization employed in Simmel's exploration of art exhibitions would justify a subtitle to the 1890 text, 'On Art Exhibitions': 'Art Exhibitions and Mental Life (*Geistesleben*)'.[31] The mental or spiritual life of contemporary individuals is Simmel's theme here, albeit with reference to art exhibitions. As we have seen, Simmel sees a close relationship between the latter and the modern metropolis. Just as the metropolis is a *mass* phenomenon in which individuals exist as differentiated entities, so this is also a general feature of modernity in which 'in the modern world the major things occur through the masses and not through individuals, the cooperation of many has replaced the solitary individual deed'.[32] This change manifests itself in art exhibitions too. No single individual work of art encapsulates the sum total of creativity of the past. Rather, the domination of the division of labour in the art world has created a situation in which our modern appreciation of art rests upon our recognition of the one-sidedness of particular artistic expressions, whose totality is only appreciated by means of according their diversity an interrelated unity.

This diversity arising out of 'the one-sidedness of the modern person, insofar as they create, is enlarged by their many sidedness, insofar as they are receptors of impressions'[33] in art exhibitions. In the latter, devoted to the appreciation and consumption of cultural products, the diversity of impressions is heightened by the spatial proximity of the most divergent artistic productions, creating a crystallization of a wealth of impressions within a confined space. Simmel suggests that:

> Just as the objects displayed themselves bring the most contradictory elements spatially close to us, so equally contradictory are the judgements, that are linked to them, approval and disapproval, admiring amazement and disparaging mockery, indifference and emotional involvement that follow in rapid sequence in the mind of the visitor, and thus in this respect too fulfil the conditions of modern enjoyment – to allow the most diverse things to pass through our senses in the smallest amount of time and space.[34]

This very openness to the most diverse entities and cultural productions produces 'two of the greatest maladies of modern artistic appreciation: the blasé attitude and superficiality'. The blasé attitude is itself 'both cause and consequence of that need for the most diverse and contradictory impressions'.[35]

Indeed, Simmel detects 'a strange contradiction in mental life (*Geistesleben*)' in modern society. There are two contradictory tendencies in our response to the contemporary world. The one leads to a weakening of our capacity for strong impressions:

> The receptivity of the modern person has become increasingly refined and nervous, their senses have become increasingly sensitive, so that instead of strong colours and their contrasts they can only cope with the pale, semi-faded tints and that the liveliness of colours harms them, just as modern parents can no longer bear the happy noise of their children.[36]

This 'shading of feelings' contrasts with the opposite tendency, namely:

> the need for great excitements, the dissatisfaction with the small stimulations and joys of the day, the insufficiency of the idyllic, that ultimately brings about a situation in which nature only still gives us satisfaction on the North Sea and in the highest peaks of the Alps.[37]

These two modern responses to the world are themselves accentuated within their own sphere as well as being two aspects of a single process. And it is not merely our perception but our bodies as a whole that are affected by them, even to the extent of generating pathological manifestations. Thus:

in the bodily realm, too, the over-excitement of the nerves leads, on the one hand, to *hyperaesthesia*, the unhealthily accentuated impact of every impression, and, on the other, to *anaesthesia*, the equally unhealthily reduced receptivity.[38]

In the context of art exhibitions, the impact of art works upon the individuals is disturbed by the spatial proximity and profusion of their display, so that it is difficult to concentrate upon a single work without being aware of the others hanging close by, thereby creating a 'confusion', a 'disturbing contemporaneity', an 'overloading' of impressions. A corresponding situation pertains in museum displays, creating a similar superficial impression, but with one difference. The relative permanence of museum displays contrasts with 'the fleeting character of the art exhibition' (Simmel speaks here of its usual 'restless eight-week life').[39]

Writing in 1890, Simmel maintains that what the visitor to art exhibitions is confronted with can usually be characterized as 'an impoverishment of motifs', especially in the untiring attempt to treat the same themes differently in genre paintings. Later, in 1896, after the commencement of the secessionist movements in Germany, he widened his critique to other styles.[40] Here, however, he reiterates the relative absence of 'the great individual entities' and, in keeping with his earlier argument, of 'the wealth of the most diverse styles and most differentiated representation of problems in modern art. This is a manifestation of the fact that 'originality has been transferred from the individual to the group',[41] to a total image of diverse strivings displayed in art exhibitions.

Modern art exhibitions are a 'characteristic indicator of the modern spirit' (*Merkzeichen des modernen Geistes*). Yet art exhibitions 'are not in fact the cause of superficiality and the blasé nature of artistic judgement, as has been ascribed to them, but rather the result of certain circumstances in the public spirit' that reveal 'the whole tone of modern impressionable life'. Its features are:

> the specialization of achievements, the concentration of the most diverse forces in the narrowest space, the fleeting haste and excited hunt for impressions, the lack of sharply formed personalities, compensated for by a great wealth of strivings, tasks, stylistic genre that are carried by whole groups.[42]

In this respect, then, art exhibitions 'form a miniature image of our intellectual currents' in modern society.

There is, too, a temporal dimension to Simmel's exploration of the exhibition in modern society. Drawing on earlier writings he briefly examines this under the notion of 'pessimism concerning the present day', but it can also be read in the context of a concept he does not use, namely historicism. Whereas Simmel himself views art exhibitions as 'symbols of

our transitional period', his critical remarks on historicist genre painting
and upon the lamented absence of great individuals in the modern world
indicate that he does not share this pessimistic response to the contemporary world. His categorization of pessimism is relevant to responses
to the metropolis and its architecture:

> The pessimism concerning the present day . . . becomes . . . an optimism con-
> cerning the past, and the myth of paradise, the dream of the golden age [and]
> the belief in the good old days are nothing other than the rosy illumination
> of a past that has been spared the shadows of the present, an unconscious
> judgement of an unsatisfying present. . . . This glorification of the past that
> the greater mass of people borrow from the idea of morality, in refined
> circles narrows down to an aesthetic glorification of the past.[43]

In turn, the beauty and creativity of the past is contrasted with a perceived
decline in artistic achievement in the present day (and a corresponding
decline in 'genius').

Simmel's interpretation of the contemporary current of pessimism can
be transposed to developments in art and architecture, as well as responses
to the modern metropolis. In the arts and in architecture, the crisis in historicism was producing an ever more laboured repetition of past motifs
as still appropriate representations of the present, as well as distinctive,
nationalistically constructed styles, such as Old German, that reappeared
both in contemporary metropolitan architecture and in exhibitions (as in
Berlin and in Dresden in 1896).[44]

Yet the extensive treatment of Simmel's analysis of a microcosm of
modern mental life in art exhibitions also reveals the extent to which,
already in 1890, he is focusing upon features of metropolitan existence
that are more fully drawn out and are placed within a different context,
both in his analysis of the money economy and in his later explorations
of the modern metropolis.

Simmel's interest in exhibitions and display is confirmed by a lecture
on 'Aesthetic Quantity' ('Über ästhetische Quantitäten'), given on 20
January 1903, two months before his metropolis lecture in Dresden.[45] The
publication of the revised version of this lecture in March 1903 suggests
the possibility that Simmel also reworked his Dresden lecture on the metropolis for its subsequent publication.[46] Unfortunately, the absence of the text
of the metropolis lecture does not permit verification of this possibility.

What the analysis of 'aesthetic quantities' does confirm is Simmel's current
interest in the representation of objects as affected by their scale and size.
Although concerned more widely with issues of size and scale – such as the
problem of representing the scale of the Alps in painting, solved, according
to Simmel, by 'the only great painter of the Alps, Segantini' – his remarks

on the representation of architecture are pertinent here. The general proposition that Simmel explores is that 'things as objects of artistic representation . . . require of themselves a quantifiable size, in order to reveal their meaning and their significance'. What he terms 'the aesthetic thresholds of objects'[47] is affected, amongst other things, by the scale of their representation and the extent to which the 'inner forces of things' manifest themselves in their representation. Simmel asks:

> how is it that small models of built structures exercise almost no aesthetic effect, or at least one that does not correspond to the effect of the identically formed built structure itself? Here I leave out of account architects whose trained fantasy allows them to expand in their imagination the full effect of the completed work, so that the problem being treated here does not arise. Yet the solution to this problem appears to me to arise out of the fact that we are physically and psychologically not in a position to feel for ourselves the load relations, the weight and bearing relations, the span and the elevation, in short the whole multilayered play of dynamic processes that creates the fundamental aesthetic attraction of architecture – that we cannot feel this in such small scale measurements. That architecture is dead and meaningless to us which does not make us *feel* how the pillars bear the timber work, how the halters of the Gothic pointed arch allow their forces to be brought together, how the cornice bears the column. Yet this empathetic understanding always only emerges above a certain absolute size of its objects. Our organs dealing with this are too crude in order to recognize psychologically the validity of the reduced relations of pressure and counterpressure of the half-metre model since they do not achieve the threshold of empathetic feeling. For ultimately empathetic feeling is feeling and must therefore, like other feelings, have a threshold in consciousness. It would appear that our architecture possesses precisely that quantitative mass that, in accordance with our physical mental structure, permits a maximum of empathetic feeling for this dynamic. Much smaller or that much larger masses – which thus overstep the *upper* threshold of empathetic feeling – we can, of course, still view and intellectually diagnose as having the same relationships of form as the aesthetically effective ones – but they are no longer aesthetically effective.[48]

Such considerations of the 'mediation of quantitative value' in the representation of things raise issues that Simmel does not take up here. Of course, his remarks on architectural models are relevant to the contemporary popularity of such models – either of individual architectural works or of whole cities – in exhibitions and museums. Similarly, Simmel is right to draw attention to a significant feature in our reception and appreciation of architectural forms in their actual state. In particular, his mention of the 'threshhold of consciousness' can be seen to anticipate Benjamin's later discussion in a metropolitan context.[49] But neither in the ensuing discussion of his lecture nor elsewhere does Simmel himself raise the question as to the extent to which architectural forms are appreciated at all in our dynamic movement in the modern metropolis. If anything, the implication of his statement in the metropolis essay to the effect that the individual is overwhelmed by built structures suggests that the distance that we maintain in order to function in the modern metropolis applies to its architecture too. Metropolitan practices may thus disregard architecture features except insofar as they, the street, and the whole built environment constrain our bodily movement and sense perception. Yet elsewhere, in his examination of social space – although not focused explicitly upon the metropolis – Simmel does explore our spatial relations in the built environment and in our interaction with others.

III

For the moment, and still remaining with *aesthetic* dimensions of the metropolis, the issue of our perception of metropolitan life is taken further by Simmel in another context. In his essay 'Philosophie der Landschaft' ('The Philosophy of Landscape', 1910) Simmel explores 'some of the presuppositions and forms' of landscape.[50] In so doing, he implies – and it must be emphasized that this is not an explicit theme of his essay – that our experience of the city is seldom one of viewing it as a landscape. Even when we are walking through open nature, our senses are drawn to particular aspects of it 'with the most diverse levels of attention'. But the very fact

> that we draw our attention to such individual elements or even this and that element taken together, we are still not yet conscious of viewing a 'landscape'. Rather, precisely such individual contents of our field of vision should no longer rivet our attention. Our consciousness must possess a new totality, a new unity, over and above its elements, that is not bound by their special significance and not mechanically constituted from them – only this is a landscape. If I am not mistaken, it has seldom been made clear that a landscape does not yet come into being through the fact that all kinds of things unfold upon a piece of the earth's surface and are immediately viewed. . . . the fact that visible things upon a piece of the earth's surface are 'nature' – if need be, however, with human works that arrange its order – and not rows of streets with department stores and automobiles, this fact does not yet make this piece of the earth's surface into a landscape. By nature we understand the infinite connection of things, the ceaseless birth and destruction of forms, the flowing unity of events that expresses itself in the continuity of temporal and spatial existence.[51]

This initial attempt to distinguish nature and landscape also draws attention to the status of the experience of urban life with its streets, stores and automobiles.

Such entities seem to belong to the world of nature, albeit a second (human) nature. But even this location is premature in the context of Simmel's distinction between nature and landscape. With respect to nature:

'A piece of nature' is really an internal contradiction. Nature has no pieces, it is the unity of a totality and in that moment in which something is plucked out of it, it is no longer in the full sense nature, because precisely only within that unbounded unity, only as a wave of that total current can it be 'nature'.[52]

In contrast, for a landscape to exist:

it is precisely the demarcation, the encapsulation in a momentary or permanent circle of vision that is always essential; its material base or its individual pieces may exist simply as nature . . . Viewing a piece of ground with all that lies upon it as a landscape means observing an extract from nature, for its part, as a unity – something totally alien to the concept of nature.[53]

There is, for Simmel, also a historical dimension to the notion of a landscape, namely that it emerges only with modernity, with 'the individualization of internal and external forms of existence, the transcendence of originally subjugated and united entities into differentiated autonomous entities'. However, in our everyday existence – including our urban life – 'what we observe, for instance, with a glance or within our momentary horizon is not yet a landscape'. Although Simmel makes no reference in this context to our metropolitan existence, it is clear that our 'momentary horizon' in the metropolis is bounded by our immediate everyday concerns, our struggle for existence, our bombardment with impressions in which things are enmeshed in everyday world (Simmel speaks of things 'interweaving in the life of an object'). In this everyday existence there is no time for extracting ourselves from our enmeshment in events. In this sense, although metropolitan existence requires an 'objective' stance vis-à-vis all that we confront, this may not include that 'distance of objectivity' with which the landscape stands over against us. And yet, at the same time as Simmel was reflecting upon the nature of landscape in 1910, some German artists were already seeking to create cityscapes of modernity that transcended the confines of traditional conceptions of the landscape. The manifestos of German Expressionism, notably in Ludwig Meidner's call to artists to turn their attention to the streets and cityscapes of the metropolis, were often directed towards realizing the immediacy of *street*scapes as well as cityscapes that challenged our orthodox notions of the landscape.[54]

Yet if Simmel viewed the creation of an autonomous realm extracted from the continuity of nature and given a new objectivity (as in landscape painting) as a presupposition for a landscape, he also reflected upon another art form that created a new entity out of natural materials. For Simmel:

> Architecture is the only art in which the great struggle between the will of the spirit and the necessity of nature results in real peace. In poetry, paint- ing and music the autonomous laws governing materials dumbly serve artistic conceptions . . . Although architecture, too, uses and distributes the weight and load-bearing power of materials according to a plan conceivable only in the human mind, within this plan the matter works by means of its own nature, carrying out the plan, as it were, with its own forces. This is the most sublime victory of the mind over nature.[55]

The context for this reflection which accords a privileged status to architec- ture compared with other arts is, again, not the modern metropolis, but rather Simmel's analysis of the significance of the ruin. Here, his attention is directed towards the consequences of the disintegration of the unity of spirit and nature that pertains to architecture. Indeed 'this unique balance . . . breaks . . . the instant a building crumbles', and natural forces come to dominate human ones. The disintegration of a building 'destroys the autonomous nature of [its] form'.[56] And although, compared to other frag- ments of a destroyed work of art, those of the ruined building remain a much more significant phenomenon, the nostalgia that it often evokes can be deceptive. Simmel draws a distinction between ruins that reveal their sources in destruction by *human beings* and those whose fascination arises from the fact that human products 'appear to us entirely as a *product of nature*'. He maintains that many Roman ruins 'lack the specific fascina- tion of the ruin' insofar as they are the product of human destruction, and that inhabited urban ruins reveal human sources of decay.

But without entering into all the nuances of his rich exploration, it should be noted that Simmel draws attention to the importance of spatial and temporal dimensions of the ruin (and of architecture). The *spatial* dimension is already present in his interpretation of architecture as the resolution of spirit and nature as 'the striving upward and the sinking downward' forces of elevation (of the spirit's creations) and embeddedness (of nature's products). The ruin also reveals its mood of peaceful resolu- tion in that it 'orders itself into the surrounding landscape without a break, growing together with it like tree and stone'.[57] The ruin's *temporal* dimension emerges from its character of being 'past':

> It is the site of life from which life has departed . . . In the case of the ruin, the fact that life with its wealth and its changes once dwelled here constitutes

an immediately perceived presence. The ruin creates the present form of a past life, not according to the contents or remnants of that life, but according to its past as such.[58]

The ruin therefore contains an 'extreme intensification and fulfilment of the present form of the past'. Hence, although the aesthetic attraction of the ruin lies in its resolution of tensions and its stimulation of appreciation – including nostalgia – for the past, it is also bound up with modernity. The fortuitous or accidental nature of the disintegration of the built structure and the immediate presentness of its 'external image and internal effect' of the past link our interest in the ruin to features of modernity. Indeed, Simmel concludes his exploration of the ruin by suggesting that our present times are fascinated with 'decay and decadence'. One might add here that precisely the same features of the ruin – its fortuitous or incidental origin and its intensification of the past *in* the present – that suggest a connection with modernity also coincide with crucial dimensions of his analysis of the adventure.

But there is one aspect of the ruin – created by human beings – that Simmel does not address, namely the proliferation of, albeit often temporary, ruins in the massive reconstruction of the modern metropolis, of which he would no doubt have been aware in Berlin. The dramatic expansion of German metropolitan centres, and especially Berlin after German unification in 1870, necessarily entailed not merely an *extension* of the metropolis into its hinterland, or the creation of new urban sites, but also a substantial *destruction* and rebuilding of existing urban spaces. It may be that Berlin did not possess a Baron Haussmann to commission on an equivalent scale what he termed 'creative destruction'. Nor was there an equivalent figure who might employ a photographer such as Charles Marville to capture both the urban structures before they were destroyed to make way for a 'new', 'modern' capital city and the act of destroying the past.[59] Instead, Simmel's instances of ruins are those of classical antiquity and not even those beloved of German romanticism in the early nineteenth century. The contemporary ruins in German metropolitan centres, including Berlin, did not require that aesthetic stance with which Simmel is concerned in his reflections on the ruin. Rather, the destruction of the city with its temporary ruins was available for *all* to see. They did not require that aesthetic distance which is necessary for our appreciation of the ruin in Simmel's sense. Indeed, the speed of destruction and reconstruction robbed the observers of the ruins the time for reflection. The face or faces of the city could be transformed so rapidly that the presentness of the past was seldom allowed to enter into consciousness at all. The faces or façades of streets were often transformed in the last quarter of the nineteenth century as rapidly as Kracauer detected in the third decade of the twentieth century in Berlin.[60]

Yet again, however, it is Simmel who causes us to reflect upon the aesthetic significance of the face, albeit the human face. Later, we will examine Simmel's reflections in his 1901 essay 'The aesthetic significance of the face', within the context of his 1903 essay on the metropolis, for its relevance to the analysis of bodies (and faces) in the city.[61] For the moment, it should be obvious that reflections on the importance of the human face are also relevant to interpretations of the faces or façades of buildings. Although the latter is not Simmel's concern, two of his observations are pertinent to the face of built structures.

The first relates to the elements affecting the total impression of a face (or façade):

> In the case of all objects that are either changeable in themselves or occur in many similar examples, much of their aesthetic character is decided by how comprehensive a change in their constituent elements must be in order to result in a change in its total impression. Here too there is a kind of ideal of energy saving: basically, an object is all the more aesthetically effective or usable the livelier it reacts as a whole to the modification of one of its smallest elements.[62]

This argument is made with reference to the human face, but the contemporary debate on abstract ornament on façades and the development of minimalist ornament on a series of similar built structures finds one of its elements elucidated here.

The second observation recalls an earlier discussion of social dimensions of aesthetics and the role of symmetry in aesthetic attraction. Symmetry is, for Simmel, 'an anti-individualistic form'. At first sight, the two dimensions of symmetry and individuality are antithetical:

> Insofar as each part of a symmetrical structure is derivable from every other part, they indicate a higher dominating principle common to them all: rationalism strives in all spheres towards a symmetrical form whereas individuality always [has] something irrational about it . . . [Yet] the face is the most remarkable aesthetic synthesis of the formal principles of symmetry and individualization: as a totality it realizes the latter, doing so in the form of the former that dominates the relations between its parts.[63]

Once more, this delineation of a feature of the human face may also be applied to the tension within the built form between symmetry and individuality – a tension that had many echoes in contemporary debates on ornamentation as well as in the principles of city planning.

Indeed, Simmel's aesthetics of metropolitan life are extended beyond a discussion of architectural models and existing architectural forms, and beyond the streetscapes of the metropolis, to the ideal forms of the city itself. In 'Sociological Aesthetics' (1896), Simmel proclaims his views on the nature of aesthetic observation and representation of things as grounded in the fact that 'in the individual element there emerges the type, in the fortuitous the law and, in the superficial and fleeting, the essence and significance of things'.[64] This implies, in turn, that 'each point hides the possibility of being redeemed into absolute aesthetic significance; out of each point, for the adequately trained eye, there is illuminated the *total* beauty, the *total* meaning of the world as a whole'.[65] But in what forms does this aesthetic significance reside?

> At the start of all aesthetic motifs there stands symmetry. In order to bring the ideal meaning and harmony into things, they must first of all be symmetrically formed, the parts of the whole must correspond with one another, they must be ordered evenly around a middle point . . . Rationalism first gains its visible structure in symmetrical forms.[66]

The sociological significance of such formations has several dimensions.

First, there is a reciprocal interaction between material purpose and aesthetic motif in the construction of systems in social formations. Purely aesthetic structures appear to emerge out of apparently purely material purposes. And the converse of this also holds. The symmetrical construction of a group – into units of ten or a hundred are Simmel's examples for military, criminal and other groupings – have their origin in 'easier overview, designation and manageability'. In such cases, 'the distinctive stylized image of society that emerged in these organizations appeared to come as a result of mere utilitarian grounds'.[67] But once in existence, such structures expanded and developed beyond their original purposes and size, whilst at the same time maintaining the fiction that they were of the same number. For Simmel this signifies the transition of the purely utilitarian into the aesthetic, the attraction of symmetry, of *architectonic tendencies* in social formations.[68]

The 'architectonic structure' of social formations and the presence or absence of ease of overview, characterization and manageability or governability and regulation, which Simmel ascribes to practical outcomes of rationalism, surely anticipates a theme subsequently developed by Foucault. Structures that facilitate a secure overview of those within them, that are capable of developing systematic means for the recognition and characterization of their 'inhabitants' and their systematic regulation also possess a *political* function.

This political function that is facilitated by some aesthetic formations, by an 'architectonic structure', is therefore another significant level that Simmel illuminates. Indeed, in some respects, he formulates this proposition more sharply than Foucault:

The tendency towards symmetry, to identically formed arrangement of elements according to universal principles is indeed, furthermore, shared by all despotic societal formations. Justus Móser wrote in 1772: 'The rulers of the General Department would very much like to have everything reduced to simple rules. In so doing we distance ourselves from the time plan of nature, that reveals its wealth in diversity, and build the path to despotism, that seeks to coerce everything in accordance with a few rules.' The symmetrical arrangement renders easier the domination of many from a single point.[69]

The ability to dominate is easier and more calculable than in the case of groupings whose 'inner structure and boundaries of the parts are irregular and fluctuating'.

Such observations by Simmel coincide, historically, with a debate on straight or crooked streets in town planning in Germany. The advocates of straight streets were associated by their opponents with the extension of Haussmann's principles of boulevard development.[70] Less than 40 years later, in 1926, the coincidence of human symmetry and rationalization was to be drawn by Kracauer in his concept of the mass ornament.[71] In turn, a decade later the mass ornament of Fascist rallies in Germany had replaced Kracauer's original exemplar, the Tiller Girls. The masses as themselves architectonic structures with the enforced synchronized bodily movements at Fascist (and Stalinist) rallies had come to complement the built structures of monumental stadiums and grand avenues.

But like Kracauer later, Simmel also drew political consequences from this interrelationship of aesthetic and practical concerns in social formations. He noted that the harmonic, unconditional relationship of the parts to the whole exercised great attractiveness to autocracies. Politically, Simmel identifies 'in contrast, the liberal state form's preference for asymmetry' with state formation in Britain as a 'liberation of the individual instance' that, in its 'rhapsodic fortuitousness', also had its own aesthetic attraction.[72] However overdrawn the comparison may have been (although the Prussian state form is not mentioned here) between contemporary Germany and Britain, it is located in the context of a comparison of the aesthetic dimension's impact upon the contemporary conflict between socialism and individualism.

As an instance of 'the rational organization of society', the socialist ideal possesses great aesthetic attractiveness since 'it seeks to make the life of the totality into a work of art such as at present cannot be possible for the life of individual elements'. Later in this essay Simmel recognizes the latter as a possibility with the development of an 'almost exclusively individualistic character' of beauty, one which his contemporaries would have recognized in the art nouveau movement's ideal of the total work of art

(*Gesamtkunstwerk*) in individual entities and structures. At all events, Simmel is convinced that an individualistically grounded society, with its heterogeneous interests and unreconciled tendencies, 'offers to the mind a restless and, as it were, uneven image; its perception constantly requires new innovations and its appreciation new efforts'.[73] Conversely, a socialist society, with its ordered centres and organic unity, offers to the observing mind 'a maximum of perceptions, a comprehensiveness of the social image with a minimum of expenditure of mental power'. The *mental life* of the two social formations is thus structurally different.

Such reflections may at first sight seem removed from a discussion of the modern metropolis. But, as we shall see, it is the *mental life* of the metropolis that is the focus of Simmel's most famous essay. Further-more, when he compares the aesthetic attractiveness of socialist forma-tion with that of a machine, 'the most extreme minimalization of resistance and friction, the harmonic interweaving of the smallest and the largest component parts'[74] and its repetition in the organization of the factory, such an association of the machine, rationalization and the metropolis was already being made by influential writers on city planning, such as Camillo Sitte. It was Sitte who, already in 1889, was defending the aes-thetic dimension of the city's physiognomy against the modern preoccu-pation with traffic, straight-lined streets and the like that was typical of what he termed the modern 'geometry man' – one of whose exemplars was, for Sitte, Otto Wagner – and his putative desire to transform the city into a functioning machine.[75]

Simmel, too, with respect to Utopian visions makes a connection between rationalization and the development of the metropolis. Socialism's interest in harmony and symmetry reveals its rationalistic impetus and its desire 'as it were, to stylize social life' in this manner. In particular:

> socialistic Utopias always construe the local individual units of their ideal cities or states according to the principle of symmetry: the localities or buildings are arranged in the form of a circle or in quadratic form. In Campanella's sun state, the plan of the imperial capital is measured math-ematically with a compass, as too are citizen's units of the day and the ranking of their rights and duties.[76]

The interaction between the aesthetic and the political realms that Simmel explores here anticipates a significant thread in later reflections upon 'the dialectic of enlightenment' by Adorno and Horkheimer and, more gener-ally, upon the ambiguity of modernity as manifested in the totalizations of 'rationally ordered social relations' (and built structures) sometimes aimed at emancipation and the 'irregular and fluctuating', fragmentary life experience that such totalizations presumed to address.[77]

More generally, reflections upon the symmetry and rational order of modern cities would focus upon a commitment to an urban monumentalism (the rationality of scale as well as order), which was evident in contemporary Germany and elsewhere, rather than in the still unrealized socialist urban Utopias. The extension of major cities opened up the possibility for the creation of monumental public spaces, even a monolithic public sphere, as the First World War approached. Later, after 1914, monuments and avenues to victory and to the dead were often to take on grotesque proportions.

IV

The essay on sociological aesthetics also reveals an interest in the *spatial* dimensions of social interaction that is subsumed there under the symmetry or asymmetry of urban spaces. In the autumn prior to giving his lecture on the metropolis in Dresden (1903), Simmel completed what are almost certainly the first major contributions to the sociology of space. The two essays on space published first in 1903 were to constitute the most substantial chapter of Simmel's major volume *Soziologie* in 1908.[78] In this respect, his treatment of spatial features of interaction went far beyond that of any other contemporary sociologists, providing a potential impetus – which was hardly taken up for decades – to explore one of the most neglected dimensions of social interaction. Although the two essays on space were published in the same year as his lecture on the metropolis, the essays explore general properties of social space rather than specific spatial features of the modern metropolis. Nonetheless, both are relevant to understanding some spatial dynamics of the metropolis.

The shorter of the two essays on space, 'Über räumliche Projektionen sozialer Formen' ('On the Spatial Projections of Social Forms'),[79] investigates 'the effects that the spatial determinants of a group experience through their social structures and energies' and commences with reflections upon state and city organization. Group organization experiences a transition from one resting upon clan affinities to 'a more mechanical, more rational and more political organization' such as the state which rests upon 'a more indifferent principle' and a less exclusive principle. A political unity requires a degree of neutrality and even indifference. Indeed, 'space as foundation of organization possesses that degree of lack of partisanship and equality of response that makes it appropriate as a correlate of state power with its similar response to the totality of its subjects'.[80] In like manner, the centralizing and, to a considerable degree, indifferent concentration in the city possesses similar features in its development:

For whereas country life encourages aristocratic, distinctive forms of existence and thereby organization on the basis of family circumstances, the city
tends towards more rationalistic, more mechanical forms of life. This crystallization around a city, on the one hand, approximates to the schematic-
localizing motifs of organization instead of the physiological whilst, on the
other, it is obviously of a more centralistic nature and enables the convergence of social forces into unified actions.[81]

However, it is not merely political but also economic organization that
encourages 'a mechanization of social elements'. The 'differentiation of
production in space' emerges in two forms. One is that of the dissolution
of itinerant traders. Travelling tradesmen remained common well into the
nineteenth century. Amongst Simmel's examples is that of the portrait
painter who 'prior to the discovery of photography still often wandered
in the nineteenth century . . . from town to town'. With the increasing
concentration of the population in cities, crafts became localized in their
urban workshops. The second form is the 'rational-organic context of
the economy' with its 'regularized division of spheres of profit', as in the
modern cartel. Spatial differentiation takes on an increasingly rational
structure.

The second dimension of spatial effects upon social forms is to be found
in the exercise of domination over people. The domination of a state power
over its subjects within its boundaries also possesses a spatial dimension
in the centralization or focus in a capital city and, in the case of a change
in the domination, a change in the location of that city. The third dimension that Simmel examines is that of the spatial localization of social entities
in their own 'houses' (families, clubs, regiments, universities, trade unions,
religious communities). The opposite of this localization tendency is to
be found in the developed money economy with its corresponding 'sociological capacity for abstraction, which makes the adjustment of rights
and duties independent of spatial proximity and from which the money
economy is both cause and effect'. The money economy's 'house' is the
metropolis, but linked to all other spatial extensions as an abstract community. Finally, Simmel draws attention to 'empty space'. The significance
of empty space lies in its spatial determination by social preconditions,
whether that be the wasteland between clans, states, etc., that establishes
boundaries (for defence); children's games where 'some kind of object is a
taboo for all'; the 'ideal vacuum' created by respectable, reserved people
in the metropolis whose distance or empty space opens up the possibility
for the unscrupulous to profit from it; or the neutrality of 'uninhabited
space' which, as a 'boundary place', might serve for commodity exchange,
where people might meet 'if not on friendly terms, at least without hostility'. In short, the exploration of 'empty space' itself 'ultimately reveals
empty space as mediator and expression of sociological interaction'.[82]

It is however, from the more substantial essay on 'The Sociology of Space' that spatial dimensions of metropolitan existence may be more readily extracted. Here Simmel draws attention to some basic features of the spatial forms that we confront in social action – the uniqueness or exclusive nature of space, spatial boundaries, the fixing of social forms in space, spatial proximity and distance and, finally, movement in space. Despite the largely ungrounded nature of this selection of spatial preconditions in social interaction, Simmel's examination of their general properties is relevant to understanding the metropolis.

First, every part of space possesses an *exclusiveness* or uniqueness. Particular social formations may be identified in different ways with particular spaces, such as states or districts of cities. Interaction between individuals and groups in states is closely identified with a specifically demarcated territory, whereas the city's 'sphere of significance and influence' extends through various differentiated functional 'waves' – economic, cultural, political – into the hinterland. Indeed, within the city there has often been a functional rather than a quantitative filling out of space, as in the medieval city with its differentiated guilds or corporations. In modern cities, the zoning of areas for designated functions is only one relatively late development of the process of spatial power designation that creates inside and outside within the metropolis itself.

Second, a feature of space is that it may be *broken into pieces* and subdivided for our purposes. In other words, it can be *framed in by boundaries*. Here Simmel specifically draws upon the analogy with the picture frame, in so far as framing has a similar significance for social groups as for works of art. Spatial framing has a wider importance that Simmel does not draw out, namely in our constitution of social experience. Nonetheless, he does indicate that a society, and forms of sociation, possess a sharply demarcated existential space in which the extensiveness of space coincides with the intensity of social relationships. This is in contrast to nature, where the setting of boundaries appears arbitrary. The social boundary, however, constitutes a unique interaction in so far as each element affects the other by setting a boundary but without wishing to extend the effects to the other element. Hence, 'the boundary is not a spatial fact with sociological consequences but a sociological fact that is formed spatially'.

Therefore, the sociological boundary signifies a quite unique interaction, in which what is significant is the interaction woven on either side of the boundary. In contrast to forms of boundary maintenance, both political and social, Simmel draws out the relationship in the city between the impulsiveness of crowds in open spaces, giving them a sense of freedom, and the tension of a crowd in an enclosed space. The indeterminacy of boundaries may also be seen in the spatial framework of darkness, in which the narrowness and breadth of the framework merge together to provide scope for fantasy – a not insignificant theme in the literary genres of the thriller and detective novel.

Simmel reflects further upon the social boundary in one of the three supplementary sections to the discussion of space (the other two being on the sociology of the sense and the stranger) where he raises a significant issue for metropolitan existence – namely, the limits of our *knowledge of others*. Elsewhere, one limit to our knowledge is extensively explored in Simmel's essay on the secret, whose maintenance is facilitated by the anonymity of metropolitan existence. Here, more general features of the boundaries of our knowledge of others are examined:

> Every instance of living together rests permanently upon the fact that each person knows more about others through psychological hypotheses than the latter reveal to a person directly and with a conscious intention. For if we had to rely only upon what is openly revealed, then on every occasion, instead of a unified human being whom we understand and with whom we can reckon, we would have before us *only a few fortuitous and uncontextu-alized fragments of a person*. Therefore, we must supplement the given fragments through inferences, interpretations and interpolations until a sufficiently whole person emerges such as we need inwardly and for the practice of life.[83]

This legitimate intervention into the Other's existence, regardless of whether it is desired by the latter or not, has to confront the Other's 'private ownership of their inner (*seelischen*) existence, their right to discretion'. There exists, then, a line between the 'unavoidable construction of the stranger's inner life' and 'psychological indiscretion'. The line between our consciousness and 'the sphere of the Other' may *vary* with social structures and contexts, but this merely confirms that 'this line stands in the closest interaction with the whole structure of social life'. The limit or boundary will be different in commercial transactions from that between parents and children, and so on. However varied such limits are in diverse social contexts, their existence serves:

> to elucidate the incomparable solidity and visibility that social boundary processes maintain through their spatialization. Every boundary is a psycho-logical, or even more precisely, a sociological occurrence; but through its investment in a line in space the reciprocal relationship, in its positive and negative sides, gains a clarity and certainty – indeed often also a rigidity – that seems to remain unobtainable to it as long as the meeting and parting of forces and laws is still not projected into a sensual form and therefore, as it were, always remains in *status nascens*.[84]

Over and above the crucial, diverse roles of socio-spatial boundaries in a metropolitan context (defining inside and outside, public and private, and concomitant stratification variables such as gender, class, ethnicity, culture, etc.), Simmel raises here the significance of Otherness that is crucial to his interpretation of metropolitan existence and our experience of the mature money economy. The concentration of individuals and groups in the metropolis and the myriad interactions in which they participate presupposes a knowledge of the Other that is not confined to 'a few fortuitous and uncontextualized fragments'. Knowledge of others is crucial for negotiating the plurality of metropolitan interactions at various levels. At the same time, our intervention into the space of the Other is often limited by what Simmel, elsewhere, calls discretion – 'the feeling that there exists a right in regard to the sphere of the immediate life contents of others'. The radius of discretion varies 'with respect to "close" individuals, to strangers and indifferent persons'.[85] These and other categories have their typical boundaries. But if the money economy – whose seat is the metropolis – socializes us into alienation and greatly extends our interactions with 'strangers' and 'indifferent' Others, the knowledge and capacity to decipher the signifiers of Otherness is essential to metropolitan life. And here we rely, in part, on our trained senses in order to distinguish features of Otherness. This makes sense of Simmel's location of his reflections on the senses in the context of a more comprehensive study of space. The reciprocal transgression of boundaries of Otherness in the glance, in smell, etc., is encountered on a massive scale in the metropolis, with its accelerated and concentrated mobility of individuals. As we shall see, this proliferation of interaction in the metropolis not merely presupposes knowledge of others and distinctive forms of 'mental life'. The circulation and interaction of individuals in the metropolis is also a circulation and interaction of bodies, of 'body life'.

A third spatial feature in social formations is the capacity for *fixing or localizing social interaction in space*. Here Simmel indicates four possibilities. First, the existence of a continuum from the completely local binding together of individuals (as in the medieval town) to a situation of complete freedom. Second, the fixing of a social form at a focal point, as in economic transactions (though Simmel points out that this derives not from the substantive immobility of a particular place but from the functions connected with the place). Third, the bringing together of otherwise independent elements around a particular space (the religious community's focus around the church). Here, Simmel draws attention to the rendezvous whose sociological significance 'lies, on the one hand, in the tension between the punctuality and fleeting nature of the occurrence, and its spatio-temporal fixing on the other'. The rendezvous also indicates that human memory is stronger on space than on time. Finally, the individualizing of place is a significant urban development (from the earlier naming of houses to their numbering and, in the Enlightenment period, occasionally the numbering and lettering of streets). The latter provides a new ordering of urban space and a new means for regulating and controlling urban populations.

The relationships between *proximity and distance* constitute the fourth dimension of social space. It would be possible to grade all social interactions on a scale of proximity or distance. In the metropolis it is distance, abstraction and indifference to those who are spatially adjacent, and close relationships to the spatially distant that are typical. The latter is a product of intellectuality that makes possible proximity to what is most remote and 'cool and often alienated objectivity between the closest individuals'. It is at this point that Simmel introduces his excursus on the sociology of the senses in his *Soziologie*, on seeing as 'perhaps the most immediate and purest reciprocal relationship that exists', and on hearing and smell, which 'remain trapped, as it were, in the human subject'.

The final dimension of space that Simmel examines is the possibility of *changing locations*. Whole groups can move their spatial determinants, as in nomadic societies, but so also can individuals with particular functions (itinerant justices) or merely travellers (and here Simmel points to the temporary intimacy of interaction between travellers temporarily abstracted from their normal milieu). What Simmel does not draw attention to, but which was a marked feature of Berlin, is the substantial migration of groups to the metropolitan centre from the east. This fifth dimension is also the context in Simmel's *Soziologie* for his excursus on 'The Stranger', which opens with its spatial referent:

> If wandering, considered as a state of detachment from every given point in space, is the conceptual opposite of attachment to any point, then the sociological form of 'the stranger' presents the synthesis, as it were, of both these properties . . . another indication that spatial relations are not only determining conditions of relationships among people, but are also symbolic of those relationships.[86]

The stranger, therefore, is an instance of the 'Other' urban figure becoming a boundary or limit, contrasting with the social boundary as the demarcating limit of others in the city and with the third 'excursus' on the senses as exploring the interaction across the boundaries of others. But the ambiguous spatial location of the stranger as both inside and outside the community, including the urban context, also open up the possibility for a distinctive social objectivity compared to those rooted in their communal contexts. This possibility – which has a wider significance for locating social preconditions for objectivity in general – is not without its perils. As Simmel suggests, 'one can also characterise objectivity as freedom. . . . This freedom, which allows the stranger to experience and to act equally both in a close relationship and from a bird's-eye view does, of course, contain *many dangerous possibilities*.[87] Not least, it is this distinctive outsider figure in the urban landscape, whose objectivity is 'composed of distance and nearness, indifference and involvement', who is often castigated as the source of 'uprisings' and disturbances to established order. This is one of several instances in which the political dimension of Simmel's explorations of social interaction and social types comes to the surface.

Thus, in various ways, Simmel's sometimes schematic investigation of spatial properties in interactional forms often reveals new features of a spatial dialectic of inside/outside, proximity/distance and so on. In particular, the concentrated spatial interactions of the metropolis are an ideal site for their exploration. It has been suggested that one of Simmel's crucial concerns is with the significance of social distance. As Donald Levine has argued:

> nearly all of the social processes and social types treated by Simmel may be readily understood in terms of social distance. Domination and subordination, the aristocrat and the bourgeois, have to do with relations defined in terms of 'above' and 'below'. Secrecy, arbitration, the poor person, and the stranger are some of the topics related to the inside–outside dimension.[88]

In the latter context, Simmel's subtle reflections on the bridge and the door, on connecting and separating could also be readily applied to the urban mechanisms for creating insides and outsides within the metropolis.[89] In turn, the inside of the exhibition can be conceived as a representation of the outside world of commodities and built structures.

V

The representation of Old Berlin in the Berlin Trade Exhibition of 1896 had its parallel also in the same year in Dresden – although in no way associated with it – with an exhibition of crafts and applied arts in Saxony on 'The Old City', which reproduced medieval and Renaissance exemplars of the city. Its exhibition catalogue declared that 'in the rooms of the past many thousands of people felt at ease, free of the cares of the present'. This exhibition 'was an imaginative recreation of an old town, complete with city wall, bastions, towers, houses, taverns and churches'.[90] According to Volker Helas, 'this temporary architecture was applauded, and elements of it promptly entered domestic architecture at the turn of the century'.[91] The retreat from the present was not uncommon in Germany, especially at the turn of the century, with a strong anti-urban tradition coinciding with several decades of the most rapid urbanization in Europe.

The Dresden of the 1903 exhibition was thus an ambiguous location. Dresden was the fifth largest city in Germany after Berlin, Hamburg, Munich and Leipzig and possessed a strong industrial sector both in Friedrichstadt and other districts. But at the same time and for several decades it already possessed another facet, described in 1878 as follows: 'Borne by the manifold charms of its landscape surroundings, Dresden, in its suburbs, possesses the character of a "city of villas" '.[92] This was especially true of Blasewitz, Loschwitz and other expanding hillside developments at the turn of the century. And in 1909, just beyond the then city boundaries, building commenced on one of Germany's most famous garden cities, Hellerau – employing architects such as Riemerschmid, Muthesius and Tessenow, and seeking to create a green idyll beyond the corrupted metropolis.[93] Yet less than a decade after the 1903 exhibition, Dresden was one of the crucial sites of an artistic avant-garde movement – *Die Brücke* – that, in part, exploded our conceptions of the metropolis and, in a sense, took quite literally Simmel's description of our experience of the modern metropolis as the bombardment of our senses with endless and varied stimuli. The German Expressionist movement also revealed the deep ambiguity in responses to the modern metropolis that oscillate between a subjective celebration of experience of it, an abhorrence of it and a radical retreat from it.[94]

In contrast, the first German Metropolitan Exhibition of 1903 in Dresden was an entirely positive display of the development of the modern metropolis. And although the invitation to exhibit went to all German cities with more than 25,000 inhabitants, it was the largest cities whose developments were often of particular interest. The more modest official catalogue of the exhibition, in comparison with the 1896 Berlin catalogue, did have in common with the latter an archaic cover illustration with a – presumably Saxon – knight in armour standing in the foreground and, in the background, the silhouette of the city.[95] The exhibition was opened by King Georg of Saxony on 20 May 1903 and ran until the end of September 1903. Although the exhibition encompassed virtually every aspect of metropolitan existence, it is interesting to note – in the light of the debate in the previous decade in Germany on the role of city planning and its aesthetic versus its practical dimensions – that the first two sections of the exhibition covered were, respectively, transport systems (including lighting, street construction and underground water, gas and sewage connections) and the extension of the metropolis. Nonetheless, as Woodhead pointed out in his survey of the exhibition, the aesthetics of the city development were not neglected. Indeed, in each German city:

> The municipality, through the building department, has jurisdiction over the decoration of the street, which is the aesthetic unit of the city, just as it

is the building unit, the sanitary unit, etc. . . . and in formulating . . . governing rules, the building department takes into account the aesthetic effect of
the street picture. . . . Lamp posts, for gas or electricity, advertising pillars,
street clocks, waiting rooms, lavatories, refreshment booths, newspaper
stands – all have a definite aesthetic value as well as utility.[96]

Yet mere rule-following could also lead to a lack of originality and a
commitment merely to making a building 'the maximum size permitted for
the sake of the rents. This produces long rows of houses all of a pattern.
The result is monotony.' Woodhead, however, detects a new development
in the past few years. Many buildings

> show a breaking away from the Renaissance style which has ruled so per-
> sistently. The *Jugend-Stil* which has replaced it is sometimes rather riotous
> and fanciful; but there is much good in this New Art, based upon frankness
> in following the lines of construction rather than upon deceit in covering
> them over; and when it sobers down somewhat, it will be very acceptable
> indeed.[97]

Woodhead's optimistic assessment of the happy convergence of an
aesthetically aware modern architecture and the needs of city planning
(with felicitous traffic and sanitary provisions, etc.) is not borne out by
the conflicts within many cities over these and other issues, nor by the
resistance to both modern architecture and city planning. What is not in
question is the positive assessment of the modern metropolis and the
practical attempts to solve its problems with new technical solutions that
were given by the exhibition itself. The significance of the Dresden exhibition was fourfold. It was the first German municipal exhibition and was
to be succeeded by more specific exhibitions and competitions on the
expansion of the modern metropolis, such as that for *Gross-Berlin* in
1910 or Düsseldorf in 1911. Second, it was a positive and even celebrat-
ory exhibition of the modern metropolis and city planning in Germany.
Third, it combined a concern for the *material* infrastructure of the city,
its streets, sewers, etc., with a display of the *aesthetic* forms that such
infrastructure could take. Finally, the tenor of the exhibition ran counter
to those who juxtaposed small town idylls to modern metropolitan existence. This was particularly important in the German context with its
powerful recent history of anti-urbanism.

The aesthetic dimension of the modern metropolis, which Woodhead
confines to the end of his report on the Dresden exhibition, is absent
from the themes examined in the series of lectures organized in Dresden
in the winter of 1902–3 prior to the opening of the metropolitan exhibition. The Gehe Foundation in Dresden inaugurated a series of lectures
on the metropolis under the direction of Theodor Petermann. With one

exception, all those invited to lecture were associated with the Leipzig circle of cultural historians and social scientists who were committed to an evolutionary, nomothetic conception of the human sciences and seeking the regulations and laws of development of society. The exception was Georg Simmel.

This 'stranger' from Berlin in the Saxon intellectual landscape apparently disturbed the continuity of the lecture series. As Petermann relates in his editorial preface to the published volume of lectures:

> According to the original plan for the individual lectures at the Gehe Foundation in the winter of 1902/3, the first three lectures were to have been devoted to the origins, the showplace and the population of metropolitan life and the three succeeding contributions were to develop the economic, intellectual and political significance of big cities.
>
> But since the stimulating deliberations of Prof. Dr. Simmel on metropolitan cities and mental life devoted attention much more to the influence of big cities on the mental life of individual metropolitan dwellers than to the intellectual collective forces of the metropolis and their collective effects, a gap in the realization of the original programme was created.[98]

The result was that Petermann was obliged to write in haste a contribution covering, in effect, what he assumed Simmel should have dealt with – 'The intellectual significance of metropolitan cities'.

The lecture series itself commenced in October 1902 and continued monthly until March 1903. The historian Karl Bücher examined historical dimensions of metropolitan development in October, the geographer Friedrich Ratzel dealt with transport and locational aspects of metropolitan centres in November, and Mayr dealt with metropolitan populations in December. In January Waentig lectured on the economic significance of the metropolis, and in February Simmel gave his lecture on the metropolis and mental life, which was followed by the final lecture in March by the historian Dietrich Schäfer on the military and political significance of the metropolis. Aside from Simmel's lecture, all lectures in the series, including Petermann's additional contribution (added subsequently to the published version), tend to treat the metropolis, to a greater or lesser extent, as a historical phenomenon. Several make extensive use of statistical evidence on the growth of German cities, sometimes in a comparative context. The contemporary, modern metropolis therefore often appears to be a subordinate issue in some of these contributions. Nonetheless, in most instances, the interpretations of the present-day metropolis that do appear in these lectures are significant. With the exception of the title of Friedrich Ratzel's lecture, all the others – including Simmel's – refer to big cities in the plural form (*Grossstädte*) of the term for the metropolis. Ratzel's lecture, in contrast, is on the geographical situation of large cities or towns (*grosse Städte*). The relevance of this distinction lies in the extensive contemporary discussion of what constituted a metropolis. It is already announced earlier in the title of an essay by Lorenz von Stein on 'The big town and the metropolis' (*Grosse Stadt und Grossstadt*).[99] As we have seen, by the turn of the century, the distinction was being made between a big city or metropolis (*Grossstadt*) and a world city (*Weltstadt*). The large number of cities and towns exhibiting in the Dresden Metropolitan Exhibition was indicative of a desire to display what Bücher termed 'the arrangements of metropolitan life' that were to be found in large and small cities.

Karl Bücher's lecture on 'Big cities in the present and in the past'[100] was devoted in large part to the history of major urban settlements from antiquity to the present day. Nonetheless, although not fully developing the reasons for the unbroken proliferation of big cities in recent decades – aspects of which were to be examined by other contributors to the lecture series – Bücher was convinced that 'our modern cities represent a new type in the total development with which no earlier form of city compares in our cultural circle'.[101] In keeping with this assertion of the qualitative newness of the modern metropolis, Bücher also declares that its inhabitants – themselves a new species – have not had time to clarify their own existence. This is because

> the metropolitan person, who indeed already forms a distinctive species of the breed of *homo sapiens*, in the unrest and haste of their existence only rarely have the time and space to concentrate attention upon themselves and to save a quiet comprehensive standpoint out of the dense tumult and bustle of the day. The whole metropolitan development that we have experienced has enveloped us in a too unexpectedly and stormy manner.[102]

Indeed, this unrest has manifested itself in metropolitan areas themselves, especially in the transformation of the stratification of the population. In the cities, 'the social contradictions confront one another more sharply here than elsewhere. A communal sense is lacking.' Nonetheless, Bücher concludes with an optimistic perspective on the modern metropolitan life which has already 'released unheard-of forces of the nation in the spheres of technology, science, art and social welfare arrangements'. Indeed, 'the modern city, the city of freely chosen labour, signifies a higher form of social existence than all other earlier urban forms, not excluding the Greek polis'.[103]

Friedrich Ratzel's lecture on 'The geographical situation of large cities'[104] explores the geographical and topographical reasons for the siting of cities. Aside from the comparative examination of such factors as the geographical and transport position, the division of labour and the population density of major cities, Ratzel occasionally comments on the contemporary topography of the modern metropolis. Thus, with respect to the perspective of the city at a distance, Ratzel describes our first impressions as follows:

> The wanderer who approaches a large city from the distance, sees first of all the brown clouds of mist and smoke that lie over it, and underneath dimly the multi-stacked profile of the high pile of buildings and right angles, an image that may remind one of the silhouette of a harsh rocky landscape. Today, the view of a modern city seldom lacks the long, blackened hallway of the railway station.[105]

Mention of the railway recalls the modern city as 'the distinctive transformed terminus of one or several transport routes, comparable perhaps with our sense organs that are the distinctive transformed ends of our nerves'. Metropolitan centres are therefore 'in large part the alluvial deposits of human beings and goods born by the streams of traffic. Questions of traffic . . . are thus, for the cities, questions of life.'[106]

Whereas other contemporaries would have seen the question of housing as the crucial question here, Ratzel focuses upon a different aspect of physical concentration whose imagery is that of extreme natural forces. The growth of the big cities is likened to 'a flooding' (*Überschwemmung*) and their emergence is that of 'a piling up (*Aufstauung*) of human beings'. The issue of circulation of human beings and goods is solved in the newer districts of major cities such as New York by broad and long streets. The 'chess board style' that we associate with modern urban design is already prefigured, as Ratzel points out, in cities such as Praunheim or Wilhelmshaven. Clearly a supporter of the straight over against the crooked street in the German debate a decade earlier between Joseph Stübben and Karl Henrici, Ratzel points out that straight streets were also present in old towns and that a defect of present-day straight streets is 'the impossibility of seeing their buildings as anything other than strictly in a line one after the other'. His final judgement on the modern German city touches upon the higher significance of the city, in a manner that unites the ideologies of the modern city with straight streets and the old city with crooked streets, insofar as 'cities are created as centres of life and as monuments for the preservation and extension of cultural goods'.[107] Often, though Ratzel does not mention this, this tension is present within the same metropolis – such as Vienna.

The growth of metropolitan centres and the features of their populations is dealt with extensively by Georg von Mayr's lecture on 'The population of the metropolis'.[108] This largely statistical exploration of features of urban populations draws upon the huge collections of statistical material that were currently available. On occasion, Mayr makes more general observations on modern cities. He draws attention to the distinctive nature of the modern metropolitan centres that are 'social individual entities of an outstanding cast'. In part, their distinctive nature is a function of size, insofar as 'the metropolitanization and especially the millionization – if the concept may be permitted – of the world city absorption of human beings is especially peculiar to the new and newest culture'.[109] Although it was not Mayr's task to explore the 'newest culture' of the metropolis, he was hopeful that statistical evidence (such as on economic life, education and criminality) might contribute to understanding the positive and negative impact of metropolitan existence upon contemporary culture.

Even though the following lecture in the series on 'The economic significance of the metropolis'[110] by Waentig also drew upon considerable statistical evidence for his topic, he was clearly more prepared than Mayr to interpret more fully the city's economic significance. Waentig chose to commence his analysis not with 'proud London', 'exciting Paris', 'patriarchal Vienna' or 'youthful Berlin' but with the embodiment of metropolitan existence – New York. It is New York that is the 'undisputable master of economic organization and technology': 'it is the metropolis that powerfully confronts the stranger as the most modern embodiment of the American spirit'.[111] The European society that has experienced similar rapid development of urbanization in recent decades is Germany. In addition, he detects a correlation between capitalist development and the modern metropolis, insofar as 'the progressive expansion of the *capitalist commercial economy* . . . has also given the impetus to the development of modern metropolitan centres'.

In the course of his exploration of the economic significance of the modern metropolis, with an accompanying differentiation of commercial and industrial cities, Waentig draws attention to a number of its interesting economic features. The concentration of an increasing proportion of national wealth in metropolitan centres is associated in part with the development of share ownership, the stock exchange, the importance of credit and the expansion of major banks, and the administration of countless enterprises in metropolitan offices and branches. The American version of the latter is one in which

> the 'captain of industry', with the 'ticker' before his eyes and his ear on the telephone, oversees from his New York office up in the clouds the progress of events and sends on his own telegraph line at lightning speed his command even to the furthest corner of the farthest West.[112]

Within the metropolis itself, it is not merely that its information and control systems extend outside, but rather that there is also an increasing use of external wealth and commodities that create the feature of the metropolis as a 'centre of consumption'. This is reflected in its being the site of refined and expensive tastes, but more generally in its expanding market halls and department stores – 'those specifically metropolitan structures for the modern satisfaction of needs'.[113] The public satisfaction of some of these needs requires the metropolis to raise its own income through taxation and to derive income from its supply of 'important mass needs' (public utilities).

Waentig concludes by exploring dimensions of the problem of the metropolis, with its 'housing question', its need to overcome the sharp contrast between rich and poor. But he sees these problems as soluble (without specifying adequately the solutions) and wishes to emphasize the significance of the modern metropolis not as 'a moloch' but as 'the pathbreaker of progress'. In this context he draws attention to the metropolis as 'a crucible of the most progressive culture', as the 'most important production site of intellectual values' and as the site in which the need for individual freedom is satisfied. Here Waentig asks 'whether the present emancipation of women would be conceivable without the metropolis?'[114] The metropolis is not merely the site for potential freedom but also for equality:

> above the rigid aristocracy of birth there rises unnoticed the new mobility of the mind, money and labour. How quickly the metropolis forgets; a happy feature for those who wish to begin a new life. Even confronted with the sexes, its levelling force does not stand still. And just as it bestows on the stubborn man the finely shaped head with the meditative glance, the agile body with the small nervous hands, so it creates the self-conscious woman with the almost manly figure, the energetic mouth and the somewhat cool but yet so clever and knowing eyes.
>
> Without doubt, the metropolis creates new human beings, entities whose most pronounced character trait is the highest *mental awareness*, whose existential principle is the greatest *life-intensity in work and pleasure*.[115]

Such concentrations of energy also imply the transformation of space (the transcendence of distance) and the increasingly fleeting experience of time in the metropolis. Never before has the effort been so intense

> to gain space for the greater diversity of pleasures, corresponding to the increased susceptibility to excitement, through the concentration of the largest amount of work achievements in the shortest time-span. The danger of excessive tension and overexcitement is not absent here. A reverse must come. And insofar as the modern metropolitan dweller, to a certain extent, elevates urban life to its highest potential, there awakens in them the longing for the country.[116]

It is the metropolitan dweller 'who has discovered the countryside aesthetically' in modern times (Waentig mentions, amongst others, the

Fontainebleau school, the 'Boys of Glasgow' and the Worpswede group). More generally, Waentig detects a dialectical turn here, insofar as 'the drive to the city has produced the drive to the countryside', and even a possible dissolving of town and countryside in the family house far from the city (as instanced by William Morris's Webb house and the country-house movement in the United States). In many respects, it is Waentig's lecture that comes closest to raising issues that were to be discussed in the next lecture in the series by Simmel, and to raising others that Simmel might have addressed.

Petermann's published contribution on 'The intellectual significance of the big cities',[117] which purportedly covers themes that Simmel should have addressed, deals with the intellectual and cultural life of the metropolis in its music, theatre, newspapers, universities and the like. The accent of his contribution can be judged by the opening thesis that the origins of a new intellectual life are to be found in 'the monastery, not in the towns and certainly not in the big cities'. The interrelationship of metropolis and modernity finds little resonance in Petermann's contribution.

The final lecture in the series – succeeding Simmel's contribution – was by the conservative historian Dietrich Schäfer on 'The political and military significance of big cities'.[118] The latter part of this largely historical treatment of the political and military dimensions of the metropolis examines the contemporary urban political situation and, in particular, their predominantly socialist complexion. Schäfer examines the current, comparative political voting patterns of several European nations and the United States. Britain and the United States are viewed as general exceptions to the predominantly socialist urban population in Germany and many other continental European societies. Schäfer concludes that there is no 'identical political character of the metropolitan popula-tion'. But in Paris and in the German Empire 'an unmistakable tendency towards extreme political views and their activation is evident today'. Why this is so requires an examination of the 'psychology of the metro-politan dweller'. In part, this is reflected in 'a spirit of contradiction arising out of the higher intellectual average development of the metro-politan person', itself emerging from the dynamism of transactions, confrontation with contradictory circumstances, diversity of opinions and viewpoints, and a sharper struggle for existence. Above all, such circum-stances lead to the increased valuation of the intellect – 'a feature that one may in a certain sense characterize as modern'. This is accompanied by such features as a 'modern metropolitan preference for extreme views of life and exaggerated evaluations of material goods that may threaten public life'.

For Schäfer, therefore, this higher intellectual development of the metro-politan person in no way guarantees 'a higher value of metropolitan intellectual culture'. Rather, the extremely diverse forms of impressions in the metropolis endanger their depth. The latter he finds in rural life:

> Happy is the child who is raised in garden and field, in forest and meadow . . . Strolling in urban parks and sandpits or children playing in the gardens cannot substitute for this, but nor too can the summer air on the beach or in the mountains or even an early introduction to the magnificence of the alpine world. All this is an emergency measure.[119]

Not surprisingly, therefore, for Schäfer, 'up to now a big city has not generated a great man'. The implication of all this is that the future lies in the metropolis developing a fuller relationship to country life (as is the case, for Schäfer, in England) to counter 'the unnaturally elevated political excitability of the metropolitan person'. The metropolis and urban life may be unavoidable for many, but our intention must be to make the metropolis centres 'in their political activity increasingly more healthy members of the unified Fatherland'. For Schäfer, The Dresden Municipal Exhibition should contribute to this task.

VI

Simmel's lecture was announced in the press as 'The metropolis and mental life' (*Die Grossstadt und das Geistesleben*), but published with the metropolis in plural as *Die Grossstädte*. The lecture was held at 8.00 pm on the Saturday evening of 21 February 1903, for which entrance tickets 'for gentlemen' (*für Herren*) were available from the Gehe Foundation.[120] What is not clear from the advertisement in the *Dresdner Anzeiger* from which these details are drawn, is whether this implied an exclusively male audience. It does draw attention to an issue for all the lectures in the series and therefore for Simmel's too: the gendered nature of the discussion of the metropolis. We will return to this issue later.

As with all the lectures in the series, Simmel's lecture was reviewed in the *Dresdner Anzeiger* (in his case, on 24 February) under the title *Die Grossstädte und das Geistesleben*.[121] The reviewer, although providing a detailed and accurate synopsis of the lecture, was somewhat disturbed by its analytical rigour and its potentially negative implications. In the published version Simmel concludes by stating that in his analysis of the metropolis 'it is not our task either to accuse or to pardon, but only to understand'. Today, this essay, and Simmel's other pieces on the city, despite their critical content, are read as revealing a positive treatment of the metropolis in the sense that it is a fundamental dimension of our experience of modernity. Simmel did not conceive of permanent escapes from the modern metropolis. Indeed, as some of his explorations of lei-sure – such as 'The Alpine Journey' – make clear, the metropolis extends its effect into distant leisure pursuits too.[122] Nor did he hate big cities, and especially Berlin, as did some of his contemporaries such as Ferdinand Tönnies.

The contemporary reviewer, however, claims that Simmel's treatment of his topic 'was basically dominated by a single viewpoint. He commenced from the standpoint that the deepest problems of modern life emerge out of the individual's claims to assert his or her independence and the distinct-iveness of their existence against the major collective powers that have created this modern life'. The reviewer concludes by taking up Simmel's thesis more specifically:

> The distinctive nature of the lecture lay in the strict adherence to the stand-point from which, from the very outset, the theme was considered: that a fundamental distinction exists between individual existence and collective forces, of which the metropolis is one, and that out of this opposition, as a result of the individual's natural drive for self-assertion, a series of import-ant mental and inner features as organs of preservation emerge, as it were, for the individual that gradually become typical qualities. Undoubtedly, a series of characteristics in the manner advanced by Simmel does exist. Whether they are the most fundamental, however, can be the subject of discussion. Yet in this precisely drawn and sharply pointed train of thought, it seems that there is no place for the following insight: namely, that the relationship of the individual to the metropolis is not merely a basic oppositional one and almost one of enmity, as can easily appear according to the construction of the lecture. The metropolis not merely 'damages' (*vergewaltigt*) the individual and gets on the individual's nerves: it also enriches the individual and elevates the individual, beyond the existing, somewhat confined and anxious concern about the preservation of his or her 'distinctiveness' (*Eigenart*), *through the tasks that it set for the individual and in whose fulfilment the individual grows!*[123]

A number of issues are raised by this contemporary critical comment-ary on Simmel's lecture. First, that the structure of the lecture is viewed as resting largely upon the opposition between the individual and collect-ive forces. Although the summary of the lecture presented by the reviewer follows closely the printed version, it may be that Simmel emphasized this opposition more in the lecture than in the published essay. Second, the negative reading of the relationship between the individual and the metropolis overlooks the significance of Simmel's approach to inter-action or reciprocal effect (*Wechselwirkung*) in this lecture as in his other works, namely the possibility of positive and negative effects in the same interaction. As the reviewer points out, the end of the lecture (and the end of the published essay) draws out the conflict between two 'types of individualism, that commencing from individual independence and that emerging from the development of personal distinctive features (*Ausbildung persönlicher Sonderart*)', both of which are nurtured in the metropolis. Third, the review, in passing, draws attention to the 'construction of the lecture', which surely deserves greater attention. Finally, the review's emphasis upon the *enrichment* of the individual through his or her relationships with the metropolis is not a feature that is excluded from Simmel's interpretation. But what is significant in the context of these lectures is the urge to be positive about the modern metropolis.

As is well known, five years later, in 1908, the last speaker in the lecture series, the historian Dietrich Schäfer, was requested to provide confidential comment upon Simmel's application for a vacant chair of philosophy at Heidelberg University.[124] Schäfer's blatantly anti-Semitic response – with its references to Simmel as 'a dyed-in-the-wool Israelite', 'a Semitic lecturer' who 'speaks exceedingly slowly', who 'spices his words with clever sayings' for an audience composed of 'the ladies' and 'an extraordinary contingent of the oriental world' – concludes with a reference to his social theory and to this 1903 lecture. For Schäfer, it is 'a most perilous error to put "society" in the place of state and church as the decisive organ of human coexistence'. A basic feature of modern society is presumably the development of the modern metropolis, but Schäfer concludes his 'substantive' criticism of Simmel with the statement that 'it is hardly possible to treat of the mental life of the metropolis in a sparser and more biased way than he did in his lecture of that title at the Gehe Foundation in Dresden'.

Perhaps the 'sparse' manner of Simmel's treatment of the metropolis would be located in the absence of a national (German) perspective on the city, clearly favoured by Schäfer and others. The Dresden exhibition was itself viewed by many as a coming to maturity of an independent German urban existence, just as the 1896 Berlin exhibition was seen as a symbolic transition to world city status for Berlin. In his introduction to the two volumes commemorating the 1903 Dresden exhibition, Robert Wuttke highlighted the more mobile or active dimension of the city compared with the state, the major economic expansion of Germany in the last decades of the nineteenth century and accompanying growth of urbanization, the expansion of metropolitan areas beyond their original boundaries, and the urban population as 'a restless, mobile mass' as amongst the significant features of the modern German city.[125] The modern dynamic impulses of metropolitan growth create a situation in which 'the city cannot have recourse to the past'. But at the same time this forward drive of urbanization in Germany had to rely upon lessons learned from abroad. Indeed, 'there was almost no sphere in which we did not borrow from suggestions from abroad'. At the present time, however, there is a need 'in the cultural spheres of the cities to shake off foreign domination and to lay the foundations for the development of genuine German energy and German spirit'. This can be mobilized by awakening the broad mass of the population's interest in 'the major cultural work of the cities' and that of the state – especially in the context of a renewed opposition between city and country.

Since we do not possess the text of Simmel's 1903 lecture on the metropolis, we do not know whether the structure of the lecture is identical with that of its published version. We do know that Simmel often revised such lectures for publication. There is also some indication that opening introductory remarks in a lecture that might be appropriate to their particular audience were sometimes not taken up in a lecture's published version. In the case of the Dresden lecture, there is some evidence that this may be the case. The review of the lecture in the *Dresdner Anzeiger* provides a substantive synopsis of its content that largely accords with the sequence of themes dealt with by Simmel in its published version. This is true of the thematic sequence from the increase in nervous life (on the second page of the published text) down to the discussion of the two types of individualism (at the end of the published text). An exception to this similarity between the report on the lecture and its published version is, in part, the opening remarks.

Although it cannot be claimed that the reviewer's opening comments are a précis of those made by Simmel himself, the fact that the immediate opening statement is similar but that the subsequent reported version contains significant differences is, at least, suggestive. After asserting that Simmel's lecture was 'basically dominated by a single viewpoint', the reviewer continues:

> He commences from the viewpoint that the deepest problems of modern life have their origin in the claim of individuals to assert their independence and the distinctiveness of their existence against *the major collective forces* which this modern life has produced. Now, in this struggle by the individual and his or her distinctiveness, metropolitan cities play a dual role. On the one hand, the latter are themselves one such *collective force* against which the individual feels called upon to struggle for his or her self; on the other hand, however, they [metropolitan cities] themselves constitute the conditions as such, the external framework as it were, within which the individual must lead his or her struggle against *all other collective forces of modern culture*. Thus, from the very outset the lecturer construes a sharp contrast between the individual and all types of *collective forces of modern culture*.[126]

The opening paragraph of the published text does not contain aspects highlighted in this putative précis of Simmel's opening remarks to the lecture.

The first, as emphasized in the quotation, is the frequent reference to 'collective forces' – whereas the published text contains one reference to 'external' forces at the end of its introductory paragraph. The second, more significantly, is the argument concerning the dual role of the metropolis in relation to the individual, as *both* a collective *force against which the individual struggles* and a collective force *which constitutes the parameter within which individuals struggle against all other collective forces*. The fact that this is a complex antinomy suggests that it may not be the reviewer's mode of introducing the overview of the lecture, but a feature of Simmel's own opening remarks. As is well known, virtually all of his essays commence with and conclude with antinomies. The Dresden essay (and almost certainly the lecture) is no exception in this respect, opening as it does with the opposition between the individual's claim to independence and the super-individual forces that confront it, and closing with the two forms of individualism.

VII

The introductory paragraph in the published version of the lecture contains an undeveloped antinomy between the body and the soul, between the products of modern life, 'the body of culture' and its soul, the external and internal existence of the individual. This is an indication of Simmel's methodological approach to the inner life, to a mental life (*Geistesleben*) that has adapted to and incorporated the products of modern culture. In other words, a central theme is the metropolis *in* mental life. But, at the same time, the assertion of the individual and the individual's resistance to objective culture points to ideals for the orientation of subjective culture, for individuality against 'collective forces'. In this respect, life within the metropolis makes possible the development of distinctive forms of individuality and intellectuality.

At the same time, however, there are a number of undeveloped references to the body in the metropolis. Although 'mental life' is the theme announced in the title, the circulation and interaction of bodies – even 'body life' – is certainly implicit at several points in the essay.[127] Often they can be amplified by reference to other relevant reflections by Simmel. Indeed, in the opening paragraph, aside from a reference to the 'transformation of the struggle with nature that primitive human beings had to lead for their *bodily* (*leibliche*) existence' into a modern struggle for existence in the metropolis, Simmel announces the theme of his essay as a focus upon 'our big cities' as one site 'where the products of specifically modern life are questioned as to their inner nature (*Innerlichkeit*), as it were, the body of culture as to its soul'. Although the body of that culture is revealed to be largely one of 'pure objectivity', facilitated by the domination of an intellectual and nervous response and defence against an estranged objective culture, the rational, calculating features of that intellectual response and the nervous reactions to external stimuli are all located in human bodies confronting an objective culture of institutions and their human agents and embodiments. The metropolis as the seat of the developed money economy and a highly developed division of labour is the site of proliferation of material wealth, as both material and intellectual private property in a capitalist economy. Elsewhere, when Simmel discusses material and intellectual property in their broadest sense as the extension of the individual, he adds a definition of property as 'that which obeys the will of the owners as, for instance (with a difference of degree only), our body, which is our first "property"'.[128] Yet in our interaction with others in the metropolis, the body takes on another significance. Our interaction with other bodies in the metropolis is governed, in part, by the fact that 'city life has transformed the struggle for livelihood into an inter-human struggle for gain, which here is not granted by nature but by other human beings'.[129] In order to participate to the maximum in that struggle, individuals must adopt functional specializations, whether in production, circulation or consumption. In this context, the body itself must become functional in order, as Mattenklott puts it, 'to reconcile the contradiction between the individual human beings and their increasingly abstract life world'.[130] The metropolis as an independent entity is itself likened to a body by Simmel:

> The most significant feature of the metropolis lies in this functional size beyond its physical boundaries: and this capacity to produce an effect (*Wirksamkeit*) reacts back in turn and gives metropolitan life its weight, importance and responsibility. Just as a person does not terminate with the limits of their body or the area (*Bezirk*) that immediately comprises their activity, but rather with the sum total of effects that extend both temporally and spatially from the person, so too a city consists first of the totality of effects that extend beyond its immediacy.[131]

Mattenklott is right to illuminate this complex affinity by reference to the reflections Simmel published two years previously on 'The Aesthetic Significance of the Face', for it is a constituent and decisive feature of body language that reveals the effect of the body beyond itself: face-work as the efficient mechanism for responding to the Other. If the distinctive achievement of the mind (*Geist*) is 'that it forms within itself the plurality of elements of the world into unities: [that] it brings together the juxtaposition of things in space and time into the unity of an image, a concept, a statement', then 'within the human body [it is] the face [which] possesses to the greatest degree this inner unity'.[132] Its slightest movements or modifications transform the whole response to a dramatic extent. Even the hand 'cannot in fact compare to the face' in this respect. The impression that individuals make is thus conditioned by their facial expressions to a considerable degree. Indeed, 'human appearance is the showplace on which inner-physiological impulses contest with physical gravity', revealing both individual and typical responses. However, 'the human being is not merely the bearer of mind, like a book . . . but rather their mental state (*Geistigkeit*) possesses the form of individuality'.[133] Of course, in metropolitan interaction that individuality has to be expressed in the context of a mass of other individuals: to seek to elevate itself beyond the typical. This suggests that the mental life of the metropolis is intimately connected with its bodily life, just as in the case of the individuals interacting and circulating within it. Hence, 'the specific mental personality is bound up with the specifically unique body . . . but *what* kind of a personality it is cannot under any circumstances be told by the body but rather only by its face'.[134] What was later to be termed 'face work' takes on additional significance in the multitude of interactions – however minimal – that we engage in within the metropolis. The speed of interactions, often their extremely fleeting nature, require a mechanism through which individuals can express their response to others. And here the face possesses a remarkable advantage over other bodily expressions. A minimum change in its parts or elements results in a change in its total impression. As Simmel indicates:

> Here too there is a kind of energy saving: an object is basically the more aesthetically effective or utilizable the more lively it reacts as a whole to the modification of the smallest element. For this reveals the refinement and strength in the context of its parts, its inner logic.[135]

If we apply this process to metropolitan interactions, then it is clear that energy saving in Simmel's sense is a constituent element in accounting for the advantages of rapid facial response to others. In terms of the *aesthetics* of metropolitan interactions, the face is also crucial insofar as 'aesthetic observation and formation transcend the indifference of things' that reign in much metropolitan interaction and circulation of individuals in the sphere of money transactions, which form a central feature of the city. Of all the face's elements, it is the eye whose minimal movement has the greatest interactional effect. No other element remains in its place, as it were, and yet seems to extend far beyond itself – 'it bores into things, it retreats back, it encompasses a space, it wanders around, it grasps the desired object as if behind it and draws it to itself'. Like the face itself, the eye manifests the 'tension between inner life (*Seele*) and appearances as the revelation and masking of each of them'.[136]

Elsewhere, in an essay on Rodin, Simmel highlights the aesthetic significance of the face in relation to modernity. In drawing a contrast between modernity and antiquity as manifested in sculpture, he argues that 'within the body, modernity emphasizes the face, antiquity the body, because the former reveals the person in the flux of their inner life, the latter more in the person's inert substance'.[137] Certainly the flux or flow of 'inner life' is crucial both to Simmel's definition of modernity in terms of emphasis upon the flow of inner life and to one of the most prominent features of metropolitan existence – the increase in nervous life. Yet the face can also hide features of inner life both in the sphere of fashion, whose crucial site is the modern metropolis, and within historicist architecture, whose façades may be totally deceptive with regard to the insides of built structures.

Although Simmel does not analyse the face specifically in a metropolitan context, his reflections nonetheless display their relevance for metropolitan interaction, whether it be 'the face in the crowd', the metropolis as the site for both secrecy and its unmasking by the 'private eye', or merely the minimal interaction of avoidance of eye contact where passengers travel in close proximity in public transport systems. Indeed, more generally, 'reciprocal reserve and indifference' are common to metropolitan density since 'bodily proximity and narrowness of space make the mental distance [between individuals] only the more visible'.[138] Again, it is Mattenklott who draws attention to the body's and the eye's response to the objectification that it confronts in the modern metropolis. That objectification (*Versachlichung*), literally 'rendered into thingness', with which Simmel commences his metropolis essay, calls forth an 'urbane intellectuality, the economically rationalized complement to the city that for its part is indeed also a product of the economization of life'.[139] In this context, the eye in the metropolis takes on another important aspect. Although Simmel is concerned with the aesthetic significance of the face and the eye, the latter's features suggest another possibility, namely that this eye

> could be that of a hunter: highly mobile and yet motionless; alert but not disturbed; encompassing everything, but itself never grasped. It is the ideal eye of the city dweller and the sociologist. As the latter, Simmel did not inquire as to the content of activities or things, of domination or exploitation, but rather as to the functional connections. . . . In order that the physiognomical gaze – which accordingly should perceive society as an organic body – should not be continually caught up in individual contents, it must immunize itself against sympathy or aversion: a cold eye.[140]

This is the response to 'the rapid crowding of changing images, the sharp discontinuity in the grasp of a single glance, and the unexpectedness of onrushing impressions' that Simmel sees as 'the *intensification of nervous stimulation*' in the modern metropolis.[141]

Somewhat abruptly in Simmel's essay on the metropolis, there is a shift in its focus upon intellectuality to the impact of the money economy, with the sudden announcement that 'the metropolis has always been the seat of the money economy'. The mode of argument may be abrupt, but the substantive connection between urbane intellectualism and the money economy is a close one, and had already been made in, especially, the final chapter of his *Philosophy of Money*. In fact, Simmel declares that the 'money economy and the dominance of the intellect are intrinsically connected'.[142] When he announces in a rare footnote at the end of the metropolis essay that the 'argument and elaboration of its major cultural-historical ideas are contained in my *Philosophy of Money*', then this may be substantiated by the recurrence of a number of themes derived from this major work in the essay. These include, thematically, the widening separation of objective from subjective culture; an increasing mental life of abstraction and the calculability and functionalization of social relations; the metropolis as a focal point of the money economy, differentiated consumption and fashion; the possibilities for individual freedom; the transformation of the individual personality in metropolitan and monetary interactions; the metropolis as the focal point of material relations and the struggle for gain; the mediation of material relations through money; and the centrality of the sphere of circulation, exchange and consumption in both the mature (capitalist) money economy and the modern metropolis.[143]

But if we return, for the moment, to the opening theme of the widening gap between objective and subjective culture, then there is one dimension of this problematic that is not alluded to in the metropolis essay, namely Simmel's earlier argument that this objective culture is gendered. In his essay on 'Female Culture' he recognizes that this objective culture is thoroughly male dominated.[144] Indeed, 'with the exception of very few areas, our objective culture is thoroughly male'.[145] This is manifested, by implication, in the dominant institutions of the modern metropolis – and Simmel does not directly reflect upon female culture in a specifically metropolitan context – and in linguistic forms identifying 'human' as 'man', in the fact that 'deficient performances in the most diverse areas are degraded as "feminine" while outstanding performances of women are celebrated as "thoroughly manly"' and in the offensive banality that designates women as "the fair sex"'.[146]

Within the metropolis and the developed money economy, a crucial factor shaping the objective culture is the division of labour, specialization and differentiation. If it is the case that this objective culture is male, then it is males who participate most fully in this culture and are most subject to its extreme differentiation and fragmentation. The alienation that Simmel ascribes to the division of labour in production and consumption in his *Philosophy of Money* does, as he recognized earlier, possess a different gendered dimension. Whereas in his essay on 'Female Culture' (1902) it is males who are subjected to the fragmentary consequences of participation in objective culture (including production), Simmel had earlier – in 'The Women's Congress and Social Democracy' (1896)[147] – recognized a significant class difference in the extent and consequences of female participation in production (outside the home) and its division of labour. Whereas for bourgeois females increased participation *in* the economic order was favoured, for working class females already subject to an (additional) inferior position within the capitalist labour process emancipation *from* that economic order was demanded.

Yet in his reflections on female culture this significant differentiating dimension is given a different interpretation. Indeed, Simmel also appears to reverse the implications of his thesis on the relation between objective and subjective culture outlined at the very start of his metropolis essay. Whereas there and elsewhere, the increasing domination of objective over subjective culture would lead to a search for preserving areas of subjective culture for facilitating personal development, and whereas the fragmentation and alienation experienced more fully in that objective culture by its male participants would lead to a male search for individual creativity within remaining spaces for subjective culture, the possibility for a new female culture is posed in the context of objective culture.

It is clearly possible, Simmel argues, for women to adapt to the male objective culture. But this culture will change only if women themselves 'accomplish something that men cannot do. This is the core of the entire problem, the pivotal point of the relationship between the women's movement and objective culture.[148] Within the objective culture of commodity production, the labour market and the production process, there already exist attempts at eliminating competition between men and women, but only by giving women differentiation tasks (i.e. 'female' tasks that are lower paid). But when Simmel comes to ask where the objectivation of the more unified, less differentiated female contribution to a new culture might be located, his answer is 'the home' – 'an aspect of life and at the same time a special way of forming, reflecting and interrelating the totality of life'.[149] Having rejected the retreat into privacy as a mode of resistance to objective culture in his *Philosophy of Money*, the home as the site of a new cultural totality is hardly convincing. Nor is it convincing as the site for a new independent female culture.

The domination of this objective culture in the metropolis and its overwhelmingly male character raises other issues. One might be whether the reserve and indifference mechanisms against the full impact of urban nervous intensity, to which Simmel ascribes considerable significance, may also be specifically male. This is supported by his assertion that 'the modes of formation and expression – by no means merely linguistic – that our culture places at the disposal of the psychic interior have essentially been created by men'.[150]

If we reflect upon the figures in Simmel's metropolitan cityscape, then the female figure present there and at the centre of the mature money economy is the prostitute. The figure of the prostitute as the symbol of female commodification in the streetscape of modernity is located as a polar opposite to Simmel's positive female identification with the home. The female figure of the prostitute as 'an ejaculation mechanism' presented as 'joy girl' in the metropolis – and these are the images Simmel evokes in his earlier pseudonymous, critical essay 'Infelices Possidentes!'[151] – is a 'leisure' commodity for male consumers, in a context in which leisure for some is labour for others. Elsewhere, in his *Philosophy of Money*, Simmel makes the reciprocal connection between prostitution and money, each sharing aspects of the other.

There is a further dimension of objective culture that Simmel does explore in his essay on the metropolis, namely its relationship to the money economy and its accompanying calculating traits. The most radical interpretation of this objective culture, which takes the principle of objectification to its logical conclusion, is that this objective culture is a *dead* culture, a culture of things and no longer that of human beings. Such an alien culture of things can be conceived as subject to its own laws, which is indeed how Simmel interprets this objective culture in his later (1911) essay on the concept and tragedy of culture, in which such a culture exists only in its *fetishized* form. If *we* reify this autonomy of objective culture, then our critique of it can be confined to a critique of culture (*Kulturkritik*) rather than a critique of the social formations (*Gesellschaftskritik*) that produce this apparent autonomy. If this objective culture is reified and closed off from human beings, then the question arises as to how its investigation is possible – at a distance, aesthetically, merely formally, etc. If such an objective culture merely exists without a *meaning* that *connects* with ourselves, then this gives justification for Simmel's study of social forms (of interaction or sociation) *in statu nascendi* or at the point of crystallization (*Verdichtung*) before they have become fully objectified or reified. Finally, if a feature of modernity is a broken-off relationship with origin (as Marx, Nietzsche and others assumed) then ostensibly we cannot search for the origin of this putative autonomous sphere of objective culture *within itself*.

Such radical reflections upon the nature of objective culture do not *directly* surface in the metropolis essay. There, still, 'intellectuality is . . . seen to preserve subjective life against the overwhelming power of metropolitan life'.[152] But this very intellectuality that creates a distance from objective (metropolitan) culture is itself connected to, and compromised by, that culture. Intellectuality is crucial to both 'the multiplicity and concentration of economic exchange' – and the latter's indifferent means – and to the preconditions for calculability. The massive increase in monetary transactions and their diversity in the metropolis is accompanied by the devaluation of quality, individuality, subjectivity and the elevation of 'a matter-of-fact attitude', a 'formal justice', indifference, a focus upon 'objective measurable achievement' and 'intellectually calculating economic egoism[s]'.[153] All these features present in the modern metropolis in monetary transactions are predicated upon an indifference to subjectivity, an 'unmerciful' objectivity that is necessary in order that the formal reciprocity of exchange, mediated by the universal equivalent of value, can operate.

This 'unmerciful' objectivity requires formal precision, exactitude, calculability and solubility. These are all features associated with intellectuality. Such features are necessary in the modern metropolis because without punctuality and precision of intersection relationships 'the whole structure would break down into an inextricable chaos'. The highly developed systems of differentiation and functional relations – what Weber and others would subsequently refer to as systems of purposive-rational action – require the complex integration of myriad temporal and spatial coordinates. And insofar as this mode of intellectuality is not merely necessary for the 'highly complex organism' of the modern metropolis in which it operates but is also extending into more areas of social relations, other modes of relating to others are increasingly and correspondingly threatened. Thus, on the one hand, in the modern metropolis:

> Punctuality, calculability, exactness are forced upon life by the complexity
> and extension of metropolitan existence. . . . These traits . . . favour the exclu-
> sion of those irrational, instinctive, sovereign traits and impulses which aim
> at determining the mode of life from within'.[154]

And where such contrary traits still exist, they are 'opposed to typical city life' and favour an 'unschematized existence'.

However, there are increasing tendencies supporting the extension of the intellectuality that typifies much of metropolitan existence. This 'calculating exactness' of practical life is nurtured by the expanding money economy and by the increasing significance of natural scientific knowledge, whose aim Simmel declares to be 'to transform the world into an arithmetic problem, to fix every part of the world by mathematical formulas'. The extension of this mode of dealing with the world is experienced most dramatically within the money economy – whose concentrated and expanding network is the modern metropolis – creating, a reduction of qualitative values to quantitative ones . . . a new precision, a certainty in the definition of identities and differences, an unambiguousness in agreements and arrangements.[155]

But unlike those of his contemporaries, such as Sombart, who viewed science and especially technology as a crucial causal factor in shaping modern metropolitan culture, Simmel views 'the condition of metropolitan life . . . [as] at once cause and effect of . . . [the calculating] trait'.

This reciprocal relationship – which is typical of Simmel's mode of argumentation and indeed, in the form of reciprocal effect, is a key feature of his methodological approach to social and cultural phenomena – enables him to open up the contradictory nature of social phenomena. In the present context, the *objective* dimensions of metropolitan mental life do not exclude what appears at first sight as their opposite, namely, 'a highly personal subjectivity'. However, the *subjective* state to which Simmel devotes the greatest amount of attention and which is viewed as the epitome of metropolitan existence – the *blasé attitude* (*Blasiertheit*) – is itself hardly an instance of a creative subjectivity, but rather is deeply compromised by its origin in a response to the dominant objective culture. Both the blasé attitude and the indifference towards others in the metropolis – and *indifference* is another related trait identified by Simmel – are associated with *distance* from objects and other persons. In both cases, we are observing *pathologies* of everyday metropolitan existence as increasingly *normal* features of urban interaction. Like other pathologies, they can acquire more extreme manifestions. Indifference, for instance, can be amplified into active distrust, reserve or even hostility, thereby creating less fluid and more inflexible demarcations in metropolitan interaction between social circles.

The blasé attitude emerges out of features of metropolitan interaction and of the money economy. In the city, 'the rapidly changing and closely compressed contrasting stimulations of the nerves', which account for increasing intellectuality in the metropolis, also generates the blasé attitude. As a source and stimulus to desires for pleasure, the metropolis 'agitates the nerves to their strongest reactivity for such a long time that they finally cease to react at all', creating 'an incapacity . . . to react to new sensations with the appropriate energy'.[156] As the site of endless distractions and 'fillings in of time and consciousness', experience of the metropolis stimulates not merely the consumption of objects but the consumption of the emotions of human subjects themselves. In this sense, the blasé attitude, for all its indifference, results from distortions of *emotional* responses, whereas the calculating attitude, as it were, is only possible as a result of heightened *intellectuality*. Simmel goes so far as to suggest that this blasé attitude afflicts metropolitan children as well as adults.

However, perhaps the more powerful source of the blasé attitude stems from the fact that 'large cities, the main seats of . . . money exchange, bring the purchasability of things to the fore . . . [and this] is why cities are also the genuine locale of the blasé attitude', whose essence is 'the deadening of differences between things'.[157] If *increasing* social differentiation is a developmental tendency in modernity, for Simmel, then that accentuation of differentiation at a variety of levels is especially evident in metropolitan centres and in the division of labour in both production and others spheres. But with the development of the mature money economy we not only experience the reduction of differentiation to a common denominator – money – but also our very participation in monetary transactions creates a *dedifferentiating* tendency in our inner response to commodification that Simmel identifies as the blasé attitude. In other words, it is not merely that money is 'the most frightful leveller' that transforms the substance of exchange relations in a developed money and commodity-dominated economy, but also that in our interactions mediated by money the latter creates an internal response, a 'mood [that] is the faithful subjective reflection of the completely internalised money economy'. This mood (*Seelenstimmung*), which sees the value of things and the differences in value between things 'in an evenly flat and grey tone', is what constitutes the blasé attitude.

The emptying out of value and value differences through the universal equivalent's focus upon 'how much?' in a developed capitalist money economy creates a kind of hollowed-out world of things. Money

irretrievably hollows out the core of things, their individuality, their distinct-ive value, their incomparability. They all swim with equal specific gravity in the constantly moving stream of money, they all lie at the same level and differentiate themselves only through the size of the piece that they cover from it.[158]

Our constant socialization into a form of alienation (as Böhringer has argued)[159] that is reinforced with every monetary transaction in the sphere of circulation of commodities also poses radical problems in the sphere of aesthetic representation. Tafuri, for example, has drawn a connection between these two spheres:

The objects all floating on the same plane, with the same specific gravity, in the constant movement of the money economy: does it not seem that we are reading here a literary comment on a Schwitters' *Merzbild*? The problem was in fact how to render active the intensification of nervous stimulation, how to absorb the shock provoked by the metropolis by trans-forming it into a new principle of dynamic development, how to utilize to the limit the anguish which 'indifference to value' continually provokes and nourishes in the metropolitan experience.[160]

In their different ways, several avant-garde artistic movements sought to give aesthetic representation to this experience. But in the metropolis itself – and in Simmel's essay – the stimulation of the nerves and even the accentuation of nervous responses in 'the concentration of human beings and things' results 'in this peculiar adaptive phenomenon of the blasé attitude in which the nerves find in the refusal to react to their stimulation their final possibility for accommodating themselves to the contents and the form of metropolitan life'.[161] Indeed, this response can culminate in an extreme pathological form in which the devaluation of the world of things is transferred into the inner devaluation of the individual, destroying the individual personality through its worthlessness. Such a possibility would open up an alternative theory to account for Durkheim's perceived increase in suicides in modern societies. Neither here nor elsewhere is this opportunity addressed by Simmel.

Instead, Simmel addresses another strategy for self-preservation in the metropolis – that of reserve and indifference to others – which is 'a no less negative behaviour of a social nature'. He adduces two reasons for the necessity for this reserve and indifference, one internal and the other external. If we were to react internally or emotionally to every person whom we met in the metropolis, then we would be 'inwardly totally atomised' and in an 'unimaginable mental state'. The second reason why reserve or even distrust is necessary in the plethora of metropolitan interactions is that 'the right to mistrust' one another is appropriate in 'the fleeting contact of criss-crossing elements of metropolitan life'. The contingent nature of many of our metropolitan interactions also renders plausible the shift from mere indifference to 'mistrust', 'aversion', 'a reciprocal estrangement' and 'repulsion', and even to 'hatred' and 'struggle' (*Kampf*). The complex networks of metropolitan interaction, the criss-crossing web of contacts, the 'extensive life of transactions' are in themselves highly differentiated, and between one another require 'an extremely varied hierarchy' of response from their participants on a scale varying from the most fleeting to the relatively permanent. In turn, that individual response can be one of 'sympathy, indifference or aversion'. Indifference is thus merely one of the responses, and not necessarily the most common one, since antipathy protects us from both total indifference and 'indiscriminate reciprocal suggestibility'. The complex hierarchy of networks of interactions, transactions and communications, each of whose components have differing rhythms – and, although not mentioned by Simmel here, spatial parameters – and forms, constitutes a totality of the metropolitan structure of life within which 'what appears . . . at first sight as dissociation is in reality only one of its elementary forms of sociation'.[162]

The discussion of the complex intersecting network of communications and transactions and the hierarchical and differentiated response to it would be one of the places in which Simmel could have readily inserted an examination of class, gender and ethnic boundaries. Although he is largely silent here on these dimensions of stratification and interactional boundaries, his analyses elsewhere on domination and subordination, the intersection of social circles, the spatial and other properties of boundaries, conflict and other dimensions indicate that a Simmelian investigation of the properties of social stratification is possible. To take but one example, the concept of 'the intersection of social circles' (the title of an essay translated into English with quite different connotations as 'The Web of Group Affiliations')[163] provides a basis for a network analysis of interactions that could be readily applied in terms of social, temporal and spatial density (intensity) of social class, gender and ethnic interactions as a means of indicating class, gender and ethnic boundaries in interactions. It is not the case that Simmel is unaware of these stratified dimensions of metropolitan interactions, but it is true that they are hardly thematized in the metropolis essay.

Instead, Simmel proceeds to draw an ostensibly positive connection between the reserve and indifference of much metropolitan interaction and the creation of a kind and amount of individual freedom. One of the crucial factors creating this personal freedom arises, for Simmel, from 'one of the major developmental tendencies of social life', namely the self-preservation and extension of the social group and the development of the individual. This is the subject of one of Simmel's substantive essays in his *Soziologie* of 1908.[164] The metropolis is a crucial instance of this developmental tendency. The transition from small town to city coincides with the weakening of the bonds of the individual to the group, the weakening in general of the inner unity of the group and the greater freedom of the metropolitan individual compared to the small town dweller. In the metropolis, the reserve and indifference that contribute to the independence of the individual are felt most keenly in the urban crowd, in which 'the bodily proximity and narrowness of space make the mental distance especially visible'. In this context, the freedom of the individual so gained may not necessarily be experienced as contributing to their well-being.

The correlation between enlargement of the group or urban circles and the *external* freedom of the individual is not the only reason why the metropolis is the site for personal freedom. Rather, the *internal* freedom of individuals transcends the merely quantitative expansion of the metropolis insofar as the city becomes the site of cosmopolitanism. Here we are looking at the extension of the effects of the metropolis far beyond its physical boundaries. To account for the development of cosmopolitanism, Simmel has recourse to an *economic* analogy in which, beyond a certain amount, wealth expands in value in geometric progression. The *intellectual* domination of the city over its hinterland grows in a similar manner. In order to illustrate the quasi-autonomous dynamic extension of cosmopolitanism, Simmel again has recourse to metaphors and analogies. The metaphor is that of the city as a web, with new threads not merely extending into the hinterland but as if growing of their own accord. The striking analogy is that of ground rent since 'within the city the unearned increment of ground rent, through the mere increase in communication, brings the owner automatically increasing profits'.[165] Similarly, the growth of metropolitan independence is not itself 'dependent upon prominent individuals' (Schäfer, it should be noted, lamented the absence of such individuals in the modern metropolis), nor are its effects confined to within its formal boundaries. Rather, just as a body in space, its effects extend far beyond its spatial and temporal boundaries.

The freedom that metropolitan existence creates for individuals is not confined to mere externalities such as 'freedom of movement' or even the 'removal of prejudices and philistinism' – however important such negative 'freedom from' dimensions may be – but rather entails the possibility for the positive freedom to express the distinctiveness and uniqueness of each individual in their 'formation of life' (*Gestaltung des Lebens*). Whether, how and where this freedom is realized in the modern metropolis is conditioned by many factors. Again, Simmel does not directly address the specific constraining dimensions of social stratification such as gender, class and ethnicity. But he does recognize that, in the context of attaining individual freedom, 'only our lack of interchangeability *with* others demonstrates that our mode of existence has not been imposed upon us *by* others'.[166]

However, crucial processes of social differentiation do not necessarily favour the differentiation of individuals in the positive sense to which Simmel alludes. One such process is the division of labour, and it is cities that are the location for 'the highest economic division of labour'. The city as expanding entity

> increasingly offers the decisive preconditions for the division of labour: a circle which, through its size is capable of receiving a highly diverse variety of services, whereas, at the same time, both the concentration of individuals and their struggle for customers compels individuals to specialize in a function in which they cannot so easily be replaced by another. What is decisive is that metropolitan life has transformed the struggle with nature for a livelihood into a struggle with other human beings, that the gain that is secured here derives not from nature but from human beings.[167]

Herein lies also a 'deeper' source of specialization aside from the struggle for gain, namely, that 'the seller must seek to generate ever new and more differentiated needs in the enticed customer', creating a 'differentiation, refinement and enrichment of the needs of the public'.

In turn, such specialization is accompanied by the 'intellectual individualization of psychological traits' in the metropolis. Simmel detects four reasons for this development. The first is the difficulty in asserting oneself in the metropolis and hence the search for what is qualitatively distinctive within a social circle. Second, metropolitan existence encourages 'the most tendentious eccentricities . . . the specifically metropolitan extravagances of mannerism, capriciousness and preciousness' as means or forms of being different, a strategy that for some may be the only mode of maintaining self-esteem through being recognized by others. Third, given 'the brevity and scarcity of contacts' with others in the metropolis, individuals must appear 'to the point, concise and as characteristic as possible' in a short space of time. Fourth, and for Simmel most importantly, the metropolis as the focal point of modern culture is characterized by the preponderance of objective over subjective mind or spirit that is embodied in the domination of objective culture over subjective culture.

But before developing this dimension further, it should be indicated here that there are many other sources in Simmel's writings that examine other aspects of the problem of individual self-assertion in a metropolitan setting. In his monograph on 'The Philosophy of Fashion',[168] Simmel maintains that the centre of fashion consciousness is the metropolis. Fashion's dialectical attraction of asserting both similarity (through imitation) and differentiation (through individuation) is appropriate to individual display in the metropolis. Individuals can reciprocally identify one another by modes of attire. At the same time, extreme dedication to fashion – including dandyism – can also serve as a mask (of accentuated fashionability, for example) beneath which individuals may preserve their inner self. Fashion serves as a largely visual means of asserting difference (or similarity). It is also associated with the generation of 'ever more differentiated needs' as an industry that is, of necessity, committed to the acceleration in the turnover time of fashion.

Although Simmel highlights the fleeting nature of many metropolitan interactions and a corresponding concentration upon brief, to-the-point interactions, his exploration of sociability as a form of interaction suggests a verbal/visual mode of sociation that is in keeping with the predominant intellectuality of many urban interactions.[169] Sociability as a form of sociation emphasizes form rather than content, a play form of interaction and even of society itself. In this respect, it also constitutes a dimension of flirtation (including intellectual flirtation). Perhaps in no other sphere of contemporary society is the 'social game' of sociability more evident than in metropolitan interactions. In the everday world it is perhaps the opposite form to the brief, matter-of-fact, pointed interactions in business or other functional transactions.

Sociability and other such forms of everyday interaction appear distanced from the objective culture that is concentrated in the metropolis as 'the genuine showcase of this culture', as 'the hypertrophy of objective culture' and 'the atrophy of individual culture'. In the metropolis, this objective culture is to be found in its

> buildings and educational institutions, in the wonders and comforts of space – conquering technology, in the formations of community life, and in the visible institutions of the state.[170]

Together with this wealth of impersonal culture, the individual is offered a multitude of distractions: 'stimulations, interests, fillings in of time and consciousness . . . [that] carry life as if in a current in which it is hardly necessary to swim for oneself'. At the same time, however, this life consists increasingly of these 'impersonal contents and offerings that tend to displace genuine personal nuances and unique features'.

In this context, it is difficult for individuals to recognize themselves in this objective culture, except as functional units within an expanding division of labour. The one-sided accentuation of skills necessitated by the division of labour and the quantitative performance required of the individual reduce the individual increasingly to a *quantité négligeable*, to a 'grain of dust' (*Staubkorn*) that confronts 'a massive organisation of things and forces', that is objective culture. In the individual's 'practices and in the obscure totality of feelings derived from them' there resides, perhaps in pathological forms, the subjective consequences of the permanent confrontation with the culture of things (*Sachkultur*). As Simmel had posited in his analysis of the money economy, we can experience 'the culture of things *as* human culture'.

Yet this bleak opposition between objective and subjective culture is not Simmel's final statement on the metropolis. He draws back from the radical possibility that this objective culture is a dead culture, or indeed a corpse. The world of total reification was left to be conceived by one of his students two decades later, in Georg Lukács's essay on reification in his *History and Class Consciousness*.[171] Instead, Simmel concludes with the unreconciled antinomies of individualism, the two forms of individualism 'nurtured by the quantitative relations of the metropolis' – 'individual independence and the cultivation of personal individuality'. This juxtaposition of individualism and individuality had been a central theme of Durkheim's studies in the previous decade, both in relation to the division of labour in modern society and its 'abnormal' forms, and in the putative high modern rates of suicide emanating from 'excessive individualism'. The essay's conclusion, therefore, returns to its opening and the problem of securing both forms of individualism in a context in which 'it is the function of the metropolis to provide the place for this struggle and its reconciliation'.

The tension contained in the essay resides not merely in the concluding statement on the simultaneous existence of these two forms of individualism but also in the potentially more negative assessments that the essay as a whole contains. However, unlike those of his contemporaries who readily passed a negative judgement on the modern metropolis, such as Tönnies, or who too readily appeared with judgements upon modern culture (including the metropolis's 'asphalt culture'), such as Sombart, Simmel – for whom antinomies were never totally resolved and for whom the dialectic never gained its synthesis – declares that 'it is not our task either to accuse or to pardon, but only to understand'.[172]

4

The City Compared

Vienna is not Berlin

We have not yet drawn any conclusion – at least I have not – whether we should judge this piece of the world, on which are crowded five million people, magnificent and majestic or raw, despicable and barbarian. Most enthusiastic – as always on travels – is Max.

Marianne Weber on New York

Verily, I say to you that Berlin would sooner grow accustomed to tradition than would Vienna to the machine.

Karl Kraus, Beim Wort Genommen

I know a country where the automats are closed on Sundays and do not function during the week.

Karl Kraus, Beim Wort Genommen

I

Few would dispute the connection between the delineation of *modernity* at the turn of the century and the development of the modern metropolis. In other words, the spirit of capitalist modernity that in different ways concerned Weber, Sombart, Simmel and others was associated with a spirit of metropolitan modernity. With few exceptions, the analyses of the development of capitalist modernity at the turn of the century take as their central focus – implicitly or explicitly – *urban* modernity. The detailed investigation of agrarian capitalism even as a historical site, with few exceptions, is not of primary concern, and still less is the impact of modernization upon rural existence.[1]

The sheer scale of urban expansion in Germany after unification offers a ready correlation between urban existence and crucial – positive or negative – features of modernity. And if the concept of modernity was problematical in social science discourse and elsewhere, then so, too, was the concept of the metropolis itself. Hence, when Sombart asks what a town or city actually is as an historical entity, as in his 1907 article but also in *Der Moderne Kapitalismus* in 1902, it may have been framed as a mere *historical* inquiry but it was simultaneously a *contemporary* issue.[2] The rapid urbanization of Germany after 1870 and, literally, the creation or building of cities (*Städtebau*) stimulated the development of a new discipline devoted to urban creation (city planning) and a debate on the nature and significance of the modern city.[3] The ostensibly merely *quantitative* expansion of urban areas produced attempts to explain the historical development of the modern city in terms of a crucial numerical threshold of dwellers. If, as was the case by 1910 (but also much earlier), it was agreed that a city should comprise a population of 100,000, then Germany possessed 49 cities. The more difficult estimation of a big city, a metropolis, whose *quantitative* expansion provided it with a *qualitative* transformation, was set at one million, giving Germany only one metropolis – Berlin – with Hamburg closely behind with a population of over 900,000.[4]

Such merely quantitative definitions of the city clearly obfuscated important differences. By 1900 Charlottenburg and by 1910 Rixdorf, Schöneberg and Wilmersdorf – all suburbs of Berlin – had achieved city status on those quantitative criteria, although all were shortly to be incorporated into Gross-Berlin. Also by 1910 Duisburg and Gelsenkirchen would join Dortmund and Essen (both cities of 100,000 population by 1900) to form part of what was, in effect, the largest urban conglomeration in the Rhine–Ruhr area, but without this conglomeration itself achieving city status.[5] Within the Austro–Hungarian Empire, Vienna's incorporation of outer suburbs in 1890 to form Gross-Wien could not count upon taking in populations the size of Charlottenburg, for example, as was the case in Berlin. Instead, Vienna's expansion rested upon natural population growth and migration. Furthermore, within the Empire, other cities such as Prague and Budapest, expanded rapidly around the turn of the century, often at a faster rate than Vienna.[6]

The sheer expansion of cities in the last third of the nineteenth century in Germany created the need for the systematization of a field of knowledge that sought to regulate urban development. The German concept of *Städtebau* reflects more closely the activity of building and expanding cities than does the English equivalent of city planning.[7] As with many other disciplines at the points and sites of their emergence, the study of the regulation of urban development was deeply contested. The concern with problems of traffic regulation and hygiene, amongst others, that was ostensibly a prime focus for city planning theorists such as Richard Baumeister or Joseph Stübben, was contested in Camillo Sitte's plea in 1889 for a city planning that concerned itself more with the aesthetics of urban planning.[8] The heated debate in the 1890s between Stübben and Sitte's supporters, ostensibly around the issue of the efficacy of 'straight or crooked streets', coincided with the hitherto largest number of German urban areas in the previous decade (i.e. 1880–90) becoming 100,000 cities.[9] That number was exceeded again in 1910, by which time no fewer than 15 such new cities had emerged in Germany.[10] Not surprisingly, therefore, the issue of urbanization (and its increasingly researched social problems) and its connection with modernity more frequently came under discussion and debate. Where there was a cultural turn in the discussion, the culture of modernity became synonymous with the culture of the metropolis. Werner Sombart, amongst others, was a social theorist who made this connection.

II

In his *Die deutsche Volkswirtschaft im neunzehnten Jahrhundert* (1903),[11] and especially in his examination at the end of this work of the relationship between economy and culture, Sombart explores some of the foundations of the emergent new society. In particular, Sombart views *massification* and *change* as two crucial cultural features of modernity. Both are present in his earlier discussion of the spirit of capitalism and, as symbolic of modern trade, the department store (as an exclusively urban phenomenon).[12] Mass and change are also crucial to his delineation of the culture of the modern metropolis. Finally, they are key features of *Amerikanismus* in exaggerated and accelerated form. In other words, the quantitative expansion of urban population, and a corresponding increase in the quantity of commodities in circulation, on the one hand, and the pervasive transformation in all spheres of society, on the other, are features of modernity most evident in modern metropolitan centres and are most accentuated in those spheres typical of American developments. If Berlin is identified as the most American city in Germany, then it will display in a heightened form the features of modernity and the corresponding impact upon urban culture that Sombart ascribes to modernity in general. For this reason, it is useful to outline briefly relevant dimensions of Sombart's delineation of the material culture of modernity.

Sombart asks whether there is anything more characteristic of modern times than their *mass nature*, the sheer quantification of both the human world and the world of goods. The dramatic increase in population in the nineteenth century and the increasing density of population in Germany (that is greater than other European countries except Britain and Italy) has produced an 'indistinguishable, unsurveyable mass' that is concentrated in metropolitan areas. This quantitative human expansion and concentration has been accompanied by an even more rapid increase in the quantity of commodities and its corresponding increase in production, factories, traffic, etc. In turn, the world of goods is characterized by a massive increase in consumption. Drawing on earlier arguments in his study of modern capitalism, Sombart refers to a 'collectivization of consumption' in department stores, in modern cities (in general utility consumption) and in rental barracks (as the consumption of urban space). The mass demand for commodities has been accompanied by less differentiated taste. This quantitative expansion extends into the *spatial* conception of things, a conception of dramatically increased spatial scale. In this context:

> The outer size of many things grows into the huge, they become 'imposing': cities, streets, dwelling blocks, railway stations, public buildings, department stores, factories, machines, bridges, ships and thousands of other such things.[13]

This treatment of the concept of mass in human quantities, quantities of commodities and size of things accords with the discovery of the concept of mass in the social sciences in the late nineteenth century. Here, the concept remains undifferentiated and its treatment undialectical.

The massification of individuals and things is accompanied by 'the characteristic *change in every structure* (*Gestalt*) in our times: movement, instability often paired with mass into a unified social phenomenon'.[14] A crucial motor for change is capitalism itself, with its ceaseless search for improving the profitability of commodities and with its harnessing of technology to this process of unending renewal. Hence 'what distinguishes our epoch . . . is the sheer size (*Massenhaftigkeit*) and hence the rapidity of change'[15] that is manifested in the reduction in the turnover time of objects. This ceaseless change generates 'a sense of uncertainty in the world of goods', a permanent 'change in the human relations of ownership to the world of goods'. Not only are we unsure as to how things will look tomorrow, and how and to what extent we can use them, but rather 'viewed from a given constellation of distribution, this form of change can be characterized as the uncertainty of existence (for its individual elements)'.[16]

Hence, although natural uncertainties may have been reduced in modern times, social and economic uncertainties have increased. Individuals are now dependent on many more factors beyond their control. Especially in the economic sphere, a characteristic of our times has become '*the univer-sality of uncertainty, uncertainty en masse*'.[17] Ownership, for instance, with its increasing dependency on market forces has become increasingly un-certain. Even landownership in the countryside has been 'mobilized'. And the same is true in an urban context: 'ownership in the city, however, has also become "more mobile" and thereby more insecure'.[18] Many categor-ies of owners and workers, Sombart argues, are sitting 'as if on a volcano' that can and does erupt at any time. The uncertainties of ownership, even leaving aside the 'agonies' of speculation, are matched by those pertaining to labour and the labour market. This also applies today to most liberal professions, where 'the mass of "the educated", that distinguishes our times from others, has here produced what is subject to change, what is insecure precisely from its own foundations'.[19] Although there are counter-tendencies against capitalist uncertainties in the form of communal economic organizations and cooperatives, they have not fundamentally affected the endemic uncertainty.

A third location of change lies in the relationship of the human world and the world of goods to their location. '*The change of place as mass phenomenon*' is a characteristic of modernity, one that manifests itself in the mobility of the mass of goods, news and communication networks, mass transport systems, changes in dwelling, mass migration (including seasonal migration and migration abroad). Indeed, viewed from the bird's-eye perspective, the German Empire is 'like an anthill in which the traveller has pierced his stick'.[20]

Such economic cultural dimensions of modernity have clearly had a significant impact upon modern intellectual culture. Thus, the effect of an emergent mass upon intellectual culture has been a broadening of the cul-tural base, an increase in cultural producers and mediators, a massive increase in literary and artistic production, a dramatic increase in pub-lished materials and a cheapening of published products. The latter would include the dramatic increase in newspapers and journals and, in the artistic–cultural realm, the significance of the feuilletons. At the collective level of cultural offerings, the increase in museums, concerts and theatres as cultural 'omnibuses' signifies their mass nature: the theatre as the 'literature omnibus', the concert as 'music omnibus' and the museum as 'art omnibus'.[21]

The crucial question for Sombart, however, is whether and how such phenomena have transformed 'the *inner essence of the new culture*'. His answer is that the domination of the mass of things over both the human mass and the individual has dramatically affected the cultural domain.

The sheer wealth of commodities and sources of satisfaction have expanded, to the extent that 'in the wealth of goods for enjoyment that grow up around us, the ideal impulses of the heart find their natural grave'.[22] This is most evident in the modern metropolis as far as Sombart is concerned.

The modern metropolis, where we dwell alongside one another 'in great stone canyons and upon hills of stone, glass and iron', is the site of a new culture – 'asphalt culture'. The 'stone deserts' of the big cities produce their own culture, their own new species of human being lacking in any real relationship to nature, 'an artificial species'. Although an examination of this new urban species must take into account the nature of social factors, such as living and working conditions, Sombart already reflects upon the 'racial fitness' of those in the suburbs of the major cities:

> Whoever assembles the bow-legged, pasty-cheeked, raceless new generation
> on the sandpiles of the city playgrounds, can easily come to the view that in
> the realm of racial formation, too, the substitution of quantity for quality
> is the really distinguishing characteristic of our age.[23]

Although such a judgement should take into account other social factors, Sombart views as less disputed the 'levelling of the distinctive cultural characteristics of individual parts of the country' and the development of a new type of person: 'in the place of rooted, concrete people of the specific localities there emerges increasingly the rootless, abstract, universal person (*Allerweltsmensch*)'.[24] In the metropolis there emerges a 'unified urban human type' that, overcome by the insecurity of existence, the struggle for existence, has been rendered 'insecure, restless and hurried'. With no time to react to changes that fill modern existence, contemporary intellectual and cultural life has become '*flatter*'.

The application of undifferentiated categories such as mass and change to the diagnosis of modernity, combined with an already pessimistic prognosing for modern metropolitan existence, indicate some of the future directions of Sombart's investigations of cultural dimensions of modernity. Only a few years later he declared his task as 'a struggle against the calamatous nature, especially of metropolitan culture', a battle in which 'we can only erect protective ramparts in order that the slimy currents of modern culture do not devastate all that surrounds us'.[25] Given such aims, it is not surprising that his cultural diagnosis of metropolitan culture should prove so negative: In contrast to a whole tradition of urban artistic and cultural avant-garde movements, Sombart could declare in 1905 that 'I cannot conceive that an artist could ever grow from the asphalt'.[26] Rather, the modern metropolis was the site of an *absent* genuine culture. And, as we shall see, so too was America – as a representation of modernity in which its crucial features of massification and endless change were present in their most accentuated form. Nowhere was this claim made so forcefully than in Sombart's comparison of Berlin and Vienna.

III

Sombart's favourable comparison of Vienna with Berlin – which contains his explicit references to *Amerikanismus* – appeared in the Berlin journal *Morgen*[27] in 1907 as a reply to an article by the Viennese writer and critic Felix Salten, which appeared earlier in the same year as itself a corrective to the romanticized outsider view of Vienna.[28] This interchange may be located in the broader context of Hermann Bahr's critical volume on Vienna[29] – which was seized by the censor when it first appeared in 1906 – and, more importantly, the 1908 volume on Vienna by Franz Servaes,[30] which makes positive reference to Sombart's article. In turn, the article by Karl Scheffler[31] in the *Österreichische Rundschau* in 1908 references Servaes and Bahr in his comparison of Berlin and Vienna. With the exception of Bahr's volume on Vienna, Sombart, Servaes and Scheffler all take up *Amerikanismus* in relation to Berlin, or at least maintain that Berlin is the most American of German cities.

The more general affinity between Berlin and American – i.e. US – cities has a longer history, as does *Amerikanismus*. For example, Max Weber, in the first of his essays on the 'Protestant Ethic', published in 1905, draws attention to Ferdinand Kürnberger's disparaging general references to Americanism as early as the 1850s.[32] But the correlation of Berlin with features of American urban life was almost certainly accentuated and accelerated following Berlin's rapid growth after 1870. Although there are many instances of hostility to Berlin as a rapidly developing urban centre that could draw upon a much more generalized hostility to urbanization in Germany on the part of significant social strata – not least sections of its intelligentsia and influential figures such as Nietzsche and Tönnies[33] – the specific affinity between Berlin and *Amerikanismus* required a connection being drawn between rapid urban expansion and the (negative) transformation of cultural life in both Berlin and American urban centres. In short, *Spreeathen* (Athens on the Spree) became *Chicago on the Spree* – as Mark Twain maintained at the turn of the century.[34] Julius Langbehn, in his *Rembrandt als Erzieher* (1890),[35] whose content was already partly revealed on its title page as having been written anonymously 'by a German', already outlined briefly the affinities between Berlin and North America. Though the rapid urban development of Berlin compares only with that of North American cities, the real significance of

their affinity becomes apparent only through examining 'the inner appearance of the city, i.e. the average mental physiognomy of its inhabitants'.
There are ethnic affinities insofar as both are 'Low German' settlements,
neither of which deny 'their common home (*Heimat*)'. The mental life in
Berlin and American cities is also similar:

> A restless commercial spirit characterizes the inhabitants of the Spree as
> much as those on the Hudson; but, of course, this unrest is a barrier in
> both instances to the blossoming of an independent spiritual life. . . . Both
> instances reveal a haste and hunt for diverse cultural achievements; both,
> however, reveal a lack of silent, quiet growth from within to the outside: *a*
> *careless cultivation of culture is practised.*[36]

Both Berlin and North American cities also have in common the fact that
a significant proportion of their expansion is due to migration (though
the more these migrants were to bring with them proponents of 'ideal
interests and self-creating intellectual forces', the better the outlook for
their respective cultures). Instead:

> North America produces countless civil engineers and Berlin countless state
> architects; but they are 'mechanical' engineers and architects. . . . The exces-
> sive culture (*Überkultur*) on this side of the ocean and the lack of culture
> (*Unkultur*) on the other confront one another in their means; but unfortu-
> nately not in their success as well. . . . This success can only be achieved
> through a single path: through creative, constructive, organized personal-
> ities; and not at all in the state–administrative but rather in the intellectual–
> cultural sense.[37]

Leaving aside the purported ethnic affinities, Langbehn's highly influential
volume already suggests parallels between Berlin and North American
cities in terms of speed of expansion, restless urban commercial spirit,
migration as a significant key to growth, and the absence of an organic
culture even when its outward forms are in evidence. These are some of
the features that were to be utilized in identifying Berlin as the site in
Germany and Europe of *Amerikanismus*.

Langbehn's reference to the Spree and the Hudson is obviously signalling
Berlin and New York, though elsewhere he sees affinities between the two
capitals, Berlin and Washington (in terms of their government architecture). But this latter comparison is seldom made in the subsequent discourse
on Berlin. Rather it is Chicago that becomes one signifier for the imperial
capital on the Spree. The fact that Chicago is not a capital city should
indicate that this comparison is neither a symmetrical nor a self-evident one.

However, as Arnold Lewis has recently shown,[38] the European interest
in Chicago was given a dramatic stimulus with the World Columbian

Exhibition held there in 1893. It should also be added here that the Midwest region around Chicago, the city itself and other cities such as Milwaukee had already attracted major waves of German migrants. The scale of expansion of Chicago in the second half of the nineteenth century suggested an apparent affinity with Berlin:

> Between 1850 and 1890 the population of London jumped from 2.3 million to 4.2 million people, Paris from 1.1 to 2.3 million, and Berlin from 387,200 to 1.5 million. These figures meant that London almost doubled (1.8 times), Paris more than doubled (2.3), and Berlin more than quadrupled (4.2) their populations. Significant population growth also characterized American cities in this forty-year period; New York's population rose 4.1 times, from 660,800 to 2.7 million. Despite these impressive statistics on both sides of the Atlantic, those of Chicago in the same period were incomparable. Its population increased 36.7 times, numbering approximately 1,100,000 people by 1890.[39]

As the world's sixth largest city by 1893, the sheer scale of urban expansion is indicative of the two cultural features of modernity outlined by Sombart in 1903 – mass and change. Amongst major capital cities in Europe, Berlin – for its part – could claim to have experienced the fastest growth in the period 1850–90.

The extensive European coverage – not least in Germany – of the Chicago exhibition of 1893 and the exhibition's success meant that it became a comparator for subsequent intended world exhibitions. Hence, according to the official catalogue and elsewhere, the Berlin Trade Exhibition of 1896 was intended as a reply both to the 1889 Paris exhibition and the Chicago Columbian Exhibition of 1893.[40] The reality was, however, otherwise. As a result of political opposition from other German states, the 1896 Berlin exhibition was neither a world exhibition nor even a German exhibition but merely a Berlin exhibition.[41] Nonetheless, many observers viewed the event as a symbolic representation of the city's elevation from a big city to a world city. But perhaps as an indication of other municipalities' opposition to Berlin, it was decided in 1897 to hold the first German Municipal Exhibition in Dresden in 1903.[42] In connection with this event, which was the first positive celebration of urban modernity in Germany, Simmel, amongst others, contributed to a prior series of lectures on the nature of the modern metropolis. In the following year, prominent German academics were invited to the 1904 St Louis exhibition and the impressions made there of American metropolitan centres had a further impact upon German conceptions of America.

The possibility of a dramatic expansion of Berlin and the growing debate on Gross-Berlin was already under way by the time Sombart published his short article on Vienna in 1907. The major exhibition of

1910 and the competition for plans for Gross-Berlin was already two decades after Vienna had expanded its city boundaries to form Gross-Wien – an enlarged Vienna that in no way compared with the more dynamic expansion of Berlin. For its part, the major restructuring of Vienna after the 1857 decision to remove the medieval fortifications and subsequently to build the Ringstrasse had already created discourses on Old versus New Vienna. The post-1890 expansion of the city provoked another, more heated discourse on modernity and New Vienna, and the threat to Old Vienna as an urban idyll.[43]

Felix Salten's brief essay in *Morgen* titled 'The Viennese Correspondent' is a critical corrective to some of the clichés associated with images of Vienna.[44] Salten argues that if the clichés concerning life in Vienna fervently held by those living in the German Empire are to be believed, the city would have collapsed long ago. The view from outside is of a city in which 'time is frittered away'; 'the city is conceived of as an extensive place of amusement' in which 'trivial people squander their money travelling in fiakers, guzzling local wine and clapping their hands singing popular ballads'. In other words, the Viennese are viewed as an 'easy living people'. However, 'one should not so seriously believe in the fact that the Viennese either merely dance waltzes or eat roast chicken (*Backhändel*)'.[45] 'Whoever was never here [in Vienna] must believe that in Vienna the people dance on their tiptoes through the streets, holding their walking stick between two fingers and performing a continuous minuette.' Their taste for these and other things is merely 'an indication of Viennese superficiality'.

Such a city is devoid of progress; it is a conglomerate of vestiges of the past. If this is the case, Salten asks:

> How are things to move forward in Vienna? This is a common difficult task for the journalists – how to explain the motionless state of a city from a thousand reasons. In Vienna, the men don't exert themselves. An easy living people . . . and all puzzles are solved. Who still wonders at the fact that such a city remains backward. What is curious about all this, however, is that Vienna is advancing rapidly. It is even now on an upturn. But no one speaks about it.[46]

Instead, much is written about 'the old Viennese culture'. However, Salten argues that this old culture 'is no longer active, no longer a living culture'. But for those in Vienna, too, who maintain its mythologically continued existence in order to assert the city's unique identity, this is a strategy for not recognizing a new Vienna. Such people 'speak of a Vienna that existed only in the dusty newspaper pages of the last century, in the books and feuilletons of local humourists, and deceive themselves that this is the real Vienna. . . . These gentlemen do not know Vienna at all. And write about it. Such things are of course quite common in journalism. Here, in fact, it is the rule.'[47] This ideology of an old culture is associated with that which is 'only possible in Vienna'. This mythology also has a political dimension:

> The fact that in our city 300,000 workers with unfurled red flags could march along the Ringstrasse, without our bourgeoisie becoming nervous and without our military receiving their marching orders, whereas in Berlin the mere rumour of an impending socialist demonstration was sufficient reason to close off the Lustgarten as well as Unter den Linden with a regiment of the guards and with artillery, does not incite our know-all to make any comparison. Everything that is foolish, unjust and backward is, for him, 'only possible in Vienna'.[48]

It is interesting to note that in his reply to Salten, Sombart does not address any political dimension of the comparison of Vienna with Berlin. This is all the more surprising given the fact that many of Sombart's contributions to *Morgen* deal with political consciousness and the contemporary situation of the socialist movement in Germany.

Before moving on to Sombart's reply to Salten, there are significant dimensions of Salten's essay worthy of mention. The juxtaposition of the Berlin view of Vienna is only one of the dichotomies explored. The opposition between new and old Vienna is also being portrayed in a somewhat muted form. If this contemporary opposition were amplified, and contemporary discourse on new Vienna explored more fully, then the correlation between proponents of a new Vienna and a favourable view of Germany and Berlin would become apparent. Thus, the dichotomy of Berlin (outside) and Vienna (inside) is complemented by Vienna (old culture) and Vienna (new culture, including that of Berlin). In other words, the polarities of Berlin and Vienna are also present *within* Vienna itself. As we shall see, Berlin as Americanism functions as a negative signifier not merely in the context of Germany but also in relation to other specific cities, notably Vienna (as culture). In this and other respects, the much broader opposition between civilization and culture was already functioning ideologically at the turn of the century both between national identities, within state formations, and between major cities. The identification of Americanism with Berlin provides another, different thesis concerning exceptionalism, both within Germany in comparison with other German cities (none of which are viewed as Americanized) and in comparison with other non-Americanized (and cultured) cities such as Vienna.

Sombart's 'north German' perspective on Vienna – as a reply to Salten – is unambiguous in its articulation of the signifiers civilization (Berlin) and culture (Vienna), Americanism (Berlin) and culture (Vienna), unculture (New York) and unculture (Berlin). In a personal retrospective, Sombart declares that a decade earlier (hence, around 1897) he shared the common north German positive evaluation of Berlin's conception of progress (and, by implication, its attendant Americanism) and negative evaluation of Vienna's lack of progress:

> Even ten years ago I found it laughable that Vienna had no nightlife and no city railway and did not increase its number of inhabitants every year by 100,000. . . . In these ten years (I believe) there occurred my development into a cultured human being and therefore I now love – Vienna.[49]

Vienna's city railway, designed by Otto Wagner and then still incomplete, was in fact officially opened in 1898. The city's population had already been increased as a result of the establishment of Gross-Wien in 1890, two decades before Berlin's 1910 enlargement.

But these and other material developments are not the focus of Sombart's interest. Rather, it is the *cultural* attributes of Vienna and Berlin that are his concern. Quite emphatically, Sombart declares Vienna to be a city of culture:

> One can really summarize the judgement on Vienna in a single word: Vienna has culture. I do not even say 'old'. Culture as such. Or, if one wishes to add an epithet to the word, then: artistic culture.[50]

This culture is evident in Vienna's 'indescribably beautiful nature', 'a breath of culture' in Schönbrunn, in the patrician dwellings in Rodaun, in the Prater – in short, in 'pastoral' Vienna. It is also evident in its music: 'Vienna is music. Is harmony. And thus, once more, culture. Wholeness, reconciliation.' This music pervades the inner city itself: 'Old Vienna as city: in each stone a song, in each street corner, in each courtyard adorned with vines, in each old palace a melodical musical piece.' Culture is evident in the city's population too: 'the Viennese: a human being. Not the fragment of a human being that we find so often in north Germany.' Culture resides also in the city's women, 'women whom one can taste, who carry with them something unique like a beautiful flower, like a beautiful animal'.

This Viennese pastoral of culture, beautiful nature, music, complete human beings not overcome by obsession with 'efficiency', attractive women, is contrasted with contemporary Berlin – 'how rapidly we become impoverished when we are still only enraptured by Berlin's nature'. What is this Berlin?

> Berlin is a suburb of New York: no more, no less. Everything of which the Berliner can be proud, New York has ten times more: it is three times as big, it grows even more quickly, it has ten times more traffic, ten times more theatres, its restaurants and amusement parks are ten times as large, its noise is ten times louder, its distances are even greater.

And what is New York? A desert. A huge cultural cemetery. Is humanity
to end up in it?![51]

This Americanism that threatens to overwhelm Berlin has a number of
distinctive features. First, it is characterized by 'the overevaluation of the
large scale, the huge, the purely quantitative'. Second, it is 'the overevaluation of technical means, about which we ultimately forget the final and
true words. As if "traffic" represents any kind of value and in the cities
not merely satisfies a sorry necessary need. The traffic about which the
American (Berliner) is so proud.' Third, the organization of things is to
provide a 'good order' through efficiency, 'as if the issue is that of "achievements" of whatever kind and not that of human beings who bring them
about. What is the use to me of the whole north German (American)
culture if I only see about me fragmented human beings, unattractive,
loathsome scoundrels.' Fourth, within 'the devastating current of modern
pseudo-culture' there is a 'proletarian-like revaluation of the old cultural
values'.

In contrast, for those of us who 'live in the desert of modern technical culture', 'Vienna, to speak in a Kantian manner, is – the regulative
idea of culture: we orientate ourselves around Vienna and Viennese
norms when we wish to know what culture is. We restore our resolve
once more with Vienna when we are overcome by disgust at modern
human development.' But Vienna too is threatened by 'progress'. If
Salten wished to ridicule the false conceptions of Vienna as ignoring
modern developments, then Sombart sees Vienna as threatened by this
progress. For Sombart, Vienna should not progress too much and should
resist the negative means-orientation of modern civilization 'as if underground railways and street cleaning and the restaurant for a thousand
people and good state administration were the end of culture'. The contrast of high and low culture is also already present in Sombart's image
of the threat to Vienna's 'culture'. In a revealing statement, he ascribes
the negative aspect of progress to the working class as itself the destroyer
of high culture:

> Vienna, too, is threatened by 'progress', like Florence, Rome and Paris. I
> spoke of Schönbrunn as a holy symbol of the highest culture: yet one
> should look out from there on the city, at how a gloomy modern prolet-
> arian district intervenes [between the city and the palace] and damages all
> fine impressions.[52]

Sombart omits to mention here that the working class did not 'choose' to
live in gloomy areas such as Meidling or Favoriten; such districts were
developed in order to house an expanding labour market.

At all events, Sombart is convinced that Vienna should not choose to be like Berlin (America):

> Do the Viennese really wish to invest their highest pride in being 'Berlin-American'? To have traffic? A 'nightlife'? To be 'efficient'? They will never totally succeed in this. For the old cultural foundation remains intact. And in order to totally give oneself up to 'modernity', in order to be totally impressed by the fact that in a single restaurant 6000 people could eat together, that every two minutes a city railway train departs: for this one would have to be completely devoid of all tradition, all culture, all qualities like the – New Yorker.[53]

Those who sought to solve even the traffic problems of Vienna in the context of a growing resistance of Old Vienna to New Vienna at the turn of the century often laid themselves open to the criticism that they were merely seeking to import American conceptions of city planning. Such people were, however, unsuccessful. Vienna's city railway went *around* the centre of the city for military reasons (no easy rapid mass access to the centre) and an *underground* railway was not built until the 1970s (in contrast to Budapest's turn-of-the-century development). But as we have seen, Sombart's juxtaposition of Berlin (America) and Vienna is concerned with *culture* or, more accurately, representations of culture, not with *actual features* of either city.

Although there was no response to Sombart's essay in *Morgen*, his stance on Vienna was taken up by the writer and critic Franz Servaes in his volume on Vienna (in a series on cultural sites) in 1908.[54] In passing, it is worth noting that the text is written as a series of 'letters to a Berlin girlfriend' who might visit Vienna and hence is an exercise in persuading a Berliner to visit the city. Servaes's representation of Vienna is that of an old city:

> Vienna is not that which, in common parlance, one terms a 'modern city'. . . .
> Of course there exists a modern veneer and an often very glittering new sheen and varnish in Vienna. . . . Yet all this is not the real Vienna. . . . The soul of this city is old and shy. One must go in search of it.[55]

There is thus an inside (the real, Old Vienna) and an outside (the modern surface) to this city. Hence it is distinguished from other cities by the fact that:

> the innermost core of its built surface is still not totally that of the 'city' pulsating with the most modern commercial city; not yet a piece of America in which warehouses are built on top of one another, where telephone and telegraph wires are the only voices on offer, and where all values are expressed exclusively in gigantic columns of figures.[56]

This city, Servaes argues, possesses much that Berlin can learn from. Indeed, 'Professor Sombart's warm and knowledgeable praise has not sunk without trace'. But however much each city can learn from the other, their historical roles are quite different:

> *Vienna has a totally different life-task compared to Berlin.* It can be expressed epigramatically as follows: Berlin wishes to 'become' (I read shortly somewhere: Berlin is 'on the way to acquiring culture'), Vienna, however, should remain Vienna.[57]

More pointedly – and beyond the cliché that Vienna remains itself – Servaes, in identifying Vienna as 'a "German" city' (and therefore overlooking one of the significant differences between Berlin and Vienna, and the empires in which they are located), views Vienna

> in the total sphere of German culture as Berlin's important and fruitful counterweight. Its task is – to present it once more epigrammatically: to be a dam and bulwark against the invasive Americanism . . . an extremely important and at the same time extraordinary difficult task.
>
> Americanism, in its greediness and soullessness, is our enemy: Europe must recognize this or otherwise it will perish. If it is conscious of this enmity (that certainly does not exclude the most urbane forms and the happiest recognition), then it will remain inwardly strong and, in possession and awareness of its old culture, will never be vanquished.[58]

One of the ironies of this binary opposition of Berlin and Vienna is that it is the most American German city that is one of the sites for the 'Ideas of 1914' less than a decade later, one of which is to preserve genuine European culture. In the present context, the implication of Servaes's – and Sombart's – argument is that Berlin is incapable of performing the task of being a 'bulwark' against Americanism.

Reflections upon the polarity of Berlin and Vienna were continued in an article by the Berlin art and architecture critic Karl Scheffler in 1908, which makes passing reference to Bahr and Servaes. Scheffler had already reflected critically in 1901 upon Berlin culture with its 'American-tempo growth', its 'Babylonian imbroglio', as a capital of 'parvenu culture' (a critique developed more fully two years earlier in Walther Rathenau's 'The most beautiful city in the world').[59] In 'Berlin as Artistic City' ('Berlin als Kunststadt', 1901), Scheffler reflects upon the impoverishment of the arts in Berlin since unification, and the fact that:

> For the first time in history, an epoch of feverish building activity does not coincide with social and artistic culture. The most vulgar profit style confronts the most inconsiderate entrepreneurs.[60]

The city's 'world bourgeoisie' is no longer trained in philosophy but 'in the halls of the stock exchange'. Scheffler sees this as, in part, a continuation of a longer process already evident in the wealthy bourgeoisie in pre-1848 Berlin, which was formed out of too many heterogeneous elements (including 'French education and Jewish mentality'). Today's wealth lies

> in the hands of speculators and city sharks; Jewish intellectuals have studied metropolitan needs in London, Paris and New York and have awakened and satisfied a desire for them with fabulous success in the German metropole. In the sandstone palaces is housed a parvenu species that knows nothing of culture and art, but rather as substitute for them promotes fashion; it does not desire what is beautiful but what is new and ascribes eternal value only to that which has a high price. For money becomes for it the measure of value of every ideal.[61]

The correlation between lack of culture, trader mentality and Jewish mentality is, of course, a thesis developed later and more fully by Sombart and is to be distinguished from the thesis that modern culture is dominated by Jews.

Scheffler's comparison of Vienna and Berlin introduces other dimensions to the metropolitan polarity. As with Sombart and Servaes, the German capital city is 'the Americanized Berlin'. This city which grew so rapidly was compelled to borrow from others its cultural features. This modern Berlin is

> a city that has emerged astonishingly quickly and continues to grow restless, a city of rapid work, without powerful traditions, without a visible history worthy of educating its citizens in, without unified forms of life and social conventions. It looked outwards to France, England and America.[62]

Berlin also looked towards Vienna, although to the Berliner, as emergent type, 'the Viennese appeared to be a person of the past, saturated, one who savours life'. Though critical of the new Viennese style, it was perceived as at least a style and not 'the Prussian–American stylelessness' prevalent in Berlin. Indeed, in a disparaging manner, Scheffler maintains that in contemporary Vienna 'Makart culture' pervades its products.

In terms of their respective position within their empires, Vienna is reminiscent of Paris ' because Vienna, too, is simultaneously a historical and a modern city, an old city and a new city in one . . . a site of old traditions, a place of conservative spirit . . . and the real living focal point of a great empire. Vienna is much more of a capital city and centre than Berlin.' The reason for this is that the German Empire is much more decentralized, such that 'each industrial and commercial city in the new empire is really the core of a metropolis, is a small-Berlin.'[63] Unlike Vienna, there is little left of Berlin's original population. The fact that

> the imperial capital lacks a local culture, that it is temporarily merely the rendezvous site for many different Germans, who have not found themselves in a new urban culture, makes this city lacking in physiognomy, weak in tradition, and gives it its American stamp: the modern Berliner stands in relation to his city much more free and much more critically unconstrained than does the Viennese to his. Berlin is a settlement of uprooted East and West Prussians, Schlesiens, Rhinelanders, however Germans, and Saxons, Jews and Poles, of Wendish and Germanic elements of peoples. Only in one thing is this still unorganized people united: in their unbroken energy for work.[64]

This negative, abstract conception of freedom, lack of physiognomy and dependency on migration is compensated for in the energy for work – another feature of Americanism, but one which Scheffler views as opening up the possibility for a new urban culture. The irony of this depiction of Berlin as dependent on external population movements is that, in the context of the Austro–Hungarian Empire with over a dozen nationalities, cultures and languages, the multicultural diversity of its capital city's population was much more marked at the turn of the century than was that of Berlin.

Instead, the external and often many internal representations of Vienna in this period seldom extended beyond the clichés of Old Vienna. Although Scheffler and Servaes deal with modern Viennese culture (though Scheffler doubts whether its products will have a lasting impact), they do not elaborate upon its positive achievements. Further, even though Servaes – as one would expect from a guide to a city that is announced as not modern – indicates some of the city's recent cultural achievements, this is not the case with Sombart's delineation of Vienna. As Birgitt Morgenbrod has pointed out:

> In Sombart's words we are not confronted – as were later generations – with the so fascinating Vienna of the *fin de siècle* with its outstanding artistic and intellectual achievements – the architecture of Otto Wagner and Adolf Loos, the music of Gustav Mahler and Arnold Schönberg, Karl Kraus's critique of language or Sigmund Freud's psychoanalysis – but rather we are confronted to a certain extent with an 'older' Vienna that seems to distance itself considerably from the inner workings of modernity with all its breaks and innovations.[65]

Rather, Sombart establishes a false continuity between past and present that allows him to retain the romantic conception of Vienna as repository

of old (high) culture. In contrast, Berlin with its asphalt culture, its Americanized culture, could hardly form the basis for a genuine urban culture as
far as Sombart was concerned. Like many anti-modernists, the possibility
of a genuine modern culture is already prejudiced at the outset by a definition of culture whose attributes are all located in the past.

The widespread identification of Berlin with Americanism around the
turn of the century – the historical conjuncture of Berlin and Americanism in Weimar Germany is different in crucial respects – creates the
possibility of another 'exceptionalism thesis'. Stated simply, it is that
unlike other metropolitan centres in Europe at the turn of the century,
Berlin is an Americanized city. The thesis was outlined by the writer and
critic Ludwig Fulda in 1913 in his essay 'Berlin und das deutsche
Geistesleben' ('Berlin and German Mental Life'), which commences with
the statement that:

> Berlin is an American city. . . . The predicate 'American' would already be
> justified with reference to its rapid expansion; but there also exist inner
> qualities. There exists the stormy drive forwards, the feverish activity, the
> unlimited desire for enterprise, the flying tempo of life, in short, all the
> characteristics that impress upon this community at large such an unre-
> strained modernity. Alongside this, there is in fact a critical overtone con-
> tained in the word. It is intended to signify that Berlin, in contrast to other
> European centres, also possesses a shadow side in common with America's
> cities: the absence of old culture, of a monumental past, of noble tradition
> and established taste.[66]

Berlin is exceptional because it is the site of 'unrestrained modernity',
an unfettered modernity that characterizes Americanism. The course of
unconstrained modernity is not held back by the past, by old cultural
values, by fixed normative rules. Everything is in motion, expanding at a
dramatic rate. This ceaseless modernity is identified with newness as such.
In Berlin, Fulda argues, 'what is new is preferred for its own sake, not
because it is good but because it is new. Newness in Berlin denotes unconditional praise.'

Fulda's identification of Berlin with modernity accords with that of
Servaes, Scheffler, Sombart and many others. But the *judgement* upon
metropolitan modernity is already implied in the latter's association with
Americanism. As is so often the case with Sombart's writings on modern
capitalism and the culture of metropolitan modernity, insights into its
features are accompanied by negative judgement. For those who supported
modernist movements emerging out of the experience of metropolitan
modernity, Berlin's identification with modernity could have positive
implications. To give but one example, outlined in the next chapter, the
Viennese critic – and analyst of Viennese literary modernisms – Egon

Friedell could view the dynamism of Berlin's modernity as an indication of a positive future over against old Vienna.[67]

Sombart's contrast between Vienna and Berlin contains an explicit longing for a retreat from metropolitan modernity, not to Vienna as such but to the romanticized imaginary version of Old Vienna, to a pastoral Vienna shared by many Viennese opponents of modernity in that city. Of course, such a retreat was only one of several available at the turn of the century. Another prominent alternative was the garden city. Yet many were sceptical of such retreats. The Viennese modernist Hermann Bahr, for instance, writing in 1910, was sceptical of attempts

> to form islands or cloisters, as it were, such as are intended by garden cities to preserve oneself from the metropolis. Garden cities can help us against land speculators, their use is hygienic, their development is to be applauded for many reasons. But if one hopes that the German spirit will gradually migrate to the garden cities in order to breathe freely away from the metropolis – of that I am not sure. For many intellectuals the garden city will be welcomed as a solution to their own personal problems. Yet it will not solve the general problem of the German spirit. It cannot be solved by emigration. Indeed, America has attempted to pack its spirit, as it were, in an undisturbed cupboard of its own: Boston. We can read in Wells's amusing portrayal what has become of this: a museum. No, the metropolitan problem can only be solved in the metropolis itself.[68]

The city as undisturbed garden with a harmonious (high) cultural existence – which is how Sombart viewed Vienna – was no solution to the problems of the modern metropolis which Sombart had outlined elsewhere. The differentiation and contradictions in modernity are real enough not to be subsumed within an undifferentiated image of America, too. If Vienna is not Berlin, then neither is Boston Chicago.

IV

This undifferentiated mode of discourse on cities in the early part of the twentieth century suggests that the concern is not so much with actual cities – though there exists a whole literature, indeed a much larger one, on urban planning, urban dwelling and urban life-forms that is exactly contemporary with it. Rather, what is at issue here is the *symbolic* significance of cities and their *representation* of other phenomena. If it can be argued that the discourse on the spirit of capitalism – that is in good part initiated by Sombart and taken up by Max Weber, Ernst Troeltsch and others – coincides with a renewed discourse on the spirit of the modern metropolis, then it should not be surprising that the putative deficiencies of capitalism could be transposed onto the modern metropolis. The modern metropolis could then function as a symbol, an imaginary, of a deficient capitalism for those opposed to modernity.

In turn, the modern metropolis came to be the signifier for modernity in Germany and elsewhere. In an extreme form, however, it was Berlin above all other German cities that came to symbolize modernity. Sombart, amongst others, drew attention to the exceptional status of Berlin by employing two strategies. The first was to accentuate the features of modernity – notably, size and quantity and the rapidity of socio-economic transformation – that he had already identified as having a significant effect upon modern culture, and to transpose them upon another symbolic representation – America – that, in turn, was identified with Berlin. Berlin becomes America. And although this thesis cannot be developed further here, America becomes Berlin or at least (north) German, not so much in Sombart's discourse but in that of his contemporaries such as Lamprecht and others. The second strategy, which seeks to highlight the specificity of Berlin, is to draw a contrast between Berlin (as America) and Vienna (as Europe), a juxtaposition that coincides ideologically with the much broader distinction between civilization (Berlin) and culture (Vienna). For its part, this polarity between Berlin and Vienna is of considerable importance in the battles over modernity in Vienna in the same period. There, the renewed polarities of 'New Vienna' and 'Old Vienna' from 1890 onwards can be seen as codifications of civilization and culture, and, in some respects, as Berlin and Vienna. Furthermore, it is not difficult to perceive in this codification another binary opposition between 'low' and 'high' culture that is present more generally in the symbolic discourse on 'America' and 'Europe', 'Berlin' and 'Vienna'.

The thesis as to the exceptionalism of Berlin, which Sombart advances and which is summarized in the statement that Berlin is America, is itself not an exceptional thesis and peculiar to Sombart. Americanism as a discourse about features of modern urban capitalism had commenced well before Sombart's intervention; it was shared and developed in both similar and different ways by several of his contemporaries; and it was continued in a different and more widely based form in Weimar Germany.[69] In the post-First World War period – and especially after the introduction of the Dawes Plan (1924), which ushered in an economic period of 'relative stabilization' until the economic collapse of 1929 – the *level* and *nature* of American investment in the German economy was much in evidence. But, in large part, the continued discourse on Americanism – as in its earlier forms before the war – was often still about cultural values rather than actual economic transformation. Similarly, Sombart, whom many contemporaries viewed as one of the most astute analysts of the German *economy*, chose to transpose his critique of *capitalism* into a critique of *culture* and a critique of *technology*.[70]

All this should force us to question the status of an exceptionalism thesis in relation to Berlin in the pre-First World War period. Unlike the exceptionalism thesis formulated by Sombart in relation to the putative absence of socialism in the United States, which offers the possibility of empirical verification or refutation (and Sombart employed a multi-causal analysis in order to verify his hypothesis), the perceived exceptionalism of Berlin as a city (and above all its Americanism) is a statement of a different order. As has been argued earlier, it is the representation of the modern metropolis as signifier of (the negative features of) modernity that was at issue. America does not figure in this discourse as substantive entity but rather as metaphor. Unlike some of the subsequent discourse in the Weimar Republic – which could at least refer to the level and significance of US investment and the introduction of 'new' modes of organizing the production process (though aspects of the 'rationalization' of production, associated with America, had already been introduced on a significant scale at least during war production, if not much earlier in the case of AEG and Siemens) – there was no recourse to empirical data in connection with the Berlin exceptionalism thesis, beyond its size and rate of growth. Of course, there existed another literature on the comparative features of German cities that emanated from a well-developed tradition of social statistics and social reform. There was also a specific comparison – which could draw upon empirical material – of Berlin with Vienna. But neither of these substantive modes of comparison was relevant to Sombart's concerns.

5

The City Designed

Otto Wagner and Vienna

Our language can be seen as an ancient city: a maze of little streets and squares, of old and new houses, and of houses with additions from various periods; and this surrounded by a multitude of new boroughs with straight regular streets and uniform houses.

Ludwig Wittgenstein, *Philosophical Investigations*

The place of this dream lay on one of the major traffic arteries that radiate out from the centre of Vienna. Even though from that time on, when world metropolises full of enormous rushing around came into being, Vienna was still only a big city, traffic in the peak hours filled this tube of streets with a dizzying stream of life, which can be best compared with swill being poured into a trough.

Robert Musil, *The Man Without Qualities*

The most modern of that which is modern in architecture are indeed our present day metropolitan cities.

Otto Wagner, *Modern Architecture*

I

Although the distinction drawn between Vienna and Berlin at the turn of the century can be seen in many of its representations or imaginaries as one *between* culture and civilization, Europe and America, tradition and modernity, the old and the new in two capital cities of extensive land empires, the ostensible struggle between such cultural representations and valorizations could also be fought out *within* a single metropolis. This was nowhere so apparent in Europe as in Vienna, in a city not merely conceived, as Olsen puts it, and as many contemporaries viewed it, *as* a work of art, but also a city in which both theoretical reflection *upon* the city as aesthetic entity was well developed by the last decade of the nineteenth century, and where the conflict between the old and the new became so intense in the period up to 1914. Yet both those who resisted the creation of a modern metropolis and those who propagated a modern city claimed that they were defending, in their different modes, the city as a work of art. Clearly the conceptions of the city as a work of art were different, perhaps even radically different as their respective proponents proclaimed. But, ultimately, it will be argued here that we can more fully understand the *resistance* to modernity by examining the modes of valorization of Old and New Vienna and what was at issue in such valorizations.

If it can be argued that modernity is experience of the tension and contradictions in modern social formations – that is, for example, between the desire to give to the modern world new modes of *ordering* and *regulating* it and the recognition of the *disintegration* of the basic categories through which we interpret and experience that world (such as time, space and causality replaced by the transitory, the fortuitous and the arbitrary); between totalization and fragmentation; between the emergence of the masses and the crisis of individual identity; between the ancient and the eternally new, etc. – then these same tensions and contradictions will be apparent in all dimensions of modern experience, including our experience of the social spaces and built environment of modernity.

It may be argued, further, that discourses on modernity and their aesthetic representations in modernisms will be that much more apparent (and possibly fruitful) where such tensions and contradictions are in evidence. The intensity of the opposition between what is old and what is new is contingent upon the existence and resilience of what is old, just as much as it is upon the emergence of the 'absolutely' new. In his unorthodox historical analysis of the 'origins' of modernity, Benjamin commenced from an excavation of 'Paris, the Capital of the Nineteenth Century', an exploration of the contradictions between the old and the new that were captured in such dialectical images as the ever-new and the ever-same (the commodity form) and the city as antiquity and the masses as modernity (the modern metropolis). The site Benjamin chose for his excavations was Paris in the mid-nineteenth century and not the ostensibly more 'modern' cities of London or, by the end of the century, Berlin. Amongst his reasons for this choice was the distinctive juxtaposition in Paris between tradition and revolution that was not to be found in either London or Berlin. In terms of the transformation of the social and built space of Paris, Benjamin focused especially upon the arcades, the grand boulevards and, replacing the arcades, the grand magasins. This transformation, in turn, transforming as it did vast, old sections of the city and creating new street configurations and interiors, committed Benjamin to investigating the complexities of Haussmannization – the most significant attempt after mid-century to establish a new regulation and order of the city, one that sought to cut through the heart of the city.[1]

The juxtaposition between the old and the new physiognomies of the city in the nineteenth century and the modes of their confrontation and transformation took different forms. Haussmann's attempt to create a north–south and east–west axis in Paris was not completely successful, although he did create extensive cuttings through the city with the linear grand boulevards. A different process of creating a new metropolitan physiognomy, faced with quite other problems, emerged in Vienna. There, the initial barrier to developing a modern metropolis was the medieval – and subsequent – fortifications around the inner city, which cut it off from its suburbs. Such a system of fortifications around the old city was still a feature of many cities and towns in Germany and Central Europe at mid-century. The solution chosen initially was to leave the inner city largely intact (Old Vienna), demolish the fortifications, and construct a ring road and ring-road zone (the first New Vienna) around the inner city which would fill the gap between it and existing suburbs. The construction of a Ringstrasse and the surrounding zone became a model for many cities in Germany (such as Cologne and Frankfurt) and Central Europe (such as Budapest or Brno). Such a Ringstrasse in Vienna commenced with imperial agreement on demolition in 1857 and, with significant exceptions, was largely complete by 1890.[2] In that year a substantial enlargement of Vienna's boundaries was agreed and, with the accompanying building regulations and, later, agreement on a new city rail infrastructure (the Stadtbahn), Vienna experienced what some contemporaries described as a 'new Renaissance' – the creation of a second 'New Vienna' succeeding the Ringstrasse zone development. This second drive to modernity and the elevation of the city from a metropolis to a world city required the construction of new social spaces, new built structures and a new conception of the metropolis.

II

Although Ludwig Wittgenstein made his own contribution to a third 'New Vienna' in the post-1918 period with the design, in 1927, of a modern house together with Paul Engelmann, a student of Adolf Loos (whose own building on the Michaelplatz overlooking the imperial palace entrance was one of the few modernist interventions into the inner core of the First District of Vienna), it is not clear that reflection upon this activity was often directly manifested in his early philosophy.[3] Of course, the *Tractatus* (1918) is concerned with a rigorous clarification and cleansing of philosophical discourse from an ostensibly positivistic standpoint, regulating that of which philosophy should concern itself or speak. Nonetheless, as Paul Wijdeveld has shown, these are indeed reflections upon architecture scattered throughout his work.[4] But there are seldom any reflections upon the *modern metropolis* within which his modernist house was to be located. However, early in the first part of his later *Philosophical Investigations* (which, like the earlier *Brown Book*, contains extensive references to building with slabs, columns, bricks, etc.) completed by 1945 in Cambridge, Wittgenstein introduces an analogy between language and a city. The context is whether or not a language is complete:

> ask yourself whether our language is complete; – whether it was so before the symbolism of chemistry and the notation of the infinitesimal calculus were incorporated into it; for these are, so to speak, suburbs of our language. (And how many houses or streets does it take before a town begins to be a town?) Our language can be seen as an ancient city: a maze of little streets and squares, of old and new houses, and of houses with additions from various periods; and this surrounded by a multitude of new boroughs with straight regular streets and uniform houses.[5]

This analogy provides a starting point for a study of Wittgenstein's philosophy by Robert John Ackermann titled *Wittgenstein's City*.[6] Although our concern is neither with Wittgenstein's philosophy as such, nor with the plausibility of Ackermann's interpretation of it, Ackermann does nonetheless provide a number of apposite reflections that are relevant to interpreting the city.

First, that the city is *segmented* in ways that were not apparent to Wittgenstein in the *Tractatus* when and where it was viewed as a 'severely regular Levittown . . . in which the total plan could be easily grasped' – though only within a single borough of language. However, although recognizing that:

> Every language game has roots in everyday life and everyday understanding . . . [t]he different areas of the City need not be isolated; they can overlap, and clearly words may have layers of use traceable to different origins in time and related to different horizons. But then some areas of the City can have sharp boundaries, especially when they correspond to the horizons of clear language games.[7]

In passing, such segmentation and boundary construction was already explored in a different context – that of the modern metropolis itself – by Simmel.

Second, this city is *surveyed* by philosophy, whose task is 'the process of surveying the City, constructing its map, using the fixed spaces of logic and grammar as the reference points for the survey'.[8] The various language games are surveyed in such a manner that 'their grammars lay out the space of possible clear assertion'.[9] Third, the role of philosophers is to provide *order* and *cleanliness* in the city. Ackermann claims that 'Wittgenstein's philosophers function as a sanitation corps within the City. They speak the local language while they sweep up and dispose of the trash, leaving the City clean and orderly. Philosophy is . . . the *activity* of putting the City in order'.[10]

Viewed from a critical distance, Ackermann highlights two further features of Wittgenstein's philosophy that are relevant to our concerns. First, that this City is *not historical*:

> Wittgenstein's City is static. The comparative age of some language games or their relative distance from behavioural roots may be noticed, but Wittgenstein does not talk historically. . . . No shift in ordinary usage as a language game, relative to practice, is ever observed.[11]

In this sense, *alternative* language games, alternative orders can only exist for him in our language. Second, if we give a historical location to Wittgenstein's own early philosophy, then it is *Vienna at the turn of the century*, a city within which many of the intellectuals had a highly critical conception of existing language games as 'exhausted or useless'. The response to this situation, Ackermann maintains, is *either to seek a new language* (or, in Wittgenstein's terms, a new language game emerging out of a new form of life) *or to overhaul the existing language*. This second path views

> the exhaustion of languages as due to an overlay of useless ornamentation that has gradually come to conceal its essentially sound basic structures. This way is Wittgenstein's. Ornamentation is to be removed and taken to the junkyard, revealing the true and beautiful basic structure. This drive for simplicity and clarity expressed itself in his life, in his architecture, and in his philosophy. Wittgenstein is a sort of archaeologist, stripping away the verbal ornaments of philosophy until layers of language are exposed whose connection with life gives them a solid meaning grounded in common human behaviour.[12]

Although Ackermann's concern is with Wittgenstein's philosophy, the features outlined here are waiting to be made relevant to aspects of the

city and architecture of Vienna. And so, too, is Wittgenstein's own statement from which we set out earlier.

Wittgenstein's analogy of language and a city seems to contain a number
of issues by means of which we can explore the analogy with Vienna. At
first glance, however, his reference to an 'ancient' city seems to contradict
this. Ancient cities that were a 'maze' would have included Mycenae, but
such ancient cities were not surrounded by new boroughs. Conversely,
the centre of Roman cities was not constructed as a maze but rather was
layed out in the manner which Wittgenstein ascribes to the 'new boroughs'
that lay beyond the centre. It is, however, the medieval city whose centre
is a maze. Indeed, although Wittgenstein's philosophy (and his philosophy as City) is not historical, this description of a city *is* historical.
It could be read as a description of Vienna in the last decades of the
nineteenth century and the early decades of the twentieth.

Read in this way, it pertains to a metropolis with an old inner centre
that has also developed over time 'with additions from various periods'.
It pertains also to a city some of whose new boroughs have been set out
in a regular and uniform manner. The inner city of Vienna accords with
Wittgenstein's description of 'an ancient city', whilst some of the new
boroughs – especial Favoriten, a district developed largely for a working-
class population – were set out in a grid system whose streets were 'regular' and whose rented apartment blocks were 'uniform'. A new borough
'with straight regular streets and uniform houses' was also designed – but
never realized – by Otto Wagner for the 22nd district of Vienna in his
1911 essay on the metropolis.[13]

The question as to when streets and houses become a town, when the
quantitative expansion of streets and houses is transposed into a qualitatively new entity – a town – can also be applied to the context of Vienna's
second extension in 1890, and to subsequent claims that this signified the
city's elevation from a city into a world metropolis. The substantiation of
this transition to a world city was made by contemporaries in a number
of ways. First, the physical extension of the city's boundaries in 1890 and
the later incorporation of other districts expanded the *size* of the city in
terms of *spatial expansion*. Yet the extension of the city boundaries in
1890 resulted in a built-up area that, even by 1902, was only slightly
larger than the area taken up by gardens and public places and forests.[14]
Nonetheless, as Petermann argued, 'the bringing together of a large number
of diversely developed city districts, composed of socially and indeed, in
part, nationally diverse populations, an agglomeration, as it were, of many
smaller towns, but with this agglomeration structurally united through a
unified city administration and a modern comprehensive transport system
– herein lies one facet of the character of a world city'.[15] Second, the increase
in population associated with the extension of the city boundaries and

its indigenous growth took the total population from over 0.8 million in 1880 to 1.36 million in 1890.[16] A feature of Vienna at the turn of the century, and one indicative of its dynamic attraction as a population centre, was that in 1900 those born out of Vienna exceeded those born within it, and that the largest age cohort was the 21–30 age group followed by the 0–10 age group. There were also significant differences in population density within the city in 1900, with the highest density in the Leopoldstadt, Ottakring, Landstrasse and Favoriten districts and the fifth lowest density in the first, inner-city district.[17] Third, the decentralization of the metropolis in terms of public buildings, schools, etc. in each district was accompanied by the availability of metropolitan facilities to all areas of the city. Again, as Petermann argued:

> In this way, centres of district life were formed, as it were, in which the inhabitants of the district can deport themselves as in small towns, whereas, on the other hand, the attractions of the whole of Vienna are readily available – a third characteristic element of the world city which determines the fact that, aside from the differences in income, the most diverse forms of life can develop alongside one another. Alongside people who participate in everything and are always in circulation, others live enclosed in close circles 'as in the country' without, however, being able to become genuine 'district dwellers', because the daily transport and the newspaper make it impossible not to take notice of the continuous transformations in the bustle of the world city.[18]

This third facet was strengthened by the filling in of the spaces between the inner and outer suburbs (in Vienna with four-storey rented apartment blocks) and with the extension of the municipal transport system (largely through the extension of the tramway network, but also through the completion between 1894 and 1900 of the city railway which did not function merely as a circular system *around* the city).

Compared with metropolitan centres such as Paris and Berlin – and these tended to be the most frequent comparisons made – Vienna possessed a much greater segmentation of language games and forms of life within its boundaries. The 'suburbs of . . . language' actually comprised different languages and forms of life based upon the migration of diverse nationalities from the Austro–Hungarian Empire. If we add this ethnic and linguistic diversity to the segmentation of social class groupings and, in turn, the gendered access to the public sphere, then Vienna reveals itself to be a much more *heterogeneous* metropolis than either Paris or Berlin.[19] However, like other modern metropolitan centres, there were many forces at work pushing in the direction of *homogeneity*.

If we return to the third facet of the world city identified by Petermann – the incorporation of previously outer districts into access to the facilities of the metropolis – then this was brought about, in part, by changes in the material circumstances of circulation and communication. The 1890s saw the electrification of the tramways, the completion of the city railway (designed by Wagner), the extension of the telephone network, the first automobile exhibition (May 1899), the introduction of automats (for chocolate and cigars) and the automat buffet – all developments highlighted by Petermann.[20] The acceleration in the sphere of circulation certainly contributed to the intensification of connections between parts of the city. But in terms of overall growth of the metropolis, Vienna could not compare with the city with which it most often considered itself in competition – Berlin. Whereas the older metropolitan centres grew more slowly in the period 1860–1900 in terms of population increase, for example, with Paris at 77 per cent and London at 135 per cent, Vienna's more substantial growth of 259 per cent did not compare with Berlin's 410 per cent increase.[21] Although this comparison does not take into account the different original base lines in 1860, such statistics abound in the comparisons of Vienna with Berlin around the turn of the century. There it is Berlin that is viewed as a modern city and Vienna as the city that is more notable for its old city beauty. It is Berlin that is often announced as merely modern, whereas Vienna contains both the old and the new. In Wittgenstein's analogy, it is the 'maze' of the inner city that is beautiful and the outer districts that are modern and unattractive. This inner–outer dialectic is absent in Berlin, which lacks the dramatic disjunction between the centre and the suburbs that is provided by the Ringstrasse zone. As we shall see, this inner–outer dichotomy recurs in the challenges to modernity in Vienna.

The controversy surrounding metropolitan and architectural modernity in Vienna in the late nineteenth century (and later) is focused upon the inner city, the Ringstrasse zone and the possibility of a new Vienna that would transform these two sectors and the surrounding districts.[22] Certainly some modern architects (notably Wagner) were intent upon giving Vienna a *new* order, a new physiognomy and, like Wittgenstein's philosophy, aimed for order and cleanliness. Where the programme of the early propagators of a modern architecture for a modern metropolis in Vienna differed from Wittgenstein's was in the relationship to *history*. Ackermann maintains that Wittgenstein's philosophy, unlike the ancient city and its maze, is not historical. It is, however, rigorously *modern*, devoted to linguistic communication in a modern (logical, useful, meaningful) manner. The removal of ornament (meaningless symbols, metaphysics) is intended to contribute to the creation (in the *Tractatus* at least) of a sign language that is governed by 'logical grammar'. As Wittgenstein declares – echoing Adolf Loos earlier – 'if a sign is useless, it is meaningless'.[23] And in his notebooks prior to completing the *Tractatus*, he declares:

'What is history to me? Mine is the first and only world' – a solipsistic declaration that has affinities both with Hermann Bahr's early statement (1889), seeking to clarify the nature of modernity, that 'I am modern . . . this means that I hate everything that already exists',[24] and with contemporary and subsequent modernist manifestos. But what was the relationship between the historical and the modern in the discourses and controversies surrounding the Viennese metropolis and its architecture in the late nineteenth century and at the turn of the century?

III

Wittgenstein's analogy of language and the city describes the latter as comprising an ancient core surrounded by new, straight and uniform districts. With the construction of the Ringstrasse zone and subsequent extensions to the city this also describes, in some respects at least, Vienna around the turn of the century. But what were the parameters within which the confrontation between the old and the new, the historical and the modern was fought out? Was this inside/outside frame the one that shaped the conflicts over modernity in Vienna?[25] In some respects, the conception of a historical (and beautiful) core surrounded by expanding modern (and ugly) extensions is not confined to Vienna. In the same period we find Simmel, for instance, indicating a similar inner/outer divide in his essay on Rome (1898), which is almost entirely concerned with the aesthetic attraction of its historical core and not with its modern expanding suburbs 'that are of uninterrupted modernity and equally uninterrupted ugliness'.[26]

Yet in order to give a comparative focus to what is at issue in the conflict over metropolitan and architectural modernity in Vienna, we should return briefly to the comparison many contemporaries made between Vienna and one other modern city in particular – namely, Berlin. It is Vienna that is embedded in a historical culture; it is Berlin that is viewed – positively or negatively – as the quintessence of metropolitan modernity. In his anonymous essay 'Die schönste Stadt der Welt' ('The Most Beautiful City in the World', 1899), Walter Rathenau laments the aesthetic unattractiveness of Berlin, 'the city of parvenus, the parvenu of cities' and calls for its aesthetic transformation into a capital that can compare with the likes of Paris and London.[27]

But as we have seen, whereas Rathenau made no reference to Vienna, Sombart explored the differences between the imaginaries of Vienna and Berlin. Sombart sought out what was distinctive about the city in comparison with Berlin, and found it in culture – 'artistic culture'.[28] This artistic culture was embodied in the city's architecture, its parks, its music – in short, in 'old Vienna as city'.[29] His sentimental portrait of Vienna was that of old Vienna, the historically embedded, culturally rich, still human city, and its contrast was with Berlin, 'a modern creation', 'a suburb of New York' that is itself a desert. A huge cultural cemetery.'[30] Whereas the superficialities of modernity predominate in Berlin, in Vienna the old cultural roots (*Kulturboden*) remains intact'.[31] This ensures that we can

> orientate ourselves by Vienna and Vienna style when we wish to know what culture is. We give ourselves strength again through Vienna when we are filled with disgust at modern human development.[32]

And insofar as Vienna is developing, Sombart fears that contemporary Vienna is already following 'the devastating current of modern false culture (*Afterkultur*)'.[33]

What implications can be drawn from Sombart's comparison of these two metropoles? There is an identification of Berlin with traffic, speed, expansion of population, facilities, amusements, in short, with the *quantitative* expansion of a *false*, *modern* culture. Vienna, by contrast, symbolizes the 'regulative cultural idea'. It is the site of a genuine culture that is embedded in the past, a city of winding streets, old palaces, alleyways, etc. Vienna is the site of (high) artistic culture; Berlin that of (low) material modern culture. Vienna's culture is embedded in 'old cultural roots', in tradition, Berlin's in the modern search for order and material achievement.

For those who sought to foster modernity in Vienna, however, Sombart's assessment of the two cities could be reversed in important respects. The Viennese critic Egon Friedell, for instance, writing on aspects of the modernist movement in Vienna in *Ecce Poeta* (1912) could draw a quite different contrast between the two metropoles. There, Friedell attacks the association of Vienna with 'old culture' and the notion that 'our modern world forms a kind of enclave of that sunken beauty of life that so many people long to return to'.[34] The beauty of earlier periods can be beautiful even today but, Friedell argues:

> it can never be a factor in our modern life. It is nothing more than a waste of time when one dreams of the historical phantoms such as 'Athens', 'Florence' or 'Weimar'. These cultures were indeed great precisely because they emerged out of the most immediate presentness of their day. Today they are dead and belong, at best, in a museum. There is only a single culture that we have to deal with: that of 1910. Everything else is self-deception. We may only ask: do we already have a culture today that corresponds to our times, a culture that does not stand in contradiction to the automobile, the torpedo boat, arc lamps and the underground railway?[35]

And, as if in response to Sombart's anti-Americanism, Friedell associates the defence of 'old culture' – 'funeral attire that is not tailored for us' – with 'the eternal lamentations concerning the Americanization of Europe'. Although it is true that 'Americanism is the crisis of modern culture, just as naturalism was the crisis of modern art', this crisis must be overcome only by going beyond Americanism but on the basis of Americanism. Indeed, 'we must first become Americans and then we can again think about being "good Europeans" '.[36]

And this is the context in which Friedell expands on his image of Berlin, the metropolis which

> has so accurately grasped its task as the capital city of the German Empire: the task of being a centre of modern civilization. Berlin is a wonderful modern machine hall, a giant electric motor that, with unbelievable precision, speed and energy completes a wealth of complex, mechanical work achievements.[37]

This positive image of the Berlin metropolis, emphasizing precisely the splendour of the machine age's technical achievements that appear in Futurist manifestos but which Sombart viewed as instances of Americanism, is contrasted once more with Vienna:

> One takes a stroll through the city and observes the monuments that have been erected in recent times, one views the furniture on which the Viennese sit, the new houses in which they live, the restaurants and cafes that they frequent and one must confess that the tastelessness (probably unavoidable in a modern metropolis) in Vienna is pursued just that much poorer and on a smaller scale than in Berlin.[38]

Instead of theatres there are show-booths for the Viennese in which is displayed 'the actor as fire-eater, as muddler, as *falsifier of life*: this is his ideal, his instinct, for the ungenuine lures the Viennese into the theatre'. For Friedell, therefore, it is the ungenuine Viennese culture that is 'false'; for Sombart it is the new modern Berlin (and New York) culture that is 'false'. As we shall see, both versions of falsity emerge in the debates on modern architecture in Vienna.

A later perspective on the comparison of Vienna with Berlin is provided by the art critic and historian Hans Tietze (who also wrote a short but incisive monograph on Otto Wagner)[39] in his history of Vienna (1931) which allows us to turn to the substantive urban and architectural context of Wagner's Vienna. Tietze maintains that Vienna, unlike Berlin, creates the impression of a 'natural city', embedded in the past. The contrast is with Berlin, which

is instinctively drawn to what is new, desirous of change, always prepared
to go along with the new, whereas Vienna's immediate feeling is to remain
with the old and then to abide with the old; Berlin's danger is snobbism,
that of Vienna, philistinism. Even as metropolis (*Grossstadt*), Vienna remains what it had been as a small city (*Kleinstadt*).

The metropolis as small city means having a stronger bonded essence
with what has been naturally given. For in the essence of the metropolitan
trait lies a propensity for the abstract, which robs concrete preconditions
of their value; the metropolis as theoretical formation has something of
an end in itself (*Selbstzweckliches*) and something autocratic about it; it
creates its terrain according to its needs and, with its large-scale activity,
stamps the human beings that live in it with a common physiognomy. . . .
If this is the essence of the metropolis . . . then its contrast with Vienna is
evident; for, more than any other city of a similar size, the latter remains
naturally coalesced (*Naturverwachsen*) and historically conditioned.[40]

This embeddedness in the past in Vienna is manifested in the built
image of the city. As Tietze states it, 'the past becomes the immediately
experienced present in the image of the city'. This is especially true of the
inner city (Wittgenstein's maze), since the maze of built-up, rebuilt and
built-upon structures created a unity that remained undisturbed by modern plans to cut through its complex configuration. Its historical structures resulted in 'the absence of a clear network of radial thoroughfares. . . .
This absence of ready accessibility in the street networks contributes to
the preservation of the unified old town character of the inner city'.[41] This
apparent isolation of the inner city was reinforced by the construction of
Vienna's *via triumphalis* – the Ringstrasse. The visual and physical effect
of sections of this boulevard rests upon the green open spaces, 'a ring that
remains devoted more to *separation* than to *connection*'.[42] In this respect,
in terms of Simmel's distinction in 'Bridge and Door', the Ringstrasse functions as a 'door' to the 'maze' of the inner city. If the Ringstrasse demarcates the inner city quite markedly, and serves central traffic, then the
Gürtel (the outer ring road) serves more peripheral and increasingly heavier
traffic. Military and security considerations kept both traffic circuits away
from the centre of the city so that the one is 'a ring around the city',
whilst the other, in the form of Wagner's city railway around the Gürtel,
is 'a railway around the city'.[43]

This distinctive physiognomy of the Vienna metropolis in comparison
with Berlin possesses other features worth mentioning. Within the 'maze'
of the old city and the 'uniform' new suburbs there existed significant
differences in composition and layout. The *size of built structures* differed
in Vienna from both Berlin and Paris in that the average ground surface
of buildings in the latter was only two-thirds that of Vienna. The tendency
to build more comprehensive structures extended in Vienna to public

buildings (Petermann cites the example of the general hospital – the Allgemeine Krankenhaus – which in Vienna housed one-and-a-half times more patients than its equivalent in Berlin – the Charité).[44] The height of the buildings was also regulated after acceptance of the 1893 building-zone plan, with the old nine city districts able to erect 4–5-storey buildings, the outer 12th to 18th districts 3-storey buildings and districts outside the city 2-storey buildings.

The *turnover* of building stock was also high in Vienna at the turn of the century. According to Petermann, in Vienna, every year between 1899 and 1903, on average 235 buildings were demolished and 661 new ones erected. Of the total building stock in 1900, only 31.6 per cent originated from the period prior to 1861 (and a significant proportion of this older stock would be in the inner-city zone). Somewhat surprisingly, Petermann maintains that in the year 1902 Vienna had the greatest percentage (3.08 per cent) of new and rebuilt building stock compared with Berlin (2.17 per cent) and Paris (1.76 per cent).[45]

The *nature and cost of the street network* varied significantly in Vienna, compared with Berlin and Paris, as a result of both the greater extent of terrain covered in Vienna and the uneven nature of its terrain. Whereas in Paris a fifth of total street surfaces were paved with wooden cobbles and two-thirds of pavements and adjoining streets were covered with asphalt, and in Berlin a quarter of all regularly cleaned streets were covered in asphalt, in Vienna only 4 per cent of the street surface was covered with a noise-free surfacing.[46] The heavier usage made of Parisian streets with their café tables, kiosks, street barrows and the like as well as greater traffic enabled more revenue to be raised in local taxes than in Vienna. Hence, as Petermann pointed out:

> In 1903 in Vienna expenditure on streets compared to revenue was greater even than in Berlin, which is justifiably proud of its outstanding streets. In Vienna, street maintenance extends over twice as much communal area as in Berlin and Paris. There are still many more streets to be constructed or to be transformed from untreated streets into surfaced streets, the terrain is much more uneven and the main factor is as follows: whereas almost the whole of Berlin is a new city and Paris has already almost completed its regulation, the latter is still in full swing in Vienna and the slogan 'ground payment for street regulation' requires, even in absolute terms, much higher contributions than in the metropoles on the Seine or on the Spree.[47]

Hence, Vienna at the turn of the century was still perceived as a city undergoing major transformation of its basic street physiognomy. Its newness was also open to contestation.

With respect to *traffic* in the Vienna metropolis, the utilization of forms of local transport by its population lagged behind that of other major

European cities, with an average of 190 annual journeys per inhabitant in Vienna, compared with 232 in Paris, 307 in London and 334 in Berlin.[48] Since its official (imperial) opening in 1898, Vienna possessed a city railway that was distinguished from city railway systems in London, Berlin and Paris by the extreme disparities in the level of the terrain which it covered. It was a city railway devoted largely to personal rather than goods' circulation. Another increasingly significant dimension of metropolitan traffic was the expansion of tourist traffic. Indicative of this growth was the increase in hotel guests in Vienna, from 181,088 in 1882 to 363,691 in 1897 and 443,713 in 1903. Thus, according to Petermann, with the exception of Paris and Berlin, no other major city on the Continent experienced such an increase in tourist traffic.[49] As Wagner, amongst others, continued to point out, this expansion required a corresponding increase in the stock of hotel accommodation in the city.[50]

In more general terms, the *economy* of the city also had distinctive traits that affected its physiognomy. As a financial centre, Vienna lay far behind London, Paris and Berlin. However, although Vienna looked less like an industrial city, having less chimneys, in the period after the turn of the century it was, after Berlin, one of the most industrialized metropoles in Europe producing mass articles. In this context, it is not surprising that those defending 'Old' Vienna had nothing to say about the industrial physiognomy of the city. But those architects such as Wagner, who prided themselves on supporting designs for 'New' Vienna, appeared hardly interested in the industrial dimensions of the city and the housing for its workers. It was, however, Wagner students such as Hubert Gessner (and his brother Franz) who designed factory buildings and an *Arbeiterheim* in the overwhelmingly working-class district of Favoriten, which possessed the most extensive street grid system in Vienna.[51] Within Wagner's architecture classes from 1894 to 1911 such concerns were the exception rather than the rule.

Wittgenstein's description of his metaphorical city includes the uniform and regular new suburbs. In Vienna, as in many other metropolitan areas, these consisted often of working-class districts with relatively high-density housing. The largest occupational grouping was that of those producing mass articles for use. Mass housing complemented this occupational concentration. An expanding occupational grouping at the turn of the century – but one that lay far behind Paris, London and Berlin – was associated with the development of department stores. Given the tendency to organize the sale of commodities in small shopping enterprises, the number of department stores (*Warenhäuser*) devoted *exclusively* to a single trading enterprise remained small and concentrated in the Mariahilfestrasse and the Kärtnerstrasse zone. Significantly, the most prestigious street in Vienna – the Ringstrasse – had (and today still has) no department stores. More typical of Vienna was the mixed building type – the *Wohn-und Geschäftshaus* – with a mixture of shopping, commerce and dwelling functions.[52] In this context, it is not insignificant that Wagner's students in the first year of study should have been required to design the apartment block and the apartment and commercial block. Only in 1902 did he set the task of designing department stores – a somewhat delayed response from someone who was intent upon producing a 'modern' metropolitan architecture and who himself had already designed and built stores in the 1890s. The exclusion of the department store from the Ringstrasse already indicated that attention was being given to the siting of particular building types. The expansion of the city in the decade after the extension of the city boundaries required more attention to its regulated growth. In keeping with this development, city planning (*Städtebau*) was added to the subjects taught at the Technical University in 1900 (and its first chair holder was Karl Mayreder).[53]

IV

Even before 1900, issues surrounding city planning and the attempts to introduce a modern architecture into the city's physiognomy had already become problematical and highly contested. In some respects at least, this process of contestation was effected by the impact of Otto Wagner upon architectural discourse in Vienna in the 1890s.

Wittgenstein's description of his city does not include its aesthetic dimension – whether it is a beautiful city, or not. But elsewhere, in his 1916 notes, he writes that:

> The artistic miracle is that the world exists. That what exists, exists.
> Is it the essence of the artistic point of view that it contemplates the world with a happy eye?
> For there is something to the opinion that the beautiful is the purpose of art.
> And the beautiful is just that what makes one happy.[54]

This connection between the beautiful and happiness, between the aesthetic and the ethical was not new, and not new in Vienna. In his provocative work on city planning, the Viennese architect and critic Camillo Sitte had already proclaimed in 1889 that the purpose of creating an aesthetically attractive city was, following Aristotle, in order to facilitate happiness.[55] Aristotle's aim of city planning, cited by Sitte, was 'to make its people at once secure and happy' and to create 'something of value and beauty'.

Sitte's aim in writing a treatise on city planning 'according to its artistic principles' was not devoid of nostalgia. The aesthetic dimension of city planning, as opposed to its purely technical dimension in 'our mathematical century', was Sitte's primary concern. The most cited exemplars of aesthetically successfully constructed squares and streets in Sitte's text are, after Vienna, drawn from Italian Renaissance and baroque cities (and especially those in Florence and Rome). Sitte writes that we must recall memories of the past to guide our planning in the present day. When we travel to Italy, in particular, the vistas of its town perspectives, squares and monuments 'all parade before our musing eye, and we savour again *the delights of those sublime and graceful things in whose presence we were once so happy*'.[56] This nostalgic opening to Sitte's treatise is complemented by a theme to which he returns towards the end of his text when he declares that:

> the impression we receive upon returning home from Venice or Florence –
> *how painfully this shallow modernity strikes us here.* This may be why the
> fortunate inhabitants of those marvellously artistic cities have no need to
> leave them, while we every year for a few weeks must *get away into nature*
> *in order to be able to endure the city for another year.*[57]

Sitte's city is Vienna, containing both felicitous arrangements within Wittgenstein's 'maze' of the inner city, and some within the new Ringstrasse zone, but also the 'shallow modernity' of its expanding modern suburbs.

Sitte's attacks upon a 'shallow modernity' were continued in two discourses. The one was continued indirectly in the 1890s by one of Sitte's German followers, Karl Henrici, against the putative obsession by Joseph Stübben (city planner and critic, author of *Der Städtebau* (1890) and joint winner with Otto Wagner of the 1893/4 competition for the General Development Plan of Vienna) with 'straight streets', traffic and hygiene.[58] This debate's general thematic focus was 'straight or crooked streets', the new versus the old, the functional versus the aesthetic city planning. This debate was conducted in one of the leading German architecture journals, the *Deutsche Bauzeitung*.[59]

Much more direct were Sitte's own more extensive confrontations with the 'shallow modernity' of the 'New' Vienna (post-1890 extension) in the populist forum of one of its newspapers, the *Neues Wiener Tagblatt*. In 1891 Sitte criticized 'the straight regular streets and uniform houses' of the new districts as 'prosaic and mentally deadening'.[60] Responding to the General Development Plan competition in 1894 and the success of Otto Wagner and Joseph Stübben, Sitte lamented 'the lack of concern for Old Vienna . . . for the world famous Viennese cosiness (*Gemütlichkeit*)' in their successful plans, as well as the absence of any principles in

Stübben's work and Wagner's 'illusory city plan fantasies' and the tendency to be 'a fanatic of the straight line'.[61]

The critique of a 'bad' modernity in Sitte's polemical writings is associated with a denial of the aesthetic attraction of many of its products and a desire to preserve what is valuable in 'Old' Vienna (largely in the inner city). Whilst those sympathetic to Sitte's position could consult the *Neues Wiener Tagblatt*, the supporters of modernity and 'New Vienna' could find support in the *Fremden Blatt*'s reviews and articles, including articles on 'Old Vienna – New Vienna', from around 1894 onwards by the critic Ludwig Hevesi (until his suicide in 1910), a consistent defender and supporter of the work of Otto Wagner.[62] What was the relationship, then, between Wagner and the 'New Vienna' and how did his conception of modernity – so evident, if not entirely consistent, in his *Moderne Architektur* manifesto of 1896 – confront both 'Old' Vienna and the products of Vienna's 'first Renaissance' (the Ringstrasse and historicism)?

V

Reviewing the Imperial Jubilee Exhibition (1898) in Vienna, Hevesi describes modernity and modernism as being:

> To serve the purpose (*Zweck*), from out of the material, in accordance with the times: here are the three given elements with which the modernist (*der Moderne*), according to the level of his talents, operates. There is no recipe.[63]

This summary of current modernist principles is an abbreviated encapsulation of Otto Wagner's modernist credo, elaborated two years previously in his *Moderne Architektur* (1896).

The focus upon the purpose (*Zweck*) or use (*Nutz*) of a building was already announced in Wagner's earliest known modernist statement, in a brief introduction to a portfolio of his own works and projects in 1889.[64] However, this early statement does not explicitly refer to modernity. And although there is a theoretical call for a new modern style in architecture – a *Nutzstil*, a utility style – it accords very little with Wagner's actual practice as manifested in most of the buildings and projects that are displayed in the volume. Yet it does signal a break with historicism insofar as it rejects the caricature of previous historical styles in architecture, even though Wagner's own declared preference is for 'a certain free Renaissance' style. Furthermore, the commitment to realism (even though Wagner judges the Eiffel Tower and the Ostend Kursaal to be too realist), is a commitment to works of art as 'the mirror image of their times',[65] utilizing 'all our circumstances and modern accomplishments in the use of materials and construction'.[66] Purpose and utility, modern appropriate materials and an architecture that accords with present modern times – these are the features that Hevesi was to ascribe to the modern architect. They are amplified in Wagner's 1896 manifesto.

Wagner's manifesto takes up themes that are already announced in his inaugural lecture of October 1894, when he succeeded Hasenauer to a chair of architecture at the Academy of Fine Arts.[67] Wagner, who had earlier been praised for his decorations and designs (in cooperation with Hans Makart) for the imperial celebration of 1879 and for his Renaissance apartment blocks in the Ringstrasse zone, must have shocked some of his audience at this lecture with his attack on historicism. Wagner denounced the dominant historicist tendency on four grounds. First, that it resulted in racing through all directions of architectural style (neo-Gothic, Renaissance, baroque, old German, etc.). Second, that its effect was to produce a situation in which ostensibly modern constructions sought to be 'exact copies' of earlier styles. Third, that certain styles were given a monopoly with respect to specific building types (in *Moderne Architektur* he gives the example of a recent competition to design a town hall, in which 52 of the 53 submissions favoured either neo-Gothic or old German styles). Fourth, that architectural styles change as rapidly as fashions, but in a context in which artistic productions are rendered deliberately old through their archaic façades and ornamentation.

In turn, Wagner's alternative proposal for a modern architecture was based upon three imperatives. First, that architecture must be 'a mirror image of its times' and hence 'art and artists should and must represent their times'. Second, a modern architecture must commence from 'the needs, the capacities, the means and achievements of *our* times'. Third, a modern architecture must give full expression to 'our conditions of life, our constructions'. Our modern architecture must therefore express 'the realism of our times'.

Such a constellation of imperatives requires a knowledge of the *present times*, its *needs and capacities, its conditions of life* and its *realism*. How this knowledge is to be acquired is hardly dealt with by Wagner. The neglect of this issue has important consequences for Wagner's programme for a modern architecture. His imperatives presuppose a detailed knowledge of modernity. This presupposes, in turn, that the metropolitan modernity to which a modern architecture is to give full expression is *legible* to those who seek knowledge of it.

But before examining Wagner's own reading of metropolitan modernity, we should draw attention to a relevant problem that Wagner himself does address. In his foreword to *Moderne Architektur*, he declares that 'the sole starting point for our artistic creation should be *modern life*'.[68] One important reason for this is that, in Wagner's opinion, the architectural landscape created by most contemporary architects is *not intelligible* (and therefore *not legible*). For the mass of the public, architecture of the present day is not legible. The reasons for this are, first, that 'the language of art [is] unintelligible'. In turn, this is because the architectural environment is expressed either in the language of the *engineer* or it is manifested in the plurality of historical styles (historicism). The second reason for this unintelligibility lies in the fact that 'what is offered is not the *work of our times*'. In other words, modern people, attuned to modern metropolitan existence, cannot read the historicist languages of forms and styles because they do not express their life circumstances. The issue of intelligibility with respect to historicism and engineering thus raises two different problems. The problem of historicism is that it is false and not true to modern life. It envelops architectural reality in *masks*. The problem of engineering is that it is not aesthetically true to modern life and lacks an architecturally modern input to its constructions. Its structures reveal *pure utility*. What is intelligible for Wagner must be neither pure mask not pure utility. He does favour both 'cladding' and usefulness, but in accordance with modern life and modern aesthetics.

Wagner concludes that this lack of intelligibility is the reason for the lack of respect for the architectural profession at the present time. Insofar as contemporary architects continue to work within 'the language of forms' of historicism or the 'applied world of forms' that is derived from the domination of archaeological or art-historical interests, then their language 'in the majority of instances remains totally unintelligible'.

Therefore, the *modern* architect urgently requires a new language of forms that is intelligible, a language that must give full expression to modern life. In short, modern forms must suit modern human beings, whereas at the present 'the language of forms of previous centuries stands in no relationship to modern human beings'. Thus, Wagner is calling for an appropriate modern language of architecture consonant with modern metropolitan needs. In terms of Wittgenstein's image of the city with its inner old core and outer new boroughs, it is Wagner's apparent intention to create a modern language appropriate to the whole city, through the transformation and expansion of the modern metropolis. But as we shall see, those opposed to this new language of modern architecture sought to prevent its penetration into the old inner core of the city. Wagner's rhetoric suggests the creation of a new language (and, in Wittgenstein's sense, a new language game) and not the cleansing and clarification of an existing language (which appeared to be Wittgenstein's later project). In order for it to be intelligible, Wagner sees the 'language game' of modern architecture as necessarily rooted in modern 'forms of life'. What their constituent elements are must be one of Wagner's central tasks if the proposed new language of forms is to be appropriate to, or even a mirror image of, them.

One problem which Wagner faced in getting his projects accepted in Vienna was that the features of metropolitan modernity that are to be found in his writings do not have any specific connection with Vienna. In terms of the contrast drawn earlier between Berlin and Vienna, it is the Berlin metropole that is recognized as modern and Vienna that is praised for its – old, traditional – (high) culture. The attempt to express those features of metropolitan modernity in Wagner's architectural projects was therefore likely to meet with considerable opposition in Vienna.

The very generality of the features of modernity recognized by Wagner presents other problems. Tafuri, for instance, has argued that:

> Wagner's words about the *form of the modern* are utterly ingenuous: the straight line, flat surfaces, functions, materials, metropolitan uniformity constitute items in a piecemeal and unenlightening list from which all significance is excluded and which does not contribute to any synthetic design. . . . It is only the surfaces of the modern that are describable for him.[69]

This theoretical deficit may well be present in Wagner's writings, but it may overlook the extent to which we do indeed experience modernity *as surface*. More focused upon the Viennese context are Friedrich Achleitner's comments upon Wagner's characterization of modernity. He maintains that, for Wagner:

> Under *modern life* everything became subsumed that could be applied in the realm of technical innovation, scientific progress but also aesthetic knowledge to architecture. This also explains the fact that Wagner's architecture displayed revolutionary elements more in the aesthetic-technological realm than in the political-societal sphere, not to mention the social realm.[70]

This places Wagner's conception of modernity – however unsystematic it may be – as one that centres around progress, rationalization and uniformity. It is a concept of modernity that contrasts with the disintegrating and discontinuous moments of modernity that were summarized by Baudelaire as the transitory, the fleeting and the fortuitous experience of metropolitan life. At the same time, as Achleitner points out, this placed Wagner in an ambiguous position in relation to those other modernist movements in Vienna at the turn of the century that emphasized disaggregation, discontinuity and disintegration. For Wagner:

> Everything that was fragmentary, open, indefinite and questioning or even problematizing was alien to him. Naturally, associated with this stance, was a formal or stylistic absolutism, that could only distance itself cynically from the relativizing, psychologizing or literarizing Viennese atmosphere.[71]

The possibility of the city as totality, of a new modern monumentalism, on the one hand, and the possibility of the fragmentary, of the small-scale, individual structure, on the other, are contrary tendencies.

Unlike some of his younger contemporaries, such as Simmel, and members of a later generation, such as Benjamin and Kracauer, Wagner did not conceive of commencing an analysis of modernity from the fragmentary (as totality), but rather set out in a positivist manner to assert the existence of real, general tendencies (however much they might often be covered over with illusion). As we have seen, the initial impulse for this approach lay in his (newly found) hostility to historicism. The neglect of 'genuine' artistic principles, a narrow utilitarianism and a rejection of a 'genuine' monumentalism had produced 'a kind of illusory architecture (*Scheinarchitektur*)'.[72] The elaborately ornamental façades, even of rented apartment blocks as if they were palaces, were, for Wagner, a swindle, with fronts 'reminiscent of Potemkin villages'[73] – a critique made before Loos's more extensive characterization of the whole city of Vienna as 'Potemkin City'[74] – ensuring that modern cities could look like ancient Rome or old Nuremberg.

A genuine modern architecture, therefore, must give full expression to modern life, one that is no longer that of the Ringstrasse (to which Wagner had himself contributed earlier). As Hermann Bahr stated in 1911, 'Otto Wagner is the opposite of the Vienna Ringstrasse. There, everything is done for effect, by Wagner for expression. There arbitrariness, here necessity. There, swindle, kitsch, theatre, here always simply what the object wishes to be.'[75] What the object wishes to be is *modern*.

The features of modernity identified by Wagner, in however unsystematic a manner, are: the notion of unlimited progress, technological development, (formal) democracy, the levelling process, acceleration in the speed of life (both in the circulation of individuals and commodities and the turnover of fashions), a new monumentalism (in which the street is also a monument), the unlimited metropolis, the transformation of metropolitan experience (the modern eye takes in less variation, longer straight lines and greater masses) and greater abstraction.[76] Several of these dimensions of modernity are manifested in the building type that Wagner viewed as the most characteristic of the modern metropolis, and therefore with whose design his students should commence their studies: the rented apartment block (*Miethaus*). Clearly, these dimensions of modernity do not constitute a coherent whole. Yet they do coalesce around a number of issues such as *abstraction* (and levelling), *circulation* (and transitoriness) and *monumentality* (and uniformity). And although Wagner's features of modernity and his treatment of them indicate the influence of an unproblematical positivist stance, the often brief incursions into the experiential consequences of modernity suggest aspects of a different mode of analysis. However, what is lacking in Wagner's discussion of modernity is a sense

5.1 Otto Wagner's last completed apartment block, 1909

of discontinuity and of contradiction. Although he applauded a realist position (certainly as early as his 1889 preface to his works, and later) and although his individual architectural projects do reveal an acute concern for their specific *genius loci*, unlike the naturalists or realists there is no evidence that he *systematically* examined the *genius loci* of modern architecture – metropolitan modernity.

5.2 Bird's-eye view of Wagner's projected 22nd district of Vienna, 1911

Let us commence with the building type in Vienna, which Wagner argued played such a great role compared with other cities – the rented apartment block – and which, in its modern forms, manifested several of the features of modernity. Wagner's students were to concentrate upon the design of the modern apartment block in their first year of study. Together with its important variant, the apartment and commercial block (*Wohn- und Geschäftshaus*), it is by far the best represented building type in the leading Viennese avant-garde architecture journal, *Der Architekt* in terms of full-page displays from 1895 to 1910, or even later.[77] But in the reaction against architectural modernism in Vienna it is not the rented apartment block as such that is viewed as problematical. Rather, it is what Wagner associates with its proliferation in Vienna and his treatment of it that is cause for concern. For Wagner, its dominance in the physiognomy of the city is related to more general processes: *levelling, uniformity* and *anonymity*. 'People's mode of life is becoming daily more alike' in the metropolis, thereby threatening the individual dwelling house and creating the 'contemporary uniformity of rented apartment blocks'. In addition, a greater number of metropolitan dwellers prefer 'to disappear in the crowd as a "number", to preserve their anonymity rather than to be pestered by nosey neighbours' in individual housing developments.[78]

The modern presuppositions behind the rented apartment block are that the apartments should be 'healthy, beautiful, comfortable and cheap', as opposed to having reference to 'tradition, cosiness and picturesque appearance'. The levelling process is assisted by new technological developments such as the electric lift (thereby making all apartments equally accessible) and is manifested in the removal of the extreme differentiation of the storeys (by size and amount of ornament) of the rented apartment block. Indeed, by 1902 Wagner was referring to the rented apartment block as a 'conglomerate of cells'. The interchangeability of life-forms, one with another, and their uniformity led Wagner to speculate upon the potential emergence in the future of other dwelling types such as 'the portable house' and 'the prefabricated house'.[79]

These processes of levelling and a tendency towards uniformity were also present in the layout of modern streets and squares – as is evident from Wagner's 1911 design for the 22nd district in Vienna. The uniformity of street structures was to create a new, modern monumentality in which the street itself was a monument. This repetition of street structures and squares was viewed by others – such as Sitte – as creating new pathologies of modern life. Already in 1889, Sitte had declared that 'in recent times a distinctive nervous illness has been observed: "agoraphobia" (*Platzscheu*)', a physical and mental aversion to large open squares and straight, broad open streets. Sitte maintained that its sufferers felt more comfortable in old squares – 'quite naturally, since one feels very much at ease in the small, old squares'. This pathology of space identified here by Sitte as agora-phobia is, for him, 'one of the newest, most modern illnesses'.[80] Sitte later accused Wagner of megalomania, for his obsession with the straight line in configuration of endless straight streets. For his part, Wagner saw in the obsession with old squares and confined spaces a source of claustrophobia.

However, only occasionally in Wagner's writings do we find discussion of the sensory and emotional features of metropolitan modernity. As someone concerned with improving the circulation of individuals in the metropolis through modern traffic systems, Wagner could not but reflect upon some of the consequences of our being in accelerating motion in the metropolis, either in the street or in the city railway. In particular, Wagner draws attention to the optical and perspectival transformation of our metropolitan experience:

> the modern eye has lost the small, intimate scale, has accustomed itself to *fewer varied images*, to *longer straight lines*, to *more extensive surfaces*, to *larger masses*. . . . Therefore, in the case of rented apartment blocks, which will indeed remain the major factors in the image of the street, the architect will seek to gain an effect through the *decoration of surfaces*, in images contrasting with one another, through *simple and correctly chosen details*, and through the *explicit accentuation of construction*.[81]

The implications for our visual grasp of built surfaces are a shift to abstract decoration of surfaces and abandonment of elaborate and diverse stucco façades (typical of historicist variants) and the greater visibility of construction elements. Thus, Wagner chooses to highlight the consequences for what he took to be the most typical building type, rather than reflect upon the consequences of the beholding subject of modernity in motion, in traffic or even in the city railway designed, after all, by Wagner with the assistance of some of his students. It is a reflection upon visual experience that runs counter to Simmel's description of metropolitan experience and to adjustment to new moving images – provided by the cinematograph.

The other dimensions of modern experience to which Wagner refers relate to socio-economic transformations in the modern metropolis. Wagner's positive (though unacknowledged) reference to Benjamin Franklin's dictum 'time is money' has several consequences for our interaction in the modern metropolis.[82] First, architects themselves must be trained to take account of the economic needs of the building process, not merely with regard to the speed of construction and other economic constraints but also with regard to the investment constraints imposed upon certain building types (the rented apartment block is also termed the interest-generating block – *Zinshaus*). Second, a general acceleration in economic and other transactions is also implicit in this dictum, and above all in the spheres of circulation, exchange and consumption. The acceleration of traffic

(*Verkehr*) requires precise spatio-temporal configurations to make it possible. As Simmel recognized, the complex interactions within the metropolis require exact calculation even though, viewed from a distance, these myriad interactions appear chaotic and unregulated.[83] The notion of human beings in accelerating motion is recognized by other contemporaries. Sitte, for example, refers to the Ringstrasse as 'a thoroughfare of human beings in motion', even though he did not wish to think through the consequences of this image.[84] Third, our actions are determined by our purposive orientation (in turn, as Max Weber was to argue, determined by a purposive rationality) in many spheres of life.[85] Wagner's focus upon purpose (*Zweck*), his plea for a useful style (*Nutzstil*) and a purpose-oriented art (*Zweckkunst*) as indicative of modernity was to prove a dangerous doctrine for the opponents of aesthetic modernisms with their continued assertion of the autonomy of the artistic sphere. That art should be in the streets and not confined to museums suggested a dangerous degree of accessibility to those for whom Viennese culture was identified with high culture. Wagner appeared to welcome the levelling which he perceived in contemporary social and political life – even though this is a remarkable presupposition to make in a society with such marked social class, ethnic, gender status *differentiation*. But 'time is money' refers not merely to the brevity of the temporal sphere. It also indicates its measurement by the universal equivalent of all values – money – and thereby presupposes a reduction to a common denomination that also functions as a *dedifferentiating* entity.[86] This dimension is highly relevant to the capitalist development of the rented appartment block and the maximization of economic returns upon such blocks.

In another context, Wagner draws out some of the consequences of the metropolis as the site of an increasingly significant *differentiating process* – fashion – for a modern architecture.[87] Modern people are acutely conscious of the latest fashions and changes in them with respect to our clothing. Yet there exists, Wagner argues, a 'disharmony in fashion and style' in the architectural realm. Why is this the case? Wagner maintains that architectural styles have always corresponded to fashions in clothing with respect to form, colour and fitting. For its part, architecture has hitherto been sensitive to the forms of its own epoch. However, historicism has destroyed this connection, creating a contrast between its rigid historical styles that do not express modernity and the general population's sense of the fashionable. The result is a contrast between the general public's sensitivity to fashion and an indifference to contemporary artistic products that do not accord with modern fashion. For fashion is easier to grasp and to influence, compared with 'rigidified' historical styles that are copies and imitations of previous condensations of taste. Wagner's imaginary instance of this disfunction is revealed when he states that:

A man in modern travelling outfit, for example, will fit in very well to the
railway station waiting room, to the sleeping car and to all our vehicles,
but what eyes we would make if we were to see, for instance, a figure in the
clothes of the Louis XV epoch using such things.[88]

How the presumed harmony between modern outfits and modern things
has arisen is not Wagner's concern. His imaginary instance reverses the
connection which he wishes to make. The outfit is produced for the architectural and travel spaces and not vice versa. More in keeping with his
intended argument is his subsequent statement that:

It is simply an artistic absurdity that men in evening attire, in lawn tennis
or bicycling outfits, in uniform or checkered breeches should spend their
life in interiors executed in the style of past centuries.[89]

Those who carry modern fashion should therefore do so in equally and
appropriately modern interiors. But again, the force of Wagner's argument
for a modern architecture should have been focused not merely on interiors
(station waiting rooms, sleeping car, vehicles) but also on the exteriors of
built structures.

An alternative account of the potential harmony between human clothing styles and the forms of other modern things might lie in the attempts
to generate a new modern style itself. The creation of a *Jugendstil* and
attempts at its universalization created an affinity between unconnected
objects, just as historicism had earlier permeated the world of things
(though possibly with greater stylistic diversification).[90] The 'casing' of
everyday objects, built structures and human attire could appear similar
despite their very different purpose (*Zweck*) and use (*Nutz*). The 'semblance' of affinities was still largely created by craft production, although by
the first decade of the twentieth century the possibilities of mass production
began to be evident. Such tensions in the modes of production of the semblance of things manifested themselves in debates and conflicts between
the architect – as building artist (*Baukünstler*) – and the engineer – as
creator of practical structures – and within the *Deutsche Werkbund* between defenders of craft production and advocates of mass production.[91]

If the semblance of harmony between modern things hides significant
tensions in the modes of producing such things, then equally Wagner's
elevation of the fashionable in the contexts of a modern architecture
revealed other important contradictions and, for some, unwelcome affinities. Many contemporaries were clearly disturbed by the correlation of
modernity (*Moderne*) with fashion (*Mode*).[92] Fashions are *transitory phenomena*, creating for only a moment *the illusion of permanence*. Fashions
exist as modes of presentation *on the surface* of everyday life. Fashions have
no depth, no connection with 'the eternal and the immutable' (Baudelaire).

And, despite Wagner's example of 'a man in modern travelling outfit' – which reveals a person 'in transit' – the preoccupation with fashion and fashionability was located by many in *the female domain*. It should be noted, in this context, that Wagner's 'master class' at the Academy of Fine Arts did not include women. Architectural study was undertaken by women in the Technical University and, later, with others such as Adolf Loos, whilst the applied arts were studied at the school of applied arts.

The contradictions in the appeal to fashion are also evident in Wagner's writing. Clearly influenced by Semper's theory of 'cladding', 'clothing' or 'dressing' buildings, Wagner nonetheless rejected the implications that such 'cladding' was merely cultural symbolic masking, that is, pertaining merely to the surface, to the façade. Rather, for Wagner, the core of architecture lay in construction, the source of all new 'forms'. Construction is that which is more basic, that which endures; 'surfacing' a building should reveal that construction and not be an arbitrary appendage of architectural style(s).

As Mary McLeod has suggested, Wagner's discussion of fashion largely ignores women's dress, applauding 'the utility and honesty of modern (i.e. male) fashion and not its attributes of masquerade and artifice. What he did not acknowledge was that the functionalism of male fashion resembled conventional interpretations of "dress" as utilitarian and relatively static'.[93] And where Wagner takes up the *negative* import of the merely fashionable, as when he remarks that 'architectural styles almost change like fashions', he introduces that correlation of fashion and superficiality (and quite possibly the association of this with female activity) which runs counter to his original positive correlation between modern architecture and fashion (as in all 'great' architecture). But this negative correlation is reserved for historicist fashionability. Nonetheless, as McLeod indicates, 'Wagner's notion of the *Zeitgeist* . . . paradoxically embodied a vision of eternal truth. The truly modern was both timely and timeless.'[94]

Wagner's somewhat positivistic response to modernity was unable to fully grasp the implications of some of the crucial features of modernity that he himself emphasized. The belief in unlimited progress would render the present as continuously transitory, always in the process of being superseded by new development. The process of permanent change would limit the timelessness demanded of aspirations to monumentality to residing only in change itself. Something of the paradoxical nature of Wagner's features of modernity is revealed in his lamentation concerning the absence of a modern monumentalism. Most of the features of modernity identified by Wagner can indeed be subsumed under the rubrics of abstraction, movement and circulation and – monumentalism.

It is true that Wagner detected a new monumentalism in what was, in effect, the *serialization* of the apartment block, the continuous façades of apartment blocks of identical height expanding along a straight-lined street. Yet he failed to recognize his own city railway design as providing a new monumental structure that embodied modernity itself. The city railway possessed both continuity and difference, structures for motion and yet static. The commitment to detail in each station and bridge, each of which is different in design but, at the same time, shares common features and surfaces that extend over several miles of urban and suburban surfaces surely commends the *Stadtbahn* for the status of a *Gesamtkunstwerk*.[95]

But Wagner's continuous call for a modern monumentality clearly refers to other structures. At one level, it is the Ringstrasse development – in which Wagner himself participated with the design of apartment blocks on the Schottenring and Universitätsstrasse, for example – that conjured up the desire to create a new constellation of monumental structures, a new *via triumphalis*, perhaps even several in the 'unlimited' metropolis. This first post-1857 'Renaissance' of Vienna, identified with the construction of the Ringstrasse and its surrounding area and largely complete by 1890, was followed by what some of Wagner's contemporaries referred to as a 'Second Renaissance', after the extension of the city boundaries in 1890.[96] The city railway structures built between 1894 and 1899 were Wagner's most extensive built structures. His one addition to the Ringstrasse *via triumphalis* – the Post Office Savings Bank (1904–5) – is actually set well back from the Ringstrasse and faces the more extensive structure – the War Ministry – the competition for which Wagner (and Loos) did not win. (It went to the conservative Ludwig Baumann.)[97]

The other highly contested space for monumental structures in the period in which the last section of the Ringstrasse was completed (the Stubenviertel, where the Savings Bank and War Ministry were located) was the Karlsplatz.[98] As Peter Haiko has documented, this proved to be the most contested space in Vienna as far as Wagner was concerned. This large square, whose ground surface was extended with the covering over of the Wien river – parallel to which was one of the city railway lines that ran to Schönbrunn and to Hütteldorf – already possessed several significant structures around its boundaries by 1890. These included the Academy of Music, the Technical University and, above all, Fischer von Erlach's baroque church (the Karlskirche). The completion of Wagner's two sections of the city railway station – then called Akademiestrasse, now Karlsplatz – providing an entrance and exit to the city railway in 1898 in the square itself, was already viewed by many to be perilously close – and a modernist affront – to Erlach's Karlskirche. In the same year, however, at the western end of the Karlsplatz the Secession building designed by Wagner's student Olbrich was completed. The opponents of the modern movement unequivocally saw this structure as an affront to a canonized Viennese architectural tradition. The modernist movements achieved no

5.3 Wagner's Karlsplatz city railway station under construction with Fischer von Erlach's Karlskirche in the background, 1898

further successes in the Karlsplatz square, with the exception of Adolf Loos's Café Museum, whose impact lay more in the transformation of the interior than of the ground floor exterior. Otto Wagner's attempts over almost two decades to execute the design of a new museum all foundered, despite support, on occasion, from the powerful Vienna mayor Dr Karl Lueger, amongst others. The same fate befell Wagner's designs for a department store, a hotel and the restructuring of the entrance to the Naschmarkt – the open market at the western end of the Karlsplatz over the enclosed sections of the city railway and the river Wien. The entrance to the Naschmarkt and the streets running westwards parallel with the city railway and the river Wien was also to have been a possible new *via triumphalis* extending to the Emperor's palace at Schönbrunn.[99] But neither this early proposal by Wagner, nor his proposed straight avenue from the very heart of the old inner city – the Stephansdom – to the southern end of the Ringstrasse (in the Stubenviertel) opening onto the Danube canal, nor the so-called Riehl plan for a radical opening up of the inner city with a new thoroughfare and the proposal for a further grand avenue from the Stephansdom to the Prater – none of these proposals came beyond the stage of proposal and discussion.[100]

Thus, in strategic areas of the metropolis, the possibility of constructing the new monumental straight street-lines that Wagner considered the source of a new monumentalism was never realized. In terms of Wittgenstein's analogy of the city and language, the emphasis he gives to the boundaries of a language game, and especially the fact that 'some areas of the City can have sharp boundaries, especially when they correspond to the horizons of clear language games', the parameters within which New Vienna – in its modernist metropolitan variants and not merely as city boundary extensions and incorporations – could overcome resistance from Old Vienna were extremely circumscribed. The differentiation of language games and forms of life was sometimes openly revealed in the opposition to Wagner and his students. One of the clearest statements is contained in a polemical piece by Joseph Bayer (1902),[101] once more opposing one of Wagner's museum designs for the Karlsplatz. Under the title 'The "Moderns" and the Historical Architectural Style', Bayer, although earlier critical of the succession of historical styles is nonetheless sceptical of the modernist position – with its philosophy of art derived, above all else, from Nietzsche, its 'subjectivism', its desire to disavow architecture's position as 'the objective art' which 'stands, as long as it is normal, in the service of general forces that constitute society' – a disavowal that is 'either a frivolity or stupidity'. For 'a flight out of history is absolutely impossible', however much the modernists might appeal to natural tendencies.

Bayer's most illuminating argument against the modern movement is expressed thus:

> It is high time to call a stop to this adventurist architectural endeavour. Modernism is indeed much less dangerous in the private construction of villas – up to now the main achievements of the latest architectural bizarre developments; *outside, one does not need to seek out its buildings. But in the city itself they cannot be avoided!* Ever since so much space has been made available here for building, for this reason we have to care the utmost for the fate of the images of the streets. Above all, what danger threatens the Karlsplatz.[102]

With approval, Bayer cites Karl Mayreder – an important competitor of Wagner's – and his dismay at the modernist tendency that 'transplants the ground of architectural experiment into the middle of the city, where its works permanently cooperate in affecting its character in prominent squares'. Such experimental works as Olbrich's Secession building, dominated as they are by 'a misunderstood individualism', are themselves uprooted from the 'people', from 'cultural development' and 'from all tradition'.[103]

The explicit appeal to an *inside* of the city, whose traditional beauty must be preserved against the encroachment of modernity, and an *outside*, where occasional 'architectural experiment' is relatively harmless, reveals both the boundaries of language games and the fear of transgression of those boundaries. Such strategies employed for the defence of 'Old Vienna' call to mind Simmel's contemporary explorations of the social boundary, the

picture frame and the bridge and the door. The objection to modernism that
is given expression by Bayer is not necessarily levelled against the movement as such, since 'outside, one does not need to seek out its buildings'
but rather its invasion of the space of tradition where, 'in the city itself
they cannot be avoided!' To extend Simmel's investigation of the picture
frame, 'Old Vienna' is already 'framed', largely though not entirely identified with the confines of 'the city itself' – which could earlier have been
merely the inner city, but by the mid-1890s could include the Ringstrasse
zone too.[104] Viewed from the distinction between the bridge (as connection)
and the door (as separation), Simmel declares that 'it makes no difference
in meaning in which direction one crosses a bridge, whereas the door displays a complete difference of intention between entering and exiting'.[105]
The contested intention here is that of *entering* a traditional cultural space
from outside. The examples of the Secession building and of all Wagner's
designs for a museum on the Karlsplatz are also instances of a *monumental* entry into the spaces of tradition, presenting a dramatic 'difference
in meaning' to the structures surrounding them. The successful monument
'cannot be avoided'.

Yet the intrusion of modernity in the city was not confined, in principle,
to individual built structures or even to designs for such structures that
were never completed. It is the case that success in building 'modernist'
structures was confined, in the inner city and even the Ringstrasse zone,
to individual buildings. Indeed, as we have seen, in the case of some
'modern' building types, such as the department store, Wagner himself was
relatively late in encouraging student design of these structures. Only in
1902 do such designs appear from his students and few were built in the
centre of the city either by them or by Wagner (whose department store
designs for the Karlsplatz came to nothing).[106]

What was more threatening to the defenders of 'Old Vienna' was the
possibility of the restructuring of the whole physiognomy of the city, a
danger epitomized in those modernists who appeared to be admirers of
Haussmann, developments in Berlin and 'Amerikanismus'. For some,
Vienna was seen as a possible bulwark against 'Gallic tendencies', Berlin's
perceived capitulation to size and quantification and to these and other
such features of America.[107]

VI

Prominent amongst those who praised straight avenues were the original
two winners of the competition to provide a general development plan for
Vienna in 1894 – Joseph Stübben and Otto Wagner.[108] It was, furthermore,

Wagner who, in his clarifications accompanying his projects as well as in his published writings, consistently made favourable reference to architectural and planning developments in Berlin.[109] And in his review of Wagner's *Moderne Architektur*, Karl Henrici (in 1897) declared that the tasks for modern architecture which Wagner outlines there 'are already solved in a practical sense in America'.[110] Similarly, in his review of Stübben's *Der Städtebau*, Henrici castigates Stübben's espousal of 'un-German' modern systems of planning and Parisian *points de vue*, instead of developing a 'national' architecture and city design. These and other issues were apparent in the negative response to modernity in Vienna, in the clash between Old and New Vienna. Modernity was identified with society, abstraction, internationalism; tradition with community, cosiness, national cultural forms. The ugly modern contrasted with the picturesque old; the cosmopolitan with the local; surface and superficiality with depth.

In this context, how did Wagner conceive of the modern metropolis, of Vienna designed as a modern expanding metropolis?[111] It is difficult to claim that Wagner's conception of a modern metropolis is pathbreaking, even though his declaration that 'the most modern of that which is modern in architecture are indeed our present day metropolitan cities' – like his insistence that a modern architecture should reflect modern life – places the metropolis at the forefront of architectural endeavour. The two major sources for Wagner's design of the metropolis are his 1893/4 submission of a general development plan for Vienna – with its detailed and specific recommendations for the city – and the much more general lecture on the metropolis of 1911 (ostensibly on metropolitan centres in general, but its accompanying illustrations and plans clearly focused upon Vienna). Additional aspects of the city's design also emerged from Wagner's discussions of specific projects.

At all events, the 1893 competition for a general development plan for Vienna was the first such competition for planning the modern metropolis. More than a decade later, the results of a similar competition for Berlin were announced in 1910. Thus, in terms of context and aside from Wagner's invitation to give a lecture on the modern metropolis at Columbia University in 1911, his 1911 reflections on the metropolis may also be read in the light of the contemporary and more significant Gross-Berlin competition of 1910 – and Wagner's lack of success in securing acceptance for his earlier plans.

In his submission Wagner compares recent developments in Vienna unfavourably with those in Paris and Germany. Vienna's tasteless orgies in building style, often generated by engineers and stonemasons, must be countered by a focus upon the purpose (*Zweckmässigkeit*) of buildings and urban planning in a context in which the dramatic expansion of circulation of individuals and commodities requires straight streets broken by monuments and squares. Yet Wagner does not favour the chequer-board grid system but rather a conception of a city expanding outwards along main arteries that intersect four ring roads – the existing Ringstrasse, a restructured, existing belt ring (*Gürtelstrasse*), a new outer ring road and an external ring road (that was intended to be more significant a generation later).

Wagner's second major proposal – with which he had some success – was the regulation of the Wien river from the contested Stubenviertel (where his Post Office Savings Bank was erected), through the Karlsplatz to Schönbrunn. The fact that Wagner was chosen to design the city rail-way project in 1894, one of whose lines was constructed largely parallel to the Wien river, necessitated the regulation of the river. The restructuring of the Karlsplatz square – but not its surrounding buildings – did take place, again as a result of the construction of the railway and a city rail station on the square, but the creation of a grand avenue equivalent to Berlin's Unter den Linden from the Karlsplatz to Schönbrunn along the Wienzeile came to nothing. The same was true of a projected avenue from the Step-hansdom to the Prater by Riehl and others (although Wagner projected an avenue from the Stephansdom to the south corner of the Ringstrasse by the Danube canal), which would have cut through the inner city.

Some of Wagner's other proposals are concerned with the distribution of essential facilities, such as the more even distribution of hospitals throughout the city for easy access, and, taking up an earlier suggestion by Semper, the creation of distribution centres at roughly equal intervals throughout the city. Such centres or *Stellen* would also provide the col-lection point for corpses to be transported to the central cemetery.

More ominously, Wagner recommended that an increase in the number of troops in military barracks be proportionate to projected increases in population. Further, given the new means of transport, such barracks could be located on the outskirts of the city rather than in the centre (and it should be remembered that the two starting points of the horseshoe-shaped Ringstrasse were occupied by military arsenals). But as an indica-tion of Wagner's attention to modern, metropolitan existence he recognized that if barracks were relocated on the periphery of the city then their officers would be detached from their necessary access to nightlife – the solution to which would be to create officers' clubs and casinos in the new barracks.

The need for 'beautiful distraction' on the part of the rest of the popu-lation was to be catered for by the creation of modern monuments, in part as an escape from the increasing levelling of modern urban life. At the same time, Wagner recognized that the proliferation of monuments should be held in check since even a major city could have only one parli-ament, town hall, etc. Again, however, the major structures designed by Wagner that could be described as 'modern monuments' and were actually built, with few exceptions, do not crucially affect the physiognomy of the city, which, in his 1911 essay on the metropolis, he judged to have the most significant influence upon the image of the city. Of the acknowledged successful modern buildings, the Kirche am Steinhof was located on the edge of the western suburbs of Vienna in a much greater complex of structures that formed, and form, the mental hospital; whilst the Post Office Savings Bank is set well back from the Ringstrasse and does not have the impact of the then Ministry of War (designed by Baumann) located opposite and actually fronting the Ringstrasse. The physiognomy of the city was transformed by the Nussdorf sleuce structure designed by Wagner as the northern entrance, in effect, to the Danube canal and, much more significantly by Wagner's design for the city railway (commenced in 1894 and opened in 1898). The railway, together with the other examples cited, constitute diverse instances of Wagner's aim from 1889 to develop a style for use or utility style (*Nutzstil*). But it is only the city railway that achieves what the Ringstrasse as a whole – with its diverse styles and monumental structures in open spaces – failed to attain, namely the status of a total work of art. It is not at all evident that Wagner himself realized that he had designed (often in cooperation with his students) such a total work of art that accorded with his desire for the monumental. Rather, up until his death in 1918, Wagner continued to insist upon a modern monumental architecture, without acknowledging that he had already made a significant impact in a city railway complex that fully accorded in every respect with what Wagner judged to be the expression of metropolitan modernity. It was not the Ringstrasse, even though one of the city railway lines, in a semi-subterranean manner, secretly connected the two 'entrances' on the Danube canal to the horseshoe course of the Ringstrasse. It was not another grand avenue, such as Wagner had conceived extending above another section of the railway from the Karlsplatz to Schönbrunn. In a somewhat irregular and incomplete manner, however, the rail 'roads' of the city railway formed two of the concentric circles around the city, whose outward extension Wagner took to be one way forward in developing the expanding metropolis.

VII

At various stages it has been argued that the resistance to modern architecture and modern urban design in Vienna after 1890, and the frequent failure of Otto Wagner and others after the mid-1890s to realize their modernist projects, can be set in the context of an opposition between conceptions of Old and New Vienna. In turn, such conceptions – seldom totally coherent and without contradictions – can be located within an opposition between an inside and outside of the city that is to a great extent, though not entirely, synonymous with the first district of Vienna as inside, and surrounding districts as outside. And to return to Wittgenstein's analogy with which we commenced, these oppositions accord, to some extent, with his distinction between the old city maze and the new suburbs. But does the analogy of old and modern language games and the implicit morphology of the city have a deeper significance? In the context of a post-1890 Greater Vienna, are the conflicts between those seeking to develop and extend a modern architecture and city planning in the heart of the metropolis and those seeking to preserve Old Vienna as a valued historical and cultural urban and architectural heritage merely fought out in cultural and symbolic discourses?

Certainly, the period immediately following the extension of the city's boundaries in 1890 and the creation of a Greater Vienna and thus, in principle at least, the possibility of a large modern metropolis, coincided with a resurgence in a literature on Old Vienna that was replete with nostalgia, a lamentation for the cosiness (*Gemütlichkeit*) of the old inner city and a representation of its people (*Volk*) as largely apolitical natural beings all expressing themselves in Viennese dialect. This expanding literature, associated with writers such as Edward Pötzl and Vincenz Chiavacci, along with many others, constituted a cultural valorization of Old Vienna.[112] It was supplemented by the end of the 1890s by a whole series of other publications on Old Vienna and by associations for the preservation and retention of historical, canonized, cultural artefacts, not least the architecture of Old Vienna. The constant polemics by Sitte against Wagner and other 'modernists' in the Vienna press (in Sitte's case, in the *Neues Wiener Tagblatt*) from 1890 onwards was joined by critics such as Bayer, Seligman and others from the turn of the century onwards in the *Neue Freie Presse*. Bayer's opposition to the modernists, highlighted by the completion of Olbrich's Secession building in 1898 and one of Wagner's submissions for a new museum adjacent to the Karlskirche, has already been cited. Modernist architecture was acceptable, he argued in 1902, as long as it remained in the 'modern' suburbs, but should not be permitted to enter the inner city area. The inside/outside confrontation was to be resolved by preserving their respective boundaries – the old as inside and, if necessary, the new as outside.

Yet a sense that more was at stake than the preservation of culture and the built structures of Old Vienna may be revealed in the intensity of other responses to Wagner's plans for the Karlsplatz. Writing to the conservative cultural critic of the *Neue Freie Presse*, A. F. Seligman, in 1909 during yet another competition for the redesigning of the Karlsplatz, Countess Pauline Metternich, as patron of the society for the preservation of art

5.4 Wagner's 1909 submission for the projected city museum (left of Karlskirche), department store (third block right of Karlskirche) and entrance to Naschmarkt (to right of Secession Building at lower right)

works in Vienna, responds to Seligman's attack on Wagner's city museum project as follows:

> I thank God that this terrible Otto Wagner is once more sent packing (*abgeblitzt*) but fear that he will rise again since he is a favourite of Lueger. Of course your article against Otto Wagner is a masterwork! It has greatly impressed me, greatly pleased me and made me happy. This arrogant, tasteless cad has deserved nothing better than that A. F. S. chop him into pieces.[113]

In a similar vein, although with a hint that much more was at issue than a few buildings in the inner city, Leopold von Andrian laments to his friend Hugo von Hofmannsthal in August 1913 that the two associations for the preservation of the inner city 'Old Vienna (*Alt Wien*) and the Preservation of the Homeland (*Heimatschutz*)' do not achieve as much as they should in preserving Old Vienna. What is at stake here, according to Andrian, is

> nothing other than the existence and greatness of Austria. If we are honest with ourselves, then we must recognize that if Old Vienna is destroyed, then we ourselves, you and I included, are to blame or at least partake in the blame. We cannot allow ourselves even the most fruitless complaining, because we must indict ourselves. In contrast, a barbarian such as Otto Wagner or some mere Christian Social city official would be much less to blame than we ourselves, for such a scoundrel (*Kerl*) has no feeling for everything that will disappear along with the old buildings (*was alles mit den alten Häusern zugrunde geht*).[114]

Given the social standing of these correspondents, it is not inappropriate to suggest here that a hierarchical aristocratic social, political and cultural order is seen to be challenged by the attacks upon Old Vienna. From the opposing camp, as it were, the rhetorical confrontation with Old Vienna can be heard in one of Otto Wagner's attacks upon attempts to preserve what he considered to be unworthy architectural objects. As one of a series of responses to a newspaper survey in 1909 on 'what Vienna needs', Wagner enters the debate on the preservation of the old War Ministry on Am Hof with the following judgement:

> What is this sacrosanct old Ministry of War? An old box. We live for the living and not for the dead. If people wish to see dead things, then they should go into a museum. We wish to live in a modern city that fulfils all our aesthetic and hygienic requirements.[115]

Transposed into the opposition of inside and outside, and leaving aside evidence that Wagner was in fact in favour of preserving much of the historical architectural heritage of Vienna, the old city as museum is located inside and the city as modern metropolis is located outside.

However, the concepts of inside and outside presuppose an absent third concept, that of the boundary that demarcates between inside and outside. Clearly many of the valorizations of Old and New Vienna do indeed seek to set and maintain boundaries, both real and imaginary. Here, Simmel's reflections upon the social boundary are worth noting, as when he claims that:

> Perhaps in the majority of all relationships between individuals and groups, the concept of the boundary is important in some respect. Everywhere where the interests of two parties lay claim to the same object, the possibility of their coexistence rests upon the fact that a border line within the object divides their spheres – whether this be as the legal boundary (*Rechtsgrenze*) of the end of a conflict or perhaps as a boundary of power (*Machtgrenze*) at its commencement.[116]

In the conflict between Old and New Vienna, we are dealing with boundaries of power that extend beyond any formal or legal boundary (as between city districts, for example). This becomes apparent when we examine the political/military valorizations of inside and outside.

The valorizations of inside and outside in the military and political context of *fin-de-siècle* Vienna were conditioned by potential or real challenges to established power in the city. The fear of revolution since 1848 and the emergence of new mass political movements contributed substantially to the valorization of the inner core of the city as the seat of political, military and bureaucratic domination. As the capital of the largest land empire in Europe (outside the Russian Empire), the preservation and concentration of power at the centre had implications not merely for the structures of power within the empire but also within the capital city itself. The preservation of a spatial concentration of power largely in the first district of Vienna necessitated limitations on access to the structures of power. Here, three examples must suffice.

It is a distinctive feature of Wagner's city railway commenced in 1894 and completed by 1899 that its four main lines go around the centre of the city and not to the centre itself. This was so apparent to contemporaries that it was suggested that central Vienna itself did not possess a city railway but rather that all the lines seemed to terminate on the outskirts of the city at Hütteldorf.[117] The military–political decision to route the city railway around the centre reflected a concern that a rapid transit system into the heart of the city (and the heart of its power) could be utilized by mass movements to gain easy access to the centre of the city. In this context, it should not be forgotten that there was a considerable military presence around the first district of the city, as evidenced by the presence of an arsenal and a barracks at each 'end' of the Ringstrasse, where it terminated at the Danube canal quay, as well as a further barracks on the Ringstrasse almost opposite the Imperial Palace grounds.

In the succeeding decade the barracks in the Stubenviertel were replaced by the new Ministry of War (designed by Baumann), Wagner's Post Office Savings Bank and other structures that completed the southern end of the Ringstrasse zone. At the same time plans were outlined for an underground railway network comprising two lines that would pass under the centre of the city (the first district) broadly on north/south and east/west axes.[118] Such plans were not realized, again in part as the result of fears of ready access to the centre of the city. Indeed, only in the 1970s did work commence on an underground rail system for the city.

The third example is of a somewhat different order but is also illustrative of the inside/outside dialectic operating politically and culturally. John Boyer has well documented the impact of the Christian Social Party's political victories in 1895 and 1896 in Vienna, creating their dominance after 1897 and up to the First World War upon the politics and culture of the capital[119] and, not least, 'the apparent collapse of political liberalism with far more devastating effect than in Germany'.[120] The dramatic shift in the political landscape after decades of bourgeois liberal domination was succeeded by Dr Karl Lueger's combination of a form of municipal socialism with a conservative Catholic and anti-Semitic ideology. In the present context, what is of significance is the building achievements of this municipal socialism: the city-owned gas works, street railways and electrical works down to 1902, the water supply innovations supplying the city from mountain sources (1910) and the new central cemetery. With the exception of the streetcars (and their entry into the first district had already been contested), these projects were located 'outside' the city's centre. They were all projects in which Otto Wagner expressed little or no interest, presumably because their monumental nature was not located in the centre of the city. Despite Wagner's not unsuccessful attempts to establish close ties with Lueger in order to secure support for his projects – not least on the Karlsplatz – the Christian Social Party's version of the modern focused too much upon 'the possibilities of technological innovation and managerial skill'[121] and in a far too confused manner upon culture, modern architecture and the modern monumentalism that Wagner so earnestly sought. Neither the core nor the periphery ultimately provided a source of cultural policy for the Christian Socials. Boyer clearly outlines the latter's cultural problematic:

> The party had no opportunity to create a second Ringstrasse and thus to emulate the Liberal Party's strategy in the 1870s and 1880s . . . [which] was not an entirely bad thing, for the few attempts of the Christian Socials to

sponsor large, representational structures ended up producing heated conflicts. . . . Although [there was] grudging consent in the Lower Austrian Diet
to Otto Wagner's plan for the church at the Am Steinhof sanitarium in
November 1903, no similar consensus could be found in the City Council
for any of Wagner's several designs for a monumental city museum. . . .
Wagner's 1902 scheme for a building on the Karlsplatz merited Karl Lueger's
personal support but ran up against opposition amongst his colleagues in
the City Council (as well as among the Viennese artistic community more
generally).[122]

For their part, Wagner's endeavours to seek the support of the Christian
Socials through Lueger would hardly have enamoured him with the aristocratic and haute bourgeois arbiters of cultural politics either. The overtly
populist Christian Social Party controlling the city's government and administration was a warning to such aristocratic-bourgeois strata of the dangers
of the populist masses' ability to take power in the centre of the city.

However, as we have seen, Old Vienna and New Vienna as inside and
outside were also modes of *cultural* valorization that were grounded in
the imaginaries of culture and civilization and symbolized in (Old) Vienna
as the bedrock of real (historical) culture and New Vienna as identical with
the modernist tendency to progressively transform the city into a version
of mere civilization as epitomized by modern Berlin. Here, the fact that
Wagner's conception of modern life – that would be 'reflected' in modern
architecture for a modern metropolis – was entirely lacking in any features that were distinctive to Vienna could only reinforce the impression
(strengthened by his occasional positive references to German developments
and to Berlin) that his vision of a modernist Vienna betrayed dangerous
affinities with modern Berlin, and hence with the introduction of mere
civilization to Vienna.

Equally significant, and ostensibly grounded in more concrete dimensions, the inside/outside opposition in Old Vienna / New Vienna also supplied
modes of *spatial valorization* of core and periphery and divergent conceptions of city planning. One dimension of spatial valorization is already
implied in the regulation of mass access to the centre of the city, namely
if we explore the topography of the lives of the poorest sections of the
population in the working-class suburbs and their relationship to the
core of the city.[123] The opposition between the culture of Old Vienna and
the civilization of New Vienna was not merely part of a cultural criticism
viewed from above that juxtaposed tradition and modernity. At a deeper
level, below the surface there lay levels of impoverishment that rendered
the working-class suburb what Maderthaner and Musner have termed 'the
suburb as the "other" of civilization'.[124] In their original study of 'the
anarchy of the suburb, the other Vienna around 1900' – by which is meant
the working-class suburbs of the city – they document a socially subordinate

culture largely ignored in studies of *fin-de-siècle* Vienna. In contrast, the working-class suburb 'appeared in contemporary reports . . . as the disorder inherent and hidden in urban order, as a cosmos of social and cultural marginality and as the epitome of urban alienation'.[125] Its population, uprooted from its quasi-feudal social status in the process of modernization and industrialization in the suburbs of Favoriten, Simmering, Meidling, Ottakring and the like, was accorded, in elite perspectives,

> a more animalistic than human existence. . . . Henceforth they dissolved into an heterogeneous mass of outsiders from bourgeois society who were experienced as threatening, from which functionality (human capital) was demanded to the same extent that their deviance (criminality, prostitution) was feared.[126]

Their domestic and impoverished existence was often hidden behind the sometimes ornamental facades of the rental barracks in working-class districts, and where the contrasts between outside and inside were extreme.

The dialectic of inside and outside is also complemented by an above and below in the topography and textuality of the city, one that rests upon

> an obstinate oscillation of hard and soft signatures of the city. . . . Through social projections, the grammar of the city creates terrains, spaces and territories as 'facts' and thus produces its inner dialectic as an oscillation of surface and depth. The deep grammar is nothing other than the *hard signature* of the city. By this we mean the structured ensemble of socially generated spaces, divisions, segregations that nonetheless appear directly as the fixed geography and topography of the city. It is the apparently ahistorical and, at first glance, ever-present order of the city. Its character of hardness is derived from its defining power over transport, communication, hierarchical placement of social actors and subcentres of production and distribution. The *soft signature* of the city is to be understood as the ensemble of aesthetic form-giving components – which means silhouette and deep perspective, ornament and context, i.e. the establishment of public and private space and ultimately also the fixing of differences as ontologized categories of *beautiful* and *ugly*, of *high* and *low*. Just as the hard signature establishes an apparently unchangeable order of centre and periphery, of inclusion and exclusion of space and social status, in which it announces the suburb as the chaotic opposite of urban order, so the soft signature appears to create a homogeneous urban body and to integrate it through an aesthetics of continuity.[127]

The homogeneity of the urban body that was being defended in Old Vienna as the beautiful old and castigated as the homogenous new in New Vienna were both subject to an aesthetic of continuity. Yet the spatial penetration of the old by the new was not only fiercely resisted (largely successfully) but was also in crucially contested sites indicative of the convergence of soft and hard signatures of the city.

There were a number of contested spaces where the possible transgression of boundaries between old and new were resisted. Originally, at a theoretical level, the debate in the *Deutsche Bauzeitung* and elsewhere from 1890 onwards on straight or crooked streets – initiated by reviews of Sitte's 1889 volume on city planning – was ostensibly a debate on general principles of city planning. In fact, however, the general debate not merely had a specific Viennese component – in that it commenced with reviews of Sitte's major work and continued in the articles by a Sitte supporter (Carl Henrici) and a critic (Joseph Stübben) who initially won the 1893/4 competition for the plans for the regulation of Vienna – but the possibility of straight streets (and grand avenues) in the core of the inner city also fed directly into the debates and spatial valorizations of Old and New Vienna.

One of the crucial contested spaces was the inner city itself. Although there had been substantial reshaping of the area around the inner city with the development of the Ringstrasse zone, finally completed with the restructuring of the Stubenviertel (including Wagner's Savings Bank) in the opening years of the twentieth century, and although there had been many instances of street realignment, there were also plans put forward for a more radical restructuring. In one of Wagner's images painted in 1897 of the completed south end of the Ringstrasse and the Quayside there are elements of his earlier 1893 plans for the regulation of the city that were imaginatively realized only on canvas. In particular, two projects are in evidence. The first is an avenue from the Stephansdom in the heart of the inner city to the southern corner of the Ringstrasse where it joins the Danube canal. The second is the development of the quayside from one end of the Ringstrasse and presumably extending to the other as a major shopping promenade. Neither of these projects in Wagner's painted imaginary Vienna were realized; nor was his projected grand avenue from the Karlsplatz to Schönbrunn. Of course, Wagner was not alone in not having his plans realized. The so-called Riehl Avenue projected in a straight line from the Stephansdom to the Praterstern in the second district was never completed and nor were similar plans drawn up by Lotz for such an avenue and for a radical realignment of the whole inner city. Had the Riehl Avenue or Wagner's grand avenue from the Karlsplatz to Schönbrunn (beneath which his city railway ran on its way to Hütteldorf and beneath which the river Wien, regulated by Wagner, also ran) been realized, the spatial valorization of the inner city would have been seriously breached. As we shall see, what was at issue here was not merely New Vienna penetrating Old Vienna but also a challenge to the economic valorization of the first district of the inner city.

5.5 Bird's-eye view of projected reconstruction of Danube canal quay and Wagner Avenue extending towards the Stephansdom, 1897

However, the inner city of Old Vienna was not entirely impregnable and closed off to individual modern structures. The most notable example of a single building, aside from Wagner's Post Office Savings Bank, and much more central to the apex of power in the inner city, was Adolf Loos's building on the Michaelerplatz overlooking the entrance to the Imperial Palace. Completed in 1911, and Loos's major city building, the Loos commercial building for the men's outfitters Goldman & Salatsch was variously denounced by its opponents as a 'sewage drain', a 'manure box' and, in view of the absence of ornamentation on the window surrounds, as 'the building without eyebrows'.[128] Hidden away in a side street off the Kärtnerstrasse, Loos also designed a modern bar. There were other individual instances of modern structures in the centre of the city. But they remained single examples that did not markedly disturb either the cultural *or* the economic valorization of the centre of the city.

The most contested substantial space in *fin-de-siècle* Vienna was, however, one that lay on the boundary of the first district, namely the Karlsplatz. In the 1880s this area was still partly covered with trees and contained a bridge over the river Wien, but the regulation of the river and the construction of Wagner's city railway with a station in the square

5.6 Wagner's 1892 projected department stores on the Karlsplatz with early design for city railway station (front right)

in the following decade removed the bridge and opened up the square. The built structures of the Ringstrasse zone along one side of the square marked the boundary of the first district. The southern end of the square opened up onto a substantial street market, the Naschmarkt, at the entrance to which Olbrich's Secession building was completed in 1898. On the western side of the square ran the fourth district (Wieden); its notable structures were the Technische Hochschule and Fischer von Erlach's baroque masterpiece, the Karlskirche. Interestingly, the lines of the two axes of this church did not point in the direction of other religious structures (such as the Stephansdom) but rather in one case to the imperial residence (the Hofburg) and in the other to the imperial palace (at Schönbrunn), thus indicating a baroque spatial configuration centring on secular power.

At one level, the bitter conflict over the Karlsplatz, which always centred around the Karlskirche, might appear in cultural discourses as a clash between the sacred (the Karlskirche) and the profane (all Wagner's Karlsplatz projects). Yet this baroque church, as has been suggested, had strong spatial ties with profane, albeit imperial, spaces. Yet over and above this largely hidden connection with the profane, were there not links with other forms of valorization at stake here?

As early as 1892 Otto Wagner had conceived of the transformation of the Karlsplatz into a large modern square complete with a department store adjacent to the Technische Hochschule. Somewhat later, though building on a much earlier proposal, he conceived of a reconstructed Naschmarkt as the entrance to a grand avenue extending to Schönbrunn. And for two decades, for various competitions, he drew up plans for a museum adjacent to the Karlskirche and, on one occasion, a hotel. The intensity of resistance to Wagner's projects increased with the completion of the city railway station on the Karlsplatz and Olbrich's Secession building in 1898. In contrast, Adolf Loos's Café Museum, also on the square, was an internal transformation of the ground floor and did not dramatically disturb the external façade. Hence, it did not attract hostility to any considerable extent. Had Wagner's plans for the new museum, together with a department store and hotel been realized, this would have made the Karlsplatz a major focus of circulation outside the first district.[129] Like the projected Riehl Avenue from the Stephansdom to the Praterstern, Wagner's proposed grand avenue from the Karlsplatz to Schönbrunn would have resulted in the flow of urban and commercial capital out of the centre of the city. The *economic* valorization of the first district would have been seriously challenged.

The economic differentiation of the first district from surrounding districts remained hidden in the cultural discourses of inside and outside. However, the dimensions of economic valorization were nonetheless vital to the dynamic tension in the urban spaces of the Viennese metropolis. This is revealed in the examination of the extent to which economic foundations of inside/outside boundaries in *fin-de-siècle* Vienna lay in land values and ground rent. Such an examination must first be located in the context of some of the more general problems that are faced in the study of land values and ground rent, but which are also relevant to the Vienna context.

VIII

Simmel's exploration of the bridge and the door,[130] which illuminates the processes of separation and connection as two sides of the same phenomenon, is relevant not merely to the inside/outside *cultural* dynamic of symbolic discourses on Old and New Vienna but also to *materialist* aspects of the relationship between inside and outside. When Simmel refers to 'the merciless separation of space' as a definite differentiation of space (including urban space), he also recognizes that such separations are more *and* less visible. Indeed, he points out that the relationship of a bridge to its banks is more apparent visually than is the relation of a built structure to its foundation 'which disappears from sight beneath it'.[131] Unwittingly, there is another spatial dimension intimated here, namely that of above and below, which is just as significant for architecture as is inside and outside.

But a built structure does not reveal that which, as Simmel suggests, 'disappears from sight beneath it'. The *economic* foundations of urban capitalist structures are located in land values and ground rent. Some aspects of the value of built structures are, of course, often revealed in their façades and their level of appointment and furbishing are conditioned by their spatial location. However, it should not be assumed that the value of an urban site is determined merely by immediate material factors. Some sites can also possess a *symbolic* significance that commands greater *material* value. Any reading of the often tortuous deliberations on the theory of ground rent – whether it be its orthodox or Marxist variants – reveals that the determination of value is anything but simple. As Marx suggested, commodities do not move around with their value stamped on their heads, and this is especially true of land as a commodity. What is of relevance to our present concerns is some aspects of the value of urban sites. Alfred Marshall, drawing on the earlier work of von Thünen amongst others in his examination of the determinants of income from land other than mere ownership or direct capital investment, speaks of a third class of incomes from land 'which are the indirect result of the general progress of society, rather than the direct result of the investment of capital and labour by individuals for the sake of gain'.[132] This class of income he refers to as a 'special *situation value*'[133] derived from advantageous location. Such income can be enhanced by a variety of improvements, including construction of additional storeys on a built structure on the site. From Marx's perspective, this 'situation value' is, as David Harvey has pointed out, a source of excess profit that can be translated into ground rent.

Indeed, in the course of his explication of Marx's theory of rent, Harvey[134] raises some pertinent issues surrounding space and location that are relevant to an understanding *inter alia* of the situation in Vienna at the turn of the nineteenth century. Marx treats land not merely as a means of production but also as a 'foundation, as a place and space providing a basis of operations'[135] for human activities. The problem is, however, that the further we move away from land as a means of production, the weaker is the force of Marx's explanatory scheme which, for his legitimate aims, was to focus upon the capitalist mode of *production*. Some of the consequent lacunae are pointed out by Harvey, as when he indicates that:

> since space is used by everyone – not just producers – we have to consider the implications of 'more favoured' locations from the standpoint of all forms of human activity, *including those of consumption*. When we leave the realm of strict commodity production, *a wide range of social and fortuitous circumstances can come into play*. The consumption preferences of the bourgeoisie are, after all, not entirely predictable, shaped as they are by changing tastes, the whims of fashion, notions of prestige and so on.[136]

The variety of activities that constitute value creation within the capitalist mode of production appear, on Marx's views, amenable to analysis on the basis of the labour power employed in them. But, as Harvey suggests, 'some – like wholesaling, retailing and money and financial functions – are more amenable to treatment on this basis than others – for example the location of *administrative, religious, "ideological" and scientific functions*'.[137] In a society such as the late Hapsburg Empire that retained strong precapitalist elements, the resistance to capitalist value creation, and indeed to its conception of value, could make the location of 'administrative, religious, "ideological" and scientific functions' fiercely contested.

Harvey thus hints at a problem for a theory of value oriented largely to the capitalist mode of production. But the problem for such a theory – and it is Marx's theory of rent that is being considered – itself reveals a significant issue that is relevant to contested urban locations in Vienna. Marx's theory of ground rent maintains that ground rent 'as the interest on some imaginary capital, constitutes the "value" of the land. What is bought and sold is not the land, but title to the ground rent yielded by it. . . . Title to the land becomes, in short, a form of *fictitious capital*'.[138]

But in a note to this argument, Harvey recognizes that other 'fictions' may also operate in the desire to hold land and, it should be added here, built structures. He notes that:

> The social incentives to hold land – prestige, symbolic importance, tradition, etc. – are also very important in practice, but we exclude them from consideration here because they have no direct root within a pure theory of the capitalist mode of production.[139]

For our purposes, however, the discourses on opposition to modernity, and to specific modernist built structures, do indeed appear to focus precisely upon a perceived threat to 'prestige, symbolic importance, tradition'.

Such reflections are very suggestive when applied to the opposition to architectural modernity in several Vienna sites but, above all, in the Karlsplatz. They indicate that we should look more closely at ostensibly symbolic conflicts over value that are evident in the turn of the century discourses on Old Vienna versus New Vienna and the cultural value of inside as opposed to outside. What appears as an *aesthetic* contestation surrounding possible modernist architectural projects might also have an *economic* foundation.

The dichotomy of inside and outside only makes sense where there is a (transcendable) boundary between the two. Again, it was Simmel who pointed out that the boundary is a social and not a spatial construction, be it imaginary or substantive (though the two are never exclusive alternatives).[140] Urban boundaries can appear as formal constructions, as in the case of administrative districts (*Bezirk*). But *socially* such boundaries are transcended, however unevenly, in terms of social, cultural, gender, ethnic access. As we have seen, the attempt to create boundaries of exclusion against modernity can also be *political*, and can also be framed *aesthetically*. In different forms, therefore, attempts to establish boundaries seek to direct circulatory flows (be they administrative, social, political, aesthetic) within prescribed paths.

But what of the circulation of commodities and capital? The real and symbolic manifestation of commodity circulation in the form of 'cathedrals of commerce', the department stores that were so evident in Haussmann's Parisian boulevards, found no place in Vienna's equivalent prestige development, the Ringstrasse. Then as now, there are no department stores either on the Ringstrasse or even along the path of its logical completion as a ring, the quay avenue along the Danube canal between the two 'ends' of the Ringstrasse. Interestingly, it was Wagner whose projected completion of the Ringstrasse along the Danube canal in 1897 clearly portrayed a series of department stores. Even less likely to be realized were, of course, Wagner's projects for a huge department store on the Karlsplatz.

More significantly, and at the same time as the opposition to architectural modernity was drawing upon the symbolic capital of Old Vienna and an 'inside' city, there was another inside/outside discourse in contemporary Vienna. The increasing concern with *the housing question* at the end of the nineteenth century in Vienna was raising the issues of land speculation, rising ground rents and land values and drawing upon an expanding body of empirical data. Prominent among the liberal economists investigating dwelling conditions in Vienna was Eugen von Philippovich. An 1894 study[141] – which applied such criteria as the number of one- and two-room dwellings as a percentage of all dwellings, the number of dwellings without kitchens and the density of dwellings (i.e. number of inhabitants) to the Vienna data for 1890 – revealed that in Vienna 47.29 per cent of inhabitants lived in one- or two-bedroom dwellings without kitchens. This compared with 36.5 per cent in Berlin, 33.1 per cent in Paris and 7.2 per cent in London. The overpopulation of the smallest one- and two-room apartments was 29.3 per cent in Ottakring, 30.8 per cent in Meidling and 31.26 per cent in Favoriten. Of course, as Philippovich points out, it is not necessarily specific districts that have the highest density of housing or the worst housing conditions, but rather specific categories of dwellings within districts.

This leads him to calculate a minimum space in the total living space per person, which he designates as 'an air space of at least 10 cubic metres and a floor space of at least 4 square metres for every person over one year of age' with a minimum height of a room as '2.5 metres, and with unfavourable lighting conditions 3.0 metres'.[142] In military barracks in Austria the minimum requirement for sleeping accommodation per head was set at 17 cubic metres, and in German military installations 13 cubic metres; the minimum requirement according to the English Poor Law was 13.5 cubic metres and in English prisons 16 cubic metres. In one of his samples of small dwellings, Philippovich found that 25 per cent did not even possess half the minimum air space.

The association of overcrowding and mortality rates is well known and becomes especially evident in a comparison of districts in Vienna. As Philippovich states:

> The first [inner city] and tenth [Favoriten] districts stand well apart from one another. In the former, only 7.43 per cent of all dwellings comprise one or two rooms and only 0.84 per cent are overpopulated; in the latter, 61.51 per cent belong to this dwelling category and 8.94 per cent are overpopulated. And, correspondingly, the annual average of mortality in the first district is 11.6 per thousand inhabitants, in the tenth 35, i.e. in the tenth district it is more than three times as high as in the first district.[143]

This contrast highlights the extreme discrepancy between the most and least favourable districts in Vienna. But the complete table of districts reveals other features. The contrast of extremes hides significant differences between conditions in the first district and adjacent districts. Here the greatest contrast is between the first district's proportion (of every hundred inhabitants) of population living in one to two rooms at 7.43 per cent and the next lowest proportion, already almost 50 per cent greater, in the fourth district (Wieden) at 14.08 per cent (with Josefstadt and Mariahilf following at over 18 per cent). There is an almost equally significant jump in mortality rates (of every 1000 inhabitants in 1891) from 11.6 in the first district to almost 17 in Wieden (fourth), Alsergrund (ninth) and Neubau (seventh).

Yet Philippovich recognizes that any examination of housing conditions must also take into account the state of the built environment itself. Indeed:

> Perhaps even worse than the dwellings that immediately endanger health are the numerous evils that derive from the total situation of the city, buildings and dwellings. Here I am referring to the narrow width of streets, the height of buildings, the lack of public spaces, playgrounds and built-upon surfaces and bathing facilities, the building density of built-up surfaces and hence limited size of courtyards, the insufficient water supplies, washing and bathing facilities in dwellings, room size in dwellings, the condition of lavatories and drainage.[144]

In this context, plans for the restructuring of Vienna – the competition was eventually won by Otto Wagner in 1894 – would not necessarily address these issues if existing building regulations remained in operation. Indeed, if they remain valid for Greater Vienna,

> 85 per cent of any building surface may be built upon, even when the buildings achieve an elevation of 25 metres, and the efforts surrounding all General Regulation Plans would be for nothing. The profit interest of the landowner will always lead to intensive building.[145]

Elsewhere, the financial rewards for urban redevelopment are exemplified in a redevelopment in the inner city in 1892, when 23 old structures were replaced by 20 new ones. In this instance:

> Hitherto, the 'old buildings partly in need of redevelopment and rebuilding' attracted 299,149 Gulden interest, but the 20 new ones erected in their place and adapted to the increased requirements of the present day raised 676,984 Gulden, and hence an increase of more than 125 per cent; despite the fact that a significant part of the land had to be given over to street widening.[146]

In general the redevelopment plans for the Greater Vienna area, which had been established through the incorporation of outer districts in 1890 and which were agreed upon in 1894 – in the year in which Philippovich's study was also published – cannot be said to have seriously addressed the issues raised with respect to the improvement of housing conditions. The needs of the 'outside' districts, which contained major concentrations of working-class population, were hardly taken into account.

Philippovich returned to the housing question at the Munich meeting of the *Verein für Sozialpolitik* in September 1901 (at which Simmel was present) with a presentation on the relationship between the land questions and the housing question.[147] Philippovich provides the following comparison of land values in the years 1860/65 with present land values:

> In the old 10 districts the value rose around 235 per cent and in the outer districts it has risen around 523 per cent. Viewed in absolute terms, however, the inner values rose from 300 to 1006, in the outer districts from 17 to 107 million [florins]. In the inner districts, the amount of the value increase was 700 million, in the outer districts, where speculation could be most in evidence, it was only not quite 100 million. Is this not revealing? We operate too often with percentage figures and hence become surprised at the extent of the increase in values. This is not sufficient. If on the Stefansplatz in Vienna the square metre price has risen from 330 to 950 florins, then this is an increase of less than 200 per cent, but in absolute terms it is much more significant in its effect than the change somewhere on the periphery from 2 to 24 florins, which indicates a rise of around 1100 per cent but in absolute terms is only 22 florins per square metre.[148]

Rather than ascribing the increase in land values to speculation in the outer districts, the argument here is that 'the source of the rising land value lies in the centre of the city'. The argument for this is that in the city centre or core

> the concentration of commercial and industrial enterprises, the historically accustomed preference to have . . . business there brings about a situation in which a competition for land takes place such that the house-owner is given the possibility of raising rents, and only when the prices are unbearable . . . does the population move out into the outer districts.[149]

This sequence of arguments certainly suggests the significance of inside and outside with respect to rental values and land values, and the crucial significance of the inner core of the city as the motor of driving force – as it were – for increases in absolute terms in land values and for increases in rental burdens to the point that the population moves into the suburbs.

It should be emphasized again that what is at issue in this extensive discussion of rental and land values is not the veracity of Philippovich's hypotheses, but rather the centrality of a core/periphery and inside/outside discourse with respect to a crucial aspect of the economy of the city. If we focus more closely upon this differentiation, we find that contemporary evidence presented by Paul Schwarz on 'the development of urban ground rent in Vienna' to the same meeting of the *Verein für Sozialpolitik* reveals a dramatic qualitative difference in the increase in land values in the first district *compared with all other districts* in the period 1860–99.[150] The explosion in land value in the first district was so great in this period that the editors of the journal had to apologize for being unable to present the complete graph of the increase in land value for the first district as a comparable graph depicting all the other districts. Indeed, the graph of ground rent for the first district *commences* in 1860 in value terms, whereas the graph for all other districts *terminates* in 1899 (at 330 florins). With respect to the first district, it should also be born in mind that large sections of it did not exist as significant sites for commercial land values on built structures in 1860, insofar as work on the Ringstrasse zone had only commenced. This makes the increase in land values in the first district all the more dramatic in the period 1860–99.

Schwarz's survey provides a detailed breakdown of land values and ground rent on properties in each of the then 19 districts of Vienna. In addition, Schwarz's general parameters for his comparisons are themselves revealing. In order to compare like with like across districts of Vienna, Schwarz selects 'a 20-metre wide, 25-meter deep regular-shaped medium building site, without regard to the individual circumstances of their being qualified for 30-year or 18-year tax exemption'.[151] Hence the comparison underestimates the actual returns on land ownership since, 'the increase in value of a building site in a better situation amounts to around 40–50 per cent with 18-year tax exemption and around 50–60 per cent for 30-year tax exemption above its existing value'.[152] Corner properties that can attract a similar premium are also excluded from the survey. Finally, the comparison of land values is undertaken 'without regard to the valorization of sites in Vienna as storage places or as cultural spaces (*Kulturgründe*)'.[153] It is worth noting here that the antinomy of commercial and cultural value lies at the heart of much of the debate surrounding contested urban sites in Vienna.

The factors that Schwarz highlights as crucial determinants of rent and interest on urban capital are traffic and transport. He maintains that:

> Commercial properties are attracted to frequent traffic and this explains why commercial outlets are visited there and that the highest rents are paid for such properties where traffic is strongest, that is, in the centre of the city and, secondly, in the radial streets that are also the main streets of the city's districts.[154]

Schwarz indicates that a commercial outlet with one entrance door and one shop window can command 4000–5000 florins rent on the Stefansplatz, Stock im Eisen, Graben and the Kärtnerstrasse, markedly higher than side streets in the same area. In some cases the value of properties can vary from one side of a shopping street to the other and from one section to another. For their part, the value of apartment blocks varies with the accessibility and quality of means of transport. Better means of transport exercise an important influence upon rents: 'with the high value of time, especially in business life, it is important to have at one's disposal the cheapest possible means of transport in all directions'.[155]

Schwarz's detailed analysis of land values and rents in all districts (and his data lead him to the conclusion that land values increased more than rents in the period 1865–99) substantiates the argument made earlier that the creation of grand avenues from the first district outwards, as envisaged by Riehl, Wagner and others, would have reduced the economic valorization of the first district. As indicated earlier, Schwarz's analysis shows that in the period 1860–99 the highest land values in other districts – from his data the sixth and seventh districts (Mariahilf and Neubau) – increased from 55 florins in 1865 to 250 in 1899, whereas in the first district they increased from 330 florins in 1865 to 850 florins in 1899.

Whatever criticism can be made concerning Schwarz's selective calculations,[156] the discrepancy between the first and other districts is confirmed by Petermann's more general data for 1900.[157] Petermann's data reveal that in the first district the annual interest on dwellings was 24.11 million kronen and on commercial properties 21.98 million. No other district could compete with these returns. The next highest, combining the second district (Leopoldstadt) with the new adjacent 20th district (Brigittenau), with double the number of buildings, was 21.91 million annual interest on dwellings and 3.17 million on commercial properties. Thus, any commercial expansion along major avenues out from the centre would jeopardize the dramatic difference between annual interest from commercial properties in the first district and those in other districts. (The comparable figures for the fourth district, which bounded on the Karlsplatz, was 11.54 million annual interest on dwellings and only 1.95 million on commercial properties.)

This economic valorization of the first district and its dramatic, substantial contrast with that of surrounding districts was, not surprisingly, absent in the dominant cultural discourses on inside and outside and on Old and New Vienna. Indeed, the possibility of a connection between the discourse on culture and that on economic valorization was hardly addressed by either those defending the putative cultural stronghold of Old Vienna or those who were addressing the glaring discrepancies between

economic circumstances in some of the surrounding working-class districts
and those in the inner core of the city. In order to find intimations of the
significance of the connection between culture and economic circumstances
we must resort to the literary representation of this epoch in Vienna
provided by Musil's *The Man Without Qualities*. This portrays the Berlin
capitalist Arnheim, who has capital and wishes to be famed for his culture, and the Austrian Count Leinsdorf, who has culture but sees the need
for capital. It is Leinsdorf, in conversation with the novel's hero Ulrich,
who reveals the Viennese connection between culture and capital when he
states:

> 'we have too much finance in modern life. But that's precisely why we must
> deal with it! Look, culture has not been pulling its weight alongside capital
> – there you have the whole secret of developments since 1861. And that's
> why we must concern ourselves with capital.' His Grace made an almost
> imperceptible pause, just long enough to let his listener know that now he
> was coming to the secret of capital, but then went on in his gloomily
> confidential tone:
> 　'You see, what's most important in a culture is what it forbids people:
> whatever doesn't belong is out. For instance, a well-bred man will never eat
> gravy with his knife, only God knows why; they don't teach you these
> things in school. That's so-called tact, it's based on a privileged class for
> culture to look up to, a cultural model; in short, if I may say so, an
> artistocracy. Granted that our aristocracy has not always lived up to that
> ideal. That's exactly the point, the downright revolutionary experiment, of
> our 1861 Constitution: Capital and culture were meant to make common
> cause with the aristocracy.'[158]

Yet whereas Leinsdorf, who is clearly more knowledgable about culture
than capital, laments the lack of unity of capital and culture, the largely
silent coincidence of culture *and* capital in the discourses on Old and New
Vienna as inside and outside is more plausible. In the debates on the
future of the Karlsplatz and on any modern development's relationships
to the Karlskirche, the ostensible separation of the sacred (the Karlskirche)
and the profane (museum, department store, hotel) is not merely a separation of culture and civilization but also of culture (as symbolic capital)
and capital (as urban capital).

The boundaries between Old and New Vienna in the *cultural* discourses
of *fin-de siècle* were not necessarily given a definite and secure demarcation in the discourses themselves. But when set alongside the compelling
economic valorizations of inside and outside in the Vienna metropolis,
the boundary of Old Vienna seemed more clearly defined. In terms of the
economic valorizations contained in commercial activity, land values and
ground rent in the first district, the possibility of that urban capital flowing

out of the inner core of the city – which would certainly have occurred had any of the grand avenues been constructed that penetrated the inner city and opened up the flow of capital outwards – clearly had to be defended against.

Such explorations of the valorizations of Old and New Vienna – which certainly require more detailed investigation – provide a new context within which Wittgenstein's analogy between his city and language games can be assessed for its relevance to Vienna. Implicit in Wittgenstein's distinction between the inner core of the city with its maze of old streets and buildings and the outer modern suburbs is the issue of the boundary between inside and outside within the same city and the boundaries of language games. It was not only Simmel who was concerned with delineating the properties of a boundary. Elsewhere in the *Philosophical Investigations* Wittgenstein reflected upon the distinctiveness or otherwise of boundaries. Again, the context is that of language games and their boundaries. He argues:

> One might say that the concept 'game' is a concept with blurred edges – 'But is a blurred concept a concept at all?' – Is an indistinct photograph an image of a person at all? Is it even always an advantage to replace an indistinct image by a sharp one? Is not the indistinct one often exactly what we need? Frege compares a concept to a district (*Bezirk*) and says: a vaguely bounded district cannot be termed a district at all. This means therefore that we cannot do anything with it. – But is it meaningless to say: 'Stand roughly there'?[159]

The concept of Old Vienna as synonymous with the first district is roughly accurate. But it has *blurred* edges. The boundary of the district (Bezirk) can be extended in cultural and other discourses. In one of the instances around which the conflicts between Old and New Vienna were fought out most vehemently – the Karlsplatz – the object against which all modernizing projects were judged – the Karlskirche – was itself not in the first district but the fourth. The cultural discourse, the language game of Old Vienna had 'blurred edges'. But the economic valorization of the first district in comparison with all other districts, generated by the 'game' of valorization of land values and ground rents that is always precise, had *definite* and defining edges or boundaries. Economic valorization only permits *precise*, 'rational' calculation of values and prices.

6

The City Dissolved

Social Theory, the Metropolis and Expressionism

Simmel's considerations on the great metropolis contained *in nuce* the problems that were to be at the centre of concern of the historical avant-garde movements.

Manfredo Tafuri, *Architecture and Utopia*

We live largely in closed spaces. These form the milieu out of which our culture grows. Our culture is, to a certain extent, a product of our architecture. If we wish to bring our culture onto a higher level then we are willingly or reluctantly impelled to transform our architecture. And this will only be possible for us to accomplish when we confront the spaces, the enclosed ones, in which we live.

Paul Scheerbart, 'Glass Architecture'

Expressionism is the mimicry of revolutionary gesture without any revolutionary foundation.

Walter Benjamin, 'False Criticism'

I

In 1863, in his essay 'The Painter of Modern Life', Charles Baudelaire introduced the concept of *Modernité* as 'the transitory, the fleeting, the fortuitous, the half of art whose other half is the eternal and the immutable'.[1] The painter of modern life was to focus upon the transitory, fleeting and fortuitous dimensions of modern experience and such experience was viewed by Baudelaire to be specifically *metropolitan*. Modernity was both a 'quality' of modern life and a new aesthetic object. As with subsequent avant-garde movements, Baudelaire's concern was with 'the fundamentally new object whose force lies solely in the fact that it is new, regardless of how repulsive and wretched it may be'.[2] The aesthetic representation of 'the ephemeral, contingent newness of the present' should capture not merely an eternal element but rather 'a relative circumstantial element which will be . . . the age, its fashions, its morals, its emotions'.[3] The focus upon everyday existence must grasp the 'rapid movement' that we find 'in trivial life, in the daily metamorphosis of external things'.[4]

Within the landscapes of the great city – 'landscapes of stone, caressed by the mist or buffeted by the sun', the modern painter must capture 'the *outward show of life* . . . [and] express at once the attitude and the gesture of human beings . . . and their luminous *explosion* in space'.[5] Like Poe's 'Man of the Crowd', the artist of modern life must be a 'passionate lover of crowds and incognitos', with a capacity to view the present, however trivial, anew. This capacity the artist shares with the convalescent who, 'like the child . . . sees everything in the state of newness; he is always *drunk*'.[6] The artist as 'passionate spectator' must 'set up house in the heart of the multitude, amid the ebb and flow of the movement, in the midst of the fugitive and the infinite'. The act of plunging oneself into the *metropolitan* crowd, into 'the multiplicity of life' commits the artist 'to become one flesh with the crowd', to enter into it 'as though it were an immense reservoir of electrical energy'.[7]

But this immersion in the dynamic flux of the metropolitan crowd, in the latest fashions as the transitory heraldry of the absolutely new, and this marvelling at 'the amazing harmony of life in the capital cities'[8] does not exhaust Baudelaire's tasks for the modern artist. In his own works – in *Les fleurs du mal* or 'Spleen' – he attempts to capture 'the savagery that lurks in the midst of civilization', its 'living monstrosities' and, not least, the 'sickly population which swallows the dust of the factories, breathes in particles of cotton, and lets its tissues be permeated by white lead, mercury and all the poisons needed for the production of masterpieces'.[9]

This delineation of modernity and the call for artists to capture our experience of it concentrates upon newness, everyday metropolitan existence, the metropolitan crowd, the dynamic movement of metropolis. Aesthetic representations of such experiences of modernity must confront the full impact and consequences of a 'transitory, fleeting and fortuitous' modern existence: the problems of representing modernity as the discontinuous and disintegrating experience of time as transitory (moments of presentness), space as fleeting (disintegrating, variable space) and causality as replaced by fortuitous or arbitrary constellations. This problematization of our 'modern' experience, and the attendant implications for human individuality and subjectivity, are evident in all modern aesthetic movements. Each aesthetic modernism feels itself to be modern in a different manner and proclaims in its manifestos it is absolutely new.

All modernist avant-garde movements have provided aesthetic representations of a 'new' object, one viewed and experienced in a new manner, and have applied new methods and techniques to their new object. No modernist movement has asserted that it is merely another artistic style; rather, it has always portrayed itself as a radical break with the past, with earlier modes of experience and representations of objects. German Expressionism, too, did not see itself as just another artistic style. As Friedrich Hübner insisted, 'expressionism is more; it signifies a change of epoch (*Zeitwende*)'. Expressionism, like other modernist movements, offers new possibilities; Expressionism 'believes in the all possible. It is the world view of Utopia. It places human beings once more at the centre of creation'.[10] But such a retrospective view of Expressionism as a cultural movement does little to illuminate its specific aesthetic focus.

Certainly a crucial site of modernity in Expressionist art is the metropolis. Overstating somewhat, Jost Hermand argues that:

> Expressionism was, from the very outset, a modernistic, avant-garde metropolitan art . . . Indeed, Expressionism was – despite the many tendencies pushing into the biological, mystical, Utopian, primal – the first really metropolitan art in Germany and thus found its logical centre in Berlin.[11]

Aside from pointing to the significance of other centres ('Die Brücke' in Dresden, 'Der blaue Reiter' in Munich, and elsewhere), such a view would require amplification of the diverse nature of Expressionist representations of the metropolis. For instance, Reinhold Heller has questioned 'whether the simple dichotomy of an Expressionist anti-urban versus a non-Expressionist celebration of the city is truly viable', and has suggested such variations in representations of the city as 'panoramic dead cities' (Egon Schiele), the 'dynamic city of animated architecture and deanimated persons' (Ludwig Meidner) or a 'focus on the city's inhabitants while subordinating architectural setting' (Ludwig Kirchner).[12] Sharing the futurist celebration of the city at night, Expressionist representations of the city – as Heller has argued – often take darkness as a theme. But equally compelling is the manner in which the artist and spectator is *in* the street, *in* the crowd, *in* the tumult of the metropolis, rather than viewing the city, as in many Impressionist representations, from a distance, from above, as a landscape from outside.

Indeed, this inclusion of the spectator in the frame of the street – thereby destroying the perspective of the flâneur posited by Baudelaire, and the very conception of a passive spectator – and his or her participation in the dynamic of the metropolis is precisely what some Expressionists declared as their aim. Such a goal is put most forcefully by Ludwig Meidner's 1914 manifesto:

> We must finally start to paint our home, the metropolis, which we love forever. Our feverish hands should paint all the marvellous and curious things, the monstrous and dramatic nature of avenues, railway stations, factories and towers upon countless canvases the size of frescoes . . . A street is not composed of tonal values [as for the Impressionists] but is a bombardment of whizzing rows of windows, racing beams of light between vehicles of all kinds and a thousand hooting spheres, scraps of humanity, advertising hoardings and threatening, formless masses of colour.[13]

The Expressionist artist's aim is to paint neither in the Impressionist nor *Jugendstil* manner, but rather to paint 'life in its plenitude: space, light and dark, heaviness and lightness, and movement of things – in short to achieve a deeper penetration of reality'. In order to confront metropolitan reality, artists must have regard for three dimensions of representation – light, viewpoint and the application of the straight line.

Whereas Impressionists saw light everywhere, Expressionists must have regard to 'heaviness, darkness, motionless matter. Light seems to flow. It cuts things to pieces. We really feel scraps of light, stripes of light, bundles of light.' Between the canyons of high buildings is 'a tumult of light and dark'. The city is in motion. 'Light sets all things in space in motion. Towers, dwellings, street-lamps seem to hang or to swim.'

The viewpoint, rather than perspective, from which the metropolis is seen is 'the most intense part of the picture and the centrepoint of composition'. It can be located anywhere but preferably below the middle of the picture. From the artist's viewpoint, it is important that 'all things . . . are clear, sharp and unmystical'. But whereas distant objects seem in perspective, 'the buildings next to us – we only grasp them with half an eye – appear to wobble and to collapse. . . . Gable, smoke-stack and window are dark, chaotic masses, fantastically shortened, ambiguous.'

Against both Impressionist and decorative tendencies, Expressionists, as 'contemporaries of the engineer, appreciate the beauty of the straight line, of geometric forms'. The straight line is crucial for portraying our cities: 'Are not all our big landscapes mathematical battlefields! What triangles, squares, rectangles and circles rush at us in the street.'

Meidner calls upon his younger colleagues to confront the metropolis and 'overflow all our exhibitions with representations of the metropolis'. Above all, the modern artist should paint

> that which is close to us, our city world! The tumultuous streets, the elegance of iron suspension bridges, the gasometers that hang in white mountains of

cloud, the roaring bright colour of omnibuses and express locomotives, the
rolling telephone wires (are they not like a melody?), the harlequinade of
the advertising pillar, and then the night . . . the big city night.[14]

In this way, Meidner hoped Expressionism would capture the dynamic
motion of metropolitan perception with its shifting standpoints, criss-
crossing images, shocking colours and contradictory confrontations.

Within such a dynamic aesthetic movement as Expressionism, it was
not merely the visual artist who called for a return to the reality and
Utopian potential of the metropolis. In a wartime essay, 'A Speech for
the Future' from the summer of 1918, Kurt Pinthus also pleaded for an
appreciation of the metropolis:

> The flight from the cities into nature will no longer be preached, for the
> stone-filled city is not the symbol of ugliness and inhumanity, nor any longer
> the asylum of impoverishment but, as a contrast to the given extended
> countryside it is formed by human beings, the work of our hands, the
> elevated temple of community, whose boisterous rhythm unites us. Here
> there beats in all houses and streets the empathetic heart of fellow human
> beings, here the eternally moving spirit calls up the deed.[15]

Yet, not all Expressionist artists responded in an equal measure to such
calls, and the attitude to the metropolis often remained what it had already
been for others earlier: deeply ambiguous.

II

However, just as the association of German Expressionism with new representations of the metropolis hides both the extent of preoccupation with
non-metropolitan themes, with nature as a contrast to urban significations,
and the diversity of responses to the metropolis, so the treatment of the
metropolis by German social theorists and commentators also reveals an
ambivalence and sometimes a hostility to urban experience. Such responses
range from an identification of the metropolis with the extreme negative
features of society, through the city as the site and exemplar of an ugly
civilization, the city as the potential source of positive aesthetic representations, to the metropolis as the necessary site for aesthetic modernisms. Many
of these responses to metropolitan experience in social theory anticipate
and certainly illuminate dimensions of Expressionist representations of the
big city.

At the most general level, the oppositions between community and society and culture and civilization were already widely disseminated prior to and in the decade of Expressionist production from 1910 to 1920. So, too, was the positive evaluation of community, culture, creativity and authentic values, and the *negative* evaluation of society, civilization, conventionality and inauthentic values. Such a juxtaposition found articulate expression in Ferdinand Tönnies's *Gemeinschaft und Gesellschaft*, first published in 1887 and reprinted many times.[16] There, the sociologist Tönnies – who hated cities and, above all, Berlin – engaged in an exploration of modern society through the polarities of community and society and the tendency for the emergence of modern society to be associated with the destruction of community. Society for Tönnies, is, 'a transitional and superficial phenomenon'. And whereas 'community is old, society is new, as a phenomenon and as a name'. Indeed, one goes into society 'as into a *strange* country', into a 'mechanical aggregate and artefact'.[17] Society is characterized by contractual exchange relations, hostility and indifference. The act of exchange is 'performed by individuals who are alien to each other, have nothing in common with one another, and confront each other in an essentially antagonistic and even hostile manner.'[18] Society thus produces a multiplicity of relations between individuals who 'remain nevertheless independent of one another and devoid of mutual familiar relationships'.[19] Similarly, conventional social life

consists of an exchange of words and courtesies in which everyone seems to be present for the good of everyone else . . . whereas in reality everyone is thinking of himself and trying to bring to the fore his importance and advantages in competition with the others.[20]

These features of *Gesellschaft* are being accelerated by contemporary processes such as urbanization, and the highest form of such societal tendencies is the metropolis.

In contrast, all the 'creative, formative and contributive activity of human beings' that is 'akin to art' belongs to the formation of community (*Gemeinschaft*).[21] Running counter to rationalization in modern society and its degradation of 'everything – objects and humans alike – to the level of means', Tönnies, in later editions of his work, looked for alternative collective elements such as cooperatives (1912) and cooperative production (1922).

It is not difficult to read into Tönnies's work – although this may not have been his intention – the search for a new community, even a nostalgia for lost communal social forms against the negativity of modern societal processes. This Utopia of an ideal community grounded in authentic social relations could be the site of genuine creativity, of 'spiritual friendship', itself 'a kind of invisible place, a mystical city and gathering, vitalized by both an artistic intuition and a creative will'.[22]

Similar conceptions of the Utopian community and the negativity of existing society abounded in Expressionist writings, which could draw upon a variety of sources of hostility to modernity. Writing during the Expressionist decade, Max Scheler, for instance, could assert that:

> 'society' is not the inclusive concept, designating all the 'communities' which are united by blood, tradition, and history. On the contrary, it is only the remnant, the rubbish left by the inner *decomposition* of communities. Whenever the unity of communal life can no longer prevail . . . we get a 'society' – a unity based on mere contractual agreement. When the 'contract' and its validity cease to exist, the result is the completely unorganized 'mass', unified by nothing more than momentary sensory stimuli and mutual contagion.[23]

Such a constellation of remnants, rubbish, decomposition, and masses united by mere sense stimuli and contagion appears in some Expressionist representations of the metropolis.

Yet this negative conception of the metropolis as exemplar of an inauthentic society was often associated with a recognition of the metropolis as a legitimate source of artistic inspiration. Thus, whilst Emil Nolde 'scorned the metropolis of Berlin as a place of decay and degeneracy', he was nonetheless 'fascinated by the splendor and sensory stimuli, by the light and shadow of nightly bustle'.[24] In other words, the horror of the metropolis as a *moral* order could be countered or fused by a fascination with its *aesthetic* order, however ugly. Flowers of evil do indeed blossom in the metropolis, as Baudelaire's depictions of modernity testified.

Yet those who argued for recognition of the *aesthetic* attraction of the metropolis had to confront not merely the powerful anti-urbanist tendencies in German society – be they the ideological idylls of a vanished village existence, the varieties of a return to nature movement or the retreat to a moral, aesthetic or religious community in the countryside – but also the powerful representation of German cities, and not least Berlin, as fundamentally ugly compared with other European cities. Certainly, many of the urban centres of the German Empire had experienced massive expansion after unification and then extensive industrialization. Thus, Berlin's population at unification in 1870 was over three-quarters of a million, but by 1895 was one million, a decade later over two million and by 1920, in Greater Berlin, was approaching four million.[25] Such an expansion was fed by mass migrations, particularly from the east. At the same time, successive phases of building and reconstruction of the city for industrial development and transportation networks within such a short period were accompanied by substantial differences in population density, threatening social inequalities, class divisions and urban impoverishment. Berlin's dramatic expansion into a major metropolis, even its elevation into a world city (*Weltstadt*) symbolized by the Berlin Trade Exhibition of 1896, meant that it was a thoroughly modern city.[26] The 1912 *Baedeker* Guide proclaimed:

> Though Berlin does not compete in antiquity or historical interest with the other great European capitals, its position as the metropolis of the German empire . . . invest it with high importance in addition to *its special and characteristic interest as the greatest purely modern city in Europe.*[27]

In contrast to the beauty of Paris or the embedded tradition of London, Berlin seemed to possess a pure modernity that was often viewed as a purely modern ugliness. In an anonymous article from 1899 entitled 'Die schönste Stadt der Welt' ('The Most Beautiful City in the World') in *Die Zukunft* (*The Future*), its author ironically contrasted London, Paris and New York with Berlin as 'the parvenu of big cities and the big city of parvenus.[28] The city's actual claim to be a metropolis rests upon 'the factory city that no one knows in the West and which is perhaps the greatest in the world', whereas its architecture is characterized by a chaotic juxtaposition of historicist styles:

> One feels oneself to be in a fevered dream . . . [in] the major thoroughfares of the West. Here an Assyrian temple structure, adjacent a patrician house from Nuremberg, further along a piece of Versailles, then reminiscences of Broadway, Italy, Egypt – dreadful premature births of polytechnic beer fantasies. A thousand misunderstood forms spring out of the walls of these petty bourgeois dwellings.[29]

And even though a city does not necessarily need beautiful buildings if it has the advantages of a striking natural setting, when it has none of these it requires

> a significant and well-planned street perspective. I am not satisfied with the expression 'street perspective' (*Strassenbild*); I prefer to say 'street landscape' (*Strassenlandschaft*) or cityscape (*Stadtbild*); for what is significant is the actual scenic total view that is created through the organization and formation of masses in the same way as a natural landscape emerges out of the group of masses of mountains and vegetation.[30]

The author's yearning for the overall street perspective would require the 'planned destruction' of the existing city and the creation (clearly in a manner reminiscent of Haussmann) of that which Berlin lacks: 'air, free prospect, perspective'.

The essay's author, Walter Rathenau (who was to figure as the character Arnheim in Robert Musil's novel of Vienna on the brink of world war, *The Man Without Qualities*), abandoned such aesthetic reflections for moral and quasi-religious ones over a decade later in works such as *Zur Mechanik des Geistes* (*On the Mechanics of the Spirit*, 1913) – reprinted 19 times by 1925.[31] It, too, contains an image of the city, but one devoid of any Utopian potential. Now, in 1912, the city no longer contains aesthetic possibilities; rather, its image is one of darkness:

> The sites of soullessness are terrifying. The wanderer who approaches the metropolis in the twilight from the depths of the countryside experiences a descent into the open tracts of misfortune. Once he has stepped through the effluent atmosphere, the dark rows of teeth of dwelling blocks open up and close off the sky. . . . thousands stand, pressed close together, with flickering eyes before the billboards of a fenced-in wilderness. Out of the courtyards stream overexhausted men and women, the spaces behind the glass cases are filled, whose inscriptions shimmer in white–blue arc-light. 'Big bar', 'hairdressing salon', 'candyshop', 'boot paradise', 'cinema', 'instalment business', 'world bazaar' – these are the places of consumption. . . . This is the night-time image of those cities that are praised and applauded as places of happiness, of longing, of intoxication, of the intellect, that depopulate the countryside, that kindle the desire of those excluded to the point of criminality.[32]

There is little doubt that Rathenau's metropolis is Berlin portrayed in quasi-expressionistic rhetoric. Yet it is possible, to discern other contemporary perspectives on the Berlin metropolis that run counter to Rathenau's pessimistic image, and to the popular negative contrast between Berlin and Vienna, between civilization and culture. Occasionally, it was the future possibilities of the most modern metropolis that were applauded, as in the Viennese critic Egon Friedell's, *Ecce Poeta* (1912).[33] There, he castigates nostalgia in Vienna in favour of a plea that 'we must become Americans' in order to become 'good Europeans':

> For this reason Berlin deserves the highest praise because it has so correctly grasped its task as the German Imperial Capital: the task of being a centre of modern civilization. Berlin is a wonderful modern machine hall, a giant electric motor, that with incredible precision, speed and energy brings forth a wealth of complex mechanical products of labour. It is true: this machine at present has no soul. The life of Berlin is the life of a cinematograph theatre, the life of a virtuoso constructed *homme–machine*. But that is enough for a start. Berlin is in the awkward adolescent years of a coming culture that we do not yet know and which must first be worked upon. Berlin examples of tastelessness are at least modern tastelessness, and they are always better than the most tasteless unmodern, because in them the possibilities for development are located.[34]

Friedell's futurist metaphors of the machine and the electric motor (perhaps referencing the image of Peter Behrens's newly built turbine hall for Rathenau's AEG factory) as positive symbols of modernity and his reference to the film draw upon dynamic elements in interpretations of the metropolis that were taken up by the Expressionists. So, too, was his insistence that, despite everything, the future lies with modernity.

Four years earlier, in his *Die Schönheit der grossen Stadt* (*The Beauty of the Metropolis*, 1908),[35] the artist and architect August Endell had more systematically challenged the conception of the modern metropolis, and Berlin in particular, as the site of ugliness. Endell argues for an orientation to present-day modern existence for a 'love of today and here', against those who shrink from the present through a return to nature (as if nature . . . were itself not exclusively nature formed by the human hand'), through a flight to art as if it were beyond the present and through a flight into the past, with nostalgia for what never existed.

In particular, Endell maintains that despite the deficiencies and ugliness of modern big cities, they contain inexhaustable sources of life and – if we view them in a new light – beauty. Although they have 'no form, no pattern', as far as their built-up structure is concerned, nonetheless cities are working structures with human beings creating their own patterns, creating 'the beauty of human patterns'. Nature, too, with its daytime and night-time 'veils' over the city and its streets can create a beauty out of apparent ugliness:

> One can walk for hours through the new parts of Berlin, and indeed get the impression that one has made no headway at all. Everything appears so uniform, despite the loud attempts to call one's attention, to stand out from one's neighbour. And yet even here, in the dreadful heaps of stone, beauty is alive. Here, too, there is nature, landscape. The changing weather, the sun, the rain, the fog form remarkable beauty out of the hopeless ugliness.[36]

Clearly Endell's call for a new aesthetic vision of the city is not a plea for Expressionism. Rather, with its mosaic of descriptions of Berlin scenes and sights, it has greater affinities with the Impressionist separation of what we see from the object itself. The city is 'enveloped', is 'veiled' by light, by darkness, etc.

However, the significance of Endell's aesthetics of modern urban life lies in its insistence upon present-day, mundane metropolitan modernity as a starting point for its aesthetic attraction, despite its ugliness, and as a search for the Utopian traces of beauty in the here and now of the metropolis. If Endell highlights the aesthetic significance of the metropolis, it was other contemporaries who drew connections between representations of the metropolis and new features of metropolitan existence.

The relationship between the economy and modern culture was investigated by several social theorists, such as the sociologist and economist
Werner Sombart, in studies of the economic transformation of modern
culture. In one[37] of several studies he examined the massive agglomeration
of people and commodities in German metropolitan centers, an agglomeration that is exemplified by mass migrations, the 'collectivization of consumption' in the cities, mass economic uncertainty and mass transport
systems ('Almost two billion people travel around annually on the streets
of the big cities in large glass boxes'). Here, Sombart highlighted the
emergence of a new urban culture:

> The distinctive nature of our technology, the distinctive nature of our social
> communal living, in large valleys of stone and upon hills of stone, glass and
> iron, have brought about a situation in which between ourselves and living
> nature . . . a mountain of dead masses of material has piled up that has
> quite specifically given our intellectual life its characteristic features. A new
> cultural foundation has thereby been created: the stone pavement; out of it
> a new culture has emerged: asphalt culture.[38]

This 'asphalt culture' extends everywhere, creating 'a species of human
being that leads its life with no genuine affinity with living nature. . . . A
species with pocket watches, umbrellas, rubber shoes and electric light:
an artificial species.' Even when this urban mass escapes the valleys of
stone for a vacation in nature, it 'hardly enters into an inner relationship
with nature', for the nature it confronts is its own creation; the 'so-called
"sense of nature" is indeed really a product of the cities'.[39] The interaction of mass (of things and people) and change (increasing tempo) creates
a levelling of cultural qualities, even 'a kind of average person', and the
insecurity of all external conditions of life 'has also made the inner core
of human beings *unstable, restless and hurried*'.[40] This condition has also
affected the artist and writer since 'they receive from outside a thousand-
fold impressions, are so bombarded with stimuli that they, too, find it
increasingly difficult to bring to fruition their personal distinctive nature.
For example, if our rich, dazzling age is not capable of developing a
distinctive architectural style is this not due to the fact that a style no
longer has the time to establish itself?'[41]

Sombart had earlier developed such themes with respect to the effects
of technology upon culture at the First German Sociological Association
Conference in Frankfurt in 1910.[42] They elicited a reply from the sociologist
Max Weber, who drew attention to the interaction between technology,
the metropolis and modern culture.[43] The issue, he maintains, as to whether
'modern technology (*Technik*), in the commonly understood sense of the

word, stands in some relationship to formal-aesthetic values must be answered, in my opinion, in the affirmative'.[44] He specifies a relationship between modern technology and aesthetics through the example of the metropolis and its 'technology', its world of things. For Weber:

> quite specific formal values in our modern artistic culture could indeed only be born due to the existence of the *modern metropolis*; the modern metropolis with its streetcars, subway, electrical and other lighting, shop-windows, concert halls and restaurants, cafés, smoke-stacks, masses of stone, and all the wild dance of tones and impressions of colour, the impressions that have their effect upon sexual fantasy and the experiences of variations in psychic make-up, which affect the hungry rabble through all kinds of apparently inexhaustible possibilities of lifestyle and happiness.[45]

The objects of metropolitan existence not merely provide a subject matter for modern artistic endeavours but also penetrate the forms of their representation. Although, in passing, Weber gives the examples of Stefan George and Emile Verhaeren, Weber's thesis here is more appropriate for an emergent Expressionist movement, with its emphasis upon an objective, disjointed culture of metropolitan technology and the attendant 'fantasies', 'dreams' and 'intensive forms of intoxication' which it conjures up.

Indeed, Weber expands upon his thesis with regard to other features of the modern metropolis and modern artistic representation. He asserts that:

> Quite distinctive formal values of modern painting . . . [and] their attainment would not have been possible for human beings who [had not experienced] the dynamic masses, the night-time lights and the reflections of the modern metropolis with its means of communication. . . . I believe that it is quite impossible that certain formal values of modern painting could ever have been realized without the impression, the absolutely distinctive impression made by the modern metropolis, hitherto never offered to human eyes before in the whole of history, forceful by day but totally overwhelming by night. And since what is visible – and this alone is of concern here – in each and every modern metropolis receives its specific quality *primarily* not from property relations and social constellations, but rather from modern technology, so here indeed is a point at which technology purely as such has a very far-reaching significance for artistic culture.[46]

Weber here not merely develops a correlation between formal artistic values and urban technology but also asserts the quasi-autonomy of this technology itself. The belief in the total autonomy of modern technology, which is *not* Weber's view, is a significant dimension of some Expressionist critiques of modern society.

III

The preface to Kurt Pinthus's major, influential anthology of Expressionist poetry, *Menschheitsdämmerung* (1919),[47] with its ambiguous twilight-and-dawn image of humanity, contains the following assertion:

> One feels ever more certainly the impossibility of a humanity that has made itself totally dependent upon its own creations, upon its science, its technology, statistics, trade and industry, upon a hypertrophied communal order of bourgeois and conventional utility.[48]

Somewhat less dramatically, the opening passage of Georg Simmel's essay 'Die Grossstädte und das Geistesleben' ('The Metropolis and Mental Life', 1903)[49] – which deals more fully with modern urban culture – commences as follows:

> The deepest problems of modern life derive from the claim of the individual to preserve the autonomy and individuality of his or her existence in the face of overwhelming social forces, of historical heritage, of external culture, and of the technology of life. . . . The person resists being levelled down and worn out by a socio-technical mechanism. An inquiry into the inner meaning of specifically modern life and its products . . . must seek to solve the equation which structures like the metropolis set up between the individual and the supra-individual contents of life.[50]

Indeed, such thematic affinities should not be surprising since, for many contemporaries, Simmel possessed an instinct for the times that rendered his reflections anticipations of not yet fully articulated positions. Writing in 1920, Friedrich Hübner, for instance, names only Nietzsche and Simmel as philosophical precursors of Expressionism: 'In philosophy Georg Simmel prepared the ground for the new mode of thought . . . with his elaboration of the concepts of "form", "self" and "life".'[51] For the moment, it is important to indicate the relevance of his essay on the metropolis and other analyses of the city for an understanding of the experiential foundations of Expressionism's representations of the big city.

The metropolis is, for Simmel, 'not a spatial entity with sociological consequences, but a sociological entity that is formed spatially'. Human interaction is experienced as different relational ways of filling in space. Social interaction and human sociation fill in space. In his essay on space, Simmel highlights a number of spatial forms confronted in interaction: the exclusiveness or uniqueness of space (such as districts in cities); boundaries of space (as in spatial framing, the picture-frame, the enclosing boundary of darkness); the fixing of social forms in space (including the rendezvous, whose significance 'lies on the one hand in the tension between punctuality and the fleeting nature of the occurrence and its spatio-temporal fixing on the other'), and the individualizing of space (as in numbering houses); spatial proximity and distance (including the abstraction and indifference of the spatially adjacent in the metropolis); and finally movement in space (the traveller, the wanderer, the stranger and the dynamic of metropolitan interactions).[52]

The metropolis is not merely the focal point of social differentiation and the complex intersection of social networks but also the location of more indefinite collectivities such as crowds. The *openness* of the city, facilitating the intersection of diverse social strata, can be contrasted with the relative isolation and social distance manifested by the 'concentrated minority' in the ghetto (as in the Berlin 'Scheunenviertel'). As for the concentrated mass, Simmel portrays the crowd in darkness in a manner that is relevant to Expressionist representations of the city at night. In a gathering in darkness, we are

> able to survey only the most immediate environment, with an impenetrable black wall rearing up behind it, [and] one feels closely pressed together with the most immediate surroundings; the delimitation against space outside the visible surroundings has reached its limiting case; this space seems to have disappeared. On the other hand, this very fact also causes the actually existing boundaries to disappear; fantasy expands the darkness into exaggerated possibilities; one feels surrounded by a fantastically indefinite and unlimited space.[53]

But, more generally, the intersection of social groups and individuals in the metropolis generates spatial constellations that provide for a total indifference to one's fellow human beings. Here the development of boundaries and social distance in the metropolis is of fundamental significance in understanding social interaction and patterns of network formation in the city. Perhaps the most striking dimension of Simmel's analysis of the metropolis lies in his examination of the psychological consequences of the endlessly dynamic interaction of networks, things, individuals and images within 'the genuine showplace of this culture', where

> in buildings and educational institutions, in the wonders and comforts of space-conquering technology, in the formations of communal life and in the visible state institutions, there is offered such an overpowering wealth of crystallized, impersonalized mind . . . that the personality cannot maintain itself when confronted with it.[54]

Simmel posits here a widening gap between objective and subjective culture – 'the atrophy of individual culture and the hypertrophy of objective culture'[55] – through a tendency for both cultures to develop a relative autonomy, with objective culture possessing a 'unity and autonomous self-sufficiency' and subjective culture emerging out of 'the subjectivism of modern times', and its attendant 'dissociation' and 'retreat' from objective culture.

Nowhere is this apparently autonomous objective culture more evident than in the metropolis, where individuals are faced with the shock of 'the rapid and unbroken change in external stimuli' that they experience 'with every crossing of the street, with the speed and diversity of professional and social life' as 'the rapid crowding of changing images, the sharp discontinuity in the grasp of a single glance, and the unexpectedness of onrushing impressions'.[56] This immediate experience of modernity as ever-changing, discontinuous and diverse impressions is depicted in Expressionist streetscapes, sometimes to the point of total bombardment of sense impressions and the attendant disorientation of the self.

However, the 'particularly abstract existence' of the metropolis originates in part in the very labyrinth of interactions themselves, which require functionality, precise differentiation, intellectuality, exactitude and calculability.[57] Thus, what appears to the individual as 'the tumult of the metropolis' with its myriad criss-crossing of abstract interactions and impressions, as 'the brevity and infrequency of meetings which are allotted to each individual' – in short, what *appears* as a *chaos* of *impressions*, shocks and *interactions* – in fact results from 'the *calculating exactness* of practical life' in the metropolis. Such calculated exactitude is necessary in order that 'the agglomeration of so many persons with such differentiated interests' are able 'to intertwine with one another into a many-membered organism'.[58]

The 'rapid and unbroken change in external and internal stimuli' in the metropolis results in a dramatic 'increase in nervous life', in the *neurasthenia* of modern human beings, in the *pathological forms* of agoraphobia and hyperaesthesia. The impossibility of otherwise retaining a stable subjectivity against the endless shocks of metropolitan existence accounts for the 'psychological distance' created by the intellect as a defence mechanism. At the same time, the heightening of intellectual, 'rational' defence mechanisms is matched by a heightening of emotional responses that remain *unsatisfied* by the 'stimulations, interests, fillings in of time and consciousness' in the metropolis.

Simmel here points to the dialectic of subjective and objective culture in which we can only fully realize our subjectivity through its externalization in objective cultural forms, and yet the latter cannot realize our desires. Hence, individuals experience a permanent 'feeling of tension, expectation and unreleased intense desires', a 'secret restlessness' that results in our endless neurotic search for momentary satisfaction in ever-new stimulations, sensations and external activities. . . . We become entangled in the instability and helplessness that manifests itself as the tumult of the metropolis, as the mania for travelling, as the wild pursuit of competition, and as the typical modern disloyalty with regard to taste, style, opinions and personal relations.[59]

This implies that 'the *inner barrier* between people that is indispensable for the modern form of life', 'the mutual reserve and indifference', and the blasé attitude are *never fully effective* against the experience of modernity as discontinuity and disintegration of experience of time, space and causality. Hence, *alienated* forms of existence can become the objective forms within which we live.

One such form, epitomizing urban society, is the blasé *attitude*, arising from 'the rapidly changing and closely compressed contrasting stimulations of the nerves', which culminates in 'an incapacity to react to new sensations with the appropriate energy'. Thus, where individuals are confronted with a mass of commodities and sensations, and where all values are reduced to exchange values, the blasé individual 'experiences all things as being of an equally dull and grey hue, as not worth getting excited about'.[60] Yet the unreleased desire for amusement and excitement has not been removed and accounts for 'the craving today for excitement, for extreme impressions, for the greatest speed in their change, for "stimulation" as such in impressions, relationships and information'.[61]

However, the metropolis does provide an 'immense abundance of machines, products and supra-individual organisations' that offer the individual 'endless habits, endless distractions and endless superficial needs', and 'fillings in of time and consciousness'.[62] This concentration of objective culture is dependent in the metropolis upon the complex intersection of networks of circulation of commodities and individuals. Simmel's analysis of metropolitan modernity emphasizes the spheres of circulation, exchange and consumption, and the accelerating tempo of changes within them.

The metropolis is thus a centre of the reification of 'a culture of things as the culture of human beings'. Just as Weber proclaims the quasi-autonomy of the technology of urban existence, so Simmel insists on the creation of a supra-individual objective culture that confronts human beings as autonomous:

> In highly developed epochs with an advanced division of labour, cultural achievements mature and grow together into an autonomous realm, as it were, things become more complete, spiritual, to some extent following ever more obediently an inner objective logic of expediency.[63]

This increasing autonomy of objective culture provides the foundation for a prevalent pessimism with regard to modern culture, namely 'the ever-wider yawning abyss between the culture of things and that of human beings'.[64] Later, Simmel brings together the apparently autonomous realm of circulation of commodities and individuals and the autonomy of the objective culture, when he declares:

> The 'fetishism' which Marx assigned to economic commodities represents only a special case of this general fate of the contents of culture. With the increase in culture these contents more and more stand under a paradox: ... originally created by human subjects ... in their intermediate form of objectivity ... they follow an immanent logic of development ... impelled not by physical necessities, but by truly cultural ones.[65]

Similarly, within the cultural sphere itself, there is a permanent struggle between life and form. Life generates form and struggles against that which it has created, impelled by an opposition to 'form *as such*, against the *principle* of form'.[66]

In 'The Conflict in Modern Culture' (1914), Simmel gives an instance of this opposition to form in the artistic realm:

> Of all the hotchpotch of aspirations covered by the general name of *futurism*, only the movement described as *Expressionism* seems to stand out with a certain identifiable degree of unity and clarity ... the point of Expressionism is that the artist's inner impulse is perpetuated in the work, or to be more precise, *as* the work, exactly as it is experienced. The intention is not to express or contain the impulse in a form imposed upon it by something external, be it ideal or real.[67]

Expressionism relies upon 'stimuli from objects in the external world' without Impressionism's 'need for the identity between the form of the cause and that of its effect'.[68] And this new art 'does not have a meaning by itself'. As abstract art, it is 'indifferent to the traditional standards of beauty or ugliness which are connected with the primacy of form. Life, in its flow, is not determined by a goal but driven by a force.' This accounts for 'the desire for completely abstract art among some sectors of modern youth [which] may stem from a passion for an immediate and naked expression of self'.[69]

Elsewhere, Simmel draws attention to an 'unmistakable mechanizing, mathematizing tendency' in recent years:

> All reconstruction of that which one terms the artist's 'calculation': the precise separation of 'planes', the schemata of the horizontal and the vertical, the triangular and rectangular in composition, the determination of contrapposto, theories of the golden section, of the visual arts as 'spatial configuration' and up to the theory of complementary colours – all this

breaks up the work of art into individual moments and elements and thereby strives to 'explain' the work of art by putting it together again out of these partial regularities and demands.[70]

Simmel finds the modern work of art in a situation that is 'analogous to the mechanistic natural sciences'. Whilst no artistic movement is mentioned here, Simmel's remarks are clearly relevant to Cubism and Expressionism. Although Simmel does not draw this inference, this new approach to the work of art, following Meidner's manifesto, is closer to our experience of the metropolis and is a representation of it in all its fragmentary images.

At the same time, the new tendency is towards the affirmation of the work of art as it is experienced by the artist's lack of reliance on existing forms. Such a tendency accords with Simmel's insistence in his *Lebensphilosophie* that life must assert itself continuously against existing reproduction of forms. In part, this is a struggle of dynamic impulses against static forms, a spontaneity of expression against a reproduced form. For Simmel, 'the essence of life is intensification, increase, growth, of plenitude and power, strength and beauty from within itself – not in relation to any definable goal but purely to its own development'.[71]

In the metropolitan context, the city is the focal point of both objective culture and the reified forms, including the reified forms of formal intellectual distance and reserve that its inhabitants adopt as a barrier to immediate life impressions. Modern artistic movements struggle against this rigidified objective culture and, in the case of Expressionism, seek to give substance to the immediate experience of metropolitan existence, in all its dynamic, rhythmic and ruptured fragmentariness. In this respect, Expressionism calls into question Simmel's conception of the metropolis in relation to a landscape. In 'The Philosophy of Landscape' ('Philosophie der Landschaft', 1910), he draws a contrast between nature and the metropolis. Referring to objects in nature, he states that 'the fact that these things observable upon a piece of earth are "nature" and not lines of streets with department stores and automobiles, this does not yet make this piece of earth into a landscape'.[72] A 'piece' of nature is an internal contradiction since nature can have no 'pieces'. By implication, the metropolis does possess pieces – of architecture, traffic, urban artefacts, social interactions. It is the pieces and fragments of 'the culture of things as the culture of human beings' that Expressionism seeks to represent in its 'streetscapes' and 'cityscapes'. There is another respect in which Expressionism's aim accords with Simmel's delineation of modern metropolitan existence, namely the attempt to represent artistically our inner experience of it. In an essay on 'Rodin' (1911), Simmel describes modernity as psychologism, the experiencing and interpretation of the world in terms of the reactions of our inner life, and indeed as *an inner world*, the *dissolution of fixed contents* in the fluid element of the soul, from which all that is substantive is filtered and whose forms are merely *forms of* motion.[73]

If we substitute subjectivism for 'psychologism' and emphasize the shift to inner lived experience (*Erlebnis*), the destabilizing of content, the preponderance of fluid forms in flux and the domination of the fragmentary, then again Simmel's delineation of metropolitan experience as the exemplar of experience of modernity becomes strikingly relevant for an understanding of at least some dimensions of Expressionism.

Finally, Simmel illustrates both the ambiguous attitude to the metropolis found in German Expressionism and the Utopian potentialities of the metropolis for human freedom. Recalling dialectics of subjective and objective culture, Simmel points out that:

> The atrophy of individual culture through the hypertrophy of objective culture is one reason for the bitter hatred which the preachers of the most extreme individualism, above all Nietzsche, harbor against the metropolis. But it is, indeed, also a reason why these preachers are so passionately loved in the metropolis and why they appear to the metropolitan person as the prophets and saviours of his or her unsatisfied yearnings.[74]

But is the metropolis a site for the realization of 'unsatisfied yearnings'? Simmel maintains it is the site for the development, in often contradictory directions, of two forms of individualism: individual independence and the elaboration of individuality. The metropolis provides 'the arena' for the struggle between these two forms of individualism and, potentially, for their reconciliation.

IV

The engagement with Expressionism, either for a relatively brief period of time or over a lifetime, was continued by two of Simmel's students: Siegfried Kracauer[75] and Ernst Bloch.[76] Whereas Kracauer developed a distinctive interest in deciphering the fields of signification in the modern metropolis that went far beyond Expressionism (though Expressionism remained a concern in his work on film), Bloch retained both a lifelong concern with the Utopian possibilities embedded in modernity and a style of writing that continued to display Expressionist impulses.

Within Kracauer's early writings, before he turned his attention to the 'insignificant superficial manifestations' of Weimar modernity, to the deciphering of the 'hieroglyphics' of spatial images in the metropolis, we find several of his confrontations with Expressionism. Towards the end of the First World War and in its immediate aftermath, Kracauer produced a series of unpublished manuscripts, one of which – 'On Expressionism: Essence and Meaning of a Movement of the Times' ('Über den Expressionismus', 1918)[77] is dedicated to investigating 'wherein the essence of this new direction in art really lies. What is at issue is not the analysis of individual works but rather the investigation of those intellectual structures that make such works possible.' A common element of Expressionism is that it is the work of a young generation 'conditioned by the total situation of our time'. Kracauer's exploration of the intellectual situation is in terms reminiscent of Simmel's earlier account of the widening separation between subjective and objective culture.

The world of external reality has a number of features, amongst which are its apparent objectivity, its conventional character and its chaotic state:

> The world of reality compared with each subjective world is a chaos. Unfettered by unified value principles, uninformed and lacking in substance, it extends itself. . . . The more it is our intention to assimilate and comprehend it, the more we abandon our original intellectual spontaneity.[78]

This conception of an objectified world of chaos is affirmed when he writes that, although 'our age is an age of lust for life', we confront a chaotic external life world in which

> lights, and shadows, buildings, paths, landscapes and cities, locomotives, human bodies, thronging masses, love, passion, lament of the lonely soul – they all turbulently swirl together in a many-formed existence; they come together in blatant opposition to one another.[79]

This reality confronting the individual appears to be governed by its own laws. Indeed, one feature stands out in contemporary intellectual life, namely 'the discovery of the autonomous nature of reality for the purpose of its ever more perfect domination'. This reality is partly created by science insofar as 'the more science elevates itself into a power of life, the more untouchable and objective the world becomes'. Along with the impersonal laws of capitalism, these forces produce the 'domination of science, of capitalism and, developing out of them, of technology'.[80]

Relations between individuals are held together only functionally by their particular interests, especially occupational interests 'as one of the major forms of contemporary communal action and intellectual cohesion'. But 'what is almost always lacking in any occupation is the existence of the human being, of his or her complete essence'. This produces a particular form of individualism in which 'the self-adjustment to a rigid reality and to the overarching totality has its corresponding reflection in a boundless, arbitrary individualism'. In other words, the form of present-day association of human beings is best expressed by the notion of civilization, the anarchy of values, and the absence of community.

Aesthetically, in order to understand Expressionism, 'one must have already confronted Impressionism: Impressionism's world is one that knows no future, it is solely the contemporary moment'. Ultimately, what is typical 'for the Impressionists is still their emphasis upon the basic principle of "l'art pour l'art" '.[81] In contrast, the new Expressionist artist 'always forcefully retains his or her active self'. And, in relation to external reality, Expressionist art

> not merely pushes reality aside but rather (primarily in painting) directly confronts it and battles with it. The Expressionist wants to destroy reality absolutely, and his or her work should not in the least be suggestive of it.[82]

Instead, the goal of this new art is 'to give expression to lived experience (*Erlebnis*) in its naked giveness as much as possible'. But although Expressionist art is deeply caught up in present life and its phenomena, nonetheless:

> A strong belief in the future and the victorious force of its nature unites the Expressionists. The Expressionist does indeed look forwards, he never languishes in the past. An enemy of the present, an adversary of reality, he strives to overcome both. . . . He is ready to engage in deeds, his basic attitude is an affirmative one.[83]

This longing for action and this waiting for genuine engagement are recurrent themes in Kracauer's early writings, as is the problematic nature of the contemporary individual. Hence his view that 'expressionism in fact is essentially nothing other than a revolt, a cry of despair of the present-day personality, enslaved and condemned to powerlessness. It is, above all, in the first instance, a *cultural* movement, in the second, an *artistic* movement'.[84] Kracauer's assessment of the latter in this manuscript is that 'a terrible danger appears to be bequeathed to Expressionist painting in particular: the danger of being unintelligible'.[85]

Only two years later, in 1920, we find Kracauer, in 'Schicksalswende der Kunst' ('Art's Turn of Fate'), declaring that 'the *Expressionist movement* in art, distinctive to our times, is ripe for its demise'.[86] Whereas, today, 'the experiences it embodies are no longer our experiences', before the First World War Expressionism responded to an 'epoch dominated above all by the spirit of the natural sciences and the spirit of the capitalist economic system', which together created an external reality of life (*Lebenswirklichkeit*) that was 'so objective and so secured within itself as no other reality before it'. The result was a transformation of 'the whole human environment' into 'a structure of horrifying impersonality' in which human beings appeared almost as mere fortuitous elements. In turn, human beings were confronted with 'a mechanized nature', with an atomized society that locked individuals into 'an invisible network of rational and objective-technical relations'[87] devoid of fundamental elements of human community.

With individuals shut off from this 'God-estranged reality', they were as if encased in 'a brazen solid wall'. In this context, it was 'Expressionism's historical merit to have forced a breach in this wall, to have reduced it to ruins'. Thus, even before the First World War, Expressionism did in art that

which the great social revolutions of the present set as their task in the realms of real life: the destruction of the powers of existence that have hitherto been valid. First of all, Expressionism unmistakably took up battle against the average reality that surrounded it![88]

Its aim was not merely the destruction of constraining forms, nor even the restoration of 'differentiated and overrefined individual persons', but rather 'the Expressionist artist felt and thought of himself or herself to some extent as a primal self (*Ur-ich*), filled with individual experiences of a totally elementary nature – a soul in search of a God, with all the attendant ecstatic convulsions'.

The consequence of this position for artistic creation is the emergence of a new art:

Paintings emerge that hardly still refer to the world of our senses. They transcend our accustomed space and the contemporaneity (*Geichzeitigkeit*) of appearances and press fragments of our perceptions into a texture of lines and body-like forms, whose structure is almost exclusively determined by the inner needs of the human being transformed into a primal self. Painter and poet endeavour to strip existing reality of its power and to reveal it for that which it actually is: a deceptive shadow-like essence, a chaos without soul, without meaning. Here, there appear things and human beings in an ostensibly known form, but their external form is only an empty mask, which the artist strips off or makes transparent in order that the true face reveals itself beneath.[89]

Such human figures as do appear in Expressionist art seem to be typical night-time figures, but they 'cast the burning torch into the buildings of our hitherto existence and inflame the ghosts into revolution. The whole essence of the outlived epoch often takes on its form in the schematic personage of the "father" and, against him, as the symbol of tradition, the preserver of what exists, there arises the "son" prepared to murder'.[90]

As an instance of this new art, Kracauer elsewhere examines the work of Max Beckmann. The modern artist's task is to reveal the outside world's 'terrible meaninglessness'. In Beckmann's cityscapes:

The thousand terrors of the street are revealed to him. People who in their innermost being are alien to one another hasten past one another or concentrate themselves in fortuitously huddled-up large masses. They meet in societies and hang around in cafés, these lavas of men, women and children, but despite their spatial proximity there is no connecting bond of one soul with another; rather, each one remains enclosed within themselves and their fate. . . . Time and again, especially in drawings and lithographs, Beckmann portrays the wild chaos that unfolds between swaying buildings on streets and squares. The high and the low, eyes of anguish, gripping hands, screaming mouths, prostitutes' wanton faces, faded masks, bestial caricature whirl around one another: a terrible turmoil above which no star has ever shone. . . . He visits the cabarets, the taverns and the wine bars and is everywhere the observer of the same theatrical game: here too a surging crowd of desires, a reciprocal search that never leads to any meeting, a confused mixture of delirious things and disoriented human beings.[91]

If the city streets are characterized by empty interactions of soulless individuals, the interiors are even more terrifying. In Beckmann's series of images of hell, the desolation becomes much more threatening. Here, and Kracauer obviously has Beckmann's 'Night' in mind:

Murderous lust prowls through the nights and organizes pogroms in which women and men are slowing martyred to death with devilish inventive genius. The whimpering pain of the victims is drowned out by the hellish din that escapes from the blood-red loudspeaker . . . the whole order of things is turned upside down.[92]

The image of the disintegration of existing reality is a powerful one in Beckmann's paintings of this period. For Kracauer, it is one in which:

The earth quakes, the temple of God shudders, and with it the rental barracks and factories also finally sink with it. All the things that our civilization has created are ripe for destruction.[93]

To Kracauer the force of Beckmann's paintings derives from the artist's inner strivings, 'the fanaticism of honesty, with which he reveals to the world that follows the whole naked horror of our times'.

The young Adorno – an admirer of Kracauer's work – detected a contradiction within Expressionist movements in their later phases. Acknowledging Expressionism's 'declaration of war' upon existing art forms, during which 'the rusty barbed-wire fence between arts and life is torn up', and its attack upon earlier art forms that 'lost sight of individual truthfulness', Expressionism, for its part, 'threatens to lose the typical' and to create its own lie that is embedded in a commitment to total subjectivity. For Adorno, 'what has become subjective and contingent remains subjective and contingent in its effect as well'.[94] The world becomes the subjective soul, 'a depiction of the self projected onto the world' without fully exploring the duality of world and self and without fully revealing the world:

> The artist, unable or unwilling, to shape the multiplicity of the world from its totality into a type, makes the individual and ultimately the contingent experiential impression the depiction of the world, and by doing so simply subordinates the soul to the totality to which he has undertaken to give artistic form. . . . Symptom of the ultimate untruthfulness is the disintegration of realities – the world, robbed of its reality, becomes a plaything in the hands of one who takes it up only for the sake of duality and not in order to explore its meaning through this duality.[95]

The representation of the typical and the real therefore required a new artistic impulse, a new orientation to the external world. Perhaps a new form of realism.

For his part, in 1920, Kracauer saw Expressionism as having fulfilled its mission of representing, artistically at least, the 'triumph of the soul over reality', the negation of the empty inner world and the awakening of 'the need for new world formations'. Although Expressionism produced new artistic means of expressing and representing reality, what was now required was to go beyond Expressionism, to realize that which it set in motion: '*the construction of a new reality in art*'. Hence, the realization of what Expressionism proclaimed must be set in motion, the creation of a new reality

> that no longer permits the advocacy, as does Expressionism, of the concerns of an abstract humanity by means of equally abstract types, but rather gives life to the general in the particular, embodying totally the human essence in accordance with its whole surging fullness.[96]

This search for concretization is one which Kracauer himself engaged upon, but only from around 1926 onwards was it fully manifested in his own rich constructions of metropolitan modernity that go far beyond the Expressionist impulses which he saw as ripe for being transcended in 1920.[97]

V

In contrast to Kracauer, Ernst Bloch retained a commitment to the Utopian impetus, at least, of German Expressionism long after its demise. Some of his own work, and above all *Geist der Utopie* (*The Spirit of Utopia*,

1918; 1923)[98] was itself a major contribution to the Utopianism of Expressionism, extensive traces of which are to be found in his later works, such as *Erbschaft dieser Zeit* (*Heritage of Our Times*, 1935)[99] and *Das Prinzip Hoffnung* (*The Principle of Hope*, 1954–9).[100] Indeed, in its mode of presentation with its 'primacy of expression over signification', Bloch's whole philosophy is, according to Adorno,

> that of Expressionism. It is preserved in the idea of breaking through the encrusted surface of life. Human immediacy wishes to make itself heard unmediated: the philosophical elements of Bloch protests against the reification of the world just like the Expressionist human subject.[101]

Bloch's *Geist der Utopie* is a radical Expressionist assertion of 'intellectual renewal', a 'confrontation of the self' (*Selbstbegegnung*) and the development of a conception of Utopia located in the here and now of the present. As Arno Münster suggests, despite the affinities with, for instance Gustav Landauer's 'mystical religious concept of revolution' – evident also in Bloch's *Thomas Münzer als Theologe der Revolution* (1921)[102] – Bloch's notion of Utopia does not presuppose any concretization in a specific socio-historical context. Rather:

> For Bloch, Utopia is from the very outset always a *tendency*, a fundamental dimension immanent in the material itself, the 'not-yet-drawn-out' of existence, that cannot be realized or represented . . . in any pre-existing model.[103]

It does not presuppose a future state of affairs but is located, hidden, waiting to be drawn out, to be expressed now. A further feature of Bloch's position is his rejection not merely of total Utopian blueprints but also of the notion that reality is a homogeneous totality. If it were, its seemingly insignificant Utopian elements could never be brought to expression. In this respect, Bloch's work in this period – despite the affinities between it and Georg Lukács's *History and Class Consciousness* with regard to a romantic anti-capitalism and variants of 'messianic Marxism' (in Bloch's case, more messianism than Marxism) – differs in its rejection of totalizations of society, reification and Utopia. Rather, for Bloch:

> Actuality and Utopia are not opposites, but 'the now' is finally the sole concern of Utopia, whether one understands it as the constant demand to throw off masks, ideologies, and transitory mythologies, or as premonition of the adequation of the process which recognises both the driving tendency and the hidden genuine reality in the now.[104]

That 'now' time of *Geist der Utopie* is one that is permeated by Expressionism. Here and elsewhere there is evidence of Bloch's reflections upon the metropolis, its buildings, its architecture.

Several such interventions are found in an early section of *Geist der Utopie*, titled 'Die Erzeugung des Ornaments' ('The Creation of the Ornament'), which is dominated by references to the Expressionism of Marc, Kandinsky, Pechstein and Kokoshka. Within this movement, whether it be 'Kandinsky who has been called the intensive Expressionist, Pechstein, the extensive Expressionist, and Marc, the great, most subjectivist and simultaneously most objectivist artist of the "concept" of the thing', they are all seeking 'to anchor the fleeting element of feeling and to embody it purely economically in firm drawing, fixed spatial relations'.[105] Today, 'we seek the magical creator who allows us to confront ourselves, to encounter ourselves', in a new environment, with a new vision that 'travels like a swimmer, like a cyclone through that which is there (*das Gegebene*)'.[106] In fact, for this new way of seeing things,

> the cinematograph is the best picture gallery, the substitute for all the great general art exhibitions of the world. This should be kept in mind by all those who must ask with each expressionist image what it represents; by what means, for instance, to their eye, that is like a mere photographic plate, hell can shrink back and resemble a street corner. For already since van Goch, this has evidently changed; we are suddenly involved in things and precisely this is what is painted; it is indeed still a visible tumult, still railings, underpasses, iron beams, brick walls, but suddenly all this overlaps in a remarkable manner, the discarded cornerstone lights up all at once and what has been drawn in all appearances, that which is incomprehensibly related, that which is lost to us, the near, far, Sais-like aspects of the world emerges in van Goch's paintings.[107]

But it is not merely the world of the metropolitan cityscape that is transformed by Expressionism. The same fate befalls still life, too, in the 'Expressionist revolution'.

> Grass is no longer grass, the multifarious disappears and that which is facelike (*das Gesichthafte*) is victorious. The thing becomes a mask, a 'concept', a fetish, a completely deformed, denaturalized formula of secret excitements towards a goal, the inner human being and the inside of the world move closer. . . . Suddenly I see my eyes, my place, my position: I am myself this drawer, and this fish, this kind of fish lying in the drawer.[108]

Bloch highlights here the intense 'materiality of things' that Expressionism reveals.

Yet it is not just the representation of still life – even in the 'new Expressionism', which uses 'things merely as memory stages of [our] . . . stubborn origins, or as punctuation marks for keeping or storing their continuous recollection' – that is significant. Still life 'can be superior to all cultures – in its escapism and intensification of small things'.[109]

The 'still life' of small things is also that with which we surround ourselves, the ornaments of our existence. They are the products of machine
production:

> The machine knew how to make everything so lifeless, technical and sub-
> human in individual elements, just as the streets of west Berlin are in their
> totality. Its actual goal is the bathroom and toilet, the most unquestionable
> and original achievements of this era. . . . Here the fact that things can be
> washed up reigns.[110]

These things of everyday existence were covered over with ornament and
style in all their heterogeneity by historicism. And here there exists –
'despite all antagonistic, malignant and negative elements that can be
read equally from the death of style in the mid-nineteenth century – the
functional connection of this epidemic of styles with the positive forces of
Expressionism'.[111]

Such 'positive forces', however, are contradictory, at least with respect
to the tension between the functional and the ornamental that exists
contemporaneously. For Bloch:

> The birth of integral technology and the birth of integral expressionism,
> accurately kept apart from each other, arise from the same magic: complete
> void of ornament on the one hand, utmost superabundance, ornamenta-
> tion on the other, but both are variables of the same exodus.[112]

Such tensions permeate architectural structures and the inability of functional form to expand stylistically. In this context:

> There will never be any Expressionist houses built if one attaches great
> importance to unified form. It is impossible to produce all of the rectan-
> gular shiny functional forms in an abundantly ornamental way, to break
> up and cover the firm windows, elevators, desks, the telephones with
> Lehmbruck's, with Archipenko's curves. The only contiguity, and in this
> instance only an apparent one, lies in places for celebrations, in exhibition
> halls, in the theatre, particularly when this space, as it is with Poelzig,
> shines into the stage itself, with the separate magic of its semblance.[113]

Later, in *The Principle of Hope*, Bloch was to argue that the architecture of Taut's 'house of heaven' or that of 'the "pancosmist" Paul
Scheerbart . . . remained fruitless'. This was because architecture 'is and
remains a social creation, it cannot blossom at all in the hollow space of
late capitalism'.[114] Nonetheless, such fantasies as were sketched and sometimes completed, even in the age of functional technology, were the product of a remarkable concentrated outburst of fantasy, testimony of Bloch's
later statement that 'ornament is the bad conscience of architecture'.[115]

In the Expressionist decade, and at least until his emigration, the site for these fantasies remained for Bloch, Berlin. As he stated in 1921: '1 do indeed believe that Berlin, the forceful, Utopian, is still of all others my city.'[116] Bloch had already detected that Utopian element in an article 'Das südliche Berlin' ('Southern Berlin') from 1916. Berlin was 'on the way to a new exuberance, in some respects to breaking through the grey life. Earlier one hoped for the same from Munich and still earlier from Vienna'.[117] The city had been for a time 'seductive, experimental'. Over a decade later, in 1928, in 'Berlin nach zwei Jahren' ('Berlin, two years later'), despite the growing crisis, Bloch could assert that 'the good element is, as we know, Berlin's dynamism, the journey into unknown stretches of heaven. To the citizen, the treadmill, when it moves rapidly, appears to be an airstrip.'[118] Still later, in 1932, in 'Berlin aus der Landschaft gesehen' ('Berlin Viewed from the Landscape'), Bloch explores Berlin's contradictory newness in the landscape, but whereas 'other cities are often mere spectres of a better past, the hollow Berlin is possibly – there is no other choice – the spectre of a better future'.[119]

In his major published work of the 1930s *Heritage of Our Times* (1935), the Utopian elements of the present become more difficult to detect and to defend, not merely against a destructive Nazism but also against ostensibly 'progressive' commentators such as Lukács and others. Almost alone within this political discourse, Bloch defends what is valuable in 'authentic Expressionism' as the 'first and most genuine form of non-representational, different dream-montage of our times'.[120] Originally, Expressionism was:

> image explosion, was torn-up surface even starting with the original, namely with the subject which violently tore up and cross-connected. Thus this subject of bourgeois-aesthetic opposition . . . definitely sought contact with the world . . . [it] covered the world with war, mounted its fragments into grotesque caricatures, mounted into the hollow spaces above all excesses and hopes of a substantial kind, archaic and Utopian images.[121]

And though Expressionism sought to explode reification, it lacked contact with the concrete means for overcoming this reification. Nonetheless, for Bloch, the genuine elements of this movement still render cultural inheritance problematic, 'simply because the Expressionist epoch so completely tore to shreds the casual routine, the conventional associations from the past'.[122] Its abrupt dislocations of the surface remain testimony to the negation of reality as homogeneity, as continuity, since 'reality is never unbroken context . . . but always still – interruption and always still fragment'.[123] For Bloch, at least, in 1938 'the inheritance of Expressionism is not yet at an end, because it has not yet been started on at all'.[124] Is the same still true today?

7

The City Rationalized

Martin Wagner's New Berlin

As intellectualism suppresses belief in magic, the world's processes become disenchanted . . . and henceforth simply 'are' and 'happen' but no longer signify anything. As a consequence, there is a growing demand that the world and the total pattern of life be subject to an order that is significant and meaningful.

Max Weber, *Economy and Society*

[Berlin is] the place in which one quickly forgets. Indeed it appears as if this city has control of the magical means of eradicating all memories. It is present-day and, moreover, it makes it a point of honour of being absolutely present-day. . . . I know of no other city that is capable of so promptly shaking off what has just occurred. . . . Only in Berlin are the transformations of the past so radically stripped from memory.

Siegfried Kracauer, 'Wiederholung'

Capitalism's core defect: it rationalizes not too much but rather too little. The thinking promoted by capitalism resists culminating in that reason which arises from the basis of human beings. The current site of capitalist thinking is marked by *abstractness*.

Siegfried Kracauer, 'The Mass Ornament'

I

When Max Weber published the first of his two articles on 'The Protestant Ethic and the "Spirit" of Capitalism' early in 1905, he introduced the concept of spirit in inverted commas, suggesting that the notion of spirit was a strange, unusual or uncomfortable one in relation to capitalism.[1] In a number of respects, Weber's articles on the spirit of capitalism can be viewed as a confrontation with Werner Sombart's *Der Moderne Kapitalismus* of 1902, a substantial and substantive study of the origins of modern capitalism that had already addressed the issue of the spirit of capitalism.[2] There, and in his study of the German economy in the nineteenth century, published in 1903,[3] Sombart's discussion of the spirit of capitalism and the metropolis were not in parentheses. For his part, Weber drew upon Benjamin Franklin as a key historical source for delineating the spirit of capitalism and, amongst Weber's contemporaries, Georg Simmel and his *Philosophy of Money* (1900).[4] However, if there was an emergent discourse and controversy surrounding the spirit of capitalism in the early years of this century in Germany, then the same was possibly true with respect to the spirit of the metropolis. These two interrelated sites of modernity – modern capitalism and the modern metropolis – were explored in greater or lesser detail by Weber, Sombart and Simmel in the early years of the twentieth century.[5] In turn, they may be viewed as part of a much wider discourse on the nature of the modern, capitalist metropolis and the search for its spirit, which is to be found in the journals and newspaper literature of the period.[6]

Given the dramatic expansion of metropolitan life in Germany since the mid-nineteenth century and its varied impact upon the consciousness and life-chances of its population, it is not surprising that there should have been a contested response to the modern metropolis, and even to its definition.[7] If the definition of a metropolis is an urban conglomeration with a population in excess of 100,000, then by 1910 there were 47 metropolitan centres in Germany (compared with one – Berlin – at the start of the nineteenth century). If the then current definition of a world city had been one with a population in excess of one million, then there was only one such city – Berlin. Its symbolic and hence mental elevation to this status occurred in 1896 on the occasion of the Berlin trade exhibition.[8] The first German municipal exhibition was held in Dresden (the fifth largest city) in 1903, the exhibition and competition for the creation of a Greater Berlin in Berlin in 1910 and the municipal exhibition in Düsseldorf in 1911. Such major celebrations of metropolitan existence only partly sublated the powerful anti-urban impulses of many social strata in Germany. The division of the city (*Stadt*) and the country (*Land*) was merely part of a wider ideological confrontation between modernity and tradition, society and community, civilization and culture and, in the appropriate context, between America and Europe, which was broadly articulated, often within emergent disciplines purporting to understand modern society, such as sociology.[9]

What this all suggests is that a series of discourses developed at the turn of the century that focused upon the nature of the modern metropolis, the directions for city building (*Städtebau*), the relationship between the development of modern capitalism and the modern metropolis and the non-material (spiritual, mental, cultural) dimensions of the modern metropolis.[10] To give some indication of the then current modes of conceptualizing the metropolis and capitalism in this period, we should note that Sombart places emphasis upon the development of an 'asphalt culture' in the modern metropolis; Simmel announces the most significant feature of mental life (*Geistesleben*) to be a dramatic increase in nervous life; the debates on the directions for city planning in the 1890s associate the spatial forms of the modern metropolis with the generation of new pathologies (for Sitte, agoraphobia; for others, amnesia); the new discussion of the emergence of modern capitalism indicates the transformation of our mental and motivational orientation to economic (and urban) life into one dominated by a restricted form of (for Weber, 'formal') rationality. In other words, without elaborating upon these developments, there is evidence of an increasing focus upon the cultural, mental and spiritual dimensions of both the modern metropolis and modern capitalism alongside a continuing exploration of their materialist aspects. The relationship between the economy, the city and their respective and interrelated 'cultures' was thus already under way.

II

This tendency to explore the spirit of the metropolis may also be seen in the critical discourse on the architecture and planning of the modern metropolis in Germany. An exemplary instance is provided by the influential writings of Karl Scheffler on the modern metropolis. His 1910 essay on 'The Metropolis' ('Die Grossstadt') opens with the following statement:

> The place where the struggle for a new architecture must be fought out is the metropolis, because there the intellectual (*geistige*) forces of the times converge together, because the metropolitan cities, as the centres of modern civilization, create the new presuppositions of a profane and ideal kind for architecture, because the idea of the metropolis slowly but surely takes over possession from the spirit of local community (*Gemeindegeist*) and the smaller towns too, and because for these reasons the whole country submits more and more to metropolitan sentiment. . . . What is absolutely decisive for the concept of the modern metropolis is not the number of its inhabitants but rather the spirit of the metropolis (*Grossstadtgeist*). It is

this spirit that builds the new architectural structures (*Architekturkörper*). . . .
For the modern metropolis is not an end [of a development] but rather a
beginning. Hence, architecture, too, does not stand under the banner of
decadence but rather under the sign of new developments.[11]

Scheffler's dichotomies between morphology and spirit, communal spirit
and metropolitan spirit, the spirit (of the modern metropolis) and the
body (of modern architecture) create the parameters within which a new
metropolitan architecture can be conceived. In particular, the focus upon
the idea of the modern metropolis enables Scheffler to explore the components of the *real* metropolis as well as the *idea* as *ideal*, i.e. the ideal
modern metropolis.

What are the features of the modern metropolis? Alongside the metropolis as centre of trade, industry, seat of government and administration, etc.,
it is above all 'the centrepoint of world economic interests', governed by
'internationally oriented, and globally expansive, economically conceived
interests in trade and manufacture'. The metropolis and its sentiments
are increasingly the dominant ones in Germany and America reinforced
by 'the natural increase in civilization (that does not always have to signify
an increase in culture)', 'the general democratization of the whole society',
the mass migrations from the land to the city, the internationalization of
the economy, and the fact that the world economy requires a money economy, which 'can only be organized in the metropolis'. The implication
that Scheffler does not draw from such a description of the modern
metropolis is that the international (world economy) orientation suggests
a further category, that of the cosmopolis and an attendant cosmopolitan
culture. As such, the cosmopolis transcends any fixed place or site. It is
spatially indeterminate insofar as the world economy's networks are continually in motion (expanding and contracting), and its culture is conditioned by the transspatial community of the money economy.[12]

If the international spirit of the world economy is one of the key dimensions of the modern metropolis, then, for Scheffler, the other is the family
as 'the primal cell of the city'. This is despite the fact that the modern
metropolis creates out of its 'huge population' merely masses of individuals,
and despite the fact that the new metropolitan population, with respect
to its sentiment for the city, is almost indifferent'.[13] The result is that the
modern metropolis has again taken on the features of a fortuitous settle-
ment (*Zufallssiedlung*). The unplanned expansion of the modern metropolis
from its centre outwards has produced 'a hypertrophied degeneration of
the old city economy', at the very same time as the modern metropolis's
'spirit' is that of 'a crystallization of the world economy'.[14]

The absence of planning and conscious overall direction in the development of the modern metropolis results from the domination of 'impersonal

capital', land speculation, and a calculated exploitation of urban capital that has worked out to the square meter the 'land value' (*Bodenwert*) but not the building value (*Gebäudewert*). This impersonal organization of the modern metropolis has contributed to its 'internal and external form-lessness',[15] which contrast markedly with the realization of the ideal metropolis. In the case of the latter:

> The ideal metropolis . . . must fulfil two requirements. First, the metropolis must include the family economy as much as the city economy – it must therefore strengthen it anew and once more create the sense of family and metropolitan sentiment; and, second, it must perfectly correspond to modern needs and be a crystallization point of interests directed towards the world economy.[16]

Such requirements appear contradictory 'since the city as enclosed dwelling place of families requires a limited number of inhabitants and a surveyable size; and the city as workplace of the world economy requires contact with hundreds of thousands'.[17] Scheffler's solution is for 'a monumental world city surrounded by a series of individualized suburban towns'.

Writing over a decade later, in 1926, in an essay titled 'Die Zukunft der Grossstädte und die Grossstädte der Zukunft' ('The Future of the Big Cities and the Big Cities of the Future') – Scheffler declares that this earlier image of the metropolis is no longer valid. Indeed, it was a Utopian vision of the future metropolis. By implication, it was an image of the future that failed to recognize that

> the fate of the metropolis coincided totally with that of the economy, society and culture. The problem of the metropolis is the problem of modern life itself.[18]

In turn, the identification of the future of the metropolis with that of life itself rapidly leads to Utopian and illusory visions of the future. But what were the Utopian visions of the metropolis in the pre-war period and what are they now? In the pre-war context, 'Utopia was that metropolitan illusion for which the concept of development, above all technical development, had become an end in itself, and in which capitalism itself appeared to have become full of fantasy and poetry'. For the present period, after the war, revolution, strikes and yet greater housing scarcity combined with the transformation of cities into 'formless giant settlements':

> the result is another kind of Utopia which one may characterize as a Utopia of pessimism and despair of the metropolis. To many, the metropolis seems merely hopeless, it appears like a synonym for the decline of the West; one makes comparisons with the phenomenon of decline in ancient Rome and sees in the future only the coming collapse.[19]

Thus, 'in the place of unlimited hope [there exists] an unlimited scepticism'.

For Scheffler, the present period (1926) is characterized by two tendencies. The first is a continuing flight from the land whose population 'has a desire for the spirit (*Geist*) of the cities'. The second is the metropolitan dweller's unrest when confronted with 'overfilled and overorganized' cities. The solution to this dilemma is for

> the metropolis to extend itself into the countryside. In other words, the country, the whole land will become city, will become metropolis, it forces the city to extend itself outwards; the broad landscape becomes filled with urban spirit (*Geist*).[20]

Such a solution is obviously a long-term one (though as we shall see, one conceived for a more immediate future by Martin Wagner). As far as Scheffler is concerned, for the present, the flight *from* the cities will remain a counter-tendency to the flight *to* the cities. The flight from the cities is a kind of 'internal colonization' of the countryside, one in which 'the spirit of the city extends across the land'. But at present this colonization exists in the form of housing estates for metropolitan dwellers and, as Scheffler points out, 'an estate (*Siedlung*) is not a village. It reckons from the outset with car, telephone and radio.' On a larger scale, it is to be found in general housing estate plans such as those for the industrial, rural area between Bitterfeld, Halle and Merseburg.

Certainly, this extension of the city to the country will be aided by new technologies (Scheffler points to 'the social and economic mission of the radio'), which, together with the general 'industrialization, mechanization of life', will extend the metropolitan spirit across national boundaries too. The metropolitan centres will become similar in architectural style as a result of their emergence out of 'universally similar needs, universally similar materials and the same forms of construction'. (In passing, it is worth noting that this constellation of needs, materials and construction was already announced in Otto Wagner's manifesto for a modern metropolitan architecture in 1896).[21]

The extension of mechanization and industrialization will transform the building process itself:

> Parts will be produced in factories and assembled together on the building site. Thus, the building craftsman will be transformed into an assembler. This mode of working determines that, to an extent still not conceived of, use will be made of the auxiliary means of typification and serialization. . . . Houses will be built in masses, in blocks, in large uniform assemblages.[22]

The future building process will commence from construction, from scaffolding, walls will no longer have their old function, and ornament will be minimal.

Finally, the extension of the city without limits has elevated 'the street into an ideal', an ideal 'that has destroyed the ideal of the city. The street has transcended the city.' But this process of extension does not stop there. The pleasure in the street is also declining and the search for a new resting place is under way:

> The old ideal of the city and the ideal of the street will be fused in metropolitan cities that are, as it were, city and street, at once extending broadly outwards and narrowly enclosed, at once cosmopolitan and communally intimate, at once metropolis and small town and, in a single phrase, city and country.[23]

The spirit of the future city is thus both cosmopolitan and local. The spirit of the metropolis lives on once more in its dissolution into another entity.

III

This somewhat extended discussion of Scheffler's conception of the metropolis and its spirit may serve as one context within which to locate the ostensibly most materialist of city planners, the city planner of Berlin in the crucial period 1926–33 – Martin Wagner. Of course there is a socialist context that should not be minimized, especially with reference to Berlin's housing policy in the Weimar period.[24] But the materialist context that has been extensively researched by Ludovica Scarpa and Manfredo Tafuri may not necessarily give us access to the changes in the conception of the city contained in Martin Wagner's work, even in this relatively circumscribed, but crucial, period. Even recourse to the fact that Wagner attended Simmel's lectures in Berlin and was influenced by Simmel's conception of the metropolis need not clarify the non-materialist dimensions of Wagner's vision of the modern metropolis.[25]

Another context in which Wagner might be located is the ostensible contrast between the earlier Expressionist visions of the Utopian metropolis and the extremely concrete deliberations by Martin Wagner with respect to public housing as an acute problem in post-First World War German cities and, above all, Berlin. Thus, if the immediate legacy of German Expressionism was both a declaration of the dissolution of the metropolis and at the same time a desire to build a Utopian metropolis, there were others ostensibly committed to realizing a new metropolis that was grounded in the practical and material problems of structuring the city. Such apparently divergent responses to the modern metropolis should not be viewed as exclusive strategies.[26] Thus, less than a decade after

Bruno Taut had declared the dissolution of the metropolis, he was working with Martin Wagner in 1925 in Berlin on the ambitious Britz housing
estate project. For his part, from 1926 to the end of the Weimar Republic,
Martin Wagner, in his capacity as *Oberbaurat* for city planning in Berlin,
was both committed to the introduction of rationalization into city planning (some of whose principles he had already outlined from 1918 onwards) and, after the economic collapse of 1929, developing a realizable
Utopia conceived as 'the flight from the prison of poverty to the paradise
of life'.

Yet despite the fact that Wagner, at Gropius's initiative, taught at the
Harvard School of Design from 1938 until his retirement, his prolific output
in the Weimar period has hardly been extensively examined in English.[27]
Indeed, the only fuller treatment remains the translation of Tafuri's critical discussion of Wagner's planning achievements, especially in relation
to housing in his *The Sphere and the Labyrinth*.[28] Yet the fullest treatment
of Wagner's work is in two other studies. The first is the centenary exhibition catalogue (1985) mounted by the Berlin Akademie der Künste, *Martin
Wagner 1885–1957*[29] whose intriguing subtitle 'Housing Construction
and Planning the World City: The Rationalisation of Happiness', partly
captures the ambiguity of Martin Wagner's exploration of the interface of city building, economy building and life building. The second work
is the only existing monograph on Wagner by Ludovica Scarpa (a former
Tafuri student), *Martin Wagner und Berlin*, published in Italian in 1983
and in German in 1986.[30] Both volumes remain invaluable sources for
investigating Wagner's work.

Drawing upon these and other earlier studies, it is possible to provide
a brief indication of Wagner's development and significance before turning
to the more detailed exploration of his conception of the metropolis. Born
in Königsberg in 1885, Martin Wagner commenced his architectural studies
in Berlin in 1905, at the same time also attending Simmel's lectures and
purportedly greatly impressed by the latter's analysis of the metropolis.
After a brief period of architectural practice in Hermann Muthesius's studio
in 1908–9, Wagner continued his studies (including economics) in Dresden
and graduated there as Diplom Ingenieur in 1910. Wagner's first extended
employment was as a city planner in the town of Rüstingen (now part of
Wilhelmshafen) from 1911 until 1914, during which time he designed several
housing estates and began publishing polemical pieces in the press. Two
months before the outbreak of the First World War, Wagner took up a
position as a studio director in the Verband Gross-Berlin. Until his brief
military service in 1918, Wagner worked on theoretical and practical projects for Berlin's redevelopment, submitted projects to architecture competitions and, in 1915, completed his doctoral dissertation (submitted to
the Technical University in Berlin) on healthy green spaces in cities (*Das*

Sanitäre Grün der Städte, published as *Städtische Freiflächenpolitik* in the same year).[31] During the war years Wagner also published on the economics of housing and worked on the implications of the process of rationalization, based on Taylorist principles, for city planning and architecture. In July 1918 he was appointed as city planner for Schöneberg, a post he abandoned in October 1920 when Schöneberg was incorporated into Greater Berlin. His most significant architectural achievement in Schöneberg was the construction of the Lindenhof housing estate. But in the post-war and post-revolutionary situation in Berlin, Wagner was increasingly active in formulating a socialist building programme and in participating in the building workers' union, the Bauhütte Berlin (independent building associations) and other organizations for the socialization of land, building and housing. In 1920 Wagner became director of a newly formed association for the promulgation and practice of socialized building, drawing together several of the organizations that had emerged in the immediate post-war period – the Verband Sozialer Baubetriebe. At the same time, Wagner used his position as the lead writer of the journal *Soziale Bauwirtschaft* to promulgate his theories on the rationalization and socialization of building. The realization of this process, in part at least, was set in motion in 1924 with the foundation of the Deutsche Wohnungsfürsorge (German Housing Association) for the provision of mass housing. As director of this association, Wagner undertook a month's study visit to the United States in 1924, the experience of which he sought to apply to German circumstances. The concrete, ostensible realization of the application of rationalization to mass housing was manifested in the Britz housing estate – in the light of its shape, also referred to as the horseshoe estate (*Hufeisensiedlung*) – designed jointly with Bruno Taut in 1925.

Late in the following year Wagner was appointed director of the Berlin city planning office, a post he held until his dismissal in 1933. These years saw the development of several important architectural and planning projects, some of them realized – such as the beach bathing facilities at Wannsee, jointly with Richard Ermisch, and at Müggelsee with Hemmings – but mostly unrealized in full, such as the trade fair complex (Messegelände), together with Hans Poelzig, and partially completed plans for the restructuring of the Alexanderplatz and the Potsdamerplatz at the heart of the world city. However, Wagner was instrumental in the development of major housing estates such as the Weisse Stadt and Siemensstadt, work on which commenced in 1929. In the same year, together with Adolf Behne, Wagner edited the short-lived Berlin journal *Das neue Berlin* (as a rival to the existing *Das neue Frankfurt*), which was a forum for modern architecture and planning but which only survived the 12 monthly issues of that year. A further visit to the United States that year was followed by one to Moscow with Ernst May, during which Wagner turned down an offer to be a city planner there. In the increasing political crisis in Berlin and Germany after the economic collapse of 1929, the rise of the Nazi party and bitter disputes between and within the left parties, Wagner remained active in putting forward new proposals (along with other architects), such as the design of an 'expanding house' (*wachsende Haus*) for the metropolitan suburbs. At the same time, the financial crisis in the Berlin metropolis and corruption within the Social Democratic Party – with respect to support for land speculation and the privatization of public bodies – led, in April 1931, to Wagner's resignation from the Social Democratic Party, of which he had been a member for a decade. In 1933 Wagner was the only member of the Berlin Academy to openly speak out against the exclusion of Heinrich Mann and Kaethe Kollwitz from that body. After the March 1933 election Wagner was dismissed from his planning post in Berlin but continued to publish theoretical work (sometimes under his wife's name) until Hans Poelzig facilitated a post for him as city planner in Istanbul in 1935. There he remained, though with few actual resources for completing projects, until his emigration to the United States in 1938, when Gropius secured him a professorship of city planning at Harvard and where he taught until his retirement in 1950. Attempts to return to Germany after 1945 proved unsuccessful. Wagner died in May 1957.

IV

Given Martin Wagner's prolific published output down to his emigration from Berlin, initially to Istanbul in 1935, it is hardly possible to do justice here to the range of his achievements. And since it is housing policies that have been given detailed treatment in English by Tafuri, the intention here will be to focus upon his conception of the modern metropolis – the world city. Hence, although some of the debate surrounding public housing policy will be alluded to here, the main concern will be with broader features of the nature and shape of the modern metropolis.

In turn, in order to understand the modern, rationalized metropolis conceived by Wagner, we must have recourse to a number of different trajectories that highlight its distinctive nature. One such trajectory has already been alluded to in Karl Scheffler's earlier prescient evocation of the tension already present within the modern metropolis conceived as a world economic centre (and its transpatial networks) and the much older notion of the city as a constellation of dwelling places. As we shall see, this tension becomes increasingly evident in Wagner's Utopian plans for a new Berlin.

A second tension is present in Wagner's conception of modernity. The equation of progress with rationalization and favouring technical solutions

to social problems, both of which recur in Wagner's Weimar writings, give
to his conception of the modern an abstract objectivity (*Sachlichkeit*) that
generates a void in this materialist modernity, a neglect of subjectivities.
Of course, Wagner was not alone in conceiving of metropolitan hetero-
topias, rigidified formations of urban form. One need only recall some of
Hilberseimer's visions in the 1920s for the modern metropolis, which he
later referred to as 'more a necropolis than a metropolis'.[32] But on a first
reading, Wagner appears to insist upon other dimensions – including non-
material ones – as crucial for a genuine modern urban form and culture.
Wagner maintains, for instance, that the negative contemporary judgements
of modern urban architecture as 'cigar-box architecture', or as 'deserving
imprisonment' because it is 'Bolshevist' and the like have their origin

> in the complete confusion between the concepts of *culture* and civilization.
> ... Civilization is a purely mechanical elevation of the external framework
> of our existence. What we today achieve in terms of *comfort* belongs to the
> realm of civilization. ... The *what* of our existence is civilization. ... Only
> the *how* belongs to the realm of culture. ... Civilization is the water closet,
> the electric light, aircraft, the radio. All these things, however, do not yet
> signify culture. Culture is *form*, is *nobility of expression*, is increased en-
> lightenment (*Bildung*), but not in the sense of quantitative knowledge.[33]

In turn, Wagner insists that art develops only out of culture, not of civilization. And modern art, in turn, grows out of modern culture. The formal-
istic separation of these spheres of civilization, culture and art and the
ideological burdening of the distinction between civilization and culture –
already a *Leitmotif* in the critique of modernity in Germany – closed off
the possibility for alternative critiques of modernity and its architectural
expressions.

Yet despite such qualifications, this essay from 1926 on 'Civilization,
Culture, Art' ('Zivilisation, Kultur, Kunst') reveals some of Wagner's
temporal reflections upon the 'spirit of the times' and contemporary
modernity. Our urban culture is clearly conditioned by 'the mechanical,
external frameworks of life, to the extent, for instance, that the change in
speed from travelling by stagecoach to travelling by aircraft must

> also give us a totally different sense of *rest* and *movement*. In the stage-
> coach one sees the smallest section of the environment move on to the next
> one in peaceful motion. In an aircraft, sections of the landscape are grasped
> with a totally different and broader field of vision. *The entities that are to
> be observed are enlarged.* One no longer sees so much the individual ele-
> ments and detail ... but rather the overall impression of the *total image*. ...
> The major lines and silhouettes move into the foreground. Whereas previ-
> ously the individual house and, accordingly, the details were the field of

tasks of the artist, so the modern architect in transformed times is confronted with the task of dealing with *street space* (*Strassenraum*) as the smallest unit of the image of the city.[34]

In a manner reminiscent of Otto Wagner, Martin Wagner goes on to argue that contemporary architects, while not ignoring the art forms of earlier ages, must 'strive for new forms of shaping that stand in bodily agreement with the spirit of the age'. In other words, 'we children of the twentieth century must develop our *own* form and our *own* style'.[35]

What does this new form of architecture and city planning look like in the context of Wagner's commitment – like that of Otto Wagner 30 years earlier – to expressing the spirit of the age? Martin Wagner, too, denounces the 'psuedo-artists and pseudo-architects' who must be confined to their actual roles as 'technicians, builders, organizers, engineers, etc.'[36] For it can only be the

intellectual broad perspective that is capable of developing the appropriate artistic form corresponding to our epoch from out of the social, economic, technical and organizational conditions of our age. From the standpoint of the communal economy, the problem of art gains a different face for us. It is indeed correct that there is no socialist art, just as there can be no German national or democratic art. Art has nothing to do intrinsically with party politics. But whoever is of the view that our whole culture is growing into a socialist one and moving from individualism to collectivism, i.e. is striving to move from the individualistic to the communal economy, must also draw their conclusions from this development for the problem of form. Thus, just as the individual will has been subordinated to a totality of wills, so modern artistic creation requires *subordination* and *ranking* (*Einreihen*), *discipline* and *order* in forms. In modern architecture there is no longer any space for the externalization of wealth or the poverty of individual elements. We turn away from the bourgeoisie's ideal of beauty with its emphasis on the personal, on the capricious and an individualistic characterization. Our ideal of beauty is no longer the accentuated individual house, but rather the sum total of houses, the street space, the square and city space.[37]

Leaving aside Wagner's obvious socialist commitment, there are again interesting parallels with Otto Wagner's delineation of modernity. Although Otto Wagner insisted that a modern architecture should reflect the process of democratization, his own cited instance of the increasingly homogeneous apartment block with its 'conglomerate of cells' is not incompatible with Martin Wagner's focus upon the totality of houses, street spaces, etc. What is taken much further by Martin Wagner is the *rational* ordering of art forms. Indeed, the categories of subordination, ranking, discipline and order are *also* appropriate to the rational organization of production and administration. As we shall see, the latter became of increasing concern to Martin Wagner in his capacity as *Oberbaurat*, as chief city planner in Berlin.

However, Wagner is more specific about the new form of modern architecture and city planning. In particular, the new architecture and planning will take account of the rhythm of the mass, the beauty of the line, undressing the body, recognition of utility and colouring. The city as machine is only hinted at in Wagner's delineation of the first of these new dimensions:

> Just as industry is striving to transform individual needs into mass needs, so we too have to create new laws of formation in accordance with the *rhythm of the mass*. This mass, that we have to form in the shape of dwelling blocks will be totally stripped (*entkleidet*) from all the stored up, lifeless, decorative wealth. It will emerge streamlined like an aircraft, an express locomotive, a motor, etc., that will reject any superfluous mass as pointless, indeed as harmful.[38]

This process of streamlining incorporates the processes of simple line creation and the stripping away of what is deemed unnecessary. Hence:

> there emerges in modern architecture a beauty of line that is revealed in the stripping away of all superfluous casings. Take note of the parallel development in female clothes. Here, too, we see how a certain *undressing* (*Entkleidung*) has taken place in the last 10 to 20 years and how one has increasingly clung to the external garment of the noble lines of the body. . . . The return to the genuinely corporeal and to the practical (*Zweckmässig*) is also to be traced back to a *mental* (*geistige*) cleansing of our creations. In architecture, too, we wish to give expression again to absolute *cleanliness* (*Sauberkeit*) and inner *sincere conviction* (*ehrliche Gesinnung*).[39]

Finally, no doubt influenced by Taut's colourful housing blocks in Magdeburg, Wagner makes a plea for colour in exteriors at least. This also has a political significance since:

> The bourgeosie also resisted *colour* in architecture because grey on grey was the old ideal of distinction. . . . Just as we require of every housewife that she turn her rooms to their best advantage, and keep the bathroom as a hygienic establishment clean, so we will also have to become accustomed to maintaining the external wall of houses and their façades clean and pure and not to shy away . . . from occasionally painting these façades with a new coat. In the colour-friendly form of our streets and city spaces is expressed the awakening to a new freedom and new life force.[40]

This gendered hierarchy of modernity, which is also present in the construction of interiors for the existence minimum in this period, is presumably to be maintained in however colourful a future.

The temporal dimension of modernity that Wagner explored from the standpoint of reflecting the spirit of the times can also be approached from another perspective, namely the relationship between the new and the old in the modern metropolis. Here at least Wagner's position is unambiguous insofar as he asserts that:

> We really do not wish to be slaves of old built structures and thereby damage the present and the future. The problem can only be to replace the highly valued old by a still higher valued new. Hence we should quite generally and rightly ask the question that the demolition of old buildings and structures should first be completed when new plans exist and really represent something of a high value. . . . It is not easy for us to correctly judge past artistic epochs. For my part, I merely conclude that each period . . . has the right to give expression to itself; however, this period has the duty before the past, the present and the future to concern itself with an expression that ennobles the present.[41]

This still confident tone with respect to the new present and future, written in 1929 before the full impact of the world economic crisis and the collapse of the German economy became evident, is clearly limited to a temporal dimension of modernity. But were there other dimensions of modernity, say of space and place, that can illuminate Wagner's conception of the modernity of the metropolis more fully?

One obvious trajectory is Wagner's response to his visits to the United States and the relevance of the urban development there for that of Berlin in particular. Responding to his second visit to the United States in 1929, Wagner is still positive concerning Berlin developments:

> German city planning at the moment experiences a new Renaissance. All predictions concerning the dissolution and the decline of cities especially metropolitan cities, remain without foundation. The attack which the false friends of the countryside made after the war upon the big cities is repulsed.[42]

And amongst the expanding German cities, Berlin 'is the metropolis of metropoles of the German Empire', 'Berlin has become a world city'.[43] This has in part been possible because the laissez-faire and fortuitous principles have been replaced by elevating the totality over individual interests.

In one respect amongst many this development can be followed through, namely with regard to traffic and the urgent problem that is present for all cities to solve: 'the *automobile* as individual *mass means of transport*'. In part, this problem arises out of modernity itself, in the fact that:

> The escape from spatial and temporal bonds lies in the essence of modern human beings. The *concentration* of millions of metropolitan dwellers within

the narrow spaces of work and dwelling pushes towards an *expansion*, towards a liberation from being bound to time and place. And this *individual* liberation to the open countryside, to free nature, to bodily regeneration, can only be provided by the automobile.[44]

Yet if the development of auto traffic that is found in American cities is transposed to Berlin, then there is a necessity for rapid action. The automobile is transforming our spatial relations in contradictory directions. For, as a means of public transport:

> The automobile kills the inner city but it connects the metropolitan dweller to the open countryside and the country dweller to the metropolis. Excursions with a three-hour journey radius – thus from Berlin to Dresden or Magdeburg – are taken for granted by the mass of the American metropolitan population just as they are enjoyed by a small stratum of wealthy people. *The automobile has created a new standard for the boundaries of the city.*[45]

Without a radical restructuring of the city through the differentiation of the varied means of transport and their separation, 'German cities, and above all the most endangered of all German cities, Berlin, are not wealthy enough to permit the revolutionary "auto" in the body of the city to come and go as it pleases'.[46] Only a 'constructive new structuring of the metropolis', including the expansion of other forms of transport such as air travel (Wagner noted that Chicago planned 20 airports in its city boundaries), can prevent the congestion caused by 'a street network not created for the automobile being fully blocked to the point of total impassability'.[47]

However, the individualistic response in the United States to economic and other problems – and Wagner cites 'Greater New York's over 16 private electricity companies, 15 different gas companies, 17 different transport companies and almost countless private and communal water works' – suggests that for all its wealth it is roughly 50 years behind German municipalities in communal provision. With respect to the American individualistic response, Wagner asks 'how this individualism in the public consumption economy is to be rendered compatible with all the goals of rationalization'.[48] And it is the process of rationalization, drawn from American models, that Wagner had already seen as crucial to accelerating housing production and which he was to increasingly favour in city planning and bureaucratic administration.

Long before the world economic crisis had seriously penetrated the German and Berlin economy, Wagner was already advocating thoroughgoing rationalization. In 1925, a year after the introduction of the Dawes Plan for stabilizing the German economy, Wagner maintained that:

the solution to the whole economic crisis lies clearly before us in its major leading ideas. Rationalization of industry, rationalization of trade, rationalization of agriculture – these are the basic leading ideas for the health of the German economy. . . . The rationalization of industry cannot be carried out without the current economic state of factories being investigated, without the factories being built anew and transferred to the completely new methods of production of the conveyor belt. The rationalization of commerce follows the path of excluding all superfluous transport and intermediary storage. The rationalization of agriculture, in turn, is dependent upon the construction of factories in the countryside that transform the raw materials on the site itself into saleable commodities, etc. This process of economic rationalization intimately affects the whole urban and rural system of housing estates (*Siedlungssystem*).[49]

Thus, for Wagner, rationalization was the solution not merely to problems of the economy but also to housing production, and, as we shall see, to the restructuring of the modern metropolis. For the moment, let us remain with the process of rationalization advocated by Wagner, not least because the frequent references to rationalization suggest that it is viewed as synonymous with modernization and – given Wagner's socialist aims – the socialization of production. The creation of 'the collective worker' (Marx) by the rationalization of large-scale production was not deemed incompatible with the socialization of production.

V

Wagner's concept of rationalization, which he applies to the economy, the building process, bureaucracy and the planning of the world metropolis, is in many respects close to that of Taylor's managerialist conception – and Taylorism was certainly being advocated in Germany in the war period, if not earlier – as well as that of Walther Rathenau and, above all, Max Weber's conception of rationalization. In addition, the rationalization advocated by Martin Wagner served to reinforce the perceived affinities between the world city of Berlin and American (i.e. US) urban developments. Since Wagner made two visits to the United States in the 1920s, it is worthwhile briefly noting once more the long-standing association of Berlin in particular with positive or, most often, negative Americanism (*Amerikanismus*), not least because this correlation represented a significant dimension of the spirit of the modern metropolis – one that served to delineate both a 'progressive' and a 'reactionary' modernism.

The spirit of 'Americanism' is thus perceived to be one of endless expansion, eternal newness, accelerating tempo of production and circulation, organization, boundless energy, and the like. So when Wagner declared that Berlin was 'amongst all the European metropoles the one that stands closest to American cities', he was clearly expressing a judgement that was not new. But in this 1929 statement (after his second US visit), part of the future of Berlin is to be glimpsed in present-day American cities. The fascination with American economic and technological developments (complete with positive references by Wagner to US President Hoover, just months before the 1929 economic crash) is certainly a general feature of the period of 'relative stabilization' in Germany (1924–9), but has particular resonance for Wagner since, for him, 'German city planning is at present experiencing a new Renaissance' propelled by 'technical and economic developments'. Throughout the decade, Wagner remained impressed by the perceived productivity gains resulting from thorough rationalization of the labour process in production. In the sphere of city planning, and especially after his appointment as city planner of Berlin in 1926, Wagner saw the need to extend the principles of rationalization to the circulation process of the metropolis and to its administration. As Max Weber had argued earlier, once the new rationality of the 'spirit' of capitalism had become established – the formal rationality of seeking the most efficient *means* to achieve a given end (whose rationality could not be assessed by this formal rationality) – the process of rationalization would permeate all major institutions in modern life (the rational organization of production, administration, state activity, state legitimation, and 'rational' justification for religion, etc). Weber was relatively silent on the rationalization of the modern metropolis. Martin Wagner sought to achieve a (planned) rationalization of the modern metropolis and, above all, Berlin.

The assumption that Taylorist principles for the rationalization of production – associated with specialization and mechanization of tasks, precise measurability and, hence, calculability of units of input and output of labour – could be applied not merely to capitalist enterprises but also to quasi-socialized production – as in Wagner's earlier building guilds employing unionized labour – was one which Wagner shared with other advocates of the rationalization and socialization of production. The subordination of labour to capital (including local state capital) could take the form not merely of what Marx had earlier defined as 'formal' subordination (in the labour contract itself) but also the 'real' subordination of labour, involving increasing substantive control of the labour process by capital (whether state or private). This is despite the fact that the presumed harmonization of labour relations in quasi-socialized production often proved illusory.

But the rationalization of building production that Wagner advocated, especially in relation to housing production, involved not merely an increase in the mechanization of production (thereby reducing the *labour time* necessary to produce individual units and, of course, the amount of labour employed) and the accompanying deskilling of labour (associated also with increasing specialization and fragmentation of tasks) but also accelerated the processes of the *standardization* of production.[50] The latter involved the *pre-fabrication* (manufacture) of units of building production, whose most rationally organized form (in terms of mass production and reduced cost) required the *serialization* and *replicability* of units. The transportation of ready-manufactured (and interchangeable) units to the site of housing production created the possibility to utilize much less skilled labour than previously. The assembly (*montage*) of ready-made units had the advantage not merely of serializing the activity of production, but also of rendering that production (construction as assembling pre-built parts) precisely measurable in terms of units of labour and time employed for completion, and thus production costs (and profits) were more precisely calculable.

Looked at from a broader perspective, this new mode of building was not merely of particular significance for Wagner, given his long-standing concern with housing, but, as Michael Hellgardt has suggested, it is a crucial instance of the built work in the age of its technological reproducibility.[51] If we return briefly to Scheffler's aims in 1910 for the modern metropolis – the provision for the family and a local city identity and provision for the crystallization of the world economy – then the first of these aims was being fulfilled by Wagner in the creation of the new housing estates (*Siedlungen*) such as Lindenhof and Britz. Neither were so constrained by the notion of the 'existence minimum' as were some of Ernst May's later Frankfurt estate developments. The extended terraced house with garden would probably satisfy Scheffler's first aim, as long as the family members of working age were in employment. More problematical, however, would be the creation of a localized city identity on the outskirts of the metropolis, where public housing estates were most often located, since the local state could acquire the building land more cheaply than in the central areas of the city.

The trend towards the creation of increasingly abstract (interchangeable) labour in housing production and other building production, favoured by Wagner, did not exhaust the possibilities and perceived need for rationalization. Max Weber had argued that the most efficient form of administration was the rationally organized bureaucracy. The organization of city planning and the increasing number of local state government departments involved in planning and building production could also be subject to rationalization. The 'rational' bureaucratic organization was always conceived as hierarchical. This implied that the apex of any such organization could give *direction* to its subordinate elements. The 'gaze of power' was always from above, a gaze unconstrained by subordinate units. But where elements of the local state government and bureaucracies are democratically elected, decision-making and direction from above is rendered that much more difficult (and, formally, more inefficient). The greater the emphasis on the need for direction from above, the more Wagner's programme for city planning became socialism from above. And the increasing call for a leadership to give direction came more and more to take on dimensions of Weber's own solution to rigidified bureaucratic organizational forms – becoming the call for charismatic leadership to restore the *dynamism* of social, economic or political development and to break out of the 'iron cage'.

On a number of occasions it is evident that Wagner viewed the modern metropolis as itself a machine. The regulation of the machine required an engineer, or at least a controller or director. Given its complexity, it could only be controlled by a bureaucratic apparatus. And in this respect some of the affinities between the latter and the machine had already been drawn out by Max Weber with regard to the *technical efficiency* of both. Weber had suggested that:

> The fully developed bureaucratic apparatus compares with other organizations exactly as does the machine with the non-mechanical modes of production. Precision, speed, unambiguity . . . continuity . . . unity, strict subordination, reduction of friction and of material and personal costs – these are raised to the optimum point in the strictly bureaucratic administration.[52]

The references to 'precision', 'speed' and the like could also be applied to the modern metropolis. But like the bureaucratic apparatus, it too could cease to find itself in this idealized state when the bureaucracies responsible for its day-to-day operations were no longer functioning efficiently. Then, those in charge of the running and planning of the city would feel the need to break out of the 'iron cage'.

VI

When we turn to Wagner's involvement in the creation of a 'new' Berlin, we find that there are two new Berlins. The first is manifested in the journal *Das neue Berlin*[53] and the specific projects – realized or unrealized – that are dealt with there and elsewhere. During the short lifespan of the journal (12 issues in 1929), the Wall Street crash and the onset of a world depression seriously compromised many projects. However, it is interesting to note how many remained under active consideration and were even completed. There also exists a second 'new' Berlin, conceived by

Wagner in a two-volume unpublished manuscript also titled *Das Neue Berlin*[54] (completed in 1932) and in a much shorter treatment of some of its main themes in a paper titled 'City Planning as Economic Planning and Planning for Life' (*'Städtebau als Wirtschaftsbau und Lebensbau'*) of October 1932.[55]

Whereas the first 'new' Berlin discourse surrounds issues such as the reconfiguration of Alexanderplatz and Potsdamer Platz, housing developments and aspects of Berlin as world city, the second 'new' Berlin discourse in 1932, located in the deepening economic and political crisis, relates to the growing discourse on the death of the metropolis and responds with a Utopian vision of a new urban development (not least in the countryside).

Thus, the 'new' Berlin discourse around 1929–30 addresses actual projects, many of which are located in the heart of the city, whereas the 'new' Berlin discourse in 1932 is locating the city in the countryside and thus returning – in part, and in very different circumstances – full circle to the Expressionist debate on the dissolution of the big city of over a decade earlier. The ambiguity of the 1932 discourse on Berlin is also revealed in the oscillation between the image of the city as machine (the technocratic Utopia) and that of the city as organism (the biological Utopia). The future of the metropolis in its 1932 vision therefore oscillates between Taylorist rationalization and variants of earlier Expressionist Utopias.

The role of the city planner, too, is different in these two discourses. The project for creating a new spirit for Berlin as world metropolis in 1929 requires dealing with anticipated expansion and acceleration. The later project of 1932 reads more like one that requires urban dispersal, if not decline. In both cases, Wagner calls for decisive leadership.

The call for direction in city planning comes to the fore in the period from 1929 onwards when Wagner is increasingly involved in the (re)creation of Berlin as world city (though already announced in 1896 and periodically reannounced, as it were, in the 1910 Greater Berlin competition and in 1920 with the actual creation of Gross-Berlin). If the creation of family dwellings in the public housing estate fulfilled, in part, the first of Scheffler's aims, then how was the crystallization of the world economy to be realized in the world city? Does the modern metropolis as world city require a world spirit? The answer given by Wagner and Adolf Behne in the preface to the short-lived journal *Das neue Berlin* in 1929 is unequivocal. The quantitative economic expansion of the city since the immediate pre-First World War period (indicated by population increase, import and export of goods to and from the city, consumption levels, savings in the Berlin Savings Bank and an increase in number of motor vehicles) reveals that its population 'have *worked* and *saved*' (though a more than fourfold increase in savings from 1913 to 1928 is *not* necessarily an indicator of positive economic growth, as Keynes was later to point out):

A city that has demonstrated such an expansive development *must* build, form itself anew, create for itself a new spirit and a new body. The new spirit of Berlin is not the spirit of Potsdam, the spirit of court society. . . . The new spirit is the spirit of the world metropolis (*Weltstadtgeist*), brings to development overwhelming forces of labour and recreation, of civilization and culture to all the other cities of a country and will produce outstanding achievements. The spirit of the world city must necessarily possess a national character with pronounced international features. Yet what it must especially appropriate to itself is the self-consciousness of its potential significance and responsibility compared with other cities in other countries. The spirit of the new Berlin is a cosmopolitan spirit, which must grow away from the parochial spirit of earlier times. This cosmopolitan spirit will also have to create the body of its city (*Stadtkörper*) according to its content and form.[56]

The tasks faced in creating the new form of Berlin as a world city that manifests this cosmopolitan spirit must be confronted with a 'cosmopolitan sense of responsibility'. Although the 'formal expression' of this world city form has not yet been found, this is not due to the absence of personnel or means for achieving it. What is lacking is:

the leadership with clear aims that can provide a comprehensive direction of all forces into a cosmopolitan tapestry. The director (*Regisseur*) of the world city of Berlin is lacking. The ordering, commanding, dynastic will has died out. Today, the world city of Berlin is not governed by a *single* democracy but by a whole system of democracies that lack decisive and unified leadership.[57]

A 'new Berlin' still remains to be created 'in a new spirit and in a new form'. Its creation, however, is hindered not so much by a bureaucratic apparatus but by a plurality of democratic bodies lacking in unified leadership. The post of director to which Wagner refers is, at the very least, ominously reminiscent of the charismatic leader.

The new form of Berlin that will embody the world city spirit first came into being with housing construction on a large scale, in the major estates (such as Britz and Zehlendorf) that created new urban forms. New forms of the metropolis will also appear in the new formation of the old city (and the need for new traffic spaces) and the large-scale dwellings in the newer areas of the city. Thus, the most transparent manifestations of the new forms embodying the world city spirit will be located in the centre of the city. They would include the reconfiguration of 'world city squares' (such as Alexanderplatz, Potsdamerplatz, Platz der Republik) and the unification of transport connections, and the representation of the world city will have major new settlements (*Gross-Siedlungen*) and recreational areas (such as the Wannsee swimming and recreation facilities).

7.1 Martin Wagner's plan for reconstruction of the Alexanderplatz, 1929

Wagner himself was actively involved in most of these projects and most of them figured in this short-lived journal *Das neue Berlin: Grossstadtprobleme*, which did not survive beyond the difficult year of 1929. Compared with the more successful *Das neue Frankfurt: Internationale Monatsschrift für die Probleme kulturelle Neugestaltung*,[58] which was published from 1926 to 1933, the Wagner and Behne Berlin journal focused exclusively upon Berlin, and its content suggested an urgent assertion of its world city status. The Frankfurt journal carried not merely articles on the new Frankfurt but also many more articles, as its subtitle suggested, on modern design in the new city, as well as contributions, amongst many others, by Behne and Wagner.

Amongst the problems covered in *Das neue Berlin* were those covering the planning and restructuring of Berlin for the expansion of *traffic*. The spirit of the world city and the cosmopolitan spirit are associated with accelerated circulation of goods and individuals. Traffic networks are circulation networks embodying, in part, that element of the spirit of the world city that is summed up in Franklin's dictum 'time is money', whose precise formation was reflected upon by Simmel when he noted that if all the clocks and watches stopped at the same time in Berlin, the whole circulation process would be rendered chaotic and grind to a halt.

The problem of traffic is a crucial element of what Scheffler earlier called 'the crystallization of the world economy'. The variation in speeds of circulation (aircraft, rail, shipping and motor vehicles, horse-drawn and pedestrian), the turnover time (amortization) of built structures to accommodate these circulation networks and the facilities for newer communication networks (telegraph, telephone, radio) all express the dynamic transformation of metropolitan (world city) existence. Although Wagner reflects, on occasion, upon air transport (the number of airports necessary in the world city), his major concern is with the structural transformation of built structures to facilitate the acceleration of traffic systems (such as giving a new form to the Alexanderplatz).

In 1929 the major traffic intersections that required a new form included the Alexanderplatz and the Potsdamerplatz. The new structuring of such

> 'squares' is determined primarily by the *new ordering* of *traffic* and the construction of *underground railways*. . . . A *world* city square is not a *small* city square. . . . The world city square is an almost permanently filled traffic sluice, whose 'clearing' point is an artery network of major traffic thoroughfares. . . . World city squares *are organisms* with distinctive formal features.[59]

Wagner claims that organically formed world city squares have not yet appeared in Europe. Their construction requires attention to a number of factors such as traffic capacity, differentiation of traffic flows (e.g. pedestrians, motor vehicles, streetcars), differentiation of traffic speeds and so on. Of particular note for the modern metropolis is the *limited lifespan* of such new squares. That limit Wagner sets at 25 years (as turnover time or amortization). This means that such spatial constellations for traffic flows are able to be totally reconstructed for new demands after 25 years. The crystallization of the world economy in such squares is therefore a transitory phenomenon. It follows from this limited lifespan that 'the buildings surrounding the square do not possess any *permanent* economic or architectural value'.[60] At the same time, such squares have to cover their costs. Hence, 'to the *flowing* traffic on the square must be juxtaposed the "*stationary* traffic" that secures the consumer power of the human masses crossing the square (shops, bars, department stores, offices, etc.)'. The flow of pedestrians as consumers must therefore also be secured. In turn, the architectural forms must create an attractive spectacle in order to draw

7.2 Wagner's and Ungabe's sketch of projected multilevel traffic interchange at the Alexanderplatz, 1929

out this power of consumption. The 'clearest form' by day and the 'characteristic, artificial effect' by night must be ensured: 'A single flowing light by day and a light flowing *out* by night produce a totally new face for the square. *Colour, form,* and *light* (advertisement) are the three major building elements for the new world city squares.' The total spatial constellation of such squares will manifest their dual functions, since 'a world city square is a *stopping point* and a *floodgate* in a single form: a stopping point for consumption power and floodgate for traffic flows'. In passing, it is worth noting here that if the Alexanderplatz and the Potsdamerplatz remain points of contention today, then so, too, does the Platz der Republik, which lacks the former's economic attractions. There,

7.3 Model of projected new Alexanderplatz, 1929

Wagner's solution was to extend the Reichstag building, thus forcing the structure of the square to be raised (with presumably *public* funding for its reconstellation). It is, however, the traffic intersection squares that aroused the greatest discussion. Marcel Breuer, justifying his plan for the Potsdamer Platz (in *Das neue Berlin*), maintained that 'the dramatic dimension of a metropolis is the traffic, and its bearer is – at the moment – the street. This drama reaches its high point in the *intersections of the main thoroughfares*; viewed in a new sense, the *squares of the city* are nothing other than these elevated points of the streets'.[61] The walls of such newly constituted squares should represent their structure in the simplest form possible, one 'whose external features merely form a basic rhythm for the permanently changing, surprising and individually multifaceted forms of colour and light of the city. They are the naked body that the changing times clothe in contemporary and diverse elements'.[62]

The new world city squares that were to be the dynamic representation of the world spirit of the metropolis were thus subject to the turnover time of urban capital in those squares, set by Wagner at 25 years. At the same time, such squares – e.g. Alexanderplatz – were to be representations of the daily differentiated circulation of traffic forms. In addition, their architectural constellation should also be consonant with their circulatory function – possibly plain, blank, curved façades that mirror the accelerated circulation. In particular, it is automobile traffic that was Wagner's

7.4 Luckhardt brothers' 1929 submission for the new Alexanderplatz. The flow of building façades mirrors traffic flows

prime concern. He suggested that 'this growing automobile traffic now appears to completely revolutionize street-level traffic in Berlin too'.[63] With a projected annual increase in such traffic of almost 40 per cent per year (as of 1929), in part as a result of a cheapening of the automobile by almost one-third of its price in 1913. Of course, writing only three years later in 1932, Wagner was to point out that Berlin's purchasing power was then less than half of what it had been in 1928. Thus, the two features of the new world squares that Wagner highlighted – their consumer power and their function as traffic sluices – were both rendered less significant long before their projected turnover time.

Nonetheless, the exclusive identification of the urban centres of modernity solely with circulation – of traffic, individuals as consumers, and commodities – is indicative of the correlation between circulation and transitoriness. This is accentuated by the 25-year turnover time that Wagner ascribes to the urban capital surrounding such centres. Had the Alexanderplatz been fully refigured in 1929, then its lifespan would have extended, on Wagner's argument, to 1954. However, its turnover time was to be accelerated by a decade – as a result of Allied bombing raids on Berlin.[64]

If the newly reconstructed world city squares were to manifest the dynamism and transitoriness of the spirit of the metropolis in modernity, then that dynamism of the human body also required spaces for expression. Whereas under the local communal liberal politics of pre-war Berlin in 1908 (in connection with the Gross-Berlin competition), '*intellectual* Berlin (*geistige* Berlin) . . . displayed very little understanding for *bodily* Berlin (*körperliche* Berlin)', the subsequent call for open recreational space in the metropolis produced 'a revolution of the body'. And whereas earlier many had to remain satisfied with 'purely mental (*geistig*) drilling', today

> what the cosmopolitan dweller needs is the fortification of body and nerves to the greatest extent. . . . Mechanized metropolitan work will find its liberation in a large-scale and thorough care of the body.[65]

The construction of such metropolitan facilities (and Wagner completed with Richard Ermisch the beach bathing and sport facilities on the Wannsee in 1930) were also intended to reduce the social and economic burdens on the public health system by keeping the population healthy through regular body exercise.

The expression of the dynamic crystallization of the world economy also required adequate representation of the world city as marketplace. One of its modes of expression is the *exhibition centre*. As early as 1896 Simmel had pointed to the significance of such exhibitions as representations of the city itself and as creating a new transitory architecture (in keeping with modernity's transitory nature). Wagner and Hans Poelzig won the competition for an exhibition and trade centre complex adjacent to the Berlin radio tower (designed by Poelzig). But Wagner makes direct comparison with the 1896 exhibition and the changed economic circumstances that no longer permit exhibition construction on the basis of 'world exhibitions'. Therefore:

> Compared with the exhibition area for the 1896 trade exhibition in the Treptower Park, which then extended 1,100,000 square metres and compared with the exhibition areas of other metropoles, the land available for the city of Berlin, at the radio tower, of 760,000 square meters is not large but nonetheless quite sufficient, because the holding of exhibitions has experienced a major transformation from extensity to intensity and from general exhibitions to specialized and trade-specific exhibitions.[66]

Yet the severity of the economic (and political) crisis ensured that the planned structures remained only partly completed for the 1931 building exhibition. In the same year Wagner left the socialist party, the SPD, in part as a result of frustration in 'directing' the creation of a new Berlin, but largely as a result of internal financial corruption in the party. On the Alexanderplatz, the crucial 'Aschinger building site', with a tax value of

7.5   Martin Wagner's model for a 'growing house', 1932

2,775,000 German marks, was actually purchased for 13,500,000 marks. As Wagner pointed out in his open letter of resignation from the party, the price of 6000 marks per square meter and the 'unbelievable 92 times [its] rentable value' spelt 'the end of any city improvement'.[67]

Nonetheless, Wagner continued to design for an expanding spirit of the city in other ways. In contrast to these major projects of reconfiguring major squares in the city centre, the extensive leisure facilities or exhibition centres, Wagner, together with others, also proposed a much more modest structure that still displayed the dynamic spirit of the city – the expanding house. Wagner's 1932 monograph on the growing house (*Das wachsende Haus*)[68] contained designs for this expanding structure – in many respects variants of the prefabricated house – by Poelzig, Gropius, Häring, Hilberseimer, Sharoun, Mendelsohn, the Tauts, Wagner himself and others. In his extensive accompanying text, Wagner calls for a planned economy to deal with the economic crisis and the recreation of a dynamic economy. Such an economy 'also requires *dynamic* building'. It 'will build *lighter, quicker* and *more frequently*' – indeed, it will favour structures 'in the process of becoming (*Werdendes*).'[69]

After examining, in typical manner, the details of costing, production and fitting as well as the planning advantages for such an expanding house in the context of an extension of the metropolis, Wagner draws out the more general context within which such structures are to be built. Although starting out from the concept of the existence *minimum*, the demarcation of the plots and the maximum utilization of space 'must also

have in mind a certain existence *maximum*',[70] even though the location of
the Utopian structures as 'the dwelling type for the five-hour day' may have
to await the transition to a communal economy. Wagner is unsure as to
where, given the economic crisis, permanent workplaces will be in the
future. However, he does recognise that:

> the *movement* (*Wanderung*) of workplaces has *commenced* with full force
> behind the dense and sheer opaque veil of the secret and private economy.
> Yet I do not know in which new spatial division these places will *terminate*.
> Cities and estates, with respect to the profitability of work places, have
> taken to *wandering*, and thus we will have to research this mobility very
> carefully before we build new dwelling spaces on a grand scale and for a
> distant future.[71]

In this sense, the spatially transitory nature of modern employment is
responded to by transitory dwelling spaces. The one follows the other
since, in city planning, too, 'the work place is primary and the dwelling
place secondary, if both are not united in one another'.[72] In this respect,
therefore, the dynamic transitory nature of the experience of modernity is
given a new embodiment in transitory dwelling.

The title of the various designs for the growing house was 'Sun, Air
and House for All' and its visitors entered

> a new world from which they appeared to require nothing other than space
> for sun, air and life. Tired and weary of the metropolis, uprooted and dis-
> appointed, they seek for themselves a new and more natural style of life.[73]

In itself, there is nothing new in 'this exodus from the stone caverns of
the cities' which commenced at the end of the nineteenth century. But
whereas the 'chains of the metropolis' were strong with respect to their
social and economic ties, with the collapse of the economy those chains
were breached. In this sense, Wagner maintains that 'the metropolis had
sinned against nature, sinned against natural thought, feelings and actions
and must therefore be *economically* weak and lose its strong magnetic
forces'. In these new economic circumstances the relationship between the
city and the country must change:

> We will only storm the machine in order to really make it into our obedient
> *slave*. If the machine is the city and nature is the country, then we will make
> the city to serve the *country* and erect a new *country* city on the old *city* land.[74]

In this context, the growing house is one means of facilitating breaking
out from 'the rigidity and limitedness of the living space of our metropolitan dweller'. What then does this growing house actually signify?

This question incorporates not only a spatial conception, but also a concept of *value* and *purpose*. The house of the future should not merely grow *spatially*, i.e. become larger through building rooms on to it, but also in the *equipment* of the individual rooms advance from the stage of simplicity to the stage of perfection. It should also transform its purpose (*Zweck*) and in the easiest manner be *capable of being rebuilt* for a changed conception of time.[75]

Symbolic of the transitory and emergent features of modernity, this growing house is, at the same time, associated with the dissolution of the metropolis.

VII

Given the intensity of the political, economic and material crisis in the German and Berlin economies, the spirit of the new Berlin was to take a different direction – at least on paper. In particular, Wagner completed a substantial manuscript in 1932 – part of which was to have been published in *Wasmuths Monatshefte*, edited by Werner Hegemann – on *Das Neue Berlin* (*The New Berlin*).[76] In this closely argued manuscript, which dealt in detail with the acute crisis in the Berlin economy, Wagner's conception of a new Berlin came, in part, to resemble Scheffler's 1926 vision (though there is no suggestion that Wagner was following him in this respect) of the new metropolis merging into the countryside. The dissolution of the metropolis – announced in a variety of forms in the Expressionist movement – reappeared in the guise of Wagner's proposal for the creation of new, young urban areas in his urban settlements of 50,000 population, which he termed his 'fifties'.

It is clear from his other writings that these new towns – Wagner's 'fifties' – are not to be identified with the garden city movement. In 'Das Problem der reinen Gartenstadt' ('The Problem of the Pure Garden City', 1926), Wagner insisted that Howard would not recognize the 'sentimental degradation of the "Garden Cities" with their small houses and gardens' to be found in Germany. Wagner maintained that 'the garden city has nothing to do with the concept of the satellite town, a form that has been discovered in order to intervene in the insanity of metropolitan development. The satellite towns, in the final instance, seek nothing less than to introduce a different *distribution* of the increase in urban population'.[77] In contrast, Wagner saw the major problem of large cities as economic. The vertical economic organization of cities, with their massive concentration in urban spaces – subsidizing building types such as the rental barracks with outlays for parks, hospitals, etc., and the excessive individual outlays for cleaning, leisure and travel costs – created false costs for arbitrarily created products. With a dramatic decline in the wealth generated in the metropolitan economy, the fixed cost burden would become that much greater. The horizontal economic organization of urban settlements, including existing cities, could create a more viable economic urban form and a genuine urban culture.

In his 1932 conception, the specific *economic* focus of Wagner's analysis of contemporary Berlin deliberately excluded a broader *political* economy of the world city that would be crucial in understanding both contemporary and future developments. Instead, Wagner asks:

> What position has Berlin in the German economic sphere? The position of Berlin as capital of the Empire, central political city, central administrative city, as financial and stock exchange city, commercial city and city of civilization and culture can remain out of discussion in the context of this analysis as unalterable (*unabänderlich*).[78]

Even at the most basic level, neither the political corruption that had led Wagner to leave the Social Democratic Party in 1931 nor the worsening political crisis in Berlin and Germany could be explained merely in narrow economic terms. From a broader perspective, the world city squares might be dynamic in terms of the circulation of traffic and consumption, but their empty and static nature in the worsening economic crisis could be filled by other forms of circulation, by what Kracauer presciently termed the 'mass ornament' of politically mobilized masses. The corporate state consolidated by Fascism could only be explained by political and socioeconomic factors. Instead, the direction of Wagner's analysis rests upon a much narrower economic focus, one that is only ostensibly broadened by reference to a fetishized machine spirit (and a false *objectivity*) and a planning for life (*Lebensbau*) (with a questionable *organicism*), which are ultimately contradictory analogies.

In order to understand Wagner's grounds for the creation of these new towns, it is necessary to follow his economic analysis of Berlin. Wagner presents a detailed account of Berlin's existing economic situation in the context of the Brandenburg regional economy surrounding the city, the German economy and the world economy. The purchasing power of all these economic regions has collapsed, and therefore crucially affected the Berlin economy. For Wagner, the reason for the dramatic decline in purchasing power lies in the fact that 'the economic leaders have not recognized the essence and significance of *machine* work'.[79] Machines have not been running to full capacity, and the utilization of the labour time set free from the planned use of machinery has not taken place within the existing free, unregulated economy.

Indeed, a substantial part of Wagner's economic analysis rests upon the *reification* of machine technology. He regards 'the machine as economic shaper (*Gestalterin*) of the economy, as the shaper of both private and public spheres of work'[80] (and hence applies to city planning too). For Wagner 'the machine has its *own* laws, is its *own* shaper, and creates its distinctive happiness'.[81] Unfortunately, it is currently controlled by dilettantes who lack the necessary knowledge to fully utilize its potential. Instead, much of the machinery is standing still. With military rhetoric, Wagner insists that a new group that understands machinery must direct the economy:

> Leader to the back! Leader to the front! Politicians and lawyers to the resting place, engineers to the front! This *must* happen and it *will* happen. And thus our *cities* will also awaken to a new life and be given a new form. *City planning* is *economic planning*, and economic planning is only possible if we work *with* the machine but not *against* the machine.[82]

The engineer recognizes that the machine has three permanent demands: 'it wishes to run permanently, it wishes to run quickly, it wishes to run cheaply'.[83] At present, the economy has collapsed, capital is on strike and labour is unemployed (and 'capital strikes because we mistreat its mother, the machine'). The engineer understands the machine and can 'move beyond the limits of the "free" non-economy and advance rapidly into the land of the planned economy'.[84] This analysis of the economy provided by Wagner is thus 'from the standpoint of the *engineer*'.

The engineer is perfectly at home in the world of machines. If the economy is reduced to a machine economy, it follows that its regulation is performed by the 'economy engineer', who 'makes us the plan for a new economic structure'.[85] The engineer is thus at the forefront of the drive to create a new economic structure. Indeed, he 'fights at the front of the planned economy against the loss economy of a liberal age'.[86] In such formulations, Wagner affirms his reduction of the economy to a machine that can best be operated by the engineer and also his exclusion of the political from the economic sphere. In fact, this elevation of the engineer takes him above and beyond the political sphere to that of a technocracy. Wagner is quite explicit about this consequence when he argues:

> When we complete the plans for a new economic structure we want engineers to lead us and not the men of politics nor the men of political doctrines. We know that this economic structure will emerge over and above all political apparatuses, all egoistic special groups and also over and above the political doctrines directed towards day-to-day successes.[87]

Such technocratic consciousness, ostensibly apolitical, can treat the economy, the state and the metropolis as a machine. The technical superiority of the machine implies the technical superiority and domination of the engineer. The support for a rationalization as envisaged by Wagner here becomes explicitly focused upon *technical* rationality.

As Max Weber pointed out, under given conditions, both the capitalist enterprise and the modern state have affinities with the machine. As far as the modern capitalist enterprise is concerned, it 'rests primarily on *calculation* and presupposes a legal and administrative system whose functioning can be rationally predicted, at least in principle, by virtue of its fixed general norms, *just like the expected performance of a machine*'.[88] For its part, in the same context, 'sociologically speaking, the modern state is an "enterprise" (*Betrieb*) just like a factory: This exactly is its historical peculiarity.'[89] Wagner's argument is ostensibly located in the context of a planned economy, but the fetishization of the machine and its identification *with* the economy as such serves to elevate the engineer to a position of technical (and political) domination.

Later in his economic analysis, Wagner makes use of Sombart's conceptualization of the basic elements of the concept of economy – spirit (*Geist*), form and technology. The contemporary economic *spirit* has abandoned the attempt to unify reason with life, the will with the deed. Instead – drawing upon another Sombart concept – 'a *trader* spirit dominates the world'.[90] The old *form* of economic life – the free play of market forces – has been rendered impossible and has led to cartellization, etc. A new economic form is emerging – 'the form of organized spatial economy with the highest possible economic impact for use'. *Technology* has been misused, since at present the 'machine is not developed for the *individual* economy but rather for the collective economy'.

In this broader context, what is Wagner's analysis and prognosis for Berlin? The concentration of economic life creates unnecessary costs, not least as far as transport is concerned. New forms cannot break out of the existing narrow, built structures. Indeed, Wagner argues:

> Berlin is still today a *pedestrian city*, but not a modern *machine* city. The whole city and street plan of Berlin, in principle and as a system, is nothing other than an enlargement of a Middle Ages – *small spaced* – pedestrian city.[91]

The new form of 'city' that Wagner proposes must depend to a much greater extent upon machine labour, and must take into account a new spatial economy. Therefore, 'we must replace the old pedestrian cities with modern ribbon cities (*Bandstädte*)'.[92] These new cities with 50,000 population will be 'new cities [built] in accord with the idea of the perfect machine'.[93]

Wagner's explication of the grounds for the deficiency of the existing metropolitan centres, and above all Berlin, and the need for new urban formations are worth closer examination. The old pedestrian cities are incapable of developing the full potentiality of the 'machine city' since their rising fixed costs and massive transport costs render them uncompetitive. Indeed, 'this false development of the machine economy in the pedestrian cities leads to the fact that metropolitan labour is 25–30 per cent more expensive than labour in small towns'.[94] Hence the need for 'the perfect machine city' since 'the machine bursts the pedestrian city asunder!'

But what of other aspects of life in existing metropolitan centres? As far as dwelling in 'the cell system of rental barracks' is concerned:

> The constriction of the self in the rental barracks results from the constriction of people in the metropolis. The metropolis suppresses natural living space for the people. It also suppresses their departure into the free and unconstrained just as it makes impossible the arrival in the great silence and loneliness of nature.[95]

Within the metropolis the space and natural distance between individuals is removed. Instead, the unnatural relationships to space predominate 'whether the metropolitan dwellers crowd through narrow alleys, whether they make their "excursions" into the fresh air in overcrowded underground or urban trains, whether they jostle with one another in a giant department store as in a beehive'.[96]

Yet Wagner also sees another, positive, potential metropolitan existence that cannot be realized at present. Granted that the metropolis is 'visibly and invisibly sick', it is also 'visibly and invisibly festive'. In fact, 'the metropolis makes Sunday into everyday and the holiday into workday!' However, this festive dimension of existence cannot be realized. Indeed, the festive element is dying in the theatre, dress balls and even in 'the major political meetings and demonstrations'. The festive dimension is dying in the metropolis because

> the conglomerates of the metropolis already deaden in us the oscillation of feeling of human beings to the mass in everyday confrontations. 'Being close to one another' has already become so mundane and unfestive in the traffic of the city, in the cinema with organ and orchestra, in the advertising fireworks of the city streets, in the mass restaurants, on the sports fields and the racing tracks that the genuinely festive . . . can no longer make an appearance! Conglomerates are amorphous and formless![97]

For Wagner, the present-day metropolis does offer a wealth of civilization. But, 'the bathtub, the water closet, the automobile, the pneumatic post – all these are culture?'

Clearly drawing upon his earlier reflections on the relationship between civilization, culture and art, Wagner asserts that:

We have forgotten that culture is no instrument of life but rather the form of life! And where is this form? Where is this reconciliation of mind and body, this bodily 'attraction' and this mental 'flight'? Where is the unity of mind and body. Has not the metropolis split up this unity and chained the mind to the 'press' and the body to the machine? How is a form of life to grow if life is split up and in ruins in its constituent parts?[98]

The way forward can only be through the creation of a new urban form that enables life to flow 'out of the amorphous mass of the metropolis, to confront the winged sunbeams, out into the organic'.

The juxtaposition of form and formlessness, the organic and the mechanical, the new towns in the countryside instead of the old metropolitan centres is reminiscent of the rhetoric of Expressionist Utopias and much more disturbing forms of organicism that were not yet realized. Despite Wagner's claim to unify economic planning with city planning and life planning, the tension between the mechanical and the organic remains in the proposal for the new cities – 'new cities with a new economy. New cities according to the idea of the perfect machine.'

There is thus a contradiction here between Wagner's more consistent analogy of the metropolis as organism and, as a result of his reification of technology, the analogy of the city as a machine. It is much easier to plan for machines than organisms. The moral rhetoric directed at 'the sin against the holy spirit of the machine'[99] (in the context of electric machines and power stations running well below their capacity) and assertions (with reference to the new form of life in the new cities) that 'the new form grows out of the organic!' are difficult to reconcile.

The new ribbon cities (Wagner also refers to them on occasion as garden cities) and machine cities will each be a 'country city in the city country'. Once created, 'the stone desert of the metropolis vanishes from the earth'. It is the metropolis that has '*destroyed* a circle of oscillation encompassing the whole community and has also left behind in history only *civilization* but no *culture*'. Instead the new ribbon city will usher in 'the age of perfect humanity and the age of the perfect machine! . . . It will lead us back again to culture, to art and to the great beliefs. Decline of the West? No! Emergence of the age of perfect humanity!'[100] Wagner insists that his 'young city is no longer Utopia and no longer Potemkin's village and representation'; the transition to the young city from 'dream to reality, contains within it no greater danger than the flight from the prison of poverty into the paradise of life'.[101]

This horizontal dispersal of the city in the country in the context of Berlin, requires 'the economic and political necessity of unifying Berlin and Brandenburg into a single economic sphere'. Other metropolitan centres also stand in a similar situation. On them, too, hangs the sword of *death* and the cross of a new *belief*. And if one wishes to bring this dying and emergence for all metropoles into a more local and personal interpretation that signifies the direction, then one can say:

> Berlin is dead
> Long live Brandenburg![102]

Anyone who has followed the debates on Berlin since 1989 will recognize the issue of the failed fusion of Berlin with the state of Brandenburg. It remains to be seen to what extent the re-location of the German capital in Berlin will solve the fiscal crisis of the local state of Berlin.

VIII

Only two years after detailing this vision of the dissolution of the metropolis and the expansion of smaller rural cities, Wagner – at the invitation of Martin Mächler and under the pseudomym of 'M. Sandow' (his wife's maiden surname), in one of the last of his publications before his emigration – returns to address the crisis of the centre of the metropolis, the problem of the redevelopment (*Sanierung*) of the inner 'city' (the term 'city' being used in German for the (old) inner core of the metropolis).[103]

The need for the redevelopment of the inner city area of Berlin is addressed from the (Expressionist) standpoint that 'the city is the city crown (*Stadtkrone*) of the metropolis'.[104] For Wagner, this city crown – for the Expressionists, this was *the* symbolic representation of the metropolis in monumental or other form – was still to be created in the Berlin city districts. However, at the present time (1934) the city core of Berlin is in need of radical redevelopment for two reasons.

First, the city core as a significant space for commodity circulation (purchasing power) is in decline, as evidenced in several indicators and factors. The decline in foreign and German visitors to Berlin is accompanied by a shift of interest to the west of the city, while local Berlin purchasing power has shifted to the north, south and east. This historical shift in commodity circulation is summarized by Wagner as follows:

> if in the period of the blossoming of the metropolis purchasing power moved to the commodity, then, conversely in the period of the death of the metropolis the commodity moved to purchasing power.[105]

This new, spatial dispersal of purchasing power away from the city centre resulted in a situation in which 'the inner city has *definitively* lost large sections of its customers'.

Second, purchasing power has itself become mobile in a number of respects. The expansion of Greater Berlin meant that those on the periphery found the way to the centre too long; the metropolitan desire for fresh air was matched by an unwillingness to go into the city at weekends; better residential areas on the periphery were created by the automobile and city rail extensions, and shops themselves became mobile with their development of suburban chainstores. In addition:

> the commodity itself became still more mobile and moved directly to the home of the customer. Technology, previous concentrated, prepared for a spreading of the commodity. The telephone called the commodity by means of the automobile to the house. But even further than that, the travelling shop and the trader began to offer the commodity in the home *without* it being ordered.[106]

This mobilization or circulation of the commodity to the periphery, to the outer districts of the metropolis, arose in part from the mobilization of dwellings themselves, as it were, in the outer districts where land was both available and cheaper.

For the inner city, this mobility meant decline and the shift of resources elsewhere. In part driven by land prices and other increased costs:

> The central postal office (*Reichspost*) moved to the Kaiserdamm, the radio to Witzleben, science to Dahlem and major industrial concerns to the west. . . . And what remained after their removal? Desolate districts, holes in building blocks, storage spaces and warehouses, dwellings that shamed human dignity, desolate cavities, etc.[107]

In this context, the transformation of the city coincides with the transformation of the outer districts and suburbs. Similarly, the problem of traffic in the city can only be that of the whole metropolis and cannot be solved merely by street widening or introducing one-way systems. The wasteful cost of underutilizing metropolitan machines (including gas, electric and waterworks as well as automobiles) that is evident in the case of traffic with uneven usage (in the city peak hours) can only be overcome, Wagner maintains, by moving to a three-shift working system that will maximize machine usage. Within the city, 'the housing quarters of the poor and the poorest with their decimated purchasing power *constrain* the development of the city and must be removed by a radical break-up of the desolate dwelling quarters'.[108] This leaves the city space for 'small parks with the most modern and quietest dwellings and small hotels' for those who have to stay in the centre to complete their work. The main building volume of the city will be for all the major administrative, commercial,

cultural, state, legal and recreational structures. Presumably, taken together, they would constitute the city crown.

The question as to how this planned reconstruction of the city was to
be carried out without the whole becoming fragmented into separate sections called for a '*leader* (*Führer*) of the City of Berlin', for leadership
'out of the labyrinth of hopeless confusion'. The leader must be a genuine
city planner, for 'no masterwork emerges from third or fourth hand:
neither an ocean liner, nor a new state and a new city'.[109] Such ominous
leadership in city planning was not carried out by Wagner, who had
already been dismissed from his position a year earlier. But he was clearly
not unsympathetic to city planning from above by a technical elite.

This technocratic dimension is commented upon by Kracauer in a
1932 article titled 'Die Techniker verteidigen sich' ('The Technocrats
Defend Themselves').[110] Reacting against the popular hostility to new
technology, Wagner and others (including the architect Hans Luckhardt,
co-designer of one of the submissions for the Alexanderplatz competition) explain:

> that it was not technology that led to the economic crisis but rather that
> the latter emerged through the false application of the means supplied by
> technology. Responsibility for the difficulties in which we find ourselves is
> accorded to the present form of the economy and not the licentiousness of
> technology claimed by the latter's opponents.[111]

For Wagner, therefore, 'society's critique of technology is answered . . . by
a critique of society'.[112] More specifically:

> City planners today, for example, as Martin Wagner testifies from his own
> experience, are handicapped by the continuous uncontrollable migration of
> production sites to the places with the lowest costs. This shifting of sites
> deriving from the drive to rationalization results in a continuous devalu-
> ation of dwellings, shops and publicly financed structures that must equally
> be confronted in the interests of rational economic activity. How should
> the latter take place? It could only occur by means of major area planning,
> whose responsibility it would be to deal with the economic viability of
> employment. But the effectiveness of such area planning would be linked,
> of course, with general considerations of the planned economy.[113]

Yet this favourable technocratic case remains one that still accords a
privileged position to the technocrat in the process of economic rationalization. Even if the dependency of technology upon economic systems is
conceded (and many, including Marx, for example, have viewed technology
as fixed capital and by no means independent), this shifts the problem of
the technocratic vision of a future economy on to the presumed *neutrality*

of the process of rationalization itself. From their different perspectives, both Weber and Kracauer (in his earlier essay on the mass ornament) had good reasons to be sceptical of such a proposition.

With respect to Wagner's Utopian urban vision, the combination of the decline of the metropolitan centres and the birth of the new ribbon cities (with a population of 50,000 and with specialized machine economies) as organic land cities has strong echoes of some Expressionist visions of the city and the country. It is perhaps all the more surprising to find it expressed in the work of such a materialist-oriented city planner as Martin Wagner, one whose message is also that there is no spirit without a body and that that body is planted on a ground whose costs are always precisely calculated.

Throughout much of Wagner's writings the spirit of the metropolis is manifested in rationalization and circulation (in *Das neue Berlin*, the electrical analogy is that of oscillation). For Wagner, the rationalization of production in a capitalist mode could only create civilization. Only the planned, socialist rationalization could create a new culture and new life form for all. In this sense, as Scarpa and others have argued, Wagner's – unrealized – aim was nothing less than the rationalization of human happiness.

Conclusion

The indescribable diversity of all the everyday language games do not penetrate our consciousness because the clothes (*Kleider*) of our language make everything alike. What is new (spontaneous, 'distinctive') is always a language game.

Ludwig Wittgenstein, *Philosophical Investigations*

The walls of the streets radiate ideologies.

Robert Musil, *The Man Without Qualities*

Space that has been seized upon by the imagination cannot remain indifferent space subject to the measures and estimates of the surveyor.

Gaston Bachelard, *The Poetics of Space*

I

A set of explorations of cityscapes of modernity that commences with the figure of the flâneur and terminates with the figure of the city planner in Berlin suggests, at first sight, a historical synchrony from around the 1830s in Paris, with the already developed contours of the flâneur's ostensibly open spaces for strolling, down to the early 1930s and the regulated spaces of the world metropolis of Berlin, with respect to both the circulation sphere (notably Alexanderplatz) and the domestic interior (oscillating between the interior, constrained space of the 'existence minimum' and the potentially dynamic space of the prefabricated 'growing house').

Yet any presumed linearity of development would be not merely deceptive but also erroneous. This can be illustrated by the figure of the flâneur.
If we have witnessed a renewed discourse on the flâneur and the practices of flânerie in recent decades, then in large part this must be due to
our rediscovery of Walter Benjamin's own analysis of this urban figure in
the late 1920s and 1930s. His historical exploration of the flâneur, later
embodied in the figure of the poet Baudelaire, presumed the figure's decline
with Haussmann's transformation of Paris. Yet it is Benjamin, reviewing
in October 1929 his friend Franz Hessel's *Spazieren in Berlin*, who asks us
to acknowledge the return of the flâneur and the possibility of Berlin as a
site for contemporary flânerie.[1] This diachronic relationship between
present and past had a deeper motive for Benjamin, since his prehistory
of modernity – of which the flâneur and flânerie constituted a not unim-
portant element – presupposed nothing less than that the reading of his
present could only be realized through blasting the past – as origin
(*Ursprung*) – into our present. At the same time, the exploration of this
ostensibly historically located figure/activity, whose habitus was most often
viewed as in decline, also provided Benjamin with crucial insights into his
own contemporary methodology.[2]

At the very least, then, the explorations undertaken in this volume
should be recognized as both diverse and interrelated, as exploring distinctive spatial dimensions of the experience of modernity and recognizing temporal affinities and disjunctions. Indeed, the spatial dimensions of
metropolitan modernity that have been explored here take up aspects of
the *production* of spaces, the *representations* of space and spatial *practices*
in urban settings. This reformulation of Henri Lefebvre's much more
detailed focus upon spatiality in *The Production of Space* and other writings has arisen out of the specific explorations of diverse thematics present
in the cityscapes of modernity.[3] It has its origin not in Lefebvre's work
but in that of Simmel, Kracauer and Benjamin.[4] Lefebvre's major work
on space makes no reference to Simmel, who also maintained that space
was socially constructed, nor to Kracauer and Benjamin. Furthermore, it
was a critical geography that took up the issue of spatiality before most
contemporary sociologists tended to focus upon the mapping of spatial
relations and networks – the horizontal planes, as it were, of spatial networks. Yet in several of his essays – notably in 'Bridge and Door' –
Simmel already drew attention to two other spatial dimensions: inside
and outside, and above and below.[5] Some of the essays in the present
volume explore aspects of these more neglected dimensions of space or
differently focused dimensions. Such spatial properties, of course, are not
unknown to architects and it is not surprising that they were developed
in the work of Kracauer, who was trained, and practised briefly, as an
architect,[6] and in Benjamin's Arcades Project, which not merely drew

upon architectonic interests but also, in his analysis of the arcade itself as a product and symbol of the origins of urban modernity, focused upon a highly complex and differentiated built structure and habitus.[7]

The figures in the metropolitan landscape who appear in these explorations therefore inhabit and create different spaces. And most of them are deeply contradictory. We commenced with the figure of the flâneur, whose seemingly aimless strolling presupposed an ability to traverse differentiated and regulated spaces of the early modernist city, which ultimately enclosed him – as Benjamin later suggested – as a parlour (*Stube*). The space of Benjamin's own flâneries in the Bibliothèque Nationale were also both regulated and open, and such flâneries did not in principle exclude those of the flâneuse. This is to be judged in the context of the late access accorded to women in universities (and their libraries). To give but one location – as a prominent site of twentieth-century modernism explored in other contexts here – women were first admitted to study at the University of Vienna only in 1897.[8] In turn, it should be noted that Otto Wagner, the leading modern architect in that city at the turn of the century, had no female students in his architecture classes from their inception in 1894 to the last cohort in 1911.

If the activity of flânerie is nonetheless predicated upon the potential openness of urban spaces and the public sphere (in which, for its part, private space could be both regulated and constrained), the figure of the detective, as representation of the urban investigator, presupposed both open public and private spaces in the metropolis – even though their accessibility was often acquired by subterfuge and deception. As we have seen with reference to the Pinkerton Agency, the latter required a training that was ignored in the subsequent representations of the private eye. In turn, the representation of the spaces of detection in the accompanying fictional forms focused upon a conception of the open city as accessible to investigation. The operation of detection, surveillance and (often armed) policing of the enclosed sites of production – manifested in the prominent role of the Pinkerton agency in strike-breaking and trade union infiltration – played little role in literary representations of detection. Indeed, a large body of that literature sited detection as far away from industrial production as possible, in the country house mystery. This was not the reality for which Pinkerton operatives were trained. Although much of the work of their detection in the second half of the nineteenth century was in connection with railroad and banking thefts in small towns and 'frontier' contexts, the Pinkerton operatives were trained in an urban milieu.

If the flâneur and the detective both relied upon the trained eye for capturing the images and figures of the metropolis, Simmel's exploration of the modern metropolis, in his most famous essay at least, focused upon the response of the emotions and the mind. Even though it is the eye that receives the greatest attention in his sociology of the senses, the body as a whole is not excluded from his analysis, not least with reference to the metropolis. Simmel's spatial analysis of the city is both that of an expanding space and, at the same time, one that is circumscribed. His astute observations on the socio-spatial boundary and his preoccupation with social distance in a variety of social contexts suggest a conception of the metropolis as a configuration of highly differentiated spaces. His analysis extends beyond the now customary differentiation of public and private space (even though its gendered dimension receives far from satisfactory treatment by Simmel). The spaces of circulation and consumption receive greater attention than those of production, which, in the context of Berlin at the turn of the nineteenth/twentieth centuries, is to overlook a crucial dimension of urban spatial relations and to ignore the potentially different spatial dynamics of industrial cities.

In turn, the spaces of circulation and their intersecting networks provide the basis for an image of the metropolis as a highly complex web of interactions verging on the chaotic (at least as far as the individual's sense perception is concerned). The sphere of circulation – of commodities, money and individuals – thus provides an image of the city as the concentration or focal point of metropolitan modernity. At the same time, however, this same circulation sphere generates a conception of the effects of metropolitan existence as being diffused far into the city's hinterland. This is most evident, elsewhere, in Simmel's treatment of the money economy as not merely having its focal point in the modern metropolis but also as capable of generating a trans-spatial community, extending far beyond the formal boundaries of the city.[9]

More significantly for spatial analysis, however, is Simmel's recognition of key modalities of space, which are articulated – albeit incompletely – in his articles on space. Beyond the explorations of spatial networks (the 'web' of social interactions is not uncommon in many of his sociological studies and their 'geometry' is occasionally referenced), their boundaries and the social distance that they engender, attention is also given to the inside and outside dimensions of spatial production, separation and connection, above and below, to fixity and diffusion in space, to the production of space in 'institutional' practices, to representation of space (as in exhibitions) and to a variety of differentiated spatial practices.

In his essay on the Berlin Trade Exhibition of 1896, but also earlier in 'On Art Exhibitions' Simmel displayed an interest in the representation of the metropolis in exhibitions. The Berlin Trade Exhibition of 1896 was viewed by contemporaries as a symbolic representation of Berlin's elevation to a world city (*Weltstadt*). But in the decades around the turn of that century, the city as imaginary took on an almost equal importance. If, in the Weimar Republic, Kracauer used the juxtaposition of Paris and

Berlin in order, in part, to contrast the historically rooted with the instantly modern metropolis, then two decades or more earlier the polarities of Berlin and Vienna were utilized for the purposes of a more ideological confrontation with modernity.

The imaginary spaces of Berlin as hypermodernity and Vienna as embodiment of historical culture do not emerge out of a rigorous historical or socio-economic comparison of the two cities. This is not because the necessary information for such comparisons was not available. On the contrary, major authorities and bureaucracies generated and had at their disposal a huge statistical- and research-based mass of relevant data. Rather, the imaginary spaces arise out of fantasies that are sometimes mediated by a third, other, space – America (the USA), or one of its cities (most often New York). Further, the possibility that one of these cities might be transformed into its other (Vienna to be Berlin, or Berlin to become New York) was posed as an unwelcome outcome by those who abhorred or felt threatened by modernity. The confrontation of these imaginary spaces was by no means confined to feuilletonistic essays and rejoinders but also entered into debates on city planning in the 1890s and later.

In the debate on city planning between Stübben (broadly in accord with Otto Wagner's position) and Henrici (a follower of Sitte) on straight or crooked streets, two representations of the metropolis confronted one another as 'modern' versus 'natural'. The conception of the modern metropolis (some of whose features Henrici denounced as 'un-German' or as displaying 'Gallic influences') putatively favoured by Wagner, Stübben and others reduced the city to a 'human storehouse' (Sitte) designed by 'geometric man' (Sitte's description of Wagner) for an abstract mass. The spaces of this modern metropolis comprised straight, boring streets, often in a grid system, creating indifference and anonymity amongst its inhabitants. Its planners were seen as preoccupied with circulation of traffic and hygiene. Aesthetically, such city design favoured symmetry, the fashionable and a preoccupation with surfaces.

In contrast, the natural, historical city and its modern variant should be 'a work of art' (Sitte) for an individualized, natural population. Its spaces were to be those of irregular (crooked) streets, pleasant streets and squares. The irregularity of the streets and the enclosed nature of the squares were to create 'cosiness', an embeddedness of the urban population, a rootedness and an intimacy. According to their respective opponents, if the space of the modern city generated the pathological response of agoraphobia, that of the natural, historical city created claustrophobia.[10]

This debate on city planning was sufficiently wide-ranging not to focus solely upon Berlin and Vienna (although Sitte's newspaper attacks on Wagner's projects did display this local context). Nonetheless, the renewed debate on Old and New Vienna, which also re-emerged in the 1890s, was effectively focused upon the historical, cultural imaginary of Old Vienna versus plans for a new, 'modern' Vienna. A decade later, as evidenced in the writings of Sombart and Servaes, the juxtaposition of Berlin/New York/modern and Vienna/culture/old was largely devoid of empirical content, and the imaginaries of Berlin as New York in Europe and Vienna as bastion of (German) culture came into their own as spatial representations that resonated with other temporary dichotomies, notably between (mere) civilization and (high) culture.

This constitutes part of the context, at least, within which resistance to Otto Wagner's projects for a new Vienna can be better understood. Wagner, too, wished to create a new Vienna as 'a work of art', but such a claim was rejected by Sitte, his supporters and the broader opposition to Viennese modernity. What were the spaces of modernity that Wagner favoured in his plea for a modern architecture appropriate to the modern metropolis?

The *production* of new spaces – whether they be Wagner's city railway system, the unrealized completion of the Ringstrasse along the quay as an extensive shopping avenue (envisaged in his 1897 painting together with an avenue from the Stephansdom to the southeast corner of the Ringstrasse and, earlier, a planned avenue from the Karlsplatz to Schönbrunn) or the various projects for restructuring the Karlsplatz itself – all involved to a greater or lesser extent the *destruction* of existing 'old' spaces. But the abstract nature of the production of new urban spaces was nowhere more apparent than in the illustrations accompanying his 1911 essay on the metropolis – be it the largely symmetrical and socially homogeneous (bourgeois) sections envisaged for the 22nd district or the vision of the expanding metropolis along radial lines and circles conceived in roughly equal spatial intervals (as a systematic web). To many contemporaries, nervous of further modernist interventions in Vienna, some of Wagner's conceptions for a modern architecture not merely involved a new planning of the city's morphology but also had serious implications for interior space that implied a new form of life.[11] The radical extension of the uniformity of the apartment block as a 'conglomerate of cells' would generate interior spaces that conformed to Wagner's belief in a levelling process in modern urban society, but would have run counter to a social structure that retained an uneasy tension between a precapitalist society, based upon estates and ranks, and a capitalist social formation based upon social class divisions. The ostensibly unifying or horizontal levelling strata of the military (and their guarded spaces) and the state bureaucracy (with both local and translocal spaces) served only to render more complex the class and status differentiations in an urban and profoundly multi-ethnic and multicultural context. Equally disturbing was Wagner's defence of the apartment block as a source of individual freedom away from the 'nosey neighbours' in individual housing systems. But most worrying of all to Wagner's opponents was that his conception of modernity and modern life in the metropolis was *in no way specific to Vienna*. His conceptions relied upon general features of metropolitan existence that could be found in many other metropolitan centres.

The neglected issue of the destruction of urban spaces, which in Vienna was often associated with the destruction of memory traces of Old Vienna and their replacement by a nostalgia for the past, has many other dimensions. One dimension, represented in some German Expressionist works, is the powerful image of the *implosion* of urban space. This is already represented most dramatically in the pre-First World War depictions of the city by Ludwig Meidner.[12] Indeed, a number of his paintings anticipate the explosive *destruction* of urban space that befell some cities during that war, but which was only realized to the full in several European metropolitan centres in the Second World War.

At the same time, however, the celebration of the bombardment of the senses in the tumult of the metropolis coincided with Utopian conceptions of new cities of glass, sometimes located in alpine locations, most notably in the Utopian visions of Bruno Taut and others. Such 'well-ventilated Utopias' (Benjamin) suggested a new urban space, translucent and open. Yet another, and related, dimension of Expressionist response to the modern metropolis was the retreat from the city to the countryside and its putative authentic existence. Such evidence of the deep ambiguity towards the metropolis was to be found not merely in artistic representations or architectural visions but also in contemporary social theory. Utopian visions of new urban space in new configurations of the city stood alongside and interacted with more concrete socialist demands – especially in the period around the failed German Revolution of 1918 – for a reconstitution of metropolitan space and its capitalist foundations.

Out of the latter impulse there emerged attempts at the planning of a socialist metropolis, but within a society that remained fundamentally capitalist with regard to urban capital. This is part of the context, at least, within which the efforts of Martin Wagner as *Oberbaurat* in Berlin during the late Weimar Republic are to be understood. But this should not be taken to imply that the socialist city planner Wagner was merely operating in the capitalist context of late Weimar Germany and therefore shaping a doomed enterprise. Rather, Wagner's conception of the metropolis was infused both with socialist Utopian intentions and a commitment to total rationalization. Yet the assumption that the process of rationalization – both economic and administrative – could be harnessed to the realization of a socialist urban Utopia without being compromised by its own (capitalist) rationalistic foundations was itself Utopian. What was anticipated as a Utopian vision of the socialist metropolis could often be actualized in dystopian urban spaces.[13]

Nonetheless, the dynamics of circulation in the modernist metropolis of 'new' Berlin are well represented in the multi-levelled transportation and circulation networks envisaged in the Alexanderplatz competition (although Wagner's own sketch of the square is certainly static compared with other submissions) and in the expandable interior spaces of the prefabricated 'growing house', instances of which were exhibited by Wagner and others in the early 1930s. In contrast, even before the world economic crisis struck Germany in 1929, the constraints of domestic interior space were already being projected in the measurement of individual figures' movements within confined cubic-metred rooms, and thus anticipating housing construction for a more radical 'existence minimum'. As Kracauer remarked 'each social stratum has a space that is associated with it'.[14] Above that existence minimum and as

> the characteristic location of the small dependent existences who still very much like to associate themselves with the sunken middle class, more and more suburbs are formed. The few inhabitable cubic metres, which cannot even be enlarged by the radio, correspond precisely to the narrow living space of this stratum.[15]

At the same time, the spaces of urban capital's circulation hubs, such as Alexanderplatz, were subject to an acceleration in their turnover time, with a maximum period of 25 years envisaged for the life of its modern architecture.

The severe economic (and political) constraints of the late Weimar years and disillusionment with socialist corruption in Berlin prompted Wagner to set out a new vision of another 'new' Berlin in 1932 (to be distinguished from the still optimistic journal *Das neue Berlin*, co-edited by Wagner in 1929). What is disturbing in the new 1932 vision of the metropolis is the confirmation of Wagner's preoccupation with formal rationalization and the prominent role given to the engineer-technician in shaping new economic and urban spaces. The illusion of mere technical solutions to economic and political problems could lead to viewing the metropolis as a technical problem requiring technical solutions. This restricted rationality, combined with leadership and direction from above, could just as readily serve quite different visions of the future from those envisaged by Martin Wagner.

II

If the present study has explored instances of spatial practices, representations of space and the production of spaces of modernity in a variety of historical configurations, then it has also drawn attention to some of the forms and modes of acquiring knowledge of these spaces of modernity, both with reference to figures in the cityscape intent upon gaining knowledge of the modern metropolis, and with respect to the researching of the city, its architecture and those who populate it. Both presuppose that the modern metropolis, despite its frequent representation as a chaos or labyrinth of interactions, signs and structures, is nonetheless intelligible.

An obvious starting point for reading the city, its streets, its architecture and its population is our everyday experience. Yet the apparent self-evidentness of such a point of departure hides a number of problems. As Simmel remarked in several contexts, that which we wish to make our problem does not immediately emerge of itself out of everyday experience. And although amongst the sociologists of his generation he is the one who paid particular attention to the everyday sphere and the surface of everyday life, he was also convinced of the necessity of exploring beneath the surface, to 'drop a sounding into the depths' (as he suggests in his essay on the metropolis).[16] Kracauer, in a different mode, also explored the metropolis 'beneath the surface' (as he titled one of his essays on Berlin).[17]

Some of the difficulties in exploring the immediacy of the everyday world are touched upon by Wittgenstein in his analysis of the nature of language and language games. Indeed, to conceive of the city as text raises issues that are reflected upon by Wittgenstein with respect to the nature of language. Some features of textuality – an, in principle, intelligible constellation of signs and symbols, a system of hieroglyphics – are necessarily presupposed. If we ask what is being said by the 'forest of symbols' (Baudelaire), by the building façades, signs, traffic and so on as 'a wealth of equally valid letters of the alphabet that together result in words, sentences and pages of an ever-new book' (Hessel), by 'the deciphering of . . . [cities'] dream-like, expressive images' (Kracauer), by each 'social hieroglyphic' (Marx) that is the product of human labour (in the metropolis, as elsewhere) – if we ask what each of these is saying, then we must confront some of the problems that Wittgenstein also faced in seeking to clarify what language is and how it is used. He maintains that 'in order to understand the nature of a statement we think of the hieroglyphic script that pictures the facts that it describes',[18] and such a hieroglyphic script could also be found in the city.

But, like Simmel and others, who insist upon an analysis beneath the surface, the question as to the nature of language, 'its function, its construction (*Bau*)' does not reveal itself to be immediately self-evident but is 'rather, something that lies *beneath* the surface'.[19] Indeed, 'the essence is hidden to us'.[20] And when we ask how what is important to us is hidden from us, we confront the self-evident nature of the everyday world:

> The aspects of things that are most important to us are hidden by their simplicity and everyday nature (*Alltäglichkeit*). (One does not notice it – because one has it permanently before one's eyes). The genuine foundations for its research do not occur to people.[21]

One of Wittgenstein's concerns is with the extreme diversity of language games – even though they are all 'games' – but again we do not recognize this because 'the clothes (*Kleider*) of our language makes everything alike'.[22] In passing, it is worth noting that with reference to money, Simmel would say that the medium of our transactions makes everything alike. That which is a means of differentiation is also a means of dedifferentiation. Is the same kind of proposition also true for architecture?

Otto Wagner's complaint against historicist architecture – with its plurality of language games played out against inappropriate and archaic forms of life – was that it was *unintelligible* to modern people. Perhaps this was also Musil's view when he stated – with obvious reference to Viennese architecture but clearly with a wider relevance – that 'the walls of the streets radiate ideologies'.[23] But although Wagner does not develop his critique, it lies at the heart of a more fundamental problem. Wagner's naive assertion that a modern architecture should reflect modern life required, on its own terms, a precise, even positivistic, analysis of the nature of that modern life in order that a modern architecture totally appropriate to it could be developed. Otherwise, the new modern architecture would itself also be unintelligible and unreadable.

One of the problems in Wittgenstein's legitimate concern with the everyday and in Otto Wagner's attention to the issue of the intelligibility of the built environment, and by implications of the metropolis in general, is that in both instances, but for different reasons, the *historical* nature of our experience of modernity is neglected. If our experience of modernity is to be any more than the endless affirmation of the ever-new that is presented to us on the surface of everyday modern life, then it must access the contradictions and differentiations of modernity that exist within it. Recognition of the historical nature of the everyday world must question any naive assumption that we are all modern in the same way. Otto Wagner's contemporaries, for example, were not located or moving in the same spatio-temporal constellation – as he increasingly and repeatedly witnessed in the oppositional movements to his projects from the mid-1890s onwards.[24] Later, when Karl Mannheim's sociology of knowledge drew attention to the 'non-contemporaneity of the contemporaneous' in his treatment of the problem of generations,[25] such disjunctions could also be given wider applicability to the study of our experience of modernity.

As we have seen, the activity of flânerie seeks to make sense of the fragmentary experiences and images of the metropolis, to search for the traces of origin. The activity of detection is one of following traces, including memory traces, in order to reconstruct the past. In contrast, the immediacy of experience of the modern metropolis, both mentally and bodily as well as in its multifarious transactions, is one theme at least in Simmel's explorations of metropolitan experience. If we were to confine our experience merely to immediacy, then its illusory dimensions would not be uncovered. Conversely, recourse to illusory and often nostalgic imaginaries of the city, as illustrated in Berlin and Vienna, as imaginary constructs fails to contrast the historically conditioned features of metropolitan life. A design of the modern city that ostensibly renders it intelligible for modern dwellers without reference to historical memory creates a mode of ostensibly intelligible city that is without memory. Indeed, the more the metropolis is viewed as a technical problem, the more this mode of problematization is distanced from everyday life. But if the issue of intelligibility is also one of meaning, then, as Wittgenstein argued by implication on the relationship between meaning and use, the meanings that adhere to metropolitan experiences of our built environment can be accessed by an investigation of the uses to which that built environment is put.

Yet the investigation of our use of the modern metropolis in the everyday world would have to explore beneath the surface of our everyday experience of it. If our experience of modernity is taken to be the modes of experiencing that which is new in modern society – and in their different ways, Simmel, Kracauer, Benjamin and others explored the experience of newness in modernity – then we should also ask what is hidden by this newness. At the very least, we would have to explore the *differentiations* and *contradictions* beneath the surface of the everyday and restore the *historical nature* of everyday experience. Such a project was intimated by Lefebvre when he argued that:

> The everyday is covered by a surface: that of modernity.... Modernity and everydayness constitute a deep structure that a critical analysis can work to uncover.[26]

One of Lefebvre's major contributions to such a critical analysis was to restore the significance of the spatial in both the everyday world and modernity. Our explorations of theoretical reflections on the spatial practices of flânerie and detection, the representations and interpretations of metropolitan spaces and the theoretical grounding of instances of spatial production in city planning and architecture are also intended to illuminate – albeit from different theoretical traditions – aspects of modernity in a metropolitan setting.

Notes

Unless otherwise indicated, translations from the German are my own.

Introduction

Epigraphs from: Siegfried Kracauer, 'Aus dem Fenster gesehen' (1931), *Schriften V.2. 1927–1931* (Frankfurt: Suhrkamp, 1990), p. 399; Robert Musil, *The Man Without Qualities*, trans. Sophie Wilkins and Burton Pike (New York: Knopf, 1995), p. 708; Anon [Walter Rathenau], 'Die schönste Stadt der Welt', *Die Zukunft*, 26 (1899), p. 41.

1 On the concept of modernity and some of its historical variants, see my *Fragments of Modernity: Social Theories of Modernity in the Works of Georg Simmel, Siegfried Kracauer and Walter Benjamin* (Cambridge: Polity, 1985; Cambridge, Mass.: MIT Press, 1986); also my 'Modernità', *Enciclopedia della Scienza Soziale 5* (Rome: Instituto Enciclopedia Italiano, 1996), pp. 754–61. For a brief overview of social theories of modernity in relation to the city, see Harold Chorney, *City of Dreams* (Toronto: Nelson, 1990).
2 Georg Simmel, 'Philosophie der Landschaft' (1910), in Michael Landmann (ed.), *Brücke und Tür* (Stuttgart: Köhler, 1957), pp. 141–52.
3 Georg Simmel, 'The Metropolis and Mental Life' (1903), in D. Frisby and M. Featherstone (eds), *Simmel on Culture: Selected Writings* (London: Sage, 1997), pp. 174–85.
4 Anon [Walter Rathenau], 'Die schönste Stadt der Welt', *Die Zukunft*, 26 (1899), pp. 36–48.
5 Ibid., p. 41.
6 Ibid., pp. 41–2.
7 See Franz Hessel, *Ein Flâneur in Berlin* (Berlin: Arsenal, 1984).

8   See Walter Benjamin, *The Arcades Project* (Cambridge, Mass.: Belknap Press, 1999).

9   See Siegfried Kracauer, *Strassen in Berlin und anderswo* (Frankfurt: Suhrkamp, 1964).

10   For a brief overview of the city as text, see my 'The Metropolis as Text: Otto Wagner and Vienna's "Second Renaissance"', *Renaissance and Modern Studies* (Nottingham), 40 (1998), pp. 1–16; also in Neil Leach (ed.), *Hieroglyphics of the City* (London: Spon, 2001).

11   W. Benjamin, 'Review of Hessel's *Heimliches Berlin*', *Selected Writings, Volume 2: 1927–1934* (Cambridge, Mass.: Belknap Press, 1999), p. 69.

12   W. Benjamin,'The Rigorous Study of Art', *Selected Writings, Volume 2*, p. 670. Translation amended.

13   Max Weber, 'Antikritisches Schlusswort zum "Geist des Kapitalismus"' (1910), *Die protestantische Ethik II. Kritiken und Antikritiken*, ed. Johannes Winckelmann (Hamburg: Siebenstern, 1972), pp. 283–345.

14   Ibid., p. 322. My emphasis.

15   G. Simmel, 'The Adventure', in Frisby and Featherstone (eds), *Simmel on Culture*, pp. 221–32.

16   See Simmel, 'The Metropolis', and ch. 3 below.

17   On Kracauer's interest in fortuitous urban constellations, see Inka Mülder, *Siegfried Kracauer* (Stuttgart: Metzler, 1985); Frisby, *Fragments of Modernity*, ch. 3.

18   See Michel de Certeau, *The Practice of Everyday Life* (Berkeley: University of California Press, 1984), pp. 91–110.

19   G. Simmel, *The Philosophy of Money* (1900), 2nd enlarged edn (London: Routledge, 1990), p. 255.

20   Ibid., p. 256.

21   Ibid., p. 257.

22   Ibid., p. 484.

23   Ibid., p. 444.

24   These figures are now available in the English translation of Benjamin, *The Arcades Project*. For a discussion of some of these figures, see Susan Buck-Morss, *The Dialectics of Seeing: Walter Benjamin and the Arcades Project* (Cambridge, Mass.: MIT Press, 1990).

25   For the fullest version of Simmel's essay on fashion, see 'The Philosophy of Fashion', in Frisby and Featherstone, *Simmel on Culture*, pp. 187–206.

26   See Priscilla Ferguson, 'The *Flâneur* On and Off the Streets of Paris', in Keith Tester (ed.), *The Flâneur* (London: Routledge, 1994), pp. 22–42.

27   W. Benjamin, 'The Return of the *Flâneur*', in his *Selected Writings, Volume 2*, pp. 262–7.

28   There is a huge literature on the emergence of the detective novel. Amongst the many historical and literary studies, see Dennis Porter, *The Pursuit of Crime* (New Haven: Yale University Press, 1981).

29   For biographies of Allan Pinkerton, see James D. Horan, *The Pinkertons* (New York: Crown, 1967); James Mackay, *Allan Pinkerton: The Eye Who Never Slept* (Edinburgh: Mainstream, 1996).

30 See G. Simmel, 'The Berlin Trade Exhibition', in Frisby and Featherstone, *Simmel on Culture*, pp. 255–8.

31 For an earlier treatment of Simmel's metropolis, see my *Simmel and Since* (London: Routledge, 1992), ch. 6.

32 For an overview of some of the literature on European and American urban life in the late nineteenth and early twentieth centuries, see Andrew Lees, *Cities Perceived: Urban Society in European and American Thought, 1820–1940* (Manchester: Manchester University Press, 1985).

33 Otto Wagner, *Modern Architecture* (1896), trans. Harry F. Malgrave (Santa Monica: Getty, 1988).

34 See Camillo Sitte, *City Planning According to Artistic Principles*, trans. George Collins and Christina Collins (New York: Rizzoli, 1985).

35 Camillo Sitte, 'Die neue Stadterweiterung', *Neues Wiener Tagblatt*, 27 Sept. 1891, p. 1.

36 For the political context of Viennese developments in the late nineteenth and early twentieth century, see Carl E. Schorske, *Fin-de-Siècle Vienna* (New York: Knopf, 1980), chs. 2, 3. More recently, see the detailed historical study by John W. Boyer, *Culture and Political Crisis in Vienna: Christian Socialism in Power, 1897–1918* (Chicago: Chicago University Press, 1995).

37 For an English translation, see O. Wagner, 'The Development of the Great City', *Architectural Record*, 31 (1912), pp. 485–500.

38 On Expressionist Utopias in general, see Timothy O. Benson et al., *Expressionist Utopias* (Los Angeles: County Museum of Art, 1993; new expanded edn, Berkeley: University of California Press, 2001). On Bruno Taut, see Iain Boyd Whyte, *Bruno Taut and the Architecture of Activism* (Cambridge: Cambridge University Press, 1982).

39 For a recent collection of essays on Bloch's work, see J. O. Daniel and T. Moylan (eds), *Not Yet: Reconsidering Ernst Bloch* (London: Verso, 1997).

40 Hiller, Behne and Wagner had studied with Simmel and, as was apparent in some of his correspondence, Mendelsohn was impressed by his philosophy.

41 There is no detailed study of Wagner's work in English. For two German sources, see Ludovica Scarpa, *Martin Wagner und Berlin* (Braunschweig/Wiesbaden: Vieweg, 1986); *Martin Wagner 1885–1957* (Berlin: Akademie der Künste, 1986).

42 On Hilberseimer's vision of the modern city, see K. Michael Hays, *Modernism and the Posthumanist Subject* (Cambridge, Mass.: MIT Press, 1992).

43 Bettine Menke, 'Das Nach-Leben im Zitat. Benjamins Gedächtnis der Texte', in R. Lachmann (ed.), *Gedächtniskunst* (Frankfurt: Suhrkamp, 1986), pp. 74–110, esp. p. 100.

44 On the general properties of viewing the city, see Richard Sennett, *The Conscience of the Eye* (New York: Norton, 1990).

45 See my *Sociological Impressionism: A Reassessment of Georg Simmel's Social Theory*, 2nd edn (London: Routledge, 1991).

46 See Georg Kamphausen, *Die Generation von 1890 und die Erfindung Amerikas*, Habilitationsschrift, Bayreuth University, 2000.

1 The City Observed

Epigraphs from: Franz Hessel, *Spazieren in Berlin* (Vienna/Leipzig: Verlag Dr Hans Epstein, 1929); reprinted as *Ein Flâneur in Berlin* (Berlin: Das Arsenal, 1984), p. 145; Walter Benjamin, 'The Return of the Flâneur' (Berlin: Das Arsenal, 1984), p. 145; Walter Benjamin, 'The Return of the Flâneur' (1930), *Selected Writings, Volume 2: 1927–1934*, trans. Rodney Livingstone et al. (Cambridge, Mass.: Belknap Press, 1999), pp. 262–3; Robert E. Park, 'Notes on the Origins of the Society for Social Research' (1939), cited in Rolf Lindner, *The Reportage of Urban Culture: Robert Park and the Chicago School* (Cambridge: Cambridge University Press, 1996), p. 100.

1   The case for Benjamin as sociologist or, at least, as someone with a major contribution to make to sociology, and certainly to the sociology of modernity has seldom been made. For a brief early attempt, see C. Neubaur, 'Walter Benjamin: Soziologe. Anmerkungen über eine Philosophie ohne Begriffe', *Freibeuter*, 15 (1983), pp. 143–9. On Benjamin in the context of a social theory of modernity, see my *Fragments of Modernity: Social Theories of Modernity in the Works of Georg Simmel, Siegfried Kracauer and Walter Benjamin* (Cambridge: Polity, 1985; Cambridge, Mass.: MIT Press, 1986), ch. 4. On Benjamin's Arcades Project, the most detailed investigation is S. Buck-Morss, *The Dialectics of Seeing: Walter Benjamin and the Arcades Project* (Cambridge, Mass.: MIT Press, 1989).
2   W. Benjamin, *Gesammelte Schriften IV* (Frankfurt: Suhrkamp, 1986), p. 172. For two reviews of Kracauer, see now: Benjamin, 'Review of Kracauer's *Die Angestellten*', *Selected Writings, Volume 2: 1927–1934* (Cambridge, Mass.: Cambridge University Press, 1996), pp. 355–7, and 'An Outsider Makes His Mark', ibid., pp. 305–11.
3   W. Benjamin, *Gesammelte Schriften III* (Frankfurt: Suhrkamp, 1972), p. 226.
4   Ibid.
5   On Benjamin and the Bibliothèque Nationale, see P. Missac, 'Walter Benjamin à la Bibliothèque Nationale', *Revue de la Bibliothèque Nationale* 10 (1983), pp. 30–43.
6   See the conference collection, H. Wismann (ed.), *Walter Benjamin et Paris* (Paris: Cerf, 1986).
7   W. Benjamin, *Gesammelte Schriften V: Das Passagen-Werk* (Frankfurt: Suhrkamp, 1982), pp. 134–5.
8   Ibid., p. 1000.
9   Ibid., p. 1009.
10 Ibid., p. 1023.
11 Ibid., p. 525.
12 W. Benjamin, 'Surrealism', in *One-Way Street and Other Writings* (London: New Left Books, 1979), pp. 225–39, esp. p. 237.
13 W. Benjamin, *Charles Baudelaire: A Lyric Poet in the Era of High Capitalism* (London: New Left Books, 1973).

14 On the broader significance of the flâneur in relation to literary production, see E. Köhn, *Strassenrausch. Flânerie und Kleine Form. Versuch zur Literaturgeschichte des Flâneurs bis 1933* (Berlin: Das Arsenal, 1989); J. Rignall, *Realist Fiction and the Strolling Spectator* (London: Routledge, 1992); D. Brand, *The Spectator and the City in Nineteenth-Century American Literature* (Cambridge: Cambridge University Press, 1991).

15 Benjamin, *Charles Baudelaire*, p. 55.

16 Ibid., p. 54.

17 Ibid., p. 170.

18 Ibid., pp. 70–1.

19 Ibid., pp. 27–31.

20 Ibid., p. 50.

21 F. Hessel, *Spazieren in Berlin* (Vienna/Leipzig: Verlag Dr Hans Epstein, 1929); most recently reissued as F. Hessel, *Ein Flâneur in Berlin* (Berlin: Das Arsenal, 1984). References are to this later edition.

22 W. Benjamin, 'Die Wiederkehr des Flâneurs', in *Gesammelte Schriften III*, pp. 194–9. For a recent translation, see 'The Return of the Flâneur', *Selected Writings, Volume 2*, pp. 262–7.

23 W. Benjamin, 'M [Der Flâneur]' in *Gesammelte Schriften V*, pp. 524–69, but also in many other passages in this volume.

24 Cited in Buck-Morss, *The Dialectics of Seeing*, p. 307.

25 Ibid.

26 See Louis-Sebastian Mercer, *Tableau de Paris* (Amsterdam: 1782–88).

27 Benjamin, *Charles Baudelaire*, p. 69.

28 Ibid., p. 40.

29 R. W. Winks, *The Historian as Detective* (New York: Harper and Row, 1969).

30 R. W. Winks, 'The Historian as Detective', in R. W. Winks (ed.), *Detective Fiction: A Collection of Critical Essays* (Woodstock, Vermont: Foul Play Press, 1988), p. 245.

31 T. W. Adorno, *Kierkegaard: Construction of the Aesthetic* (Minneapolis: University of Minnesota Press, 1989), p. 42.

32 Benjamin, *Gesammelte Schriften V*, p. 554.

33 Benjamin, *Charles Baudelaire*, p. 40.

34 Ibid.

35 Hessel, *Ein Flâneur in Berlin*, p. 8.

36 Benjamin, *Charles Baudelaire*, p. 40.

37 Ibid, p. 41.

38 W. Benjamin, *Gesammelte Schriften V*, p. 529.

39 Ibid., p. 540.

40 Ibid., p. 1232.

41 Ibid., p. 541.

42 Ibid., p. 969.

43 Ibid.

44 Ibid., p. 526.

45 Ibid., p. 525.

46 D. J. Grossvogel, *Mystery and its Fictions: From Oedipus to Agatha Christie* (Baltimore/London: Johns Hopkins University Press, 1979), p. 99.

47   Benjamin, *Gesammelte Schriften V*, p. 541.
48   Ibid., p. 530.
49   Ibid., p. 437.
50   Ibid., p. 527.
51   Ibid., p. 1215.
52   Ibid., p. 559.
53   Benjamin, *Charles Baudelaire*, p. 41.
54   Benjamin, *Gesammelte Schriften V*, p. 559. See Siegfried Kracauer, *Offenbach and the Paris of his Time* (London: Constable, 1937).
55   Benjamin, *Gesammelte Schriften VII* (Frankfurt: Suhrkamp, 1989), p. 743.
56   Benjamin, 'Die Wiederkehr des Flâneurs', p. 195.
57   Ibid., p. 194.
58   Ibid., p. 196.
59   Ibid., p. 195.
60   Hessel, *Ein Flâneur in Berlin*, p. 273.
61   Benjamin, *Gesammelte Schriften V*, p. 1091.
62   S. Lackner, 'Von eines langen, schwierigen Irrfahrt', *Neue deutsche Hefte*, 26 (1979), p. 55.
63   W. Benjamin, 'N [Theoretics of Knowledge; Theory of Progress]', *The Philosophical Forum*, XV, 1–2 (1983–4), pp. 1–40, esp. p. 7. Now also in Benjamin, *The Arcades Project* (Cambridge, Mass.: Belknap Press, 1999), pp. 456–88.
64   Benjamin, *Gesammelte Schriften V*, p. 1033.
65   Ibid, p. 528.
66   Benjamin, *Gesammelte Schriften III*, p. 400. For a recent translation, see 'Excavate and Memory', *Selected Writings, Volume 2*, pp. 576–7.
67   Ibid., p. 401.
68   M. Opitz, 'Lesen und Flanieren. Über das Lesen von Städten, vom Flanieren in Bücher', in *Aber ein Sturm weht von Paradies her. Texte zu Walter Benjamin* (Leipzig: Reklam, 1992), pp. 162–81.
69   Opitz, 'Lesen und Flanieren', p. 178.
70   Ibid., p. 179.
71   Ibid., pp. 180–1.
72   R. L. Herbert, *Impressionism: Art, Leisure and Parisian Society* (New Haven / London: Yale University Press, 1988), esp. ch. 2.
73   Cited in Köhn, *Strassenrausch*, p. 200.
74   Ibid., p. 201.
75   Ibid., p. 207.
76   D. Frisby, *Sociological Impressionism: A Reassessment of Georg Simmel's Social Theory*, 2nd edn (London: Routledge, 1991). This volume first appeared in 1981.
77   My subsequent studies of Simmel include *Georg Simmel* (London: Tavistock, 1984); *Fragments of Modernity*; and *Simmel and Since* (London: Routledge, 1992).
78   Cited in my *Sociological Impressionism*, p. 72.
79   M. Christen, 'Essayistik und Modernität. Literarische Theoriebildung in Georg Simmels *Philosophische Kultur*', in *Deutsche Vierteljahrsschrift für Literaturgeschichte und Geistesgeschichte*, 66, 1 (1992), pp. 129–59, esp.

p. 140. For a useful discussion of Simmel's essay form from another perspective, see H. Böhringer, 'Das Pathos der Differenzierung. Der philosophische Essay Georg Simmels', *Merkur*, 39, 4 (1985), pp. 298–308.

80 G. Simmel, *The Philosophy of Money*, 2nd enlarged edn (London: Routledge, 1990), p. 55. On the construction of the text, see pp. 513–34.

81 R. Lindner, *Die Entdeckung der Stadtkultur. Soziologie aus der Erfahrung der Reportage* (Frankfurt: Suhrkamp, 1990); in English as *The Reportage of Urban Culture: Robert Park and the Chicago School* (Cambridge: Cambridge University Press, 1996). Lindner's stimulating study contains a wealth of insights on the connection between reporting and sociology.

82 Cited in Linder, *The Reportage*, p. 38.

83 Ibid., p. 61.

84 See 'Robert E. Park's "Notes on the Origins of the Society for Social Research", with an introduction by L. R. Kurtz', *Journal of the History of the Behavioral Sciences*, 18 (1982), pp. 332–40, esp. pp. 336–9.

85 Cited in Lindner, *The Reportage*, p. 175.

86 On Mayhew as social investigator, see E. Yeo and E. P. Thompson, *The Unknown Mayhew* (London: Merlin, 1971; New York: Schocken, 1972).

87 On Kracauer, see my *Fragments of Modernity*, ch. 3; I. Mülder, *Siegfried Kracauer* (Stuttgart: Metzler, 1985); M. Kessler and T. Y. Levin (eds), *Siegfried Kracauer. Neue Interpretationen* (Tübingen: Stauffenburg Verlag, 1990); for a detailed bibliography of his work, see T. Y. Levin, *Siegfried Kracauer. Eine Bibliographie seiner Schriften* (Marbach: Deutsche Schillergesellschaft, 1989).

88 S. Kracauer, *Soziologie als Wissenschaft* (1922), in S. Kracauer, *Schriften I* (Frankfurt: Suhrkamp, 1971), p. 60.

89 Letter from Kracauer to Bloch, 27 May 1926.

90 See Kracauer, *Offenbach and the Paris of his Time*.

91 S. Kracauer, 'Ein paar Tage Paris' (1931), *Schriften 5.2* (Frankfurt: Suhrkamp, 1990), p. 298.

92 S. Kracauer, *Theory of Film. The Redemption of Physical Realtity* (New York: Oxford University Press, 1960), p. 72. On Kracauer's theory of realism, see Dagmar Barnouw, *Critical Realism: History, Photography and the Work of Siegfried Kracauer* (Baltimore: Johns Hopkins University Press, 1994).

93 Kracauer, *Theory of Film*, p. 50.

94 Ibid., pp. 50–1.

95 Most of Kracauer's articles in the *Frankfurter Zeitung* are now available in S. Kracauer, *Schriften 5*, ed. Inka Mülder-Bach (Frankfurt: Suhrkamp, 1990). Additional articles are to be found in Siegfried Kracauer, *Berliner Nebeneinander. Ausgewählte Feuilletons 1930–1933)*, ed. Andreas Volk (Zurich: Edition Epoca, 1996) and S. Kracauer, *Frankfurter Turmhäuser. Ausgewählte Feuilletons 1906–1930*, ed. Andreas Volk (Zurich: Edition Epoca, 1997). Kracauer's *Die Angestellten* is available in English translation as *The Salaried Masses: Duty and Distraction in Weimar Germany* (London: Verso, 1998), with an introduction by Inka Mülder-Bach. Some of Kracauer's most famous essays are now available in S. Kracauer, *The Mass Ornament: Weimar Essays*, trans., ed., and intro. T. Y. Levin (Cambridge, Mass.: Harvard University Press, 1995).

96   For a discussion, see my *Fragments of Modernity*, ch. 4. Some of the Berlin
     essays are available in S. Kracauer, *Strassen in Berlin und Anderswo* (Berlin:
     Das Arsenal, 1987). See also S. Kracauer, *Schriften 5. Aufsätze* (Frankfurt:
     Suhrkamp, 1990).
97   See Kracauer, *Die Angestellten*, in *Schriften I* and *The Salaried Masses*.
98   Kracauer, *Schriften I*, p. 216, *The Salaried Masses*, p. 32.
99   Ibid.
100 Ibid.
101 See the unpublished review in T. Y. Levin, *Siegfried Kracauer*, p. 39.
102 S. Kracauer, 'Der operierende Schriftsteller', *Frankfurter Zeitung*, 17 Feb.
     1932.
103 S. Kracauer, 'Unter der Oberfläche', *Frankfurter Zeitung*, 11 Sept. 1931.
104 S. Kracauer, 'The Challenge of Qualitative Content Analysis', *Public Opinion
     Quarterly*, 16, 4 (1952–3), pp. 631–42.
105 Ibid., p. 642.
106 S. Kracauer, 'Einige Angaben über mich' (1934) in inside cover of
     T. Y. Levin, *Siegfried Kracauer*.
107 Benjamin, *Gesammelte Schriften III*, p. 226. For a recent translation, see
     Selected Writings, Volume 2, p. 355.

2   The City Detected

Epigraphs from: Edgar Allan Poe, 'Marginal Notes' (1845), *Essays and Reviews*
(New York: The Library of America, 1984), p. 1370; Ludwig Wittgenstein, *Philo-
sophical Investigations* (Oxford: Blackwell, 1974), p. 228 (translation amended);
Dashiell Hammett, 'From the Memoirs of a Private Detective' (1923), cited in
Diane Johnson, *Dashiell Hammett: A Life* (New York: Fawcett Columbine, 1983),
p. 44.

1   On the significance of Benjamin's explorations of his methodology, see
    D. Frisby, *Fragments of Modernity: Social Theories of Modernity in the Works
    of Georg Simmel, Siegfried Kracauer and Walter Benjamin* (Cambridge:
    Polity, 1985; Cambridge, Mass.: MIT Press, 1986); S. Buck-Morss, *The
    Dialectics of Seeing: Walter Benjamin and the Arcades Project* (Cambridge,
    Mass.: MIT Press, 1990); G. Gilloch, *Myth and Metropolis* (Cambridge:
    Polity, 1996).
2   For a discussion of this in the context of other discourses see Marie-Christine
    Leps, *Apprehending the Criminal: The Production of Deviance in Nineteenth-
    Century Discourse* (Durham: Duke University Press, 1992).
3   For a discussion of Sue's success (and of that of his imitator G. W. M.
    Reynold's), see Richard Maxwell, *The Mysteries of Paris and London*
    (Charlottesville: University Press of Virginia, 1992).
4   See Louis Chevalier, *Laboring Classes and Dangerous Classes in Paris During
    the First Half of the Nineteenth Century* (Princeton: Princeton University
    Press, 1973). For a perceptive account of British 'crime waves' and especially
    the fear of 'garrotting' in the mid-1850s in London, see Geoffrey Pearson,
    Hooligan: A History of Respectable Fears (London: Macmillan, 1983).

5   Maxwell, *The Mysteries*, p. 19.
6   Dana Brand, cited in Tony Bennett (ed.), *Popular Fiction* (London: Routledge, 1990), p. 214. Brand's monograph is titled *The Spectator and the City in Nineteenth Century America* (Cambridge: Cambridge University Press, 1991).
7   Honore Balzac, 'Ferragus. Chief of the Dévorants', in *The Mysteries of Honore Balzac* (New York: Juniper Press, n.d.), pp. 257–382.
8   Balzac, 'Ferragus', pp. 259–60.
9   Emile Gaboriau, *Monsieur Lecoq* (1869) (New York: Dover, 1975), p. 5. On Gaboriau's significance in the French context of the development of the detective novel, see Roger Bonnist, *Emile Gaboriau ou la naissance du roman policiers* (Paris: Vrin, 1985).
10 Emile Gaboriau, *File No. 113* (1867) (New York: Charles Scribners Sons, 1900), p. 49.
11 See Winifred Hughes, *The Maniac in the Cellar: Sensational Novels of the 1860s* (Princeton: Princeton University Press, 1980). For the later period, see Lyn Pykett, *The Improper Feminine: The Women's Sensational Novel and the New Woman Writing* (London: Routledge, 1992).
12 Charles Dickens, *Bleak House* (London: Chapman & Hall, 1853), pp. 1–2.
13 Charles Dickens, *Our Mutual Friend* (London: Chapman & Hall, 1869).
14 Walter Thornbury, *Old and New London: A Narrative of its History, its People, and its Places*, 6 vols (London: Cassell, Petter & Galpin, n.d.).
15 Ibid., vol. 1, p. 1.
16 Ibid.
17 Cited in Bennett, *Popular Fiction*, p. 214.
18 Ibid., p. 215.
19 Michel Foucault, *Discipline and Punish* (Harmondsworth: Penguin, 1979), esp. pp. 68–9.
20 These features are a summary of those elaborated in Franco Moretti, *Signs Taken For Wonders* (London: Verso, 1988), esp. chs 4 and 5.
21 Ibid., ch. 5.
22 Ibid., p. 143
23 Ibid.
24 Ibid., p. 144.
25 See the discussion below.
26 Moretti, *Signs*, p. 149.
27 Siegfried Kracauer, *Der Detektivroman* (MS 1922–5); now in his *Schriften I* (Frankfurt: Suhrkamp, 1971), pp. 103–204. For a discussion of Kracauer's theory of the detective novel see my 'Siegfried Kracauer and the Detective Novel', *Theory, Culture & Society*, 9, 2 (1992), pp. 1–22.
28 Kracauer, *Schriften I*, pp. 105–6.
29 Colin Watson, *Snobbery With Violence* (London: Eyre & Spottiswood, 1971).
30 See my discussion in 'Siegfried Kracauer and the Detective Novel'.
31 For a discussion of Benjamin see my 'Walter Benjamin and Detection', *German Politics and Society*, 32 (Summer 1994), pp. 89–106.
32 See Ernst Bloch, 'A Philosophical View of the Detective Novel', in *The Utopian Function of Art and Literature: Selected Essays* (Cambridge, Mass.: MIT Press, 1988), pp. 245–64.

33   See Michael Denning, *Mechanic Accents* (London: Verso, 1987).

34   Anon, 'Sensational Novels', *Quarterly Review*, 113 (January–April 1863), pp. 481–514.

35   Some of these differences are explored in Dennis Porter, *The Pursuit of Crime: Art and Ideology in Detective Fiction* (New Haven: Yale University Press, 1981).

36   Cited in Richard Layman, *Shadow Man: The Life of Dashiell Hammett* (New York: Harcourt Brace, 1981), pp. 45–6.

37   In making this distinction, there are echoes of the distinction made, in a different context, by Hannah Arendt between *animal laborans* and *homo faber* in *The Human Condition* (Chicago: University of Chicago Press, 1958).

38   Cited in Layman, *Shadow Man*, p. 46.

39   Ibid., p. 47.

40   Ibid., pp. 79–80.

41   Steven Marcus, 'Introduction', Dashiell Hammett, *The Continental Op* (London: Macmillan, 1974), p. xxiv.

42   Ibid., pp. xxv–xxvi.

43   See Layman, *Shadow Man*, ch. 2.

44   Cited in Layman, *Shadow Man*, p. 10.

45   Pinkerton World Headquarters Archive. Appended to application of John Fraser.

46   Ibid.

47   John Fraser file, Pinkerton Headquarters Archive.

48   Cited in Layman, p. 50. Elsewhere Hammett expands upon the techniques of shadowing: 'You simply saunter along somewhere within sight of your subject, and, barring bad breaks, the only thing that can make you lose him is over-anxiety on your part. . . . You don't worry about a suspect's face. Tricks of carriage, ways of wearing clothes, general outline, individual mannerisms – all as seen from the rear – are much more important to the shadow than faces.' Cited in Diane Johnson, *Dashiell Hammett: A Life* (New York: Fawcett Columbine, 1985), p. 18.

49   Histories of the Pinkerton Agency include: James D. Horan, *The Pinkertons: The Detective Dynasty That Made History* (New York: Crown Publishers, 1967).

50   Wayne G. Broehl Jr., *The Molly Maguires* (New York: Vintage, 1968), p. 135.

51   Allan Pinkerton, *The Spy of the Rebellion* (Hartford: Winter & Hatch, 1883).

52   Dashiell Hammett, 'Poisonville' (*Black Mask*, November 1927). The actual title was 'The Cleansing of Poisonville', which, with three other parts, appeared in book form as *Red Harvest* (New York: Knopf, 1929).

53   A statement by the Agency on 1 June 1921 was sent by Superintendent George Bangs to all offices justifying 'secret work undertaken for employers amongst employees'.

54   *General Principles and Rules of Pinkerton's National Detective Agency* (New York: Jones Printing Company, 1878), pp. 37–8. My emphasis.

55   Joachim Schlör, *Nachts in der grossen Stadt. Paris. Berlin. London 1840–1930* (Munich: Artemis & Winkler, 1991); in English as *Nights in the Big City* (London: Reaktion Books, 1998).

56 See also the discussion of the scares in the 1850s in London in Geoffrey Pearson, *Hooligan.*

57 Edgar Alan Poe, 'The Man of the Crowd', *The Popular Tales of Edgar Allan Poe* (New York: Wood & Clarke, n.d.), pp. 493–4.

58 Ibid., p. 495.

59 Ibid., p. 497.

60 Edward Winslow Martin, *The Secrets of the Great City: A Work Descriptive of the Virtues and the Vices, the Mysteries, Miseries and Crimes of New York City* (Philadelphia: National Publishing Company, 1868).

61 Ibid., p. 15.

62 Ibid., p. 16.

63 Matthew Hale Smith, *Sunshine and Shadow in New York* (Hartford: J. B. Burr and Hyde, 1872).

64 Ibid., p. 707.

65 Ibid., p. 708.

66 In Europe, this post-1848 fear of insurrection and its consequences for city planning has more often been argued for Baron Haussmann's Paris. But other cities (including Vienna) were affected.

67 It is interesting to note that in the contract into which John C. Fraser entered with the Agency on 29 March 1886, he is already described as 'an Operative'.

68 Janet Wolff, 'The invisible flâneuse', *Theory, Culture & Society*, 2, 3 (1985), pp. 37–48.

69 Cited in Horan, *The Pinkertons*, p. 342.

70 Cited in Broehl, *The Molly Maguires*, p. 142.

71 *General Principles and Rules*, p. 6.

72 Ibid., p. 7.

73 Ibid., pp. 10–11.

74 Ibid., p. 11.

75 Ibid., pp. 11–12.

76 Ibid., p. 12.

77 Ibid., p. 15.

78 George S. McWatters, *Knots United or, Ways and By-Ways in the Hidden Life of American Detectives* (Hartford: Burr & Hyde, 1871).

79 Ibid., pp. 648–50.

80 *General Principles and Rules*, pp. 22–3.

81 Ibid., p. 24.

82 Ibid., p. 36.

83 Ibid., p. 39.

84 Ibid., p. 40.

85 Ibid., pp. 40–1.

86 Ibid., p. 42.

87 Ibid., pp. 43–4.

88 Ibid., pp. 44–5.

89 See Wolfgang Schivelbusch, *Disenchanted Night* (Berkeley: University of California Press, 1988).

90 George Simmel, 'Written Communication', in K. H. Wolff (ed.), *The Sociology of George Simmel* (Glencoe, Ill.: Free Press, 1950), pp. 352–5.

91　*General Principles and Rules*, p. 45.

92　Ibid., pp. 46–7.

93　Ibid., p. 50.

94　Ibid., p. 51.

95　Ibid., p. 57.

96　Despite the continued use of informers, Pinkerton always insisted that the occupation of the detective was 'modern', and therefore to be distinguished from earlier police practices.

97　*General Principles and Rules*, p. 51.

98　'Waters', *Recollections of a Detective Police-Officer* (London: Ward, Lock, and Tyler, 1875; reprinted London: Covent Garden Press Ltd, 1972), ch. III, 'X.Y.Z.'.

99　Letter in Pinkerton World Headquarters Archive.

100　Letter in Pinkerton World Headquarters Archive.

101　William A. Pinkerton, 'The "Yeggman": Bank Vault and Safe Burglar of To-Day', paper read by William A. Pinkerton to the Annual Convention of the International Association Chiefs of Police, St Louis, Miss., 6–11 June 1904 (Agency Archives).

102　The accompanying photographs are probably from the Pinkerton Agency files.

103　W. A. Pinkerton, 'The Yeggman', p. 14.

104　Ibid.

105　This case is discussed in Horan, *The Pinkertons*, pp. 252–79

106　Anonymous notebook in Scott–Dunlap files, Pinkerton World Headquarters Archive.

107　Ibid.

108　Report in files, Pinkerton World Headquarters Archive.

109　Horan suggests five ghost writers but, in keeping with 'ghosting', provides no names.

110　Allan Pinkerton, 'Preface', *Claude Melnotte as a Detective* (Chicago: Keen, Cooke & Co., 1875).

111　These are detailed in Horan, *The Pinkertons*.

112　Allan Pinkerton, *Professional Thieves and the Detective* (Chicago: A. G. Nettleton & Co., 1881), pp. 185–286.

113　This was common practice in popular publishing.

114　See Denning, *Mechanic Accents*.

115　Ibid.

116　For instance, the file on Sophie Lyons, suspected of membership of several criminal gangs but never apprehended, suggests that she was under intermittent surveillance for over 20 years.

117　The American part of Arthur Conan Doyle's *The Valley of Fear* (1915) draws upon the *The Molly Maguires and the Detectives* (New York: G. W. Dillingham, 1877). See O. D. Edwards 'Introduction' to *The Valley of Fear* (Oxford: Oxford University Press, 1993), pp. xxx ff.

118　Reprinted and cited in Layman, *Shadow Man*, pp. 45–6.

119　Dashiell Hammett, *The Continental Op*.

120　Ibid., p. 47.

121 Ibid., p. 63.
122 Max Weber, 'Bureaucracy', in Hans H. Gerth and C. Wright Mills (eds), *From Max Weber* (London: Routledge & Kegan Paul, 1948), pp. 196–244, esp. p. 196.
123 Ibid., p. 197.
124 Ibid., p. 199.
125 Ibid., p. 213.
126 Ibid.
127 Ibid., p. 214.
128 Ibid., p. 244.
129 Ibid., p. 197.
130 Ibid., p. 215.
131 Ibid., p. 233.
132 See 'The Pinkertons', *The Detective*, March 1887.
133 Ibid.
134 Allan Pinkerton, *Thirty Years a Detective* (Chicago: G. W. Dillingham, 1889), p. 27.
135 Cesare Lombroso, *L'Homme criminel* (1876), 2nd edn (Paris, 1887–8).
136 Gustave le Bon, *The Crowd* (Marietta: Larlin Corporation, 1982); Gabriel Tarde, *Les Lois de l'imitation: Etude sociologique*, 2nd edn (Paris: Alcan, 1895).
137 Francis Galton, *Finger Prints* (London: Macmillan, 1892), p. 148; reprinted in 1965 by DaCapo Press, New York.
138 Ibid., pp. 152–3.
139 Ibid., p. 154.
140 See E. D. Forgues 'Studies in English and American Fiction' (1846), reprinted in I. M. Walker (ed.), *Edgar Allan Poe: The Critical Heritage* (London: Routledge, 1986), pp. 205–19, esp. p. 206.
141 On the use of photography see John Tagg, *The Burden of Representation* (London: Macmillan, 1988), ch. 3; see also Tom Gunning, 'Tracing the Individual Body: Photography, Detectives and Early Cinema', in Leo Charney and Vanessa R. Schwartz (eds), *Cinema and the Invention of Modern Life* (Berkeley: University of California Press, 1995), pp. 15–45. In the context of 'scientific' detection, it is interesting to note that Hammett was extremely sceptical of such methods. 'Many devices of "scientific" detecting are excellent when kept to their places, but when pushed forward as infallible methods, they become forms of quackery, and nothing else. . . . There is no doubt that fingerprints are a valuable part of the anti-criminal arsenal, but they are only a part of it. As evidence goes, I favour what is usually called "circumstantial evidence" as against the testimony of witnesses. . . . Neither have I much faith in experts who claim infallibility in any field except, perhaps, abstract mathematics.' Cited in Johnson, *Dashiell Hammett*, pp. 17–18.
142 See Ian Hacking, *The Taming of Chance* (Cambridge: Cambridge University Press, 1990).
143 Albert Camus, *The Rebel* (New York: Vintage Books, 1961). Cited in R. I. Edenbaum, 'The Poetics of the Private Eye', in David Madden (ed.),

Tough Guy Writers of the Thirties (Carbondale: Southern Illinois University Press, 1968), pp. 80–103, esp. pp. 94–5.

144 Ibid.

145 See Walter Benjamin, 'Erfahrung und Armut', *Gesammelte Schriften II.1* (Frankfurt: Suhrkamp, 1980), pp. 24–5. For a recent translation, see 'Experience and Poverty', *Selected Writings, Volume 2: 1927–1934* (Cambridge, Mass.: Belknap Press, 1999), pp. 731–5, esp. pp. 731–2.

146 Ibid., p. 25.

147 See, for example, M. Christine Boyer, 'Crimes in and of the City' and Margaret Crawford, 'Investigating the City: Detective Fiction as Urban Interpretation', in Diana Agrest, Patricia Conway and Leslie K. Weisman (eds), *The Sex of Architecture* (New York: Harry N. Abrams, 1996), pp. 97–118, 119–26.

148 See the essays in Joan Copjec (ed.), *Shades of Noir* (London: Verso, 1993).

149 Anon, 'Pinkerton's Men', *The World*, 19 Sept. 1875.

150 Letter in Pinkerton World Headquarters Archive.

151 See Schivelbusch, *Disenchanted Night*.

152 Elaine S. Abelson, *When Ladies Go A-Thieving* (Oxford: Oxford University Press, 1989).

153 See my *Metropolitan Architecture and Modernity: Otto Wagner's Vienna* (Minneapolis: University of Minnesota Press, 2001), ch. 2.

154 On Geddes, see Volker M. Welter and James Lawson (eds), *The City after Patrick Geddes* (Frankfurt: Peter Lange, 2000).

155 See Marie de Thézy, *Marville. Paris* (Paris: Hazan, 1994).

156 See my *Fragments of Modernity*, ch. 3.

157 Cited in my *Fragments of Modernity*, ch. 4.

158 Eugene Sue, *The Mysteries of Paris* (London: Chapman and Hall, 1844).

159 See, for example, Gerda Breuer and Ines Wagemann, *Ludwig Meidner* (Stuttgart: Hatje, 1991).

160 See Walter Benjamin, 'Die Wiederkehr des Flâneurs', *Gesammelte Schriften III* (Frankfurt: Suhrkamp, 1980), p. 196; 'The Return of the Flâneur', *Selected Writings, Volume 2*, p. 262.

161 See George Simmel, 'The Secret and the Secret Society' (1908), in K. H. Wolff (ed.), *The Sociology of George Simmel* (Glencoe, Ill.: Free Press, 1950), pp. 330–76.

162 Reprinted in D. Frisby (ed.), *Georg Simmel: Critical Assessments*, vol. 3 (London: Routledge, 1994).

163 Birgitta Nedelmann, 'Secrecy as a Macrosociological Phenomenon: A Neglected Aspect of Simmel's Analysis of Secrecy', in Frisby, *Georg Simmel*, vol. 3, pp. 202–21.

164 Simmel, 'The Secret', p. 330.

165 Ibid., p. 317.

166 Ibid., p. 19.

167 Nedelmann, 'Secrecy', p. 213.

168 Ibid., p. 214.

169 On the significance of things as traces, see Moretti, *Signs*; Christoph Asendorf, *Batteries of Life* (Berkeley: University of California Press, 1994).

170 Simmel, 'The Secret', p. 322.
171 Georg Simmel, *The Philosophy of Money*, 2nd enlarged edn (London: Routledge, 1990), esp. ch. 5.
172 Simmel, 'The Secret', p. 322.
173 Ibid., p. 323.
174 Nedelmann, 'Secrecy', p. 216.

3 The City Interpreted

Epigraphs from: Georg Simmel, 'Über Massenverbrechen', *Die Zeit*, 2 Oct. 1897, p. 4 (now in *Gesamtausgabe 1*, ed. Klaus C. Köhnke (Frankfurt: Suhrkamp, 1999), p. 388); Arthur Conan Doyle, 'The Field Bazaar' (1896), reprinted in *The Return of Sherlock Holmes*, ed. Richard Lancelyn Green (Oxford: Oxford University Press, 1993), p. 321; Louis Wirth, 'A Bibliography of the Urban Community' (1925), in Robert E. Park and Ernest W. Burgess, *The City* (Chicago: University of Chicago Press, 1967), p. 219.

1 G. Simmel, 'Berliner Gewerbe Ausstellung', *Die Zeit*, 8, 25 July 1896, pp. 59–60; in English as 'The Berlin Trade Exhibition', trans. Sam Whimster, in D. Frisby and M. Featherstone (eds), *Simmel on Culture: Selected Writings* (London: Sage, 1997), pp. 255–8.
2 G. Simmel, 'Die Grossstädte und das Geistesleben', *Die Grossstadt. Jahrbuch der Gehe-Stiftung zu Dresden*, 9 (1903), pp. 185–206; in English as 'The Metropolis and Mental Life', trans. Hans Gerth, in Kurt H. Wolff (ed.), *The Sociology of George Simmel* (Glencoe, Ill.: Free Press, 1950), pp. 409–24, and in Frisby and Featherstone, *Simmel on Culture*, pp. 174–85.
3 Simmel's essay on the stranger appeared only as an *excursus* to his much longer chapter on space in his *Soziologie*. The context is therefore the study of space. See G. Simmel, 'Exkurs über den Fremden', in *Soziologie* (Leipzig: Duncker & Humblot, 1908), pp. 685–91.
4 To give but one example, Walter Benjamin's 'The Work of Art in an Age of Mechanical Reproduction', one of his most widely read essays, is devoted to a theme that is announced on the very first page of Simmel's *Philosophy of Money*, but whose context is largely ignored. See G. Simmel, *The Philosophy of Money*, 2nd enlarged edn (London: Routledge, 1990), p. 53 (which is p. 1 of the 'Preface').
5 G. Simmel, 'Das Geld in der Modernen Kultur', *Neue Freie Presse*, 12 August 1896. In English as 'Money in Modern Culture', in Frisby and Featherstone, *Simmel on Culture*, pp. 243–55.
6 See Simmel, *Philosophy of Money*.
7 On Lamprecht, see Roger Chickering, *Karl Lamprecht: A German Academic Life (1856–1915)* (New Jersey: Humanities Press, 1993).
8 See discussion below (V) and Woodruff D. Smith, *Politics and the Science of Culture in Germany, 1840–1920* (New York: Oxford University Press, 1991), esp. ch. 11.
9 See Karl Lamprecht, *Deutsche Geschichte*, Ergänzungsbände (Berlin: R. Gärtners Verlagsbuchhandlung, 1902).

10   See below.
11   Howard Woodhead, 'The First German Municipal Exposition (Dresden 1903)', *American Journal of Sociology*, 9 (1904), pp. 433–58, esp. p. 433; 612–30; 812–31; 10 (1905), pp. 47–63.
12   Somewhat surprisingly, Simmel did not comment upon this major competition for plans for the expansion of Berlin.
13   G. Simmel, 'Über Kunstausstellungen', *Unsere Zeit*, 26 Feb. 1890, pp. 474–80.
14   See G. Simmel, 'Soziologische Ästhetik', *Die Zukunft*, 17 (1896), pp. 204–16.
15   Simmel, 'Über Kunstausstellungen', p. 475.
16   Simmel, 'Soziologische Ästhetik', p. 205
17   Simmel, 'Über Kunstausstellungen', pp. 479–80.
18   G. Simmel, 'The Berlin Trade Exhibition', p. 255.
19   For another view of the exhibition's significance, see Alfred Kerr, *Mein Berlin* (Berlin: Aufbau Verlag, 1999), pp. 100–10.
20   See Paul Lindenberg, *Pracht-Album der Berliner Gewerbe-Ausstellung* (Berlin: The Werner Company, 1896).
21   On the impact of the Chicago Columbia Exhibition on European architecture, see Arnold Lewis, *An Early Encounter with Tomorrow* (Urbana/Chicago: University of Illinois Press, 1997).
22   Klaus Strohmeyer, ' "Berliner Gewerbe-Ausstellung". Annotationen zu einem Text von Georg Simmel', *Ästhetik und Kommunikation*, 18, 67/68 (1988), pp. 107–9.
23   Simmel, 'The Berlin Trade Exhibition', p. 255.
24   Ibid.
25   Ibid., p. 256
26   Ibid.
27   Ibid., pp. 256–7.
28   Ibid., p. 257.
29   Ibid.
30   Ibid., p. 256.
31   Simmel, 'Über Kunstausstellungen'. Simmel refers in the text to the concept of mental life.
32   Ibid., p. 474.
33   Ibid., p. 475.
34   Ibid., p. 476.
35   Ibid.
36   Ibid.
37   Ibid., p. 477.
38   Ibid. My emphasis.
39   Ibid., p. 478.
40   Ibid., p. 479.
41   Ibid.
42   Ibid.
43   Ibid., p. 474.
44   On Dresden see below (V and VI).

45   G. Simmel, 'Über ästhetische Quantitäten', *Aufsätze und Abhandlungen 1901– 1908* (Frankfurt: Suhrkamp, 1995), pp. 184–9.

46   There is some evidence that the lecture was reworked. See the discussion below (VI). For the revised version of the aesthetics lecture, 'Die ästhetische Quantität', see Simmel, *Aufsätze und Abhandlungen*, pp. 190–200.

47   Simmel, 'Über ästhetische Quantitäten', p. 187.

48   Simmel, 'Die ästhetische Quantität', pp. 192–3.

49   On the significance of the threshhold in Benjamin's analysis of metropolitan modernity, see Winfried Menninghaus, *Schwellenkunde* (Frankfurt: Suhrkamp, 1986).

50   G. Simmel, 'Philosophie der Landschaft', in *Brücke und Tür* (Stuttgart: Köhler, 195), pp. 141–52.

51   Ibid., p. 141.

52   Ibid., p. 142.

53   Ibid.

54   On Meidner, see ch. 6 below.

55   G. Simmel, 'Der Ruin', *Der Tag*, 22 Feb. 1907; in English as 'The Ruin', in Kurt H. Wolff (ed.), *George Simmel: 1858–1918* (Columbus: Ohio State University Press, 1958), pp. 259–66, esp. p. 259. Translation amended.

56   Ibid.

57   Ibid., p. 263.

58   Ibid., p. 265.

59   For a recent biography of Haussmann, see David P. Jordan, *Transforming Paris* (New York: Free Press, 1995).

60   On Kracauer's analysis of Berlin, see my *Fragments of Modernity: Social Theories of Modernity in the Works of Georg Simmel, Siegfried Kracauer and Walter Benjamin* (Cambridge: Polity, 1985; Cambridge, Mass.: MIT Press, 1986), ch. 3

61   G. Simmel, 'Die ästhetische Bedeutung des Gesichts', *Der Lotse*, 1, 2 (1901), pp. 280–4. For an English translation, see 'The Aesthetic Significance of the Face', in Wolff, *Georg Simmel*, pp. 276–81.

62   Ibid., p. 280. Translation amended.

63   Ibid.

64   Simmel, 'Soziologische Aesthetik', *Aufsätze und Abhandlungen 1894 bis 1900*, ed. H.-J. Dahme and D. P. Frisby (Frankfurt: Suhrkamp, 1992), pp. 197– 214, esp. p. 198.

65   Ibid., p. 199.

66   Ibid., pp. 201–2.

67   Ibid., p. 202.

68   Ibid., p. 203. My emphasis.

69   Ibid., p. 204.

70   See David van Zenten, *Building Paris* (Cambridge: CUP, 1994).

71   S. Kracauer, 'The Mass Ornament', in *The Mass Ornament*, trans. and intro. by T. Y. Levin (Cambridge, Mass.: Harvard University Press, 1995), pp. 75–86.

72   Simmel, 'Soziologische Aesthetik', p. 205.

73   Ibid., p. 206.

74 Ibid., p. 205.
75 See C. Sitte, *City Planning* (New York: Rizzoli, 1985).
76 Simmel, 'Soziologische Aesthetik', pp. 205–6.
77 See Z. Bauman, 'Moderne und Macht: Die Geschichte einer gescheiterte Romanze', in Romana Schneider and Wilfried Wang (eds), *Moderne Architektur in Deutschland 1900 bis 2000* (Ostfildern-Ruit: Hatje, 1998), pp. 13–31.
78 See G. Simmel, 'Der Raum und die räumlichen Ordnungen der Gesellschaft', *Soziologie* (Leipzig: Duncker & Humblot, 1908), pp. 614–708.
79 G. Simmel, 'Über räumliche Projektionen sozialer Formen', *Zeitschrift für Sozialwissenschaften*, 6 (1903), pp. 287–302.
80 Ibid., p. 288.
81 Ibid., p. 289.
82 Ibid., p. 296.
83 Simmel, *Soziologie*, p. 624. My emphasis.
84 Ibid., p. 625.
85 G. Simmel, 'Discretion', in Wolff, *The Sociology of George Simmel*, p. 322.
86 G. Simmel, 'The Stranger', in Wolff, *The Sociology of Georg Simmel*, pp. 402–408, esp. p. 402. Translation amended.
87 Ibid., p. 405.
88 D. N. Levine, 'Simmel at a Distance', *Sociological Focus*, 10, 1 (1977), p. 16.
89 G. Simmel, 'Bridge and Door', in Frisby and Featherstone, *Simmel on Culture*, pp. 170–4. For a recent discussion of Simmel's explorations of space and the city, see Iain Borden, 'Space Beyond: Spatiality and the City in the Writings of Georg Simmel', *Journal of Architecture*, 2 (1997), pp. 313–35.
90 V. Helas, 'Essay', in P. Gössel and G. Louthäiser (eds), *Villa Architecture in Dresden* (Cologne: Taschen, 1991), p. 35.
91 Ibid., p. 134.
92 Ibid., p. 66.
93 On Hellerau, see Kristiana Hartmann, *Deutsche Gartenstadtbewegung* (Munich: Heinz Moos, 1976).
94 See ch. 6 below.
95 Woodhead, 'The First German Municipal Exhibition', 10, p. 55.
96 Ibid., p. 56.
97 Ibid.
98 T. Petermann, 'Vorbemerkung des Herausgebers', *Die Grossstadt. Jahrbuch der Gehe-Stiftung zu Dresden* (Dresden: Zahn & Joensch, 1903).
99 L. von Stein, 'Grosse Stadt und Grossstadt', *Nord und Süd*, LIII (1888), pp. 62–78.
100 K. Bücher, 'Die Grossstadt in Gegenwart und Vergangenheit', in Petermann, *Die Grossstadt*, pp. 1–32.
101 Ibid., p. 29.
102 Ibid., p. 4.
103 Ibid., p. 30.
104 F. Ratzel, 'Die geographische Lage der grossen Städte', in Petermann, *Die Grossstadt*, pp. 33–72.
105 Ibid., p. 39.

106   Ibid., p. 44.
107   Ibid., p. 72.
108   G. von Mayr, 'Die Bevölkerung der Grossstädte', in Petermann, *Die Grossstadt*, pp. 73–146.
109   Ibid., p. 77.
110   H. Waentig, 'Die wirtschaftliche Bedeutung der Grossstädte', in Petermann, *Die Grossstadt*, pp. 147–84.
111   Ibid., p. 150.
112   Ibid., p. 165.
113   Ibid., p. 165–6.
114   Ibid., pp. 181–2.
115   Ibid., p. 182.
116   Ibid., p. 182–3.
117   T. Petermann, 'Die geistige Bedeutung der Grossstädte', *Die Grossstadt*, pp. 207–30.
118   D. Schäfer, 'Die politische und militarische Bedeutung der Grossstädte, in Petermann, *Die Grossstadt*, pp. 231–82.
119   Ibid., pp. 279–80.
120   According to the advertisement in the *Dresdner Anzeiger*
121   For the lecture, see G. Simmel, 'Die Grossstädte und das Geistesleben', in Petermann, *Die Grossstadt*, pp. 185–206. For the review see *Dresdner Anzeiger*, 24 Feb. 1903.
122   See G. Simmel, 'The Alpine Journey', in Frisby and Featherstone, *Simmel on Culture*, pp. 219–21.
123   *Dresdner Anzeiger*, 24 Feb. 1903, p. 3.
124   D. Schäfer, cited in Lewis A. Coser, 'The Stranger in the Academy', in L. A. Coser (ed.), *Georg Simmel* (Englewood Cliffs; Prentice Hall, 1965), p. 39.
125   R. Wuttke (ed.), *Die deutsche Städte*, vol. 1 (Leipzig: Friedrichs Brandstetter, 1904), esp. pp. xx and xxii.
126   *Dresdner Anzeiger*, 24 Feb. 1903, p. 3.
127   For a discussion of this dimension of Simmel's essay, see Gerd Mattenklott, 'Der mythische Leib: Physiognomisches Denken bei Nietzsche, Simmel und Kassner', in K. H. Böhrer (ed.) *Mythos und Moderne* (Frankfurt: Suhrkamp, 1983), pp. 138–56.
128   G. Simmel, 'Discretion', in Wolff, *The Sociology of Georg Simmel*, p. 322.
129   Simmel, 'The Metropolis', in Frisby and Featherstone, *Simmel on Culture*, p. 182.
130   Mattenklott, 'Der mythische Leib', p. 146.
131   Simmel, 'The Metropolis', p. 182. Translation amended.
132   Simmel, 'Die ästhetische Bedeutung des Gesichts', *Brücke und Tür* (Stuttgart: K. F. Köhler, 1957), p. 153, 'The Aesthetic Significance of the Face', p. 276.
133   Ibid., p. 278. Translation amended.
134   Ibid.
135   Ibid., p. 280. Translation amended.
136   Ibid., p. 281. Translation amended.

137 G. Simmel, 'Rodin', *Philosophische Kultur* (Leipzig: Klinkhardt, 1911), p. 202.
138 Simmel, 'The Metropolis', p. 179.
139 Mattenklott, 'Der mythische Leib', p. 146.
140 Ibid., p. 147.
141 Simmel, 'The Metropolis', p. 175.
142 Simmel, *The Philosophy of Money*, p. 411.
143 See my *Simmel and Since* (London: Routledge, 1992), chs 5–7.
144 G. Simmel, 'Female Culture' (1902), *On Women, Sexuality and Love*, trans. and intro. G. Oakes (New Haven: Yale University Press, 1984), pp. 65–101. For critiques of Simmel's position, see Rita Felski, *The Gender of Modernity* (Cambridge: Harvard University Press, 1995), ch. 2; Inka Mülder Bach, ' "Weibliche Kultur" und "Stahlhartes Gehäuse", in Sigrun Anselm and Barbara Beck (eds), *Triumph und Scheitern in der Metropole* (Berlin: Dietrich Reimer, 1987), pp. 115–40.
145 Simmel, 'Female Culture', p. 67.
146 Ibid.
147 G. Simmel, 'The Women's Congress and Social Democracy' (1896), in Frisby and Featherstone, *Simmel on Culture*, pp. 270–4.
148 Simmel, 'Female Culture', p. 75.
149 Ibid., p. 92.
150 G. Simmel, 'Flirtation', *On Women, Sexuality and Love*, p. 148.
151 *'Infelices Possidentes!'*, in Frisby and Featherstone, *Simmel on Culture*, pp. 259–62.
152 Simmel, 'The Metropolis', p. 176.
153 Ibid.
154 Ibid., p. 177.
155 Ibid.
156 Ibid., p. 178.
157 Ibid., p. 179.
158 Ibid., p. 178. Translation amended.
159 See H. Böhringer, 'Die "Philosophie des Geldes" als ästhetische Theorie', in H. J. Dahme and O. Rammstedt (eds), *Georg Simmel und die Moderne* (Frankfurt: Suhrkamp, 1984), pp. 178–82, esp. p. 182.
160 M. Tafuri, *Architecture and Utopia* (Cambridge, Mass.: MIT Press, 1968), pp. 88–9.
161 Simmel, 'The Metropolis', p. 178.
162 Ibid., p. 180.
163 See G. Simmel, *Conflict and the Web of Group Affiliations* (Glencoe, Ill.: Free Press, 1955).
164 G. Simmel, 'Die Erweiterung der Gruppe und die Ausbildung der Individualität', *Soziologie*, pp. 791–863.
165 Simmel, 'The Metropolis', p. 182.
166 Ibid. Translation amended. My emphasis.
167 Ibid.
168 See 'The Philosophy of Fashion', in Frisby and Featherstone, *Simmel on Culture*, pp. 187–206.

169 G. Simmel, 'The Sociology of Sociability', in Frisby and Featherstone, *Simmel on Culture*, pp. 120–30.
170 Simmel, 'The Metropolis', p. 184.
171 G. Lukacs, *History and Class Consciousness* (London: Merlin, 1971).
172 Simmel, 'The Metropolis', p. 184.

4 The City Compared

Epigraphs from: Marianne Weber, cited in Hans Rollmann, ' "Meet Me in St Louis": Troeltsch and Weber in America', in Hartmut Lehmann and Günther Roth (eds), *Weber's 'Protestant Ethic': Origins, Evidence, Contexts* (Cambridge: Cambridge University Press, 1993), p. 368; Karl Kraus, *Beim Wort Genommen* (Munich: Kösel, 1955), p. 263; ibid., p. 264.

1   An exception is Max Weber's interest in ancient agrarian societies and contemporary development in East Elbe. On the other hand, the examples discussed in the 'Protestant Ethic' thesis suggest an implicit urban context. Simmel's *Philosophy of Money* does not focus upon a consistent site but rather upon the transition from an undeveloped money economy to a mature money economy (with many agrarian examples in the former). Durkheim's explorations of the pathologies of modernity in *The Division of Labour in Society* (Basingstoke: Macmillan, 1984) and *Suicide* (London: Routledge, 1952) are located in an urban context.
2   See Werner Sombart, 'Der Begriff der Stadt und das Wesen der Städtebildung', *Archiv für Sozialwissenschaft und Sozialpolitik*, 25 (1907), pp. 1–9; W. Sombart, *Der Moderne Kapitalismus* (Leipzig: Duncker & Humblot, 1902).
3   For a recent history of the German concerns, see Brian Ladd, *Urban Planning and Civic Order in Germany* (Cambridge, Mass.: Harvard University Press, 1990).
4   For a contemporary discussion, see Sigmund Schrott, *Die Grossstädtische Agglomerationen des Deutschen Reiches. 1871–1910* (Breslau: W. G. Korn, 1912).
5   Ibid., p. 4.
6   For contemporary comparisons of Vienna with other major cities, see Reinhard E. Petermann, *Wien im Zeitalter Franz Josephs I* (Vienna: Lechner, 1908).
7   The German concept was the subject of extensive debate in the 1890s. See Ladd, *Urban Planning* and n. 9 below.
8   A translation with a valuable introduction of Sitte's 'City Planning According to Artistic Principles' is to be found in G. R. Collins and C. C. Collins, *Camillo Sitte: The Birth of Modern City Planning* (New York: Rizzoli, 1986), pp. 138–302.
9   See Schrott, *Die Grossstädtische Agglomerationen*, p. 4. On the debate between Joseph Stübben and Karl Henrici, see my *Metropolitan Architecture and Modernity* (Minneapolis: Minnesota University Press, 2002).
10 Schrott, *Die Grossstädtische Agglomerationen*, p. 4.
11 W. Sombart, *Die deutsche Volkswirtschaft im neunzehnten Jahrhundert* (Berlin: Georg Bondi, 1903).

12   These and other features of modern capitalism are examined in Sombart's *Der Moderne Kapitalismus.*

13   W. Sombart, *Die deutsche Volkswirtschaft*, p. 461.

14   Ibid.

15   Ibid., p. 462.

16   Ibid.

17   Ibid., p. 464.

18   Ibid., p. 465.

19   Ibid., p. 467.

20   Ibid., p. 472.

21   Ibid.

22   Ibid., p. 480.

23   Ibid., p. 485.

24   Ibid.

25   Cited in Friedrich Lenger, *Werner Sombart 1863–1941. Eine Biographie* (Munich: Beck, 1994), p. 162. This is an invaluable source on Sombart's work.

26   Cited in Lenger, *Werner Sombart*, p. 165.

27   W. Sombart, 'Wien', *Morgen*, 19 July 1907, pp. 172–5.

28   F. Salten, 'Der Wiener Korrespondent', *Morgen*, 1907, pp. 113–16.

29   Hermann Bahr, *Wien* (Stuggart: Carl Krabbe Verlag, 1906).

30   Franz Servaes, *Wien: Briefe an eine Freundin in Berlin* (Leipzig: Klinkhardt & Biermann, n.d. [1908]).

31   Karl Scheffler 'Wien–Berlin', *Österreichische Rundschau*, XVII (1908), pp. 450–6.

32   For the shortened reference in English, see Max Weber, *The Protestant Ethic and the Spirit of Capitalism* (London: Allen & Unwin 1930), p. 192, n. 3. For a valuable exploration of the history of the image of America in German cultural life, see the catalogue by Becke Sell Tower with an essay by John Czaplicka, *Envisioning America* (Cambridge, Mass.: Busch-Reisinger Museum, Harvard University, 1990).

33   For the anti-urban discourses in historical and comparative perspective, see Andrew Lees, *Cities Perceived: Urban Society in European and American Thought, 1820–1940* (Manchester: Manchester University Press, 1985).

34   For an overview of this transformation, see Jochen Boberg, Tilman Fichter and Eckhart Gillen (eds), *Exerzierfeld der Moderne. Industriekultur in Berlin in 19. Jahrhundert* (Munich: Beck, 1984).

35   Julius Langbehn, *Rembrandt als Erzieher* (1890) (Leipzig: C. L. Hirschfeld, 1922) (77th–84th edn) esp. pp. 263–5.

36   Ibid., p. 264.

37   Ibid.

38   Arnold Lewis, *An Early Encounter with Tomorrow: Europeans, Chicago's Loop, and the World's Columbian Exhibition* (Urbana/Chicago: University of Illinois Press, 1997).

39   Ibid., p. 1.

40   For a contemporary account see Julius Lessing, 'Die Berliner Gewerbeausstellung', *Preussische Jahrbücher*, LXXXVIII (1896), pp. 276–94.

41   On its significance for Berlin, see Georg Simmel 'The Berlin Trade Exhibition',
     in D. Frisby and M. Featherstone (eds), *Simmel on Culture: Selected Writings*
     (London: Sage, 1997), pp. 255–8.

42   For a description of the Dresden Exhibition by one of Albian Small's students,
     see Howard Woodhead, 'The First German Municipal Exposition (Dresden
     1903)', *American Journal of Sociology*, 9 (1904), pp. 433–58; 612–30; 812–31;
     10 (1905), pp. 47–63.

43   See Carl E. Schorske, *Fin-de-Siècle Vienna* (New York: Knopf, 1980),
     ch. 2. See also my *Metropolitan Architecture and Modernity*.

44   Salten, 'Der Wiener Korrespondent'.

45   Ibid., p. 114.

46   Ibid.

47   Ibid., p. 116.

48   Ibid.

49   W. Sombart, 'Wien', p. 172.

50   Ibid.

51   Ibid., pp. 173–4.

52   Ibid., p. 174.

53   Ibid.

54   Servaes, *Wien*.

55   Ibid., p. 5.

56   Ibid., p. 7.

57   Ibid., pp. 130–1.

58   Ibid., p. 133.

59   Anon [Walter Rathenau], 'Die schönste Stadt der Welt', *Die Zukunft*, 26
     (1899), pp. 36–48.

60   Karl Scheffler, 'Berlin als Kunststadt', *Der Lotse*, II (1901), pp. 257–63, esp.
     p. 257.

61   Ibid., p. 260.

62   K. Scheffler, 'Wien–Berlin', p. 451.

63   Ibid.

64   Ibid., p. 456.

65   Brigitt Morgenbrod, ' "Träume in Nachbars Garten". Das Wien-Bild im
     Deutschen Kaiserreich' in Ganolf Hübinger and Wolfgang J. Mommsen (eds),
     Intellektuellen im Deutschen Kaiserreich (Frankfurt: Fisher, 1993), pp. 111–
     25, esp. p. 116.

66   Ludwig Fulda, 'Berlin und das deutsche Geistesleben', *Der Greif*, I (1913/
     1914), pp. 185–99.

67   Egon Friedell, *Ecce Poeta* (Berlin: Fischer, 1912).

68   Hermann Bahr, 'Der Betrieb der Grossstadt', *Die neue Rundschau*, XXI, 4
     (1910), pp. 697–705, esp. pp. 704–5.

69   On American production methods and their influence in Berlin, see 'Die
     Fabrik wird zur Maschine', in Boberg, Fichter and Gillen, *Exerzierfeld der
     Moderne*, pp. 324–35; for another contemporary's reflections, see Karl
     Lamprecht, *Americana* (Frieburg: Hermann Heyfelder, 1906); for a Weimar
     discussion see, for example, Adolf Halfeld, *Amerika und der Amerikanismus*
     (Jena: Diederichs, 1928).

70 See Lenger, *Werner Sombart*; Jeffrey Herf, *Reactionary Modernism* (Cambridge, Cambridge University Press, 1984), ch. 6; Arthur Mitzman, *Sociology and Estrangement* (New York: Knopf, 1973), Part III.

5 The City Designed

Epigraphs from Ludwig Wittgenstein, *Philosophical Investigations* (Oxford: Blackwell, 1974), p. 8; Robert Musil, *The Man Without Qualities* (New York: Knopf, 1995), p. 1706; Otto Wagner, *Modern Architecture* (1896), trans. Harry Malgrave (Santa Monica: The Getty Center, 1988), p. 103 (translation amended).

1   On Haussmann's project, see David Jordan, *Transforming Paris* (New York: Free Press, 1995) and David van Zenten, *Building Paris* (Cambridge: Cambridge University Press, 1994).
2   On the Ringstrasse's development, see Carl E. Schorske, *Fin-de-Siècle Vienna* (New York: Knopf, 1981), ch. 2.
3   On the relation between his architecture and philosophy, see Nana Last, 'Transgressions and Inhabitations: Wittgenstein's Spatial Practices', *Assemblage*, 35 (1998), pp. 36–47.
4   See Paul Wijdeveld, *Ludwig Wittgenstein: Architect* (London: Thames & Hudson, 1994).
5   Ludwig Wittgenstein, *Philosophical Investigations*, 3rd edn (London: Routledge, 1974), p. 18.
6   Robert J. Ackermann, *Wittgenstein's City* (Amherst: University of Massachusetts Press, 1988).
7   Ibid., p. 13.
8   Ibid., p. 15.
9   Ibid., p. 14.
10 Ibid., p. 204.
11 Ibid., pp. 217–18.
12 Ibid., p. 207.
13 See Otto Wagner, *Die Grossstadt* (Vienna: Schroll, 1911).
14 See Paul Kortz, *Wien am Aufang des XX. Jahrhunderts* (Vienna: Gerlach & Wiedling, 1905).
15 Reinhard E. Petermann, *Wien im Zeitalter Kaiser Franz Josephs I* (Vienna: R. Lechner, 1908).
16 Ibid., p. 144.
17 Kortz, *Wien*, p. 39.
18 Petermann, *Wien*, p. 111.
19 On the significance of the heterogeneity of the city and the Empire more generally for architectural development, see Akos Moravänszky, *Competing Visions* (Cambridge, Mass.: MIT Press, 1998).
20 See Petermann, *Wien*.
21 Ibid., p. 143.
22 See David Frisby, *Metropolitan Architecture and Modernity: Otto Wagner's Vienna* (Minneapolis: Minnesota University Press, 2002).

23 Ludwig Wittgenstein, *Tractatus Logico-Philosophicus* (London: Routledge, 1961), p. 31.
24 Reinhard Farkas, *Hermann Bahr. Prophet der Moderne* (Vienna: Böhlau, 1987), p. 43.
25 See Frisby, *Metropolitan Architecture.* Also Beatriz Colomina, *Privacy and Publicity: Modern Architecture as Mass Media* (Cambridge, Mass.: MIT Press, 1994).
26 Georg Simmel, 'Rom', *Die Zeit*, 15, 28 May 1898, p. 19.
27 Anon [Walter Rathenau], 'Die schönste Stadt der Welt', *Die Zukunft*, 26 (1899), pp. 36–48.
28 Sombart, 'Wien', *Morgen*, 19 July 1907, p. 172.
29 Ibid., p. 173.
30 Ibid.
31 Ibid., p. 174.
32 Ibid.
33 Ibid., p. 175.
34 Egon Friedell, *Ecce Poeta* (Berlin: Fischer, 1912).
35 Ibid., p. 259.
36 Ibid., p. 260.
37 Ibid.
38 Ibid.
39 See Hans Tietze, *Otto Wagner* (Vienna/Berlin: Rokola Verlag, 1922).
40 Hans Tietze, *Wien* (Vienna/Leipzig: Dr Hans Epstein, 1931), p. 40.
41 Ibid., p. 379.
42 Ibid., p. 384. My emphasis.
43 Ibid., p. 386.
44 See Petermann, *Wien*, p. 132.
45 Ibid., p. 132.
46 Ibid., p. 254.
47 Ibid., p. 168.
48 Ibid., p. 199.
49 Ibid., p. 200.
50 Otto Wagner, 'Hotel Wien' (1910), in Otto Antonia Graf, *Otto Wagner. Das Werk des Architekten*, 2 (Vienna: Böhlau, 1985), pp. 619–24.
51 On the significance of Hubert Gessner in particular, see the unpublished manuscript by Markus Kristan, 'Hubert Gessner'.
52 On department stores in Vienna, see Andreas Lehne, *Wiener Warenhäuser 1865–1914* (Vienna: Deuticke, 1990); on the Wohn- und Geschäftshaus, see Ursula Prokop, *Wien. Aufbruch zur Metropole* (Vienna: Böhlau, 1994).
53 By implication, city planning was not taught as a separate subject by Wagner at the Akademie.
54 Cited in Wijdeveld, *Ludwig Wittgenstein*, p. 187.
55 See Camillo Sitte, *City Planning According to Artistic Principles* (New York: Rizzoli, 1985), p. 138.
56 Ibid.
57 Ibid., p. 278. Translation amended. My emphasis.
58 See Frisby, *Metropolitan Architecture.*

59   Ibid., ch. 2.
60   See Camillo Sitte, 'Die Regulierung des Stubenviertels', *Neues Wiener Tagblatt*, 5 Mar. 1893.
61   Ibid.
62   Many of Hevesi's articles are collected in two volumes. See L. Hevesi, *Acht Jahre Sezession* (1906) (Klagenfurt: Ritter Verlag, 1986) and *Altkunst – Neukunst. Wien 1894–1908* (1909) (Klagenfurt: Ritter Verlag, 1986).
63   Hevesi, *Acht Jahre Sezession*, p. 45.
64   Otto Wagner, *Einige Skizze, Projekte und ausgeführte Bauwerke* (1889) (Tübingen: Wasmuth, 1984).
65   Ibid., p. 41, n. 99.
66   Ibid., p. 40, n. 95.
67   On Wagner's appointment, see Walter Wagner, *Die Geschichte der Akademie der bildende Künste* (Vienna: Rosenbaum, 1967).
68   See O. Wagner, *Modern Architecture*, trans. Harry F. Malgrave (Santa Monica: Getty, 1988), p. 60.
69   Manfredo Tafuri, 'Am Steinhof – Centrality and "Surface" in Otto Wagner's Architecture', in G. Peichl (ed.), *Die Künst des Otto Wagner* (Vienna: Akademie der bildenden Künste, 1984), p. 62.
70   Friedrich Achleitner, 'Der Glanz des Können's', *Wiener Architektur* (Vienna: Böhlau, 1996), p. 34.
71   Ibid.
72   O. Wagner, 'Moderne Architektur', in Otto Antonia Graf, *Otto Wagner*, vol. 1 (Vienna: Böhlau, 1985), p. 281.
73   Ibid.
74   Adolf Loos, 'Potemkin City', *Spoken into the Void* (Cambridge, Mass.: MIT Press, 1982), pp. 95–7.
75   Hermann Bahr, 'Otto Wagner', *Essays* (Leipzig: Insel, 1912), pp. 113–16, esp. pp. 113–114.
76   For a fuller discussion, see Frisby, *Metropolitan Architecture*.
77   Ibid., ch. 3.
78   Otto Wagner, 'Die Grossstadt', in Graf, *Otto Wagner*, vol. 2 (Vienna: Böhlau, 1985), p. 646.
79   Ibid.
80   See Sitte, *City Planning*, p. 245.
81   Wagner, *Modern Architecture*, p. 109. Translation amended.
82   This same dictum plays a significant role, too, in Max Weber's delineation of the spirit of capitalism.
83   See ch. 3.
84   With some exceptions, Sitte viewed much of the Ringstrasse development as aesthetically acceptable.
85   Weber came to view the penetration of purposive rational action into the spheres of life as a universal tendency.
86   As with other effects of the developed money economy, Simmel's analysis in *The Philosophy of Money* suggests the dialectical interplay between differentiation and dedifferentiation in universal money exchange.
87   See Wagner, *Modern Architecture*, pp. 76–8.

88 Ibid., p. 77.

89 Ibid., p. 118.

90 The case for this process of connecting disparate objects is made in Christoph Asendorf, *Batteries of Life* (Berkeley: University of California Press, 1993).

91 See Frederic J. Schwartz, *The Werkbund* (New Haven: Yale University Press, 1996).

92 This is true of those not unsympathetic to Wagner's positive assessment of the role of fashion in architecture. See, for instance, Victor Höfert, 'Modern', *Wiener Bauindustrie-Zeitung*, 17 Jan. 1895, p. 1.

93 Mary McLeod, 'Undressing Architecture: Fashion, Gender and Modernity', in D. Fausch et al. (eds), *Architecture: In Fashion* (Princeton: Princeton Architectural Press, 1994), p. 53.

94 Ibid.

95 The city railway has a better claim to being a total work of art than does the Ringstrasse.

96 Notably by Freiherr von Feldegg, 'Wiens zweite Renaissance', *Der Architekt*, 1 (1895), pp. 1–2.

97 On Baumann, see Rudolf Kolowrath, *L. Baumann. Architekt zwischen Barock und Jugendstil* (Vienna: Compross Verlag, 1985).

98 On the history of Wagner's unsuccessful projects on the Karlsplatz, see Peter Haiko and Renata Kassal-Mikula (eds), *Otto Wagner und das Kaiser Franz Josef-Stadtmuseum. Das Scheitern der Moderne in Wien* (Vienna: Historisches Museum der Stadt Wien, 1988).

99 This is contained in Wagner's winning submission to the competition for a General Regulierungsplan for Vienna in 1894. Perhaps the two apartment blocks on the Linke Wienzeile (including the 'Majolikahaus') are a later indication of how that grand avenue might have looked.

100 Wagner depicted part of this projected avenue from the Stefansdom to the Ring Kai in one of his illustrations (1897) for the Kaiser's Jubilee Exhibition of 1898.

101 Joseph Bayer, 'Die Moderne und die historischen Baustyle', *Neue Freie Presse*, 3 Apr. 1902.

102 Ibid.

103 Ibid.

104 This suggests an interesting dialectic between inside and outside that goes beyond the more frequently noted opposition between the private and the public.

105 G. Simmel, 'Bridge and Door', in D. Frisby and M. Featherstone (eds), *Simmel on Culture: Selected Writings* (London: Sage, 1997), p. 173.

106 One of the exceptions is Otto Wagner's Neumann department store, built in the fashionable Kärtnerstrasse in 1893. For other developments, see Andreas Lehne, *Wiener Warenhauser 1865–1914*, with contributions by Gerhard Meissl and Edith Hahn (Vienna: Franz Deuticke, 1990). For the last year before the Great War, see Ursula Prokop, *Wien. Aufbruch zur Metropole* (Vienna: Böhlau, 1994).

107 See ch. 4.

108 See my *Metropolitan Architecture*, ch. 2.

109 Ibid., ch. 3.
110 Karl Henrici, 'Moderne Architektur', *Deutsche Bauzeitung*, 31 (1897), pp. 14–20.
111 The following argument is an abridged version of a more detailed treatment in my *Metropolitan Architecture*.
112 This literature expands in volume on every occasion that a 'new' Vienna comes into being – whether it be the Ringstrasse zone, the Greater Vienna enlargement of 1890, the new Vienna after 1918, a new Vienna after 1938, 1945 and 1955. In the period we are examining, the literary contributors to Old Vienna, also occasionally ventured into satire of the modern 'new' Vienna. See, for example, Edward Pötzl, *Moderner Gschnas* (Vienna: Robert Mohr, 1900).
113 Cited in Elisabeth Springer, *Geschichte und Kulturleben der Wiener Ringstrasse* (Wiesbaden: Franz Steiner, 1979), p. 610–11.
114 Letter to Hugo van Hofmannsthal 18 Sept. 1913 in Hugo von Hofmannsthal and Leopold von Andrian, *Briefwechsel* (Frankfurt: S. Fischer, 1967), p. 203.
115 O. Wagner, 'Nur keine Mäcene!', *Illustriertes Wiener Extrablatt*, 11 Apr. 1909. I wish to thank Gehard Meissl for drawing my attention to this reference.
116 G. Simmel, 'Exkurs über die soziale Begrenzung', *Soziologie* (Leipzig: Duncker & Humblot, 1908), p. 624.
117 Anton Czepelka, 'Stadtbahnen in Europa, Amerika und – Wien', *Die Zeit*, 18 Nov. 1899, p. 101.
118 See Karl Hochenegg, 'Projekt, betreffend elektrische Untergrundbahnen durch die Innere Stadt Wien', *Zeitschrift des Österreichischen Ingenieur- und Architekten-Vereines*, LX1, 25 June 1909, pp. 413ff.
119 John W. Boyer, *Culture and Political Crisis in Vienna* (Chicago: Chicago University Press, 1996).
120 Ibid., p. xi.
121 Ibid., p. 10.
122 Ibid.
123 See Wolfgang Maderthaner and Lutz Musner, *Die Anarchie der Vorstadt. Das andere Wien um 1900* (Frankfurt: Campus, 1999).
124 Ibid.
125 Ibid., p. 86.
126 Ibid.
127 Ibid., pp. 80–2.
128 See Hermann Czech and Wolfgang Mistelbauer, *Das Looshaus* (Vienna: Löcker Verlag, 1984), p. 89. On Loos's response to modernity, see Janet Stewart, *Fashioning Vienna. Adolf Loos's Cultural Criticism* (London: Routledge, 2000).
129 For the wider context of the uncompleted projects for rebuilding sections of the city, see *Das Ungebaute Wien 1800–2000. Projekte für die Metropole* (Vienna: Historisches Museum, 2000), esp. sections V, VI, VII.
130 Simmel, 'Bridge and Door'.
131 Ibid., p. 172.
132 Alfred Marshall, *Principles of Economics*, 8th edn (London: Macmillan, 1930), p. 441.
133 Ibid.

134 David Harvey, *The Limits to Capital* (Oxford: Blackwell, 1982), ch. 11.
135 Ibid., p. 337.
136 Ibid., p. 339–40.
137 Ibid., p. 340. My emphasis.
138 Ibid., p. 367.
139 Ibid., n. 20.
140 See Simmel, 'Exkurs'.
141 Eugen von Philippovich, 'Wiener Wohnungsverhältnisse', *Archiv für soziale Gesetzgebung und Statistik*, VII (1894), pp. 215–76.
142 Ibid., p. 226.
143 Ibid., p. 237.
144 Ibid., p. 249.
145 Ibid., p. 250.
146 Ibid., pp. 248–9.
147 E. von Philippovich, 'Korreferat', *Schriften des Vereins für Sozialpolitik*, XCVIII (1902), pp. 43–56.
148 Ibid., pp. 46–7.
149 Ibid., p. 48.
150 Paul Schwarz, 'Die Entwicklung der Städtischen Grundrente in Wien', *Schriften des Vereins für Sozialpolitik*, XCIV, 1 (1901), pp. 35–143.
151 Ibid., p. 36.
152 Ibid.
153 Ibid., p. 39.
154 Ibid., p. 48.
155 Ibid., p. 54.
156 See for example, Emil Lederer, 'Bodenspekulation und Wohnungsfrage', *Archiv für Sozialwissenschaft und Sozialpolitik*, 25 (1907), pp. 613–48, esp. pp. 637ff.
157 Petermann, *Wien*, p. 141.
158 R. Musil, *The Man Without Qualities*, trans. Sophie Wilkins and Burton Pike (New York: Knopf, 1995), p. 919.
159 L. Wittgenstein, *Werkausgabe*, vol. 1 (Frankfurt: Suhrkamp, 1984), p. 280.

6   The City Dissolved

Epigraphs from: Manfredo Tafuri, *Architecture and Utopia* (Cambridge, Mass.: MIT Press, 1968), p. 88; Paul Scheerbart, 'Glass Architecture', in Rose-Carol Washton Long (ed.), *German Expressionism* (Berkeley: University of California Press, 1995), pp. 127–8 (translation amended); Walter Benjamin, 'False Criticism' (1930), *Selected Writings, Volume 2: 1927–1934* (Cambridge, Mass.: Belknap Press, 1978), p. 506.

The author would like to acknowledge the assistance of the staff of the Deutsches Literaturarchiv, Marbach, for access to material by Siegfried Kracauer, and Dr Karlheinz Weigand, Director of the Ernst-Bloch-Archiv, Ludwigshafen, for access to material by Ernst Bloch.

1   C. Baudelaire, 'The Painter of Modern Life', in C. Baudelaire, *The Painter of Modern Life and Other Essays*, trans. and ed. J. Mayne (London: Phaedron, 1964), pp. 1–40.

2   W. Benjamin, *Gesammelte Schriften I.3* (Frankfurt: Suhrkamp, 1980), p. 1152.

3   Baudelaire, 'The Painter of Modern Life', p. 1.

4   Ibid., p. 4.

5   Ibid., p. 8.

6   Ibid.

7   Ibid., p. 9.

8   Ibid., p. 11.

9   Cited in W. Benjamin, *Charles Baudelaire: A Lyric Poet in the Era of High Capitalism*, trans. H. Zohn (London: New Left Books, 1973), p. 74.

10   F. M. Hübner, 'Der Expressionismus in Deutschland' (1920), in P. Raabe (ed.), *Expressionismus. Der Kampf um eine literarische Bewegung* (Zurich: Arche, 1987), pp.133–46, esp. p. 136. The volume is a valuable source of documentation on Expressionism.

11   J. Hermand, 'Das Bild der "grossen Stadt" in Expressionismus', in K. R. Scherpe (ed.), *Die Unwirklichkeit der Städte* (Reinbek: Rowohlt, 1988), pp. 61–79, esp. p. 66. On literary Expressionism and the metropolis, see S. Vietta and H. G. Kemper, *Expressionismus* (Munich: Fink, 1975).

12   R. Heller, ' "The City is Dark": Conceptions of Urban Landscape and Life in Expressionist Painting and Architecture', in G. B. Pickar and K. E. Webb (eds), *Expressionism Reconsidered* (Munich: Fink, 1979), pp. 42–56, esp. p. 45. More generally, see C. Brockhaus, 'Die ambivalente Faszination der Grossstadterfahrung in der deutschen Kunst des Expressionismus', in H. Meixner and S. Vietta (eds), *Expressionismus – sozialer Wandel und Kunstlerische Erfahrung* (Munich: Fink, 1982), pp. 84–106.

13   L. Meidner, 'Anleitung zum Malen von Grossstadtbilder', in G. Brever and I. Wagemann, *Ludwig Meidner. Zeichner, Maler, Literat* (Stuttgart: Hatje, 1991), vol. 2, pp. 290–2. The contrast with Impressionism could be beyond representation to social organization. Writing in 1917, Karl Scheffler argued that the Berlin Secessions were inappropriate for the new movement since 'expressionism . . . cannot really make use of this intimate group [the Secession]. The spirit that has captured our young artists and dominates them more every day rejects limits and boundaries; it seeks a direct link to the masses, it strives for breadth, universality, loudness – its essence is democratic, not patrician.' (Cited in P. Paret, *The Berlin Secession* (Cambridge, Mass./London: Belknap, 1980), p. 233).

14   Ibid. For a discussion of this text, see H. Brüggemann, 'Grossstadt und neues Sehen', in Brever and Wagemann, *Ludwig Meidner*, vol. 1, pp. 48–56. In detail, see G. Leistner, *Idee und Wirklichkeit. Gehalt und Bedeutung des urbanen Expressionismus in Deutschland, dargestellt am Werk Ludwig Meidners* (Frankfurt/Bern/New York: Peter Lang, 1989). More generally, on changes in perception, see C. Asendorf, *Ströme und Strahlen* (Giessen: Anabas, 1989).

15   K. Pinthus, 'Rede mit die Zukunft', in W. Rothe (ed.), *Der Aktivismus 1915–1920* (Munich: DTV, 1969), pp. 116–33, esp. p. 131.

16 F. Tönnies, *Gemeinschaft und Gesellschaft* (Leipzig: Fues's Verlag, 1887). For an English translation, see F. Tönnies, *Community and Association*, trans. C. P. Loomis (London: Routledge, 1955). On representations of the city, see A. Lees, *Cities Perceived: Urban Society in European and American Thought, 1820–1940* (Manchester: Manchester University Press, 1985); A. Sutcliffe (ed.), *Metropolis 1890–1940* (London: Mansell, 1984), esp. p. 2.

17 F. Tönnies, 'Zur Einleitung in der Soziologie', *Zeitschrift für Philosophie und philosophische Kritik*, 115 (1899), p. 248.

18 Ibid., p. 242.

19 Tönnies, *Community and Association*, p. 87.

20 Ibid., p. 89.

21 Ibid., pp. 95–6.

22 Cited in H. Liebersohn, *Fate and Utopia in German Sociology 1870–1923* (Cambridge, Mass.: MIT Press, 1988), p. 36.

23 M. Scheler, *Ressentiment*, trans. W. W. Holdheim and intro. by L. A. Coser (Glencoe, Ill.: Free Press, 1961), p. 166.

24 Cited in Donald E. Gordon, *Expressionism: Art and Idea* (New Haven/London: Yale University Press, 1987, p. 136. On the sexual – and sexist – representations of 'decay and degeneracy' in Expressionist and later portrayal of the city, see B. I. Lewis, '*Lustmord*: Inside the Windows of the Metropolis', in C. W. Haxthausen and H. Suhr (eds), *Berlin, Culture and Metropolis* (Minneapolis/Oxford: University of Minnesota Press, 1990), pp. 111–40; also Maria Tatar, *Lustmord: Sexual Murder in Weimar Germany* (Princeton: Princeton University Press, 1995).

25 Figures cited in Haxthausen and Suhr, *Berlin*, p. xxii, n. 13. For detail on German urbanization, see J. Reulecke, *Geschichte der Urbanisierung in Deutschland* (Frankfurt: Suhrkamp, 1985).

26 The Berlin Trade Exhibition of 1896 is discussed by, amongst others, Georg Simmel. Cf. G. Simmel, 'Berliner Gewerbe Ausstellung', *Die Zeit*, 8, 25 July 1896, pp. 59–60; G. Simmel, 'The Berlin Trade Exhibition', in D. Frisby and M. Featherstone (eds), *Simmel on Culture: Selected Writings* (London: Sage, 1997), pp. 255–8.

27 K. Baedeker, *Berlin and its Environs*, 5th edn (Leipzig: K. Baedeker, 1912), p. v.

28 Anon [W. Rathenau], 'Die schönste Stadt der Welt', *Die Zukunft*, 26 (1899), pp. 36–48, esp. p. 37. For a fuller discussion of this article and of Endell (below), see L. Müller, 'The Beauty of the Metropolis', in Haxthausen and Suhr, *Berlin*, pp. 37–57.

29 Ibid., p. 40.

30 Ibid., p. 41. The notion that Berlin and other cities were developing without a structure was widespread. Karl Scheffler saw the city as 'an unnaturally extended, formless city economy'. See K. Scheffler, *Die Architektur der Grossstadt* (Berlin: Cassirer, 1913), pp. 3–39, esp. p. 21.

31 W. Rathenau, *Zur Mechanik des Geistes* (Berlin: S. Fischer, 1913).

32 Ibid., pp. 40–1.

33 E. Friedell, *Ecce Poeta* (Berlin: S. Fischer, 1912).

34 Ibid., p. 260.

35 A. Endell, *Die Schönheit der grossen Stadt* (Stuttgart: Strecker & Strecker, 1908. Now available as *Die Schönheit der grossen Stadt* (Berlin: Archibook, 1984). References are to this edition.

36 Ibid., p. 34.

37 W. Sombart, *Die deutsche Volkswirtschaft im neunzehnten Jahrhundert* (Berlin: G. Bondi, 1903).

38 Ibid., p. 415.

39 Ibid., p. 416.

40 Ibid., p. 419.

41 Ibid., p. 420.

42 W. Sombart, 'Technik und Kultur', *Verhandlungen des Ersten Deutschen Soziologentages, 1910* (Tübingen: Mohr, 1911), pp. 80–97. On Expressionist literary responses to technology, see also K. Daniels, 'Expressionismus und Technik', in H. Segeberg (ed.), *Technik in der Literatur* (Frankfurt: Suhrkamp, 1987), pp. 351–86.

43 M. Weber, 'Diskussionsrede zu W. Sombarts Vortrag über Technik und Kultur', in M. Weber, *Gesammelte Aufsatze zur Soziologie und Sozialpolitik* (Tübingen: Mohr, 1988), pp. 449–56. For another discussion of Weber see S. Whimster, 'The Secular Ethic and the Culture of Modernism', in S. Whimster and S. Lash (eds), *Max Weber: Rationality and Modernity* (London: Allen & Unwin, 1987), pp. 259–90.

44 Ibid., p. 453.

45 Ibid., p. 453.

46 Ibid., pp. 453–4.

47 K. Pinthus (ed.), *Menschheitsdämmerung* (1919) (Hamburg: Rowohlt, 1990).

48 Ibid., p. 26.

49 G. Simmel, 'Die Grossstädte und das Geistesleben', *Die Grossstadt. Jahrbuch der Gehe-Stiftung zu Dresden*, 9 (1903) pp. 185–206; in English as 'The Metropolis and Mental Life', in K. H. Wolff (ed.), *The Sociology of Georg Simmel*, Glencoe, Ill., Free Press, 1950, pp. 409–24. References are to this translation by H. Gerth (which has been reprinted in Frisby and Featherstone, *Simmel on Culture*, pp. 174–85).

50 Ibid., p. 409.

51 Hübner, 'Der Expressionismus', p. 139.

52 See G. Simmel, 'Soziologie des Raumes', *Jahrbuch für Gesetzgebung. Verwaltung und Volkswirtschaft*, 27 (1903), pp. 27–71. In English as 'The Sociology of Space', in Frisby and Featherstone, *Simmel on Culture*, pp. 137–70; also G. Simmel, 'Über räumliche Projektionen sozialer Formen', *Zeitschrift für Sozialwissenschaft*, 6 (1903), pp. 287–302. The discussion here and below relies upon D. Frisby, *Simmel and Since* (London / New York: Routledge, 1992), pt 2. Simmel's relevance for the interpretation of metropolitan art and architecture has been noted, for instance, by Manfredo Tafuri: 'Simmel's considerations on the great metropolis . . . contained *in nuce* the problems that were to be at the center of concern of the historical avant-garde movements.' Cf. M. Tafuri, *Architecture and Utopia* (Cambridge, Mass.: MIT Press, 1976), pp. 88ff; cf. also M. Müller, *Schöne Schein* (Frankfurt: Athenaum, 1987), esp. pp. 29ff.

53   G. Simmel, 'Soziologie des Raumes', in *Soziologie* (Leipzig: Duncker & Humblot, 1908), pp. 704–5.

54   Simmel, 'The Metropolis', p. 410. The constellation of city, abstraction and money economy were to receive a conservative interpretation in Spengler's highly popular volumes. Cf. Oswald Spengler, *Der Untergang des Abendlandes*, vol. 2 (Munich: Beck, 1923). Spengler's interpretation of the metropolis owes not a little to the reworking of Simmel's themes.

55   Ibid., p. 422.

56   Ibid., p. 410.

57   G. Simmel, *The Philosophy of Money*, 2nd edn, trans. T. Bottomore and D. Frisby (London/New York: Routledge, 1990), esp. ch. 6.

58   Simmel, 'The Metropolis', p. 412.

59   Simmel, *The Philosophy of Money*, p. 484.

60   Ibid., p. 256. In the metropolis article, Simmel equates the blasé attitude with 'a faithful subjective reflection of a completely internalized money economy. . . . All things float with equal specific gravity in the constantly moving stream of money. All things lie on the same level.' Commenting on this passage, Manfredo Tafuri writes: 'The objects all floating on the same plane, with the same specific gravity, in the constant movement of the money economy: does it not seem that we are reading here a literary comment on a Schwitter *Merzbild*? . . . The problem was, in fact, how to render active the intensification of nervous stimulation; . . . how to absorb the shock provoked by the metropolis by transforming it into a new principle of dynamic development; how to "utilize" to the limit the anguish which "indifference to value" continually provokes and nourishes in the metropolitan experience.' (*Architecture*, pp. 88–9)

61   Ibid., p. 257.

62   Ibid., p. 483; Simmel, 'The Metropolis', p. 422. Translation amended.

63   G. Simmel, 'Vom Wesen der Kultur', *Brücke und Tür* (Stuttgart: Köhler, 1957), pp. 86–94, esp. p. 94. In English as 'On the Essence of Culture', in Frisby and Featherstone, *Simmel on Culture*, pp. 40–6, esp. p. 45.

64   G. Simmel, 'Die Zukunft unserer Kultur', *Brücke und Tür*, pp. 95–7, esp. p. 95. In English as 'The Future of Our Culture', in Frisby and Featherstone, *Simmel on Culture*, pp. 101–3.

65   G. Simmel, 'On the Concept and Tragedy of Culture', *The Conflict in Modern Culture and Other Essays*, trans. and ed. K. P. Etzkorn (New York: Teacher's College Press), p. 42.

66   G. Simmel, 'The Conflict in Modern Culture' (1914), *The Conflict*, p. 71. Translation amended.

67   Ibid., pp. 15–16.

68   Ibid., p. 16.

69   Ibid., p. 18.

70   G. Simmel, 'L'art pour L'art', *Zur Philosophie der Kunst* (Potsdam: Kiepenheuer, 1922), p. 79.

71   In P. Lawrence (ed.), *Georg Simmel: Sociologist and European*, trans. D. E. Jenkinson et al. (New York: Barnes and Noble, 1976), p. 228.

72   G. Simmel, 'Philosophie der Landschaft' (1910), *Brücke und Tür*, p. 141.

73 G. Simmel, 'Rodin' (1911), *Philosophische Kultur*, 3rd edn (Potsdam: Kiepenheuer 1923), pp. 179–97, esp. p. 196.

74 Simmel, 'The Metropolis', p. 422.

75 On Kracauer, see I. Mülder, *Siegfried Kracauer* (Stuttgart: Metzler, 1985); D. Frisby, *Fragments of Modernity: Social Theories of Modernity in the Works of Georg Simmel, Siegfried Kracauer and Walter Benjamin* (Cambridge: Polity, 1985; Cambridge, Mass.: MIT Press, 1986), ch. 3; M. Kessler and T. Y. Levin (eds), *Siegfried Kracauer* (Tübingen: Stauffenburg Verlag, 1990).

76 On Bloch, see P. Zudeick, *Der Hintern des Teufels. Ernst Bloch. Leben und Werk* (Moos/Baden-Baden: Elster, 1987).

77 S. Kracauer, *Über den Expressionismus. Wesen und Sinn einer Zeitbewegung* (1918), MS, 81 pp., Siegfried Kracauer Nachlass, Deutsches Literaturarchiv, Marbach.

78 Ibid.

79 S. Kracauer, *Das Leiden unter dem Wissen und die Sehnsucht nach der Tat* (*c.*1917), MS, Siegfried Kracauer Nachlass, p. 246.

80 S. Kracauer, *Über den Expressionismus*, pp. 60–6.

81 Ibid., p. 18.

82 Ibid., p. 36.

83 Ibid., p. 46.

84 Ibid., p. 72.

85 Ibid., p. 77.

86 S. Kracauer, 'Schicksalswende der Kunst' (1920), *Schriften 5.1 (Aufsätze 1915–1926)*, ed. I. Mülder-Bach (Frankfurt: Suhrkamp, 1990), pp. 72–8, esp. p. 72. The crisis in Expressionism around 1920 is also commented upon by, amongst others, Kracauer's younger friend, Theodor Adorno. Cf. T. W. Adorno, 'Expressionismus und künstlerische Wahrhaftigkeit', *Die neue Schaubühne*, 2, 9 (1920), pp. 233–6.

87 Ibid., p. 73.

88 Ibid., p. 74.

89 Ibid., p. 75.

90 Ibid., p. 75.

91 S. Kracauer, 'Max Beckmann', *Die Rheinlande*, 31, 3 (1921), pp. 93–6, esp. p. 95.

92 Ibid., p. 96.

93 Ibid.

94 T. W. Adorno 'Expressionismus und künstlerische Wahrhaftigkeit, *Die neue Schaubühne*, 2, 9 (1920), pp. 233–6. In English as 'Expressionism and Artistic Truthfulness: Towards a Critique of Recent Literature', in Theodor W. Adorno, *Notes To Literature*, vol. 2, ed. Rolf Tiedemann (New York: Columbia University Press, 1992), pp. 257–9, esp. p. 258.

95 Ibid., p. 259.

96 Kracauer, 'Schicksalswende der Kunst', p. 78.

97 See Frisby, *Fragments of Modernity*, ch. 3; Mülder *Siegfried Kracauer*.

98 E. Bloch, *Geist der Utopie* (Munich/Leipzig: Duncker & Humblot, 1918; 2nd enlarged edn 1923). The original was written between April 1915 and

May 1917. There are significant differences in the two texts. Most references here are to the 1918 edition. Zudeick has captured the Expressionist content of this volume as follows: 'In "Geist der Utopie" Bloch played through the whole repertoire of the Expressionist sense of life, and he was master of this keyboard like hardly anyone else: critique of bourgeois society, mendacity, mediocrity, the constraint of bourgeois moral conceptions, anti-intellectualism, the mechanization and commercialization of society, the emptiness and anomic nature of human relationships, and out of all these things the longing for a new humanity, a new religiosity, a fraternal-socialistic future society.' (Zudeick, *Der Hintern des Teufels*, pp. 66–7).

99   E. Bloch, *Erbschaft dieser Zeit* (Zurich: Oprecht & Helbling, 1935); E. Bloch, *Heritage of Our Times*, trans. N. and S. Plaice (Berkeley/Los Angeles: University of California Press, 1991).

100   E. Bloch, *Das Prinzip Hoffnung*, 3 vols, rev. edn (Frankfurt: Suhrkamp, 1959); E. Bloch, *The Principle of Hope*, 3 vols, trans. N. Plaice, S. Plaice and P. Knight (Oxford: Blackwell, 1986).

101   T. W. Adorno, 'Blochs *Spuren*', *Noten zur Literatur*, vol. 2 (Frankfurt: Suhrkamp, 1961), pp. 144–5. In English as 'Bloch's *Spuren*', in Adorno, *Notes to Literature*, pp. 200–15.

102   E. Bloch, *Thomas Münzer als Theologe der Revolution* (Munich: Kurt Wolff Verlag, 1921).

103   A. Münster, *Utopie, Messianismus und Apokalypse im Frühwerk von Ernst Bloch* (Frankfurt: Suhrkamp, 1982), p. 126.

104   Cited in W. Hudson, *The Marxist Philosophy of Ernst Bloch* (New York: St Martins Press, 1982), p. 40.

105   Bloch, *Geist der Utopie*, p. 44. On Bloch's theory of ornament, see G. Raulet, *Natur und Ornament* (Darmstadt/Neuwied: Luchterhand, 1987), pp. 63–121.

106   Bloch, *Geist der Utopie*, p. 50.

107   Ibid., pp. 50–1

108   Ibid., p. 51.

109   E. Bloch, *The Utopian Function of Art and Literature: Selected Essays*, trans. J. Zipes and F. Mecklenburg (Cambridge, Mass.: MIT Press, 1988), p. 101. This volume contains a translation of 'The Creation of the Ornament' from the second edition of *Geist der Utopie*.

110   Bloch, *Geist der Utopie*, p. 21.

111   Ibid., pp. 22–3.

112   Bloch, *The Utopian Function*, p. 83.

113   Ibid., p. 82.

114   Bloch, *The Principle of Hope*, vol. 2, p. 737. Somewhat ironically, Walter Benjamin, more critical of Expressionism, refers to Taut's 'Alpine Architecture' as 'a well-ventilated Utopia'. More significantly, Benjamin sees Scheerbart's plea for glass architecture as a plea for an architectural material that leaves behind no traces: 'Things made from glass have no "aura". Glass is everywhere the enemy of secrets. It is also the enemy of possession.' (W. Benjamin, 'Erfahrung und Armut', *Gesammelte Schriften II.1*, pp. 213–19)

115　E. Bloch, 'Architektur und Utopie', Alpbach 1972, typescript Ernst Bloch Archiv.

116　Cited in Zudeick, *Der Hintern des Teufels*, p. 95.

117　E. Bloch, 'Das südliche Berlin', *Zeit-Echo*, 15 (1915–16), pp. 235–8. Part of this text is incorporated into *Geist der Utopie*, pp. 303–4.

118　E. Bloch, 'Berlin nach zwei Jahren', *Die Weltbühne*, 24 (1928), pp. 32–3.

119　E. Bloch, 'Berlin aus der Landschaft gesehen', *Frankfurter Zeitung*, 7 July 1932.

120　Bloch, *Heritage of Our Times*, p. 204. The 'dream-montage' is most often associated with surrealism, which proved a major influence upon Benjamin despite his subsequent critical regard for it. Bloch, too, saw its possibilities, especially in the improvised, revue form of Benjamin's *One-Way Street*, with its emphasis on the fragmentary. What Bloch found absent was the 'concrete intention': 'Even one-way streets have a destination.' On Bloch's own fragmentary *Spuren*, see K. L. Berghahn, 'A View Through the Red Window: Ernst Bloch's *Spuren*', in A. Huyssen and D. Bathrick (eds), *Modernity and the Text* (New York: Columbia University Press, 1989), pp. 200–15.

121　Bloch, *Heritage of Our Times*, p. 240.

122　Ibid.

123　Ibid., p. 253.

124　Ibid., p. 250.

7　The City Rationalized

Epigraphs from Max Weber, *Economy and Society*, ed. Günther Roth and Klaus Wittich (Berkeley: University of California Press, 1978), p. 56; Siegfried Kracauer, 'Wiederholung' (1932), *Schriften 5.3. Aufsätze 1932–1965* (Frankfurt: Suhrkamp, 1990), p. 71; Siegfried Kracauer, 'The Mass Ornament' (1927), *The Mass Ornament*, trans. Thomas Y. Levin (Cambridge, Mass.: Harvard University Press, 1995), p. 81.

1　Max Weber, 'Die protestantische Ethik und der "Geist" des Kapitalismus', *Archiv für Sozialwissenschaft und Sozialpolitik*, 20 (1905), pp. 1–54; 21 (1905), pp. 1–110.

2　Werner Sombart, *Der moderne Kapitalismus* (Leipzig: Duncker & Humblot, 1902).

3　Werner Sombart, *Die deutsche Volkswirtschaft im neunzehnten Jahrhundert* (Berlin: Georg Bondi, 1903).

4　Georg Simmel, *The Philosophy of Money* (1900), 2nd enlarged edn, trans. T. Bottomore and D. Frisby (London/New York: Routledge, 1990).

5　Simmel is usually associated with a preoccupation with the modern metropolis, although Sombart and Weber made greater contributions to the history of the city. On the city in classical social theory, see Harold Chorney, *City of Dreams* (Toronto: Nelson, 1990).

6　See, for example, Peter Fritsche, *Reading Berlin 1900* (Cambridge, Mass.: Harvard University Press, 1996).

7　See ch. 4.

8   See ch. 3.

9   For the varied response within sociology, see Chorney, *City of Dreams*.

10 See Andrew Lees, *Cities Perceived: Urban Society in European and American Thought, 1820–1940* (Manchester: Manchester University Press, 1985).

11 Karl Scheffler, 'Die Grossstadt', *Die neue Rundschau*, 21 (1910), pp. 881–97.

12 Ibid., p. 882.

13 Ibid., p. 886.

14 Ibid., p. 885.

15 Ibid., p. 887.

16 Ibid., p. 888.

17 Ibid., p. 889.

18 Karl Scheffler, 'Die Zukunft der Grossstädte und die Grossstädte der Zukunft', *Neue deutsche Rundschau*, 37 (1926), p. 522.

19 Ibid., p. 523.

20 Ibid., p. 529.

21 See Otto Wagner, *Modern Architecture*, trans. Harry F. Malgrave (Santa Monica: Getty, 1988).

22 Scheffler, 'Die Zukunft der Grossstädte', p. 534.

23 Ibid., p. 536.

24 Crucial aspects of this policy are examined in Manfredo Tafuri, *The Sphere and the Labyrinth* (Cambridge, Mass.: MIT Press, 1987), ch. 7.

25 Cited in Ludovica Scarpa, *Martin Wagner und Berlin* (Braunschweig/Wiesbaden: Vieweg, 1986), p. 9.

26 On the crucial role of Bruno Taut, see Iain Boyd Whyte, *Bruno Taut and the Architecture of Activism* (Cambridge: Cambridge University Press, 1982). For other visions of the modern city in the Weimar Republic, such as those of Hannes Mayer and especially Ludwig Hilberseimer, see K. Michael Hays, *Modernism and the Posthumanist Subject* (Cambridge, Mass.: MIT Press, 1992).

27 'Socialisation and Rationalisation of Housing in the Weimar Republic: The Work of Martin Wagner', in Architectural Association and Goethe Institute (eds), *Social Housing in Weimar Republic* (London: Architectural Association, 1978), pp. 54–74.

28 Tafuri, *The Sphere*, ch. 7.

29 *Martin Wagner. 1885–1957. Wohnungsbau und Weltstadtplanung. Die Rationalisierung des Glücks* (Berlin: Akademie der Künste, 1986).

30 Scarpa, *Martin Wagner*.

31 M. Wagner, *Städtische Freiflachenpolitik* (Berlin: Carl Heymans Verlag, 1915).

32 On Hilberseimer, see Hays, *Modernism*, esp. pp. 241–78.

33 Martin Wagner, 'Zivilisation, Kultur, Kunst', *Wohnungswirtschaft*, 3, 20/21, 26 Oct. 1926, pp. 165–8, esp. p.165. For a fuller discussion of this essay, see Martin Kieren, 'Von der Wirtschaft zur Wissenschaft', in *Martin Wagner. 1885–1957*, pp. 66–82.

34 M. Wagner, 'Zivilisation, Kultur, Kunst', p. 165.

35 Ibid., p. 166.

36 Ibid.

37 Ibid.
38 Ibid., p. 167.
39 Ibid., pp. 167–8.
40 Ibid., p. 168.
41 M. Wagner, *Die Baugilde*, 11, 19 (1929), p. 1577.
42 M. Wagner, 'Deutsche Städtebau-Ausstellung "1930 gegen 1900"', *Städtebauliche Probleme in amerikanischen Städten und ihre Rückwirkung auf den deutschen Städtebau* (Berlin: Deutsche Bauzeitung, 1929), p. 5.
43 Ibid.
44 Ibid.
45 Ibid., p. 10.
46 Ibid., p. 6.
47 Ibid., p. 10.
48 Ibid., p. 77.
49 M. Wagner, 'Englische Gartenstädte', *Wohnungswirtschaft*, 2, 17/18 (1925), p. 136.
50 For one of the many advocacies of rationalization in house building by Wagner, see M. Wagner, 'Gross-Siedlungen. Der Weg zur Rationalisierung des Wohnungsbaues', *Der Aufbau* (Vienna), 1, 6 (1926), pp. 81–96.
51 See Michael Hellgardt, 'Das Bauwerk im Zeitalter seiner technischen Reproduzierbarkeit', *Martin Wagner 1885–1957*, pp. 83–98.
52 Max Weber, *Economy and Society*, ed. G. Roth and C. Wittich (Berkeley: University of California Press, 1978), p. 973. Cited in Rogers Brubaker, *The Limits of Rationality* (London: Allen & Unwin, 1984), p. 21.
53 This journal has been reprinted in extract form as *Das Neue Berlin* (Berlin: Birkhäuser Verlag, 1985).
54 There are two copies of this manuscript. The original is in the Special Collections of the Frances Loeb Library in the Harvard Graduate School of Design. A second copy, without precise dates, is in the Archiv der Akademie der Künste, Berlin.
55 This 17-page manuscript, dated 20 October 1932, is in the Archiv der Akademie der Künste, Berlin.
56 Adolf Behne and Martin Wagner (eds), 'Das neue Berlin – die Weltstadt Berlin', *Das Neue Berlin* (Berlin: Deutsche Bauzeitung, 1929), p. 5.
57 Ibid.
58 For a selection of writings from this journal, see Heinz Hirdina (ed.), *Neues Bauen Neues Gestalten. Das neue Frankfurt/die neue Stadt. Eine Zeitschriften zwischen 1926 und 1933* (Dresden: Verlag der Kunst, 1984). The selection also contains articles by Wagner.
59 M. Wagner, *Städtebauliche Probleme der Grossstadt* (Berlin: Deutsche Bauzeitung, 1929), pp. 13–14.
60 Ibid., p. 14.
61 M. Breuer, 'Verkehrsarchitektur', Behne and Wagner, *Das neue Berlin*, p. 136.
62 Ibid., p. 141.
63 M. Wagner, *Städtebauliche Probleme der Grossstadt*, p. 11.
64 On the Potsdamer Platz, see Vittorio Magnago Lampugnani and Romana Schneider, *Ein Stück Grossstadt als Experiment. Planungen am Potsdamer*

Platz in Berlin (Stuttgart: Hatje, 1994); on the Alexanderplatz, see Peter Behrens, *Berlin Alexanderplatz* (Kaiserslautern: Pfalzgallerie Kaiserslautern, 1993). See also Tilmann Buddensieg, 'Der Weltstadtplatz', *Berliner Labyrinth* (Berlin: Wagenbach, 1993), pp. 83–94.

65 M. Wagner, 'Freiflächenpolitik', Behne and Wagner, *Das neue Berlin*, p. 109.
66 M. Wagner, 'Eine Studie über die Gestaltung des Berliner Ausstellungsgelände', *Wasmuths Monatshefte. Baukunst und Städtebau*, 15 (1931), pp. 33–40, esp. p. 34.
67 Letter from Wagner, in *Wasmuths Monatshefte*, p. 196.
68 M. Wagner, *Das wachsende Haus. Ein Beitrag zur Lösung der Städtischen Wohnungsfrage* (Berlin/Leipzig: Deutsches Verlagshaus Bong, 1932).
69 Ibid., p. 1.
70 Ibid., p. 35.
71 Ibid., p. 36.
72 Ibid.
73 Ibid., p. 40.
74 Ibid.
75 Ibid., p. 41.
76 *Das Neue Berlin*, MS, 1932. See n. 54.
77 M. Wagner, 'Das Problem der reinen Gartenstadt', *Wohnungswirtschaft*, 3, 18/19 (1926), pp. 156–9, esp. p. 156.
78 M. Wagner, *Das Neue Berlin I*, MS, p. 40.
79 Ibid., p. 130.
80 Ibid., p. 8.
81 Ibid., p. 9.
82 Ibid., p. 10.
83 M. Wagner, 'Städtebau als Wirtschaftsbau und Lebensbau' (see n. 54), p. 2.
84 Ibid., p. 5.
85 Ibid., p. 6.
86 Ibid., p. 5.
87 Ibid., pp. 5–6.
88 Weber, *Economy and Society*, p. 1394. Second emphasis mine.
89 Ibid.
90 M. Wagner, *Das Neue Berlin*, MS, p. 133.
91 Ibid., p. 78.
92 Ibid., p. 132.
93 M. Wagner, 'Städtebau als Wirtschaftsbau', p. 14.
94 Ibid., p. 13.
95 Ibid., p. 9.
96 Ibid.
97 Ibid., p. 10.
98 Ibid.
99 M. Wagner, *Das Neue Berlin*, MS, p. 250.
100 M. Wagner, 'Städtebau als Wirtschaftsbau', p. 11.
101 M. Wagner, *Das Neue Berlin*, MS, p. 420.
102 Ibid., p. 362.

103   M. Sandow, 'Die Sanierung der Berliner "City"', *Deutsche Bauzeitung*, 8 (1934), pp. 142–6.

104   Ibid., p. 144.

105   Ibid., p. 142.

106   Ibid.

107   Ibid.

108   Ibid., p. 144.

109   Ibid., p. 146.

110   S. Kracauer, 'Die Techniker verteidigen sich', *Frankfurter Zeitung*, 28 June 1932; reprinted in Siegfried Kracauer, *Berliner Nebeneinander*, ed. Andreas Volk (Zurich: Edition Epoca, 1996), pp. 211–14.

111   Ibid., p. 212.

112   Ibid., pp. 213–14.

113   Ibid., p. 214.

Conclusion

Epigraphs from Ludwig Wittgenstein, *Philosophical Investigations* (Oxford: Blackwell, 1974), p. 50; Robert Musil, *The Man Without Qualities* (New York: Knopf, 1995), p. 1759; Gaston Bachelard, *The Poetics of Space* (Boston: Beacon Press, 1964), p. 212.

1   W. Benjamin, 'The Return of the Flâneur', in Walter Benjamin, *Selected Writings, Volume 2: 1927–1934* (Cambridge, Mass.: Belknap, 1999), pp. 262–7.

2   For a discussion of Benjamin's methodological approaches to the city, see Graeme Gilloch, *Myth and Metropolis* (Cambridge: Polity, 1996).

3   H. Lefebvre, *The Production of Space* (Oxford: Blackwell, 1991).

4   As in my *Fragments of Modernity: Social Theories of Modernity in the Works of Georg Simmel, Siegfried Kracauer and Walter Benjamin* (Cambridge: Polity, 1985; Cambridge, Mass.: MIT Press, 1986).

5   G. Simmel, 'Bridge and Door', in D. Frisby and M. Featherstone (eds.), *Simmel on Culture: Selected Writings* (London: Sage, 1997), pp. 170–4.

6   On Kracauer's architecture, see Gerwin Zohlen, 'Siegfried Kracauer. Architekt und Schriftsteller', in M. Kessler and T. Y. Levin (eds), *Siegfried Kracauer. Neue Interpretationen* (Tübingen: Stauffenburg Verlag, 1990), pp. 325–44.

7   See W. Benjamin, *The Arcades Project* (Cambridge, Mass.: Belknap Press, 1999).

8   See W. Heindl and M. Tichy (eds), *'Durch Erkenntnis zu Freiheit und Glück . . .' Frauen an der Universität Wien (ab 1897)* (Vienna: WUV Universitätsverlag, 1990).

9   This is argued in David Harvey, *Consciousness and the Urban Experience* (Oxford: Blackwell, 1985), ch. 1.

10   Some of the pathologies of modern space have been explored in recent studies. See Anthony Vidler, 'Psychopathologies of Modern Space: Metropolitan Fear from Agoraphobia to Estrangement', in Michael S. Roth (ed.), *Rediscovering History: Cutlure, Politics and the Psyche* (Stanford: Stanford University Press,

1994), pp. 11–29; on the gendered nature of such pathologies, see Esther da Costa Meyer, 'La Donna è Mobile', in Louise Durning and Richard Wrigley (eds), *Gender & Architecture* (Chichester: John Wiley, 2000), pp. 155–70.

11   On interior and exterior spaces in the context of private and public space, see Beatriz Colomina, *Privacy and Publicity: Modern Architecture as Mass Media* (Cambridge, Mass.: MIT Press, 1994).

12   See G. Brever and I. Wagemann, *Ludwig Meidner. Zeichner, Maler, Literat* (Stuttgart: Hatje, 1991).

13   The German vision of a rational modern metropolis was also apparent in the conceptions of other architects such as Hannes Mayer and Ludwig Hilberseimer: S. K. Michael Hays, *Modernism and the Posthumanist Subject: The Architecture of Hannes Mayer and Ludwig Hilberseimer* (Cambridge, Mass.: MIT Press, 1992).

14   S. Kracauer, 'On Employment Agencies', in N. Leach (ed.), *Rethinking Architecture* (London: Routledge, 1997), p. 59.

15   Ibid.

16   G. Simmel, 'The Metropolis and Mental Life', in D. Frisby and M. Featherstone (eds), *Simmel on Culture: Selected Writings* (London: Sage, 1997), p. 177.

17   See S. Kracauer, 'Unter der Oberfläche', *Frankfurter Zeitung*, 11 July 1931.

18   L. Wittgenstein, *Tractatus logico-philosophicus: Werkausgabe I* (Frankfurt: Suhrkamp, 1984), p. 27.

19   L. Wittgenstein, 'Philosophische Untersuchungen', *Tractatus logico-philosophicus*, p. 293.

20   Ibid.

21   Ibid., p. 304.

22   Ibid, p. 570.

23   R. Musil, *The Man Without Qualities* (New York: Knopf, 1995), p. 1759.

24   This aspect of non-contemporaneity was highlighted by Loos: 'I live in the year 1908, but my neighbour lives approximately in the year 1900 and one over there lives in the year 1889.' In A. Loos,'Ornament and Crime', *The Architecture of Adolf Loos* (London: Arts Council, 1987), p. 101.

25   On Mannheim's sociology of knowledge, see my *The Alienated Mind: The Sociology of Knowledge in Germany 1918–33*, 2nd edn (London: Routledge, 1992), ch. 3.

26   Henri Lefebvre, 'The Everyday and Everydayness', *Yale French Studies*, 73 (1988), pp. 7–11, esp. pp. 10–11.

Bibliography

Abelson, Elaine S., *When Ladies Go A-Thieving*. Oxford: Oxford University Press, 1989.

Achleitner, Friedrich, *Wiener Architektur*. Vienna: Böhlau, 1996.

Ackermann, Robert J., *Wittgenstein's City*. Amherst: University of Massachusetts Press, 1988.

Adorno, Theodor W., *Kierkegaard: Construction of the Aesthetic*. Minneapolis: University of Minnesota Press, 1989.

Adorno, Theodor W., 'Expressionism and Artistic Truthfulness: Towards a Critique of Recent Literature', in *Notes to Literature*, vol. 2, ed. Rolf Tiedemann. New York: Columbia University Press, 1992, pp. 257–9.

Agrest, Diana, Patricia Conway, Leslie K. Weisman (eds), *The Sex of Architecture*. New York: Harry N. Abrams, 1996.

Anon, 'Sensational Novels', *The Quarterly Review*, 113 (January-April 1863), pp. 481–514.

Anon, 'Pinkerton's Men', *The World*, 19 Nov. 1875.

Anon [Walter Rathenau], 'Die schönste Stadt der Welt', *Die Zukunft*, 26 (1899), pp. 36–48.

Anon [Julius Langbehn], *Rembrandt als Erzieher*. Leipzig: C. L. Hirschfeld, 1922.

Arendt, Hannah, *The Human Condition*. Chicago: University of Chicago Press, 1958.

Asendorf, Christoph, *Ströme und Strahlen*. Giessen: Anabas, 1989.

Asendorf, Christoph, *Batteries of Life*. Berkeley: University of California Press, 1994.

Baedeker, Karl, *Berlin and its Environs,* 5th edn. Leipzig: K. Baedeker, 1912.

Bahr, Hermann, *Wien*. Stuttgart: Carl Krabbe Verlag, 1906.

Bahr, Hermann, 'Der Betrieb der Grossstadt', *Die neue Rundschau*, XX1, 4 (1910), pp. 697–705.

Bahr, Hermann, 'Otto Wagner', *Essays von Hermann Bahr*, ed. H. Kindermann. Vienna: Böhlau, 1980, pp. 283–5.

Balzac, Honore, *The Mysteries of Honore Balzac*. New York: Juniper Press, n.d.

Barnouw, Dagmar, *Critical Realism: History, Photography and the Work of Siegfried Kracauer*. Baltimore: Johns Hopkins University Press, 1964.

Baudelaire, Charles, 'The Painter of Modern Life', *The Painter of Modern Life and Other Essays*. London: Phaedron, 1964, pp. 1–40.

Bayer, Joseph, 'Die Moderne und die historischen Baustile', *Neue Freie Presse*, 3 Apr. 1902.

Behne, Adolf and M. Wagner (eds), *Das Neue Berlin*. Berlin: Deutsche Bauzeitung, 1929.

Benjamin, Walter, *Gesammelte Schriften*. Frankfurt: Suhrkamp, 1972–91.

Benjamin, Walter, *Charles Baudelaire: A Lyric Poet in the Era of High Capitalism*. London: New Left Books, 1973.

Benjamin, Walter, *One-Way Street and Other Writings*. London: New Left Books, 1979.

Benjamin, Walter, 'Berliner Kindheit um Neunzehnhundert', *Gesammelte Schriften VII.1*, ed. R. Tiedemann and H. Schweppenhauser. Frankfurt: Suhrkamp, 1989, pp. 385–432.

Benjamin, Walter, *The Arcades Project*. Cambridge, Mass.: Belknap Press, 1999.

Benjamin, Walter, 'A Berlin Chronicle' (1932), *Selected Writings, Volume 2: 1927–1934*. Cambridge, Mass.: Belknap Press, 1999, pp. 595–637.

Benjamin, Walter, 'Review of Hessel's *Heimliches Berlin*', *Selected Writings, Volume 2: 1927–1934*. Cambridge, Mass.: Belknap Press, 1999, pp. 69–71.

Benjamin, Walter, 'The Rigorous Study of Art', *Selected Writings, Volume 2: 1927–1934*. Cambridge, Mass.: Belknap Press, 1999, pp. 666–72.

Bennett, Tony (ed.), *Popular Fiction*. London: Routledge, 1990.

Benson, Timothy O. et al., *Expressionist Utopias*. Los Angeles: County Museum of Art, 1993; University of California Press, 2001 expanded edn.

Berghahn, Klaus L., 'A View Through the Red Window: Ernst Bloch's *Spuren*', in A. Huyssen and D. Bathrick (eds), *Modernity and the Text*. New York: Columbia University Press, 1989, pp. 200–15.

Bloch, Ernst, 'Das südliche Berlin', *Zeit-Echo*, 15 (1915–16), pp. 235–8.

Bloch, Ernst, *Thomas Münzer als Theologe der Revolution*. Munich: Kurt Wolff Verlag, 1921.

Bloch, Ernst, *Geist der Utopie*. Munich/Leipzig: Duncker & Humblot, 1918; 2nd enlarged edn 1923.

Bloch, Ernst, 'Berlin nach zwei Jahren', *Die Weltbühne*, 24 (1928), pp. 32–3.

Bloch, Ernst, 'Berlin aus der Landschaft gesehen', *Frankfurter Zeitung*, 7 July 1932.

Bloch, Ernst, 'Architektur und Utopie'. Alpbach: 1972. Typescript, Ernst Bloch Archiv, Ludwigshafen.

Bloch, Ernst, *The Principle of Hope*, 3 vols. Oxford: Blackwell, 1986.

Bloch, Ernst, *The Utopian Function of Art and Literature: Selected Essays*. Cambridge, Mass.: MIT Press, 1988.

Bloch, Ernst, *Heritage of Our Times*. Berkeley: University of California Press, 1991.

Boberg, Jochen, Tilman Fichter and Eckhart Gillen (eds), *Exerzierfeld der Moderne. Industriekultur in Berlin im 19. Jahrhundert*. Munich: Beck, 1984.

Böhringer, Hannes, 'Die "Philosophie des Geldes" als ästhetische Theorie', in H. J. Dahme and O. Rammstedt (eds), *George Simmel und die Moderne*. Frankfurt: Suhrkamp, 1984, pp. 178–82.

Böhringer, Hannes, 'Das Pathos der Differenzierung. Der philosophische Essay George Simmels', *Merkur*, 39, 4 (1985), pp. 298–308.

Bon, Gustave Le, *The Crowd*. Marietta: Larkin Corporation, 1982.

Bonnist, Roger, *Emile Gaboriau ou la naissance du roman policiers*. Paris: Vrin, 1985.

Borden, Iain, 'Space Beyond: Spatiality and the City in the Writings of Georg Simmel', *The Journal of Architecture*, 2 (1997), pp. 313–35.

Boyer, John W., *Culture and Political Crisis in Vienna: Christian Socialism in Power, 1897–1918*. Chicago: Chicago University Press, 1995.

Brand, Dana, *The Spectator and the City in Nineteenth Century American Literature*. Cambridge: Cambridge University Press, 1991.

Breuer, Marcel, 'Verkehrsarchitektur', *Das neue Berlin*. Berlin: Deutsche Bauzeitung, 1929, pp. 136–41.

Brockhaus, C., 'Die ambivalente Faszination der Grossstadterfahrung in der deutschen Kunst des Expressionismus', in H. Meixner and S. Vietta (eds), *Expressionismus – sozialer Wandel und kunstlerische Erfahrung*. Munich: Fink, 1982, pp. 84–106.

Broehl Jr., Wayne G., *The Molly Maguires*. New York: Vintage, 1968.

Brubaker, Rogers, *The Limits of Rationality*. London: Allen & Unwin, 1984.

Bücher, Karl, 'Die Grossstadt in Gegenwart und Vergangenheit', in *Die Grossstadt. Jahrbuch der Gehe-Stiftung zu Dresden*. Dresden: Zahn & Joensch, 1903, pp. 1–32.

Buck-Morss, Susan, *The Dialectics of Seeing: Walter Benjamin and the Arcades Project*. Cambridge, Mass.: MIT Press, 1990.

Buddensieg, Tilmann, 'Der Weltplatz', *Berliner Labyrinth*. Berlin:Wagenbach, 1993, pp. 83–94.

Camus, Albert, *The Rebel*. New York: Vintage Books, 1961.

Chevalier, Louis, *Laboring Classes and Dangerous Classes in Paris During the First Half of the Nineteenth Century*. Princeton: Princeton University Press, 1973.

Chickering, Roger, *Karl Lamprecht. A German Academic Life (1856–1915)*. New Jersey: Humanities Press, 1993.

Chorney, Harold, *City of Dreams*. Toronto: Nelson, 1990.

Christen, Markus, 'Essayistik und Modernität. Literarische Theoriebildung in Georg Simmel's *Philosophische Kultur*', *Deutsche Vierteljahrschrift für Literaturgeschichte und Geistesgeschichte*, 66, 1 (1992), pp. 129–59.

Colomina, Beatriz, *Privacy and Publicity. Modern Architecture as Mass Media*. Cambridge, Mass.: MIT Press, 1994.

Copjec, Joan (ed.), *Shades of Noir*. London: Verso, 1993.

Coser, Lewis A., 'The Stranger in the Academy', *Georg Simmel*. Englewood Cliffs: Prentice Hall, 1965, pp. 29–39.

Daniel, J. O. and J. Moylan (eds), *Not Yet: Reconsidering Ernst Bloch*. London: Verso, 1997.

Daniels, K., 'Expressionismus und Technik', in H. Segeberg (ed.), *Technik in der Literatur*. Frankfurt: Suhrkamp, 1987, pp. 351–86.

De Certeau, Michel, *The Practice of Everyday Life*. Berkeley: University of California Press, 1984.

Denning, Michael, *Mechanic Accents*. London: Verso, 1987.

Dickens, Charles, *Bleak House*. London: Chapman & Hall, 1853.

Dickens, Charles, *Our Mutual Friend*. London: Chapman & Hall, 1869.

Doyle, Arthur Conan, *The Valley of Fear*. Oxford: Oxford University Press, 1993.

Endell, August, *Die Schönheit der grossen Stadt*. Stuttgart: Strecker & Strecker, 1908; Berlin: Archibook, 1984.

Farkas, Reinhard, *Hermann Bahr. Prophet der Moderne*. Vienna: Böhlau, 1987.

Ferguson, Priscilla, 'The Flâneur On and Off the Streets of Paris', in Keith Tester (ed.), *The Flâneur*. London: Routledge, 1994, pp. 22–42.

Foucault, Michel, *Discipline and Punish*. Harmondsworth: Penguin, 1979.

Friedell, Egon, *Ecce Poeta*. Berlin: Fischer, 1912.

Frisby, David, *George Simmel*. London: Tavistock, 1984.

Frisby, David, *Fragments of Modernity: Social Theories of Modernity in the Works of Georg Simmel, Siegfried Kracauer and Walter Benjamin*. Cambridge: Polity, 1985; Cambridge, Mass.: MIT Press, 1986.

Frisby, David, *Sociological Impressionism: A Reassessment of Georg Simmel's Social Theory*, 2nd edn. London: Routledge, 1991.

Frisby, David, 'Siegfried Kracauer and the Detective Novel', *Theory, Culture & Society*, 9, 2 (1992), pp. 1–22.

Frisby, David, *Simmel and Since*. London: Routledge, 1992.

Frisby, David, 'Walter Benjamin and Detection', *German Politics and Society*, 32 (1994), pp. 89–106.

Frisby, David, 'Modernità', *Enciclopedia della Scienza Soziale*, 5. Rome: Instituto Enciclopedia Italiano, 1996, pp. 754–61.

Frisby, David, 'The Metropolis as Text: Otto Wagner and Vienna's "Second Renaissance"', *Renaissance and Modern Studies* (Nottingham), 40 (1998), pp. 1–16.

Frisby, David, *Metropolitan Architecture and Modernity: Otto Wagner's Vienna*. Minneapolis: Minnesota University Press, 2002.

Frisby, David (ed.), *Georg Simmel in Wien. Texte und Kontexte aus der Wien der Jahrhundertwende*. Vienna: WUV Universitätsverlag, 2000.

Fritsche, Peter, *Reading Berlin 1900*. Cambridge, Mass.: Harvard University Press, 1996.

Fulda, Ludwig, 'Berlin und das deutsche Geistesleben', *Der Greif*, I (1913/14), pp. 185–99.

Gaboriau, Emile, *File No. 113* (1867). New York: Charles Scribners & Sons, 1900.

Gaboriau, Emile, *Monsieur Lecoq* (1869). New York: Dover, 1975.

Galton, Francis, *Finger Prints*. London: Macmillan, 1892.

Gilloch, Graeme, *Myth and Metropolis*. Cambridge: Polity, 1996.

Gordon, Donald E., *Expressionism: Art and Idea*. New Haven: Yale University Press, 1987.

Graf, Otto Antonia, *Otto Wagner. Das Werk des Architekten*, vol. 2. Vienna: Böhlau, 1985.

Grossvogel, D. J., *Mystery and Its Fictions: From Oedipus to Agatha Christie*. Baltimore: Johns Hopkins University Press, 1979.

Hacking, Ian, *The Taming of Chance*. Cambridge: Cambridge University Press, 1990.

Haiko, Peter and Renata Kassal-Mikula (eds), *Otto Wagner und das Kaiser Franz Josef-Stadtmuseum. Das Scheitern der Moderne in Wien*. Vienna: Historisches Museum der Stadt Wien, 1988.

Halfeld, Adolf, *Amerika und der Amerikanismus*. Jena: Dietrichs, 1928.

Hammett, Dashiell, *Red Harvest*. New York: Knopf, 1929.

Hammett, Dashiell, *The Continental Op*, ed. Steven Marcus. London: Macmillan, 1974.

Haxthausen, C. and H. Suhr (eds), *Berlin: Culture and Metropolis*. Minneapolis: University of Minnesota Press, 1990.

Helas, V., 'Essay', in *Villa Architecture in Dresden*, ed. P. Gössel and G. Louthaiser. Cologne: Taschen, 1991.

Heller, R., ' "The City is Dark": Conceptions of Urban Landscape and Life in Expressionist Painting and Architecture', in G. B. Pickar and K. E. Webb (eds), *Expressionism Reconsidered*: Munich: Fink, 1979, pp. 42–56.

Hellgardt, Michael, 'Das Bauwerk im Zeitalter seiner technischen Reproduzierbarkeit', in *Martin Wagner. 1885–1957*. Berlin: Akademie der Künste, 1987, pp. 83–98.

Henrici, Karl, 'Moderne Architektur', *Deutsche Bauzeitung*, 31 (1897), pp. 14–20.

Herbert, Robert, L., *Impressionism: Art, Leisure and Parisian Society*. New Haven: Yale University Press, 1988.

Herf, Jeffrey, *Reactionary Modernism*. Cambridge: Cambridge University Press, 1984.

Hermand, Jost, 'Das Bild der "grossen Stadt" in Expressionismus', in K. R. Scherpe (ed.), *Die Unwirklichkeit der Städte*. Reinbek: Rowohlt, 1988, pp. 61–79.

Hessel, Franz, *Spazieren in Berlin*. Vienna/Leipzig: Verlag Dr Hans Epstein, 1929.

Hessel, Franz, *Ein Flâneur in Berlin*. Berlin, Arsenal, 1984.

Hevesi, Ludwig, *Acht Jahre Secession*. Klagenfurt: Ritter Verlag, 1986.

Hevesi, Ludwig, *Altkunst – Neukunst. Wien 1894–1908*. Klagenfurt: Ritter Verlag, 1986.

Hirdina, Heinz (ed.), *Neues Bauen, Neues Gestalten. Das neue Frankfurt/die neue Stadt. Eine Zeitschrift zwischen 1926 und 1933*. Dresden: Verlag der Kunst, 1984.

Höfert, Victor, ' "Modern" ', *Wiener Bauindustriezeitung*, 17 Jan. 1895, pp. 249–50, 265–6.

Horan, James D., *The Pinkertons*. New York: Crown, 1967.

Hübner, F. M., 'Der Expressionismus in Deutschland', in P. Raabe (ed.), *Expressionismus. Der Kampf um eine literarische Bewegung*. Zurich: Arche, 1987, pp. 133–46.

Hughes, Winnifred, *The Maniac in the Cellar: Sensational Novels of the 1860s*. Princeton, N.J.: Princeton University Press, 1980.

Jordan, David P., *Transforming Paris*. New York: Free Press, 1995.

Kerr, Alfred, *Mein Berlin*. Berlin: Aufbau Verlag, 1999.

Kessler, Michael and T. Y. Levin (eds), *Siegfried Kracauer. Neue Interpretationen*. Tübingen: Stauffenburg Verlag, 1990.

Kieren, Martin, 'Von der Wirtschaft zur Wissenschaft', in *Martin Wagner. 1885–1957*. Berlin: Akademie der Künste, 1987, pp. 66–82.

Köhn, Eckhardt, *Strassenrausch. Flânerie und kleine Form. Versuch zur Literaturgeschichte des Flâneurs bis 1933*. Berlin: Arsenal, 1989.

Kolowrath, Rudolf, *L. Baumann. Architekt zwischen Barock und Jugendstil*. Vienna: Compross Verlag, 1985.

Kortz, Paul, *Wien am Anfang des XX. Jahrhunderts*. Vienna: Gerlach & Wiedling, 1905.

Kracauer, Siegfried, *Das Leiden unter dem Wissen und die Sehnsucht nach der Tat* (*c*.1917), MS, Siegfried Kracauer Nachlass, Deutsche Literaturachiv, Marbach.

Kracauer, Siegfried, *Über den Expressionismus. Wesen und Sinn einer Zeitbewegung* (1918), MS, 81 pp., Siegfried Kracauer Nachlass, Deutsches Literaturarchiv, Marbach.

Kracauer, Siegfried, 'Max Beckmann', *Die Rheinlande*, 31, 3 (1921), pp. 93–6.

Kracauer, Siegfried, 'Unter der Oberfläche', *Frankfurter Zeitung*, 11 July 1931.

Kracauer, Siegfried, 'Der operierende Schriftsteller', *Frankfurter Zeitung*, 17 Feb. 1932.

Kracauer, Siegfried, *Offenbach and the Paris of His Time*. London: Constable, 1937.

Kracauer, Siegfried, 'The Challenge of Qualitative Analysis', *Public Opinion Quarterly*, 16, 4 (1952–3), pp. 631–42.

Kracauer, Siegfried, *Strassen in Berlin und anderswo*. Frankfurt: Suhrkamp, 1964.

Kracauer, Siegfried, *Theory of Film: The Redemption of Physical Reality*. New York: Oxford University Press, 1965.

Kracauer, Siegfried, *Schriften I*. Frankfurt: Suhrkamp, 1971.

Kracauer, Siegfried, 'Schicksalswende der Kunst', *Schriften 5.1*. Frankfurt: Suhrkamp, 1990, pp. 72–8.

Kracauer, Siegfried, *Schriften 5*. Frankfurt: Suhrkamp, 1990.

Kracauer, Siegfried, *The Mass Ornament: Weimar Essays*, trans. and ed. T. Y. Levin. Cambridge, Mass.: Harvard University Press, 1995.

Kracauer, Siegfried, *Berliner Nebeneinander. Ausgewählte Feuilletons 1930–1933*, ed. Andreas Volk. Zurich: Edition Epoca, 1996.

Kracauer, Siegfried, *Frankfurter Turmhäuser. Ausgewählte Feuilletons 1906–1930*, ed. Andreas Volk. Zurich: Edition Epoca, 1997.

Kracauer, Siegfried, *The Salaried Masses: Duty and Distraction in Weimar Germany* (1930). London: Verso, 1998.

Kristan, Markus, 'Hubert Gessner', unpublished MS.

Lackner, S., 'Von eines langen, schwierigen Irrfahrt', *Neue deutsche Hefte*, 26 (1979), pp. 48–69.

Ladd, Brian, *Urban Planning and Civil Order in Germany*. Cambridge, Mass.: Harvard University Press, 1990.

Lamprecht, Karl, *Deutsche Geschichte. Ergänzungsbände*. Berlin: R. Gärtners Verlagsbuchhandlung, 1902.

Lamprecht, Karl, *Americana*. Freiburg: Hermann Heyfelder, 1906.

Lampugnani, V. M. and R. Schneider, *Ein Stück Grossstadt als Experiment. Planungen am Potsdamer Platz in Berlin*. Stuttgart: Hatje, 1994.

Last, Nana, 'Transgressions and Inhabitations: Wittgenstein's Spatial Practices', *Assemblage*, 35 (1998), pp. 36–47.

Lawrence, Peter (ed.), *Georg Simmel: Sociologist and European*. New York: Barnes & Noble, 1976.

Layman, Richard, *Shadow Man: The Life of Dashiell Hammett*. New York: Harcourt Brace, 1981.

Lees, Andrew, *Cities Perceived: Urban Society in European and American Thought, 1820–1940*. Manchester, Manchester University Press, 1985.

Lehne, Andreas, *Wiener Warenhäuser 1865–1914*. Vienna: Deuticke, 1990.

Leistner, G., *Idee und Wirklichkeit. Gehalt und Bedeutung des urbanen Expressionismus in Deutschland, dargestellt am Werk Ludwig Meidners*. Frankfurt/ Bern: Peter Lang, 1989.

Lenger, Friedrich, *Werner Sombart 1863–1941. Eine Biographie*. Munich: Beck, 1994.

Leps, Marie-Christine, *Apprehending the Criminal: The Production of Deviance in Nineteenth-Century Discourse*. Durham, N.C.: Duke University Press, 1992.

Lessing, Julius, 'Die Berliner Gewerbeausstellung', *Preussische Jahrbücher*, LXXXVIII (1896), pp. 276–94.

Levin, Thomas Y., *Siegfried Kracauer. Eine Bibliographie seiner Schriften*. Marbach: Deutsche Schillergesellschaft, 1989.

Levine, Donald N., 'Simmel at a Distance', *Sociological Focus*, 10, 1 (1977), pp. 618–27.

Lewis, Arnold, *An Early Encounter with Tomorrow*. Urbana/Chicago: University of Illinois Press, 1997.

Lewis, B. I., '*Lustmord*: Inside the Windows of the Metropolis', in C. W. Haxthausen and H. Suhr (eds), *Berlin: Culture and Metropolis*. Minneapolis: University of Minnesota Press, 1990, pp. 111–40.

Liebersohn, Harry, *Fate and Utopia in German Sociology, 1870–1923*. Cambridge, Mass.: MIT Press, 1988.

Lindenberg, Paul, *Pracht-Album der Berliner Gewerbe-Ausstellung*. Berlin: The Werner Company, 1896.

Lindner, Rolf, *Die Entdeckung der Stadtkultur. Soziologie aus der Erfahrung der Reportage*. Frankfurt: Suhrkamp, 1990.

Lindner, Rolf, *The Reportage of Urban Culture: Robert Park and the Chicago School*. Cambridge: Cambridge University Press, 1996.

Loos, Adolf, 'Potemkin City', *Spoken Into The Void*. Cambridge, Mass.: MIT Press, 1982, pp. 95–7.

Lukács, Georg, *History and Class Consciousness*. London: Merlin, 1971.

Mackay, James, *Allan Pinkerton: The Eye Who Never Slept*. Edinburgh: Mainstream, 1996.

McLeod, Mary, 'Undressing Architecture: Fashion, Gender, and Modernity', in D. Fausch et al. (eds), *Architecture: In Fashion*. Princeton, N.J.: Princeton Architectural Press, 1994, pp. 38–123.

McWatters, George S., *Knots Untied or, Ways and By-Ways in the Hidden Life of American Detectives*. Hartford: Burr and Hyde, 1871.

Madden, David (ed.), *Tough Guy Writers of the Thirties*. Carbondale: Southern Illinois University Press, 1968.

Martin Wagner. 1885–1957. Wohnungsbau und Weltstadtplanung. Die Rationalisierung des Glücks. Berlin: Akademie der Künste, 1986.

Martin, Edward Winslow, *The Secrets of the Great City: A Work Descriptive of the Virtues and Vices, the Mysteries, Miseries and Crimes of New York*. Philadelphia: National Publishing Company, 1868.

Mattenklott, Gert, 'Der mythische Leib: Physiognomisches Denken bei Nietzsche, Simmel und Kassner', in K. H. Böhrer (ed.), *Mythos und Moderne*. Frankfurt: Suhrkamp, 1983, pp. 138–56.

Maxwell, Richard, *The Mysteries of Paris and London*. Charlottesville: University Press of Virginia, 1992.

Mayr, G. von, 'Die Bevölkerung der Grossstädte', in *Die Grossstadt. Jahrbuch der Gehe-Stiftung zu Dresden*. Dresden: Zahn & Joensch, 1903, pp. 73–146.

Meidner, Ludwig, 'Anleitung zum Malen von Grosstadtbilder', in G. Bever and I. Wagemann, *Ludwig Meidner. Zeichner, Maler, Literat*. Stuttgart: Hatje, 1991, vol. 2, pp. 290–2.

Menninghaus, Winfried, *Schwellenkunde*. Frankfurt: Suhrkamp, 1986.

Missac, Pierre, 'Walter Benjamin à la Bibliothèque Nationale', *Revue de la Bibliothèque Nationale*, 10 (1983), pp. 30–43.

Mitzman, Arthur, *Sociology and Estrangement*. New York: Knopf, 1973.

Moravanszky, Akos, *Competing Visions*. Cambridge, Mass.: MIT Press, 1998.

Moretti, Franco, *Signs Taken For Wonders*. London: Verso, 1988.

Morgenbrod, Brigitt, ' "Träume in Nachbars Garten". Das Wien-Bild im Deutschen Kaiserreich', in Ganolf Hübinger and Wolfgang J. Mommsen (eds), *Intellektuellen im Deutschen Kaiserreich*. Frankfurt: Fischer, 1993, pp. 111–25.

Mülder, Inka, *Siegfried Kracauer*. Stuttgart: Metzler, 1985.

Mülder Bach, Inka, ' "Weibliche Kultur" und "Stahlhartes Gehäuse". Zur Thematisierung des Geschlechtsverhältnisses in den Soziologien Georg Simmels und Max Webers', in Sigrun Anselm and Barbara Beck (eds), *Triumph und Scheitern in der Metropole*. Berlin: Dietrich Reimer, 1987, pp. 115–40.

Müller, Lothar, 'The Beauty of the Metropolis', in C. Haxthausen and H. Suhr (eds), *Berlin: Culture and Metropolis*. Minnesota: University of Minnesota Press, 1990, pp. 37–57.

Müller, Michael, *Schöne Schein*. Frankfurt: Athenäum, 1987.

Münster, Arno, *Utopie, Messianismus und Apokalypse im Frühwerk von Ernst Bloch*. Frankfurt: Suhrkamp, 1982.

Nedelmann, Birgitta, 'Secrecy as a Macrosociological Phenomenon: A Neglected Aspect of Simmel's Analysis of Secrecy', in D. Frisby (ed.), *George Simmel: Critical Assessments*, vol. 3. London: Routledge, 1994, pp. 202–21.

Neubaur, Christine, 'Walter Benjamin. Soziologe. Anmerkungen über eine Philosophie ohne Begriffe', *Freibeuter*, 15 (1983), pp. 143–9.

Opitz, Michael, '*Lesen und Flanieren. Über das Lesen von Städten, vom Flânieren in Bücher*', in '*Aber ein Sturm weht von Paradies her'. Texte zu Walter Benjamin*. Leipzig: Reklam, 1992, pp. 162–81.

Paret, Peter, *The Berlin Secession*. Cambridge, Mass.: Belknap Press, 1980.

Park, Robert E., ' "Notes on the Origins of the Society for Social Research", with an introduction by L. R. Kurtz', *Journal of the History of the Behavioural Sciences*, 18 (1982), pp. 332–40.

Pearson, Geoffrey, *Hooligan: A History of Respectable Fears*. London: Macmillan, 1983.

Peter Behrens. Berlin Alexanderplatz. Kaiserslautern: Pfalzgallerie Kaiserslautern, 1993.

Petermann, Reinhard E., *Wien im Zeitalter Franz Joseph I*. Vienna: Lechner, 1908.

Petermann, Theodor, 'Die geistige Bedeutung der Grossstädte', *Die Grossstadt. Jahrbuch der Gehe-Stiftung zu Dresden.* Dresden: Zahn & Joensch, 1903, pp. 207–30.

Petermann, Theodor, 'Vorbemerkung des Herausgebers', in *Die Grossstadt. Jahrbuch der Gehe-Stiftung zu Dresden.* Dresden: Zahn & Joensch, 1903.

Pinkerton, Allan, *Claude Melnotte as a Detective.* Chicago, Ill.: Keen, Cooke & Co., 1875.

Pinkerton, Allan, *General Principles and Rules of Pinkerton's National Detective Agency.* New York: Jones Printing Company, 1878.

Pinkerton, Allan, *Professional Thieves and the Detective.* Chicago, Ill.: A. G. Nettleton & Co., 1881.

Pinkerton, Allan, *The Spy of the Rebellion.* Hartford, Conn.: Winter & Hatch, 1883.

Pinkerton, Allan, *Thirty Years a Detective.* Chicago, Ill.: G. W. Dillingham, 1889.

Pinthus, Kurt, 'Rede mit die Zukunft', in W. Rothe (ed.), *Der Aktivismus. 1915–1920.* Munich: DTV, 1969, pp. 116–33.

Pinthus, Kurt (ed.), *Menschheitsdämmerung.* Hamburg: Rowohlt, 1990.

Porter, Dennis, *The Pursuit of Crime.* New Haven, Conn.: Yale University Press, 1981.

Prokop, Ursula, *Wien. Aufbruch zur Metropole.* Vienna: Böhlau, 1994.

Pykett, Lyn, *The Improper Feminine: The Women's Sensational Novel and the New Woman Writing.* London: Routledge, 1992.

Rathenau, Walter, *Zur Mechanik des Geistes.* Berlin: S. Fischer, 1912.

Ratzel, Friedrich, 'Die geographische Lage der grossen Stadt', in *Die Grossstadt. Jahrbuch der Gehe-Stiftung zu Dresden.* Dresden: Zahn & Joensch, 1903, pp. 33–72.

Raulet, Gerard, *Natur und Ornament.* Darmstadt/Neuwied: Luchterhand, 1987.

Reulecke, J., *Geschichte der Urbanisierung in Deutschland.* Frankfurt: Suhrkamp, 1985.

Rignall, John, *Realist Fiction and the Strolling Spectator.* London: Routledge, 1992.

Salten, Felix, 'Der Wiener Korrespondent', *Morgen* (1907), pp. 113–116.

Sandow, M. [pseud. M. Wagner], 'Die Sanierung der Berliner "City"', *Deutsche Bauzeitung*, 8 (1934), pp. 142–6.

Scarpa, Ludovica, *Martin Wagner und Berlin.* Braunschweig/Wiesbaden: Vieweg, 1986.

Schäfer, Dietrich, 'Die politische und militärische Bedeutung der Grossstädte', in *Die Grossstadt. Jahrbuch der Gehe-Stiftung zu Dresden.* Dresden: Zahn & Joensch, 1903, pp. 231–82.

Scheffler, Karl, 'Berlin als Kunststadt', *Der Lotse*, II (1901), pp. 257–63.

Scheffler, Karl, 'Wien-Berlin', *Österreichische Rundschau*, XVII (1908), pp. 450–6.

Scheffler, Karl, 'Die Grossstadt', *Die neue Rundschau*, 21 (1910), pp. 881–97.

Scheffler, Karl, *Die Architektur der Grossstadt.* Berlin: Cassirer, 1913.

Scheffler, Karl, 'Die Zukunft der Grossstädte und die Grossstädte der Zukunft', *Neue deutsche Rundschau*, 37 (1926), pp. 522–36.

Scheler, Max, *Ressentiment.* Glencoe, Ill.: Free Press, 1961.

Schivelbusch, Wolfgang, *Disenchanted Night.* Berkeley: University of California Press, 1988.

Schlör, Joachim, *Nights in the Big City*. London: Reaktion Books, 1998.

Schorske, Carl E., *Fin-de-Siècle Vienna*. New York: Knopf, 1980.

Schrott, Sigmund, *Die Grössstadtische Agglomerationen des Deutschen Reiches. 1871–1910*. Breslau: W. G. Korn, 1912.

Schwartz, Frederic J., *The Werkbund*. New Haven, Conn.: Yale University Press, 1996.

Sennett, Richard, *The Conscience of the Eye*. New York: Norton, 1990.

Servaes, Franz, *Wien. Briefe an einer Freundin in Berlin*. Leipzig: Klinkhardt & Biermann, n.d.

Simmel, Georg, 'Über Kunstausstellungen', *Unsere Zeit*, 26 Feb. 1890, pp. 474–80.

Simmel, Georg, 'Berliner Gewerbe Austellung', *Die Zeit*, 8, 25 July 1896, pp. 95–6.

Simmel, Georg, 'Das Geld in der modernen Kultur', *Neue Freie Presse*, 13, 18 and 25 Aug. 1896; now in *Gesamtausgabe 5*, ed. H.-J. Dahme and D. P. Frisby. Frankfurt: Suhrkamp, 1992, pp. 178–96.

Simmel, Georg, 'Soziologische Aesthetik, *Die Zukunft*, 17 (1896), pp. 204–16; now in *Gesamtausgabe 5*, ed. H.-J. Dahme and D. P. Frisby. Frankfurt: Suhrkamp, 1992, pp. 197–214.

Simmel, Georg, 'Rom', *Die Zeit*, 15, 28 May 1898, pp. 137–9; now in *Gesamtausgabe 5*, ed. H.-J. Dahme and D. P. Frisby. Frankfurt: Suhrkamp, 1992, pp. 301–10.

Simmel, Georg, 'Die Grossstädte und das Geistesleben', in *Die Grossstadt. Jahrbuch der Gehe-Stiftung zu Dresden*. Dresden: Zahn & Joensch, 1903, pp. 185–206; now in *Gesamtausgabe 7*, ed. R. Kramme, A. Rammstedt and O. Rammstedt. Frankfurt: Suhrkamp, 1995, pp. 116–31.

Simmel, Georg, Über raumliche Projektionen sozialer Formen', *Zeitschrift für Sozialwissenschaften*, 6 (1903), pp. 287–302, now in *Gesamtausgabe 7*, ed. R. Kramme, A. Rammstedt and O. Rammstedt. Frankfurt: Suhrkamp, 1995, pp. 201–20.

Simmel, Georg, 'Der Ruin', *Der Tag*, 22 Feb. 1907; now in *Gesamtausgabe 8*, ed. A. Cavalli and V. Krech. Frankfurt: Suhrkamp, 1993, pp. 124–30.

Simmel, Georg, *Soziologie*. Leipzig: Duncker & Humblot, 1908; now also *Gesamtausgabe 11*, ed. O. Rammstedt. Frankfurt: Suhrkamp, 1992.

Simmel, Georg, 'L'art pour l'art' (1912), *Zur Philosophie der Kunst*. Potsdam: Kiepenheuer, 1922, pp. 79–86; now in *Gesamtausgabe 13*, ed. K. Latzel. Frankfurt: Suhrkamp, 2000, pp. 9–15.

Simmel, Georg, 'Rodin' (1911), *Philosophische Kultur*, 3rd edn. Potsdam: Kiepenheuer, 1923, pp. 179–97.

Simmel, Georg, 'Discretion' (1906), in K. H. Wolff (ed.), *The Sociology of Georg Simmel*. Glencoe, Ill.: Free Press, 1950, pp. 320–4.

Simmel, Georg, 'The Secret and the Secret Society' (1908), in K. H. Wolff (ed.), *The Sociology of Georg Simmel*. Glencoe, Ill.: Free Press, 1950, pp. 330–76.

Simmel, Georg, 'Written Communication' (1908), in K. H. Wolff (ed.), *The Sociology of Georg Simmel*. Glencoe, Ill.: Free Press, 1950, pp. 352–5.

Simmel, Georg, *Conflict and the Web of Group Affiliations*. Glencoe, Ill.: Free Press, 1955.

Simmel, Georg, 'Philosophie der Landschaft' (1910), in Michael Landmann (ed.), *Brücke und Tür*. Stuttgart: Köhler, 1957, pp. 141–52.

Simmel, Georg, 'The Aesthetic Significance of the Face' (1901), in K. H. Wolff (ed.), *George Simmel: 1858–1918*. Columbus, Ohio: Ohio State University Press, 1958, pp. 276–81.

Simmel, Georg, 'The Ruin' (1907), in K. H. Wolff (ed.), *Georg Simmel: 1858–1918*. Columbus, Ohio: Ohio State University Press, 1958.

Simmel, Georg, *On Women, Sexuality and Love*. New Haven, Conn.: Yale University Press, 1984.

Simmel, Georg, *The Philosophy of Money*, 2nd enlarged edn, ed. David Frisby. London: Routledge, 1990.

Simmel, Georg, 'Über ästhetische Quantitäten' (1903), *Aufsätze und Abhandlungen 1901–1908*. Frankfurt: Suhrkamp, 1995, pp. 184–9.

Simmel, Georg, 'The Adventure' (1910), in D. Frisby and M. Featherstone (eds), *Simmel on Culture*. London: Sage, 1997, pp. 221–32.

Simmel, Georg, 'The Alpine Journey' (1895), in D. Frisby and M. Featherstone (eds), *Simmel on Culture*. London: Sage, 1997, pp. 219–21.

Simmel, Georg, 'The Berlin Trade Exhibition' (1896), in D. Frisby and M. Featherstone (eds), *Simmel on Culture*. London: Sage, 1997, pp. 255–8.

Simmel, Georg, 'Infelices Possidentes!' (1893), in D. Frisby and M. Featherstone (eds), *Simmel on Culture*. London: Sage, 1997, pp. 259–62.

Simmel, Georg, 'The Metropolis and Mental Life' (1903), in D. Frisby and M. Featherstone (eds), *Simmel on Culture*. London: Sage, 1997, pp. 174–85.

Simmel, Georg, 'Money in Modern Culture' (1896), in D. Frisby and M. Featherstone (eds), *Simmel on Culture*. London: Sage, 1977, pp. 243–55.

Simmel, Georg, 'The Philosophy of Fashion' (1905), in D. Frisby and M. Featherstone (eds), *Simmel on Culture*. London: Sage, 1997, pp. 187–206.

Sitte, Camillo, 'Die neue Stadterweiterung', *Neues Wiener Tagblatt*, 27 Sept. 1891.

Sitte, Camillo, 'Die Regulierung des Stubenviertels', *Neues Wiener Tagblatt*, 5 Mar. 1893.

Sitte, Camillo, *City Planning According to Artistic Principles* (1889), trans. Georg and Christina Collins. New York: Rizzoli, 1985.

Smith, Matthew Hale, *Sunlight and Shadow in New York*. Hartford: J. B. Burr and Hyde, 1872.

Smith, Woodruff D., *Politics and the Science of Culture in Germany, 1840–1920*. New York: Oxford University Press, 1991.

Sombart, Werner, *Der Moderne Kapitalismus*. Leipzig: Duncker & Humblot, 1902.

Sombart, Werner, *Die deutsche Volkswirtschaft im neunzehnten Jahrhundert*. Berlin: Georg Bondi, 1903.

Sombart, Werner, 'Der Begriff der Stadt und das Wesen der Städtebildung', *Archiv für Sozialwissenschaft und Sozialpolitik*, 25 (1907), pp. 1–9.

Sombart, Werner, 'Wien', *Morgen*, 19 July 1907, pp. 172–5.

Sombart, Werner, 'Technik und Kultur', *Verhandlungen des ersten Deutschen Soziologentages, 1910*. Tübingen: Mohr, 1911, pp. 80–97.

Spengler, Oswald, *Der Untergang des Abendlandes*. Munich: Beck, 1923.

Stewart, Janet, *Fashioning Vienna: Adolf Loos's Cultural Criticism*. London: Routledge, 2000.

Strohmeyer, Klaus, ' "Berliner Gewerbe-Ausstellung". Annotationen zu einem Text von Georg Simmel', *Ästhetik und Kommunikation*, 18, 67/68 (1988), pp. 107–9.

Sue, Eugene, *The Mysteries of Paris*. London, Chapman and Hall, 1845.

Sutcliffe, A., *Metropolis: 1890–1914*. London: Mansell, 1984.

Tafuri, Manfredo, *Architecture and Utopia*. Cambridge, Mass.: MIT Press, 1968.

Tafuri, Manfredo, 'Am Steinhof: Centrality and "Surface" in Otto Wagner's Architecture', in G. Peichl (ed.), *Die Kunst des Otto Wagner*. Vienna: Akademie der bildende Kunste, 1984, pp. 61–75.

Tafuri, Manfredo, *The Sphere and the Labyrinth*. Cambridge, Mass.: MIT Press, 1987.

Tagg, John, *The Burden of Representation*. London: Macmillan, 1988.

Tatar, Maria, *Lustmord: Sexual Murder in Weimar Germany*. Princeton, N.J.: Princeton University Press, 1995.

Thézy, Marie de, *Marville. Paris*. Paris: Hazan, 1994.

Thornbury, Walter, *Old and New London: A Narrative of its History, its People, and its Places*. London: Cassell, Petter & Galpin, n.d.

Tietze, Hans, *Otto Wagner*. Vienna/Berlin: Rokola Verlag, 1922.

Tietze, Hans, *Wien*. Vienna/Leipzig: Dr Hans Epstein, 1931.

Tönnies, Ferdinand, *Gemeinschaft und Gesellschaft*. Leipzig: Fues's Verlag, 1887.

Tönnies, Ferdinand, 'Zur Einleitung in die Soziologie', *Zeitschrift für Philosophie und philosophische Kritik*, 115 (1899), pp. 240–51.

Tönnies, Ferdinand, *Community and Association*. London: Routledge, 1955.

Tower, Becke Sell, *Envisioning America*. Cambridge, Mass.: Busch Reisinger Museum, Harvard University, 1990.

Vidler, Anthony, *Warped Space: Art, Architecture and Anxiety in Modern Culture*. Cambridge, Mass.: MIT Press, 2000.

Vietta, S. and H. G. Kemper, *Expressionismus*. Munich: Fink, 1975.

Waentig, H., 'Die wirtschaftliche Bedeutung der Grossstadt', in *Die Grossstadt. Jahrbuch der Gehe-Stiftung zu Dresden*. Dresden: Zahn & Joensch, 1903, pp. 147–84.

Wagner, Martin, *Städtische Freiflachenpolitik*. Berlin: Carl Heymans Verlag, 1915.

Wagner, Martin, 'Gross-Siedlungen. Der Weg zur Rationalisierung des Wohnungsbaues', *Der Aufbau* (Vienna), 1, 6 (1926), pp. 81–96.

Wagner, Martin, 'Das Problem der reinen Gartenstadt', *Wohnungswirtschaft*, 3, 18/19 (1926), pp. 156–9.

Wagner, Martin, 'Zivilisation, Kultur, Kunst', *Wohnungswirtschaft*, 3, 20/21, 26 Oct. 1926, pp. 165–8.

Wagner, Martin, *Städtebauliche Probleme im amerikanischen Städten und ihre Rückewirkung auf den deutschen Städtebau*. Berlin: Deutsche Bauzeitung, 1929.

Wagner, Martin, *Städtebauliche Probleme der Grossstadt*. Berlin: Deutsche Bauzeitung, 1929.

Wagner, Martin, 'Eine Studie über die Gestaltung des Berliner Ausstellungsgelände', *Wasmuths Monatshefte. Baukunst und Städtebau*, 15 (1931), pp. 33–40.

Wagner, Martin, *Das neue Berlin*, 2 vols. MS, 1932, Special Collections, Graduate School of Design Library, Harvard University.

Wagner, Martin, *Städtebau als Wirtschaftsbau und Lebensbau*, MS, 1932, Archiv der Akademie der Künste, Berlin.

Wagner, Martin, *Das wachsende Hans. Ein Beitrag zur Lösung der städtischen Wohnungsfrage.* Berlin / Leipzig: Deutsches Verlagshaus Bong, 1932.

Wagner, Otto, *Die Grossstadt.* Vienna: Schroll, 1911.

Wagner, Otto, 'The Development of the Great City', *Architectural Record,* 31 (1912), pp. 485–500.

Wagner, Otto, *Einige Skizze Projekte und ausgeführte Bauwerke.* Tübingen: Wasmuth, 1984.

Wagner, Otto, *Modern Architecture,* trans. Harry F. Malgrave. Santa Monica: Getty, 1988.

Wagner, Walter, *Die Geschichte der Akademie der bildende Künste.* Vienna: Rosenbaum, 1967.

Walker, I. M. (ed.), *Edgar Allan Poe: The Critical Heritage.* London: Routledge, 1986.

'Waters', *Recollections of a Detective Police-Officer.* London: Ward, Lock and Tyler, 1875.

Watson, Colin, *Snobbery with Violence.* London: Eyre & Spottiswood, 1971.

Weber, Max, 'Die protestantische Ethik und der "Geist" des Kapitalismus', *Archiv für Sozialwissenschaft und Sozialpolitik,* 20 (1905), pp. 1–54; 21 (1905), pp. 1–110.

Weber, Max, *The Protestant Ethic and the Spirit of Capitalism.* London: Allen & Unwin, 1930.

Weber, Max, 'Antikritisches Schlusswort zum "Geist des Kapitalismus" ' (1910), in M. Weber, *Die protestantische Ethik II. Kritiken und Antikritiken,* ed. Johannes Winckelmann. Hamburg: Siebenstern, 1972, pp. 283–345.

Weber, Max, *Economy and Society,* ed. G. Roth and C. Wittich. Berkeley: University of California Press, 1978.

Weber, Max, 'Diskussionsrede zu W. Sombarts Vortrag über Technik und Kultur', *Gesammelte Aufsätze zur Soziologie und Sozialpolitik.* Tübingen: Mohr, 1988, pp. 449–56.

Welter, Volker M. and James Lawson (eds), *The City after Patrick Geddes.* Frankfurt: Peter Lange, 2000.

Whimster, Sam, 'The Secular Ethic and the Culture of Modernism', in S. Whimster and S. Lash (eds), *Max Weber: Rationality and Modernity.* London: Allen & Unwin, 1987, pp. 259–90.

Whyte, Iain Boyd, *Bruno Taut and the Architecture of Activism.* Cambridge: Cambridge University Press, 1982.

Wijdefeld, Paul, *Ludwig Wittgenstein. Architect.* London: Thames & Hudson, 1994.

Winks, Ronald W., *The Historian as Detective.* New York: Harper and Row, 1969.

Winks, Ronald W., 'The Historian as Detective', in R. W. Winks (ed.), *Detective Fiction: A Collection of Critical Essays.* Woodstock, Vermont: Foul Play Press, 1988.

Wismann, H. (ed.), *Walter Benjamin et Paris.* Paris: Cerf, 1986.

Wittgenstein, Ludwig, *Tractatus Logico-Philosophicus.* London: Routledge, 1961.

Wittgenstein, Ludwig, *Philosophical Investigations.* London: Routledge, 1974.

Wolff, Janet, 'The invisible flâneuse', *Theory, Culture & Society,* 2, 3 (1985), pp. 37–48.

Woodhead, Howard, 'The First German Municipal Exposition (Dresden 1903)', *American Journal of Sociology*, 9 (1904), pp. 433–58; 612–30; 812–31; 10 (1905), pp. 47–63.

Yeo, E. and E. P. Thompson, *The Unknown Mayhew*. London: Merlin, 1971; New York: Schocken, 1972.

Zenten, David van, *Building Paris*. Cambridge: Cambridge University Press, 1994.

Zudeick, Peter, *Der Hintern des Teufels. Ernst Bloch. Leben und Werk*. Moos & Baden-Baden: Elster, 1987.

Index